Social Capital versus Social Theory

Initially, social capital was used to reveal how family affects schooling; in the past decade, it has come to explain why nations, communities, and individuals are rich or poor in every respect. No area of socio-economic analysis and policy has been left untouched by what the World Bank describes as the missing link to development, from Russia and the Third World to the ghettos of North America.

Ben Fine traces the origins of social capital through the work of Becker, Bourdieu and Coleman, and comprehensively reviews the literature across the social sciences. *Social Capital versus Social Theory* is uniquely critical of social capital, explaining how it avoids a proper confrontation with political economy and, as a result of its origins and evolution, has become chaotic. The following major themes are addressed:

- the shifting relationship between economics and other social sciences as economics forces itself upon neighbouring disciplines
- how scholarly integrity is being prejudiced by the concepts of "publish or perish" and punditry
- how social capital purports to steer a delicate course between neo-liberalism and statism, whilst in fact neglecting political economy, power and conflict
- how a genuine interdisciplinarity across the social sciences requires a place for political economy together with, rather than a retreat into, cultural and social theory

This highly topical text will be of great interest to advanced students, researchers and academics, as well as professionals involved in public policy.

Ben Fine is Professor of Economics and Director of the Centre for Economic Policy for Southern Africa at the School of Oriental and African Studies.

Contemporary political economy series
Edited by Jonathan Michie
Birkbeck College, University of London, UK

This series presents a fresh, broad perspective on the key issues in the modern world economy, drawing in perspectives from management and business, politics and sociology, economic history and law.

Written in a lively and accessible style, it presents focused and comprehensive introductions to key topics, demonstrating the relevance of political economy to major debates in economics and to an understanding of the contemporary world.

Global Instability
The political economy of world economic governance
Edited by Jonathan Michie and John Grieve Smith

Reconstructing Political Economy
The great divide in economic thought
William K. Tabb

The Political Economy of Competitiveness
Employment, public policy and corporate performance
Michael Kitson and Jonathan Michie

Global Economy, Global Justice
Theoretical objections and policy alternatives to neoliberalism
George F. DeMartino

Social Capital versus Social Theory
Political economy and social science at the turn of the millennium
Ben Fine

A New Guide to Post Keynesian Economics
Steven Pressman and Richard Holt

Social Capital versus Social Theory

Political economy and social science
at the turn of the millennium

Ben Fine

London and New York

First published 2001
by Routledge
11 New Fetter Lane, London EC4P 4EE

Simultaneously published in the USA and Canada
by Routledge
29 West 35th Street, New York, NY 10001

Routledge is an imprint of the Taylor & Francis Group

© 2001 Ben Fine

Typeset in Baskerville by Taylor & Francis Books Ltd
Printed and bound in Great Britain by Clays Ltd, St Ives PLC

British Library Cataloguing in Publication Data
A catalogue record for this book is available from the British Library

Library of Congress Cataloging in Publication Data
Fine, Ben.
    Social Capital versus Social Theory: Political Economy and
    Social Science at the Turn of the Millennium / Ben Fine.
    Includes bibliographical references and index.
    1. Social sciences – philosophy.
    2. Economics – philosophy. I. Title.
    H61.15 .F56 2000
    306.3–dc21   00-032176

ISBN 0–415–24179–0 (hbk)
ISBN 0–415–24180–4 (pbk)

Contents

Acknowledgements

In bits and pieces, even in chunks, parts of this book have been published elsewhere, although all of the text has been revised and updated. I am grateful for the opportunity to draw on earlier writings and, in particular, to thank *Economy and Society* and Routledge for Fine (1999c), the latter also for Fine (2001a and 2001b) and Fine and Rose (2001), Berg for Fine (1998b), *International Papers in Political Economy* for Fine (1999a) and *Development and Change* and the Institute for Social Studies (ISS), The Hague, for Fine (1999b). This book was written whilst in receipt of a Research Fellowship from the UK Economic and Social Research Council (ESRC) under award number R000271046 to study "The New Revolution in Economics and Its Impact upon Social Sciences". Much of it was drafted whilst visiting the Department of Economics, University of Melbourne. Otherwise my professional, intellectual and personal debts are too heavy, complex and intertwined to list. I thank all concerned with the hope that, on balance, I have given as good as I have got.

Part I

1 Introduction and overview

Why social capital?

The last two decades have been unkind to political economy. The 1970s had witnessed unprecedented success – in response to the post-war boom and its demise, the political radicalisation of the 1960s, the liberal expansion of higher education, and an ideological climate in which the contentious issue was whether Keynesianism, welfarism and decolonisation were enough by way of state intervention. Political economy and political economists flourished as never before, alongside journals, books and *Capital*-reading groups. Most of this has been thrown into reverse following the rise of monetarism, concerns about gaining employment, increasingly conservative and uniform curricula, and a questioning of whether Keynesianism, welfarism and the post-colonial state are too much by way of obstruction to the global market. Political economists within economics departments have been left high and dry, increasingly needing or choosing to conform with orthodoxy in teaching and research and with little prospect of enjoying sympathetic support from colleagues, let alone arrival of, or replacement by, like-minded scholars.[1] Indeed, possibly more than any other discipline, economics has become dominated by its own neoclassical orthodoxy, one which is widely recognised from outside to be far removed from economic realities, to be totally intolerant of other approaches, and to be equally ignorant of its own history as a discipline as well as its fellow social sciences. Further, its supposedly rigorous and scientific commitment to mathematical modelling and statistical methods have become so demanding for both students and academics that breathing space scarcely exists to allow for more circumspect considerations. How could you, for example, tell students during or after three years of hard grind that a few simple criticisms suffice to render that effort essentially worthless other than in learning what economics is really like, no matter how its results might be presented informally or for popular consumption. In short, anyone interested in economies, especially from a progressive and/or critical perspective, would surely give economics a wide berth. Indeed, students have been voting with their feet, the vocationally inclined streaming in hordes to accounting, business and finance, and the less self-interested seeking refuge in the "softer" and more relevant social sciences.[2]

To someone who had benefited considerably from the earlier rise of political economy, and given more than twenty years back in return, its prospects seemed particularly bleak in the 1990s. Three fundamental tasks presented themselves: how to sustain commitment to socialism, to Marxism and to political economy. I was particularly concerned with how the next generation of political economists would be born. My own experience would not be replicated: following a degree in mathematics, providing an easy passage over the technical barriers to the discipline, and three years of fully-funded postgraduate study in economics, a university position was readily available in the early 1970s despite commitment to political economy. From the subsequent experience of my own PhD students, the prospects for academic jobs have only been diminished, if not eliminated, by revealing an interest in political economy. Quite apart from any ideological stigma and associated worries about acceptability of future research output, work on political economy entailed lost advantage in the increasingly fierce competition by mainstream publications with the growing legion of clones, formally trained in the esoteric techniques and ploughing a furrow down their narrow specialisms.[3]

In addition, as already mentioned, systemically and often both institutionally and personally, the discipline of economics has become more and more intolerant of alternatives – in teaching, research, appointments and publications. The fate of political economy at Cambridge in the UK is indicative, as past traditions have suffered under the assault from mainstream orthodoxy. Paradoxically, though, the more esoteric and unworldly the latter's content – and the more vulnerable to criticism from outside – the more secure has been its internal stranglehold. Whilst intellectually crippled, mainstream economics has never been more secure. As a result, with considerable reluctance, I came to the view that economics as a discipline had been lost to political economy. Essentially, it has been squeezed from two directions in the process of excluding it from any effective participation even as critical conscience, let alone viable alternative, to the orthodoxy. First, mainstream economists have had no need to debate with political economy. For political economists to engage with them, it has been necessary to accept their methodological and theoretical terrain, and tease out inconsistencies as the entry price for being allowed to posit an alternative view. My own experience now suggests that even such levels of compromise have become insufficient to gain recognition with few exceptions. Rather, the twist in the tail to be provided by political economy has rarely been allowed to wag the mainstream dog in criticism of the orthodoxy. Publication would be refused or require neutering revision.

Second, political economy has, paradoxically, increasingly come under pressure from developments within economics itself. As will be apparent in the next section, many of its central concerns have been appropriated and transformed by the very discipline that it preceded and with which it is essentially inconsistent. Most notable are the new political economy, the new institutional economics, the new industrial economics, and so on, as these, respectively, purport to deal in politics, institutions, monopoly and other previously neglected aspects of economic reality. As Hodgson (1994a, p. 22) records, "as yet, the 'political economy' term does not itself provide a secure defence against the ravages of economic imperialism."[4]

In short, the squeeze on political economy has had the effect of robbing it both of its subject matter and its subjects. The process of engaging with the mainstream has overtaken the provision of alternatives and increasingly slipped into one of succumbing to its dubious charms, an outcome marking much of US radical political economy. In this light, the prospects for securing the future of political economy seemed much brighter by locating endeavour within other social sciences, less alien to its methods, more intellectually tolerant, and where its importance continued to be recognised alongside its traditional variables of class, power, conflict, and so on. These too, however, had not escaped unscathed, if to a lesser degree, from the influences that had rendered political economy unpalatable to economics. In addition, the rise of postmodernism had done much to divert attention away from political economy, partly by accident and partly by denigrating design. Much more alarming was my discovery that the very same developments within economics that had squeezed out political economy had also been the basis for launching an assault on the subject matter of the other social sciences. I return to this in the next section, but it led me to the conclusion that the tasks of reviving and retaining political economy within social science needed to be undertaken side by side with defending it against the incursions of a new imperialism of economics.[5] For it has become apparent that colonisation of other disciplines by the dismal science had been taking the insidious form of informal and unwitting transposition of concepts that would, hopefully, have been rejected had their origin and content been more fully recognised. Yet, once entertained, such colonising notions proved guests reluctant to depart, ingratiating themselves as if new-found family members.

Against this personal and intellectual background, it is now easy to explain how social capital became an object of my own study. Having worked previously on consumption, the work of both Gary Becker and Pierre Bourdieu had been familiar to me, one mainstream ideologue within economics, the other deriving, at least in part, from Marxist traditions, respectively. Remarkably, Becker (1996) published a book that used the notion of social capital. It had also been deployed by Bourdieu more than a decade earlier. I was immediately determined to discover the relationship between the two uses and its relevance for the hypothesis of colonisation of other social sciences by economics (Fine 1999a). Consequently, it was my (mis)fortune to be keenly attuned to the significance of social capital at an extremely early stage in its meteoric rise and evolution.

The rest, as the saying goes, is history, and what follows is its result. I found myself chasing a target that moved and multiplied at a pace that defied my capacity to catch up. But, before getting down to substance, a few preliminaries are in order. First, this book is heavily marked by its origins. Whilst written by an economist and, to a large extent, taking economics as its starting point, it ranges across the social sciences as a whole. As a result, it is liable to be tough reading since social science is characterised by narrow specialisation within disciplines despite increasing, often nominal, commitment to interdisciplinary endeavour. At times, some will have difficulties with the material covered that lies outside their own discipline and, at other times, will find the treatment of their own discipline insufficiently penetrating and extensive. Nonetheless, there is much here that challenges the existing literature both within each of the disciplines and across them. But depth and breadth across the social sciences has been one amongst a number of balances that has necessarily been struck in composing the overall content.

Second, whilst primarily a critical commentary on social capital, and without seeking to be either definitive or comprehensive, the book has relevance for much broader concerns, over and above those already laid out. The most important, to which I return in the closing chapter, is to shed light on the state of social theory and its associated intellectual, mainly academic, life at the turn of the millennium.

Third, to some extent it is a shabby life, and the standards of scholarship – even when not motivated by the imperatives of publishing or perishing and gaining external funding – often simultaneously reach the highest standards in some respects whilst plummeting to the lowest depths in others. At times, I do not hesitate from saying so, verging on the use of ridicule and contempt and, thereby, violating the politeness and respect that are conventional in most academic discourse.[6] Too bad I am tempted to respond unless this defeats the purpose of being taken seriously. This is not a consequence of exercising hostile vengeance against economists who readily dismiss the slightest deviation from their methods and assumptions as being "unscientific" and lacking "rigour", on the basis of a total ignorance of the debates and uncertainties that surround such terms.[7] Gentle and subtle humour would be best in such circumstances, but blunt weapons can hardly be set aside. For much that passes as the highest scholarship is ridiculous and contemptuous. Failure to say so must surely contribute to its persistence even if in milder forms, not least as the supposedly more balanced gain credibility by distancing themselves from the extremes. Nor is this a victimising of the fledgling academics who need guidance in broadening their vision from narrow to wider horizons. We are dealing, for example, with the likes of Nobel prize winners who believe that the world should be understood on the basis of given biologically determined preferences without regard to the literature on such absurdities, and who are ridiculed by their own, more reasonable, colleagues. More generally, if *scholars* and *intellectuals*, those who peddle in ideas, use words like social, capital, trust, ethnicity, civil society, and so on, then they surely open themselves to ridicule and contempt if they do not engage with the corresponding literature superficially if at all. Possibly in less dramatic terms, although needing to be set against the making and results of economic and social policy, economists and social scientists might refer to Hobsbawm's (1997, p. 277) closing assessment on history, when written from a religious or ethnic perspective without regard to the truth:[8]

> Unfortunately, as the situation in large parts of the world at the end of our millennium demonstrates, bad history is not harmless history. The sentences typed on apparently innocuous keyboards may be sentences of death.

Third, and moving to a much more mundane level, as already indicated, the social capital literature has expanded beyond recognition within a few years. I cannot hope to have covered it all, or to deal evenly with what I have covered. At times, I am guilty of superficiality both in relative and absolute terms. At other times, my own devious interests, and capabilities, have taken me to the most arcane level of detail. Such imbalances are in part accidental, depending on what literature has been available, when and how. Had I been writing the book afresh rather than on the basis of contributions already studied for and drafted over the past five years, I would do it differently. But, by the time it was done, I would face exactly the same problem once again. This all taken for granted, I called a flexible stop on consulting the literature around the turn of the millennium, although there is surely slippage on either side.[9] I have also pushed towards making each chapter as self-contained as possible although, in part, relying upon cross-reference between chapters. This has probably meant a slight amount of repetition across the book as a whole but, hopefully, this has been kept to a minimum. Fourth, much material has been downloaded from the internet, either in draft prior to publication or as the only way of accessing published material for lack of local availability of relevant journals. This has meant that pages for citations cannot always be given, and the rooting out of such, when published versions have materialised, has not been assiduously pursued. Last, I am grateful for being able to draw upon my own existing publications and drafts, on which many have usefully commented. Thanks to them and also to those who have assisted in my endeavours, especially those who have done so secure in the knowledge that the results would be unpalatable to them.

The revolution in and around economics

Until the end of the post-war boom, mainstream economics had been dominated by what might be termed a complacent Keynesianism.[10] It was presumed to underpin the macroeconomic policy that would guarantee full employment whilst microeconomics provided a rationale for government intervention in detail to correct market imperfections. The Keynesian compromise between macro and micro, and between theory and policy, were rudely shattered both by the stagflation of the 1970s and the associated intellectual and ideological assaults launched by neo-liberalism. In short, in the 1970s, economics as a discipline was suffering from perhaps its greatest internal crisis of self-confidence. Over the post-war period, microeconomics had developed ever-more sophisticated and esoteric models of the ideal conditions necessary for the existence and stability of a market economy based on optimising agents. But macroeconomics was thrown into disarray by stagflation, not least because the failure of Keynesianism and interventionism gave rise to the neo-liberal alternative of presuming that markets work well if left alone – just as market economies were performing as badly as at any time for fifty years!

After a brief interlude of Milton Friedman's crude monetarism, the discipline was saved from its doldrums by the new classical economics. It draws upon a new technique: that of rational expectations, the idea that, in effect, each economic agent acts upon the same, consistent economic model, fully deploying the information available. This simple, wildly unrealistic, assumption appeared to give rise to dramatic implications – that all previously estimated macroeconomic models were inappropriate for policy making, and government could not effectively and systematically intervene to shift the path of the economy.[11] Economic fluctuations became primarily understood as the consequence of responses to shocks by optimising and efficient economic agents who would neutralise systematic government intervention by anticipating its intended impact. With the rise of neo-liberalism, government expenditure was perceived to be excessive and government intervention as inducing inefficiency. Far from perfect competition and general equilibrium being the ideal from which deviations in the form of market imperfections justified state intervention, the ideal of attaining the free market and minimal state gave rise to what Carrier and Miller (eds) (1998) refer to as the new economic virtualism – the imperative to remould the world to conform to an imagined ideal of perfectly working markets spread as wide and deep as possible.

But the triumph of neo-liberalism, and its academic counterpart in the new classical economics, is far from a complete picture. For, it did not take long for the economics profession to embrace rational expectations which, for technical reasons, considerably ratcheted up the levels of mathematical and statistical techniques required. It was also realised that the results of the new classical economics depended less upon rational expectations as such and more upon the accompanying assumption of instantaneous market-clearing in all markets – in other words, that supply and demand are brought into equality with one another at all times and at once by price movements (by analogy with the trading in foreign currencies through computer links). In the case of real business cycle theory, for example, fluctuations in (un)employment are freely chosen with workers seeking to labour more (less) when productivity, and hence wages, are randomly higher (lower).

As a result of its content and results, the new classical economics served a number of crucial functions for the discipline. It rescued it from the analytical stagnation attached to the Keynesian/monetarism debate. On the one hand, it posed instantaneous market clearing as an extreme against which other models could react. On the other hand, it prompted the introduction of rational expectations into models that had not used this assumption previously. It pushed economics as a discipline further down the route of esoteric modelling in which mathematical and statistical technique prevails over conceptual advance. In addition, the new classical economics posed an intellectual challenge to its opponents in the form of explaining why prices might not adjust instantaneously in some markets. By resuscitating Say's Law of markets, that supply creates its own demand, in the context of rational expectations, in a risky world subject to random shocks, the discipline established an extreme standard against and from which an agenda of less extreme mainstream alternatives have subsequently been able to prosper.

For, in a perverse way, neo-liberalism had the advantage of forging a link between micro and macro, even if in the negative or vacuous sense of emphasising the leaving of the micro "supply-side" to the market, with the macro demand-side also looking after itself apart from accommodating, not excessive, targeting of the money supply, government expenditure, etc. It further undermined confidence in the state by questioning its efficiency and motivation in view of rent seeking and corruption. In short, economic theory confronted two challenges: on the one hand, why are market imperfections so important; on the other hand, why would an improvement be guaranteed by intervention given government may be worse than market failure?

Over the past two decades, these challenges have been met by what I have termed a revolution in or, more exactly, around economics.[12] Briefly, as before, emphasis has been placed upon market imperfections, only with the new twist that these are also perceived to be the consequence of informational imperfections and asymmetries around sale and purchase. Consider, for example, the market for health insurance. Individuals are liable to know more about their health than insurers who may, nonetheless, have information about the average health of their (potential) customers. At a given premium price, only those with relatively poor health will apply.

Consequently, there are three possible outcomes as a result of what is known as adverse selection. First, markets may clear (supply equal demand) at too high a price since the most healthy would take out insurance at a lower price but cannot be offered it by insurers ignorant of their lower risk (and if there were lower premiums for the healthy, everyone would present themselves as healthy). Second, the market may not clear, with demand exceeding supply, since the insurers might decide only to take a certain amount of risk but do not raise their premiums for fear of driving away a disproportionately large number of relatively healthy customers. Third, it is possible for markets to be absent altogether. Any level of premium, whether high or low, for the aged and infirm, for example, may only attract such bad risks on average as to be loss making. It is also possible, in view of what is known as moral hazard, that, once insured, customers take insufficient care of themselves since their behaviour cannot be monitored and they know that any medical bills will be covered.

A number of points need to be made about what Stiglitz (1994) has termed the information-theoretic economics on which this account has been based. First, information can be gathered on individuals to temper the asymmetry through medical check-up and histories, on smoking, etc. But this is to incur what are known as transaction costs, and there will always be the potential for these to outstrip the value of rectifying residual informational imperfection.

Second, there is nothing specific about insurance markets although these might, in some respects, be thought to suffer from significant informational imperfections of particular types. But the argument about different information available to buyers and sellers is general and can be found in any market. Particularly favoured, for example, are those for finance, where banks are concerned about the credibility of their customers, and for labour markets where employers need to assess the skills, work effort and loyalty of their employees.

Third, marking a distinctive and remarkable development for economics as a discipline, there has been, most important for my account, a new-found capacity to address economic *and* social structure, apparently non-optimising such as customary behaviour or social norms, and the formation of institutions.[13] How is this possible? In the case of employment, for example, the optimising employer may well structure the labour market, offering a real wage below which the unemployed of the same qualities as the employed are prepared to work. The labour market becomes structured between employed and unemployed, and can also be structured across the employed. More generally, imperfect information may lead to market structures on the basis of proxy variables such as gender, for example. If, on average, it is believed that women are liable to leave work to raise a family, then all women will be treated as such. This can have the knock-on effect of lowering their incentive to be trained, consolidating their comparative disadvantage (relative to husbands) in the labour market and providing a rationale for being assigned to household responsibilities.

Thus, imperfect information leads optimising individuals to structure markets, and for these to be reproduced and consolidated. In addition, the theory suggests an explanation both for the formation of (non-market) institutions and for apparently non-optimising behaviour. For these can be the optimal response for handling informational asymmetries outside the market, in order to build up trust between contracting parties, for example, or mutual reputations.

The reason why such results are significant is that they appear to square the circle as far as mainstream economics' relations with the other social sciences are concerned. For, previously, it was necessary to take the social, institutions and customary behaviour as given with the latter taken to be irrational. Now, even on the continuing basis of methodological individualism, this need no longer be the case. The explanatory scope of the basic neoclassical principles has been considerably widened to incorporate what has previously been considered to be the analytical terrain of the other social sciences.

This is why I refer to a revolution around economics. For it reverses a central feature of the marginalist revolution of the 1870s that established modern mainstream economics. It forged a sharp separation of the economy from the rest of society and an exclusive pre-occupation with the economy as market relations. The new information-theoretic approach to economics addresses both the economic and the non-economic, and their interaction. As a result, it is colonising the other social sciences in a variety of ways, with a variety of results and to a greater or lesser extent. This is evidenced by a whole new range of sub-disciplines – the new institutional economics, the new political economy, the new development economics, the new household economics, etc.[14]

Even so, imperialistic designs by economics on the other social sciences are far from new. Because of its deploying universal categories – such as production, consumption and utility – it has long made incursions to incorporate non-economic behaviour within its compass as part and parcel of what would now be termed rational choice analysis. Only, however, with recent developments within the discipline has it been able to offer an analysis of the social, institutional and customary without which it has always tended to meet a frosty reception from other social sciences.

But, despite examining economic and non-economic simultaneously, current developments do not restore economics to its position from before the marginalist revolution. Unlike classical political economy, the theory remains rooted in methodological individualism, albeit with optimisation in the context of imperfect and asymmetric information. In this and other respects, it shares more features with traditional neoclassical economics than it sheds. For it continues to depend upon the same universal – and hence asocial and ahistorical – categories, including an unproblematic notion of information itself. In this respect, however, it does claim to address historical specificity but not in terms of its conceptual apparatus. Rather, it is acknowledged that economies (and societies) are path dependent and subject to multiple equilibria. History matters only in the sense of having laid down social and economic structures and customs in the past from which follows a deterministic if stochastic evolutionary outcome.

Having now studied the colonisation of the other social sciences by economics, I would draw some general, and harsh, conclusions about how it proceeds as far as the economists' practices are concerned.[15] First, it tends to be parasitical upon the other social sciences, picking up ideas that have originated there and reworking them through the new economic principles. This does not have to be so, however, since the process can also be marked by mathematical formalism and inventive speculation – about how households are run, for example. Second, contributions are often profoundly ignorant of existing literature since they only need pick up and run with a single idea gleaned from another discipline and uprooted from its analytical and contextual traditions. Third, ignorance is often complemented by arrogance in believing that new results within economics are original whereas they will have long been known and even better understood within other disciplines. Fourth, the ignorance and arrogance is often accompanied by contempt for the failure of the other social sciences to have adopted the methods by which economists have proven their results.

From an analytical perspective, however, the most important feature of economics' incursions into other social sciences is its reductionism. This has a number of components. Economics is dependent upon methodological individualism of a special type – exclusive reliance upon utility maximisation. For technical tractability in its formal modelling, it will often reduce analysis to a few variables or factors. These are liable to be ahistorical or asocial, stripped of context and universalised, most notably in the use of notions such as utility, production function, etc., and especially – as will be seen – in the understanding of social capital itself (in the understanding both of social and of capital). Inevitably, a corollary is the total absence of any interpretative content to the concepts deployed. Economists remain untouched by postmodernist influences even though they have, for example, become concerned with the economic effects of ethnicity (quite apart from gender). In other words, the conceptual apparatus of economists is totally unreconstructed. With concepts taken as given and unproblematic, the relationship between theory and practice tends to be based on a direct leap into econometrics where data represent the world as it is and by which theories can be tested. Whether in pure, often speculative theory, or from empirical work, policy conclusions are readily posited in the form of correcting market imperfections as long as the state is benevolent or no worse than the market.

So much for the way in which economists have addressed the other social sciences. But how have its colonising designs been received? Initially, consider the intellectual climate as far as the other social sciences are concerned. Oversimplifying and overgeneralising, there is now something of a retreat from the excesses of postmodernism. It has had a lasting effect or set the context for much "postpostmodernism". As such, for my purposes, it has been marked by a number of important aspects. First, postmodernism has witnessed a flight from the objective to the subjective, with an associated rise in the appeal of theoretical relativism (one theory or view is as valid as another is). Second, as a result, social theory has found eclecticism to be more acceptable. Arguments and concepts can be picked up from different sources and combined together without regard to their separate, let alone their mutual, consistency. Third, the economy, especially production, has been perceived to be unduly privileged, leading to a focus upon the non-economic, especially consumption and culture. Fourth, interest in the so-called new social movements has tended to discredit, and shift attention way from, class analysis. Fifth, novel forms of discourse have arisen, not least in discourse theory itself, with new analytical formalisms in the study of symbolic representation, and in the critical deconstruction of meaning, etc.

Jean Baudrillard has been a leading figure in the postmodernist movement. In the context of consumption, Fine and Leopold (1993, Chapter 19) have argued that his particular flight of fancy arises out of the use of the notion of the symbolic value of objects. It has allowed an exclusive pre-occupation with the redefinition of the meaning of the use value of commodities without reference to their material properties. By the latter is not simply meant the objects of consumption in terms of their physical properties but also the influence of the material cultures surrounding the activities by which they become consumed, not least in being produced as exchange values for the market. Significantly, Slater (1997, p. 158) perceives Baudrillard as having reduced consumption to a matter of signs alone:[16]

> Barthes and Baudrillard ... merely adopt Veblen's general idea that the only real function of goods is to signify status. They then generalize this to all classes and translate it into semiotic terms. Baudrillard takes this furthest, to the point of arguing that we no longer consume things but only signs.

Now the period of postmodernist pre-occupation with consumption and its paraphernalia in isolation from the economic has passed its peak. Yet, in the hands of Baudrillard, for example, it continues to exert an influence. These two points are ably illustrated by contributions such as the aptly named, *Forget Baudrillard*, in which Rojek and Turner (1993) point out that he has become viewed as a figure of unique importance, subtle and powerful, but equally ludicrous and maladroit. Whilst, by implication, most will not have gone as far as Baudrillard, it is also important to recognise that most have gone some of the way, and that the detachment from the material realities of life is not confined to the world of consumption alone. Rather, the flight from exchange value to the virtual world of use values is equally, more fundamentally, an abandonment of the world of capital and capitalism.[17] By the same token, the flight from capital is of necessity a flight from the economy and, hence, from economics. Consequently, quite apart from its own analytically inhospitable environment as far as social theory is concerned, mainstream economics has commanded a near monopoly of its subject matter without challenge in the period of postmodernism, especially with the declining influence of radical political economy over the past twenty years. In this respect, however, it is also crucial to recognise that mainstream economics, and much of the heterodoxy, does not have a theory of consumption as such.[18] To be more precise, consumption is treated as if it were production – with individuals maximising the utility they can produce under the constraints imposed by the price system.[19] At most, the economics of consumer theory is a theory of the demand for quantities of goods. The activities and especially the meanings associated with consumption are simply set aside.

Postmodernism has exploited this duality in economic theory – the appropriation of the economic but the abandonment of consumption. For it has abandoned the economic and appropriated consumption, albeit in its own way.[20] The one exception that proves the rule is where postmodernism has confronted the economic, as in theories of post-Fordism, neo-Fordism or flexible specialisation. Here we find that deference is paid to the economy alone at the expense of engaging with postmodernist notions of consumption at all except as fragmented demand. For post-Fordist notions of consumption are confined to the unjustified and unspecified assertion that mass consumption of uniform goods has given way to the demand for fast changing, differentiated and customised products. This suffices to support a particular view of the modern era as one based on new forms of flexible production.[21]

Of course, economics was remarkably, and uniquely across the social sciences, untouched by the impact of postmodernism. However, as the latter's influence wanes, social sciences other than economics are strengthening their interest in the material world, of which economic issues form a part. In short, postmodernism and economics stand at two opposite extremes, in both method and subject matter, with a partial vacuum in the huge void between them. As a result, other social sciences are particularly vulnerable to the colonising incursions of economics, especially in view of its new-found micro-foundations, as long as postmodernist concerns with the construction of use value can be set aside. For this and other reasons, it would be a mistake to see economics as simply sweeping unhindered and uniformly across the other social sciences.

First, even if economics has become more attractive or acceptable in view of its ability to address the social, it is still riddled with problems from the perspective of other social sciences. Second, whilst economics is heavily reliant upon formal mathematical models, this is not usually characteristic of the other social sciences. Consequently, the results from economics tend to be incorporated in an informal fashion reflecting the character of the recipient discipline just as, for example, human capital has been deployed in a variety of ways across the social sciences without necessarily reflecting precisely its initiating meanings within economics. Third, by the same token, the extent and nature of influence of a colonising economics depends upon the intellectual traditions and momentum of its host. The outcome will inevitably be uneven from discipline to discipline and from topic to topic. For example, in contrast to the influence of human capital theory, the explosive growth of interest in consumption across the social sciences has been more or less unaffected by economics, not least because it is heavily concerned with the meaning of objects as well as their provision.[22]

In general, within economics itself, the new theory has advanced in the form of relatively sophisticated mathematical models – as extraordinarily esoteric in their content as they are ambitious in their reductionist claims. The world is explained by (informational) market imperfections. The results, however, tend to be readily translated into informal propositions that are often striking in their simplicity – the idea that institutions and history matter, for example. Consequently, the influence of the new economics can be felt without explicit recognition of the methodology and assumptions upon which it is based. Further, because the new takes the old economics as its starting point, it only reintroduces the social as a result of informational imperfections and the historical as path-dependence. In this respect, the new theory is richer than the old in terms of analytical structure. On the other hand, it has a much wider, even unlimited, scope of application set against which its broader analytical framework is most modest if not totally inadequate. Paradoxically, as a result, the social and historical for the new theory is otherwise an empty canvas upon which the other social sciences, however coherently, can fill out their own landscape and detail. Such can even be interpreted as civilising a rampant economics by bringing the insights of other social sciences to bear upon it. By doing so, social theory is no longer reduced to market imperfections and their non-market consequences, as for economists, but can be attached to a greater or lesser extent to such notions. Thus, power, conflict, and class, for example, can either be eschewed altogether (as is most common) or interpreted informationally in terms of greater access to resources or knowledge, as strategies within game theory, or collectively rationalised on an individualistic basis. As Gibbons (1997, p. 127) perceptively puts it:

> Game theory is rampant in economics ... game-theoretic models allow economists to study the implications of rationality, self-interest and equilibrium, both in market interactions ... and in nonmarket interactions.

A further factor in the impact of economics imperialism is the extent to which a rational choice approach has a presence (and can be strengthened). Such allows a seamless entry of the methods of mainstream economics, albeit augmented by information-theoretic analysis and its incorporation of the social or whatever on the basis of methodological individualism. For those pre-disposed to reject rational choice and methodological individualism more generally, an understandable response is to retreat from the explicit or implicit incursions of economics into their discipline. The economic can be eschewed altogether, drawing upon an easy critical dismissal in the wake of the postmodernist, and earlier, insight that (the meaning of) objects that economics and its disciples take as given are socially constructed. Whilst preserving a space for itself, such a response is equally to concede that occupied by the economic, within economics itself as well as its application in other disciplines.

In a nutshell, then, economics is seeking to colonise other social sciences and is succeeding, albeit with mixed results, to an unprecedented extent. In part, this reflects developments within economics itself whereby it perceives itself as being capable of addressing the social despite its dependence upon methodological individualism. In addition, the other social sciences are unevenly retreating from the extremes of postmodernism and, not surprisingly, in the return to the real, they are seeking to incorporate an economic content. Whether by accident or design, economics as a discipline has set itself the task of seizing this newly created opportunity; but what it has on offer is totally unacceptable to those rejecting rational choice, unless it be veiled in the analytical vernacular of its host. Consequently, it is essential that other social sciences remain deeply suspicious and critical of the analytical gifts being proffered by economics, despite what are often attractive appearances to the contrary. There is no short cut to the (re)incorporation of the economic which depends upon a full and proper account of the political economy of contemporary capitalism.

Overview

Most of the colonisation of the other social sciences by economics falls somewhere between these two extremes of uncritical acceptance and critical retreat. Social capital, in what is by now its diverse range of uses, epitomises all of the observations laid out above. As will be seen, its very name is highly significant, with capital taken as economic and individualistic, only for it to be qualified by bringing back in the social as, by implication, the non-economic. In contrast, Chapter 2 establishes that capital is an economic category and, in reality, is itself social, thereby creating an oxymoron for the mirror image of social capital, the notion that some other type of capital is not social. Why, then, has it proved so popular? To a large extent, it is a consequence of the power of capital itself. In a sense, this involves an inversion of Berman's (1982) discussion of modernity in terms of Marx's *Communist Manifesto* dictum, "All that is solid melts into air". For the notion of social capital depends upon making capital out of the ephemeral or, at least, the non-economic, quite apart from stripping the economic of its social content. Chapter 2 discusses this in terms of the enigma and fluidity of capital. Because its underlying social relations are difficult to identify and, yet, reappear in many forms and are facilitated by, or depend upon, a host of other conditions, any or all of these are potentially identified as capital irrespective of the extent to which they are rooted in capitalist society and its pre-conditions. In short, a sort of capital- and capitalism-fetishism, by analogy with commodity fetishism, reigns supreme. The failure to specify capital properly in its social and historical context allows it to roam freely over any number of non-economic or social characteristics, whether attached to capitalism or not.

Chapter 2 opens Part II of the book that is primarily concerned with the origins and evolution of social capital. It provides the background for the critical assessment of four writers, each of whom, in a different way, allows for the notion to be placed in perspective, both in its foundations and in its subsequent meteoric rise. At last, having tried the patience of the reader with the first two chapters of preliminaries, social capital is addressed directly. But is this a false dawn? For Chapter 3 focuses on the work of Gary Becker and how he, somewhat surprisingly, came to incorporate social capital into his thinking. This requires some consideration of his so-called economic approach to social theory prior to the later dependence upon social capital. How could someone embrace such a concept who had previously pathologically denied the social as a result of an approach based on methodological individualism and society as if a market? The answer requires consideration of how Becker's virtual world without social capital proved incapable of addressing all of the social phenomena he sought to explain. Social capital is forced upon the economist in order to fill out an otherwise incomplete universe.

To some extent, then, this and the next chapter on Bourdieu reflect my own starting point in addressing social capital – how I first came to study it and how it concerns the shifting relationship between economics and other social sciences. More generally, although economics is not the discipline making the major contribution to the study of social capital, it is immanently its alter ego, either in method and methodology or, more narrowly, in hypothesising that economic effects arise out of non-economic factors. Laying out the views of both Becker and Bourdieu at the outset has the further advantage of marking the analytical boundaries that contain social capital for they lie at opposite extremes. Becker defines social capital as any social, or non-market, interaction with a continuing effect; essentially, it fills out whatever is left over after (the presumption of) taking account of other types of capital, such as natural, physical, and human (or personal more generally) capital. This has become a standard procedure for the literature, with the leftovers ranging over networks, customs, institutions, civil society, the family, and so on, with an equally varied range of applications or outcomes, from the economy to government to criminality, etc. What is a remarkable paradox, however, is that Becker should be the economist at the forefront in deploying the notion of social capital. His earlier, crude form of colonising the social sciences was based on society as if market without otherwise allowing for the social to exist. For this he has been roundly criticised by his fellow economists for relying too exclusively on the supposed rationality of the optimising individual and for extending such analysis into arenas where it is inappropriate. Their preference has been to emphasise how the social arises out of rational and, subsequently, historically evolved responses to market imperfections. However, this is precisely the basis on which Becker proceeds to rationalise his use of social capital.

There are two important implications. First, Becker's use of social capital in advance of his more rounded and reasonable colleagues is a striking demonstration that the distance between him and them is extremely narrow and increasingly academic. Essentially, there is a single mainstream economic approach to the economic and its relationship to the non-economic or social. Second, the economist's use of social capital is based on what can be represented by the formula, $e = (mi)^2$, where e stands for economics and mi stands both for methodological individualism and market imperfections. In addition, $ss = e$; social science can be reduced to the corresponding economic approach. In short, and not surprisingly, the contribution to social capital by economics is inevitably based on methodological individualism and a corresponding reductionism of the social to rational choice in response to market imperfections.

Such economic interpretations of social capital do effectively reduce its objects of study from air to the solid, treating social relations as if physical capital in all but form. In contrast, Chapter 4 considers Bourdieu's contribution. It provides a remarkable illustration of how even a scholar attuned to the social and historical boundedness of categories has, nonetheless, fallen prey to the illusions attached to capitalism. For Bourdieu, capital and its various manifestations can be treated as if open to projection both across various aspects of capitalist society as well as to other modes of production. Not surprisingly, this leads Bourdieu to posit a variety of types of capital – the cultural and the symbolic, for example, as well as social capital. In retrospect, however, his saving grace is a continuing analytical commitment to the idea that such capitals are socially and historically limited to the circumstances that create them. In other words, they are contextual and constructed. This has two important implications for Bourdieu's continuing position within the evolving literature. First, and foremost, his analytical insights are simply set aside despite his occasionally being acknowledged as an initiator of the social capital concept. For, as social capital gathers momentum in its indiscriminate application across the social sciences, there is no place for it to be grounded historically or socially. Second, the other forms of capital highlighted by Bourdieu become equally anonymous, being confined to prominence only within specialised fields. For reference to the symbolic and the cultural inevitably render the social and historical unavoidable. Social capital can only reign supreme by excising the cultural, the symbolic and Bourdieu.

In place of Bourdieu, James Coleman is much more likely to be lauded as the inspiration for social capital. His founding work on social capital is the subject of Chapter 5. In what has become a traditional procedure for the literature, a simple hypothesis, in his case concerning the positive relationship between supportive family background and (Catholic) schooling, was extrapolated into a general theory of social capital, in terms of both sources and effects. Rarely referenced in the subsequent literature, however, has been any study of Coleman's own analytical background. He had been a long-standing and extremely active campaigner for the application of rational choice in the study of sociology. By the end of the 1980s, social capital proved a successful instrument for this project where previously rational choice had failed to gain acceptance when offered in other guises. This is especially so of a literature that has become even less acknowledged than the rational choice origins of social capital. For social exchange theory, in which Coleman was a major participant, also sought to address social theory on the basis of individual choice. In particular, how is the micro to be related to the macro, and the individual to the social, and, ultimately, how is the meaning of social exchanges (understood as the sum of individual interactions) to be incorporated? It effectively failed under the weight of its own inconsistencies. Undeterred, Coleman transformed social exchange to social capital, reinvigorated individual as rational choice, and shifted analytical emphasis away from psychological and other factors towards the economic, scarcely acknowledging the significance of the earlier literature even as he himself continued to contribute to it. In addition, no doubt partly explaining Becker's early interest in social capital, he and Coleman had a close working relationship at the University of Chicago. Whilst Coleman claims to have been bringing sociological insights to economics, the opposite seems closer to the truth.

One of the, again rarely observed, ironies of Coleman's contribution, irrespective of its analytical merits, is that subsequent research has revealed his empirical results concerning the relationship between familial background and schooling to be highly questionable once other correcting variables are taken into account. Such inconvenient niceties are legion in the case of Robert Putnam's contributions, covered in Chapter 6. If Coleman is a founding family member, foisting rational choice and economic reductionism on an often-unsuspecting audience, Putnam has become the crown prince of social capital. His initial contribution concerned differential regional development in north and south Italy, with government performance explained by uneven incidence of social capital in the form of horizontal civic association, laid down almost a millennium previously. Transported in truly Machiavellian style to the United States, however, Putnam's hypothesis verges on self-parody as its citizens are perceived to have fallen victim to "bowling alone", losing their great Tocquevillean civic traditions, not least in devoting undue attention to television sets. From a social asset built over centuries in Italy, social capital is now subject in the United States to rapid transformation in quantity and quality, and capable of addressing, possibly reversing, economic and social malaise. Unfortunately, from a scholarly point of view, each of Putnam's case studies has been subject to battery after battery of devastating theoretical and empirical critiques.

As a result, he has perpetrated what I term a "benchkin", named for a classic example of what is a very common form of "scientific progress" within economics. Theory, not necessarily original, is put forward to explain what subsequently proves to be false empirical evidence. Paradoxically, when this is revealed, far from the original contribution being rejected, it grows in stature, appearing to draw strength and support from the considered criticisms that are levelled against it. Look at all of these established scholars, politicians and social commentators, including the popular media, taking this issue seriously. There must be something to it, and prominence grows especially where it strikes an ideological chord, like the decline of civic America. In, through and beyond Putnam's hands, social capital has become a benchkin of enormous proportions with his work becoming the most cited across the social sciences in the 1990s.

This is reflected in Chapter 7 in providing an extensive if still partial review of the literature. It is not simply that social capital has extended its reach both theoretically and empirically across social theory as a whole, to the extent of claiming that those who have not used it explicitly have, in fact, done so unwittingly. Rather, the evolving and expanding literature is marked by two, closely related aspects, that prove futile in exhausting its gargantuan analytical appetite. On the one hand, criticism serves merely to provide for missing factors that need to be incorporated – the horizontal and the vertical, the individual and the social, the micro, meso and macro, the public and the private, the upside and the downside, ethnicity, race and gender, formal politics, trade unionism, and the internet, and, if pushed, power, conflict and inequality. It is a matter of putting Humpty together again after the fall from the rational choice wall. In other words, social capital becomes a dumping ground for synthesis across the social sciences. This even extends to social and historical context and meaning itself. On the other hand, then, with the last point reflecting the re-incorporation of Bourdieu following his previous excision, social capital proceeds by bringing back in all the factors that were excluded in its initial formulation under the rational choice framework set down by Coleman. There is, however, one more or less unavoidable exception: that is the failure to bring back in the economic, capital, as social in any sense other than as, a possibly disguised, information-theoretic analysis based on $ss = e = (mi)^2$. In this respect, no matter how much the traditional variables of social science are included within social capital, both to answer criticism and to expand its frontiers, it will never satisfactorily address the relationship between the economic and the social. The irony is the extent to which social capitalists see themselves as civilising economists where, effectively, they leave them unchallenged.

Part III addresses the role of social capital in development studies, specifically confronting the impact made by the World Bank that has heavily promoted social capital in its own work and that of others. Chapter 8 seeks to explain why social capital should have been so important to the World Bank. First, the World Bank's general approach has shifted from the Washington to the post-Washington consensus. Pioneered by its Chief Economist, Joe Stiglitz, during the second half of the 1990s, the post-Washington consensus is nothing neither more nor less than the revolution in and around economics as applied to development studies. It seeks to replace the debate, attached to the Washington consensus, over state versus market, in which the International Monetary Fund (IMF) and the World Bank favoured the market, with a debate over the extent and incidence of market imperfections and the corresponding role for a less than perfect state. In other words, the post-Washington consensus is more state-friendly and more social-friendly than its predecessor but it is still reductionist to the information-theoretic analysis of market imperfections in order to explain both economic and non-economic alike. Within the World Bank, the post-Washington consensus has created an opening for social theorists who have otherwise been dominated by economists, both in numbers, focus and influence. They have been quick to seize it. But it is an opportunity that has strict limitations, serving more to facilitate unchanged economic policies and policy analysis rather than to challenge them. The point is not that the research and ideology of the World Bank has no influence on its operations and on wider external research and policy debates. This is argued to be uneven from issue to issue. Rather, the reintroduction of the social has the troubling dual aspect both of rhetorically smoothing the acceptance of at most marginally altered economic policies and analysis and of broadening the scope of justifiable intervention from the economic to the social in order to ensure policies are successful. Social, and covert political, engineering is to complement economic engineering, with social capital providing a client-friendly rhetoric.

Against this general background, Chapter 9 reviews the World Bank's work on social capital, most notably through close examination of what has come out of its dedicated website. Not surprisingly, the propositions of the previous part of the book are all borne out in the specific context of development studies and the research environment and endeavours of the World Bank. In addition, it is revealed how influential the World Bank has been in incorporating previously dissident voices and ideas. This all reflects a continuing failure to assess critically the economic basis on which the post-Washington consensus has been built. Accordingly, within the World Bank, limited horizons are being set in bringing "the social" to the attention of economists. In order for social theorists to be taken seriously, they cannot question core economic analysis even in departing the world previously ruled by the neo-liberal Washington consensus. Part III is completed by a more technical chapter concerned with theoretical issues raised by the problem of how social capital might be measured, drawing upon standard literature from within economics. By reviewing similar issues in the context of capital theory, social choice theory, and the formation of social norms, the underlying problems with social capital are confirmed from another angle. In addition, some light is thrown on the way in which the concerns associated with the use of social capital might be more usefully addressed.

Part IV is confined to a single chapter that places the discussion of social capital in the wider context of the way in which social theory is manufactured today. To a large extent, what has come before leaves the impression of deeply pessimistic prospects. Research has been far from scholarly in the round, is subject to fashions and dictated by personal motivation of the sort summarised by "publish, raise external funding and conform or perish". Nor is this simply a matter of vulgar materialism on the part of scholars and their institutions although this should not be underestimated. For some are only too aware of the limitations imposed by notions such as social capital. Indeed, they have pointed them out in passing only to carry on using the notion on the grounds that it is better to compromise at this stage with an economism that has been unduly reductionist and committed to the market. In this light, analytical ambitions are clipped to conform to what is perceived to be achievable, a sort of scholarly Third Way, more attuned to opening up an agenda or two than confronting directly the power, conflicts and contradictions associated with capitalism.

But this is to accept too bleak a picture of what can be achieved. As already suggested at the outset in this chapter, there are those who, in the retreat from postmodernism, are genuinely concerned to examine the economic realities that are central to outcomes in contemporary capitalism. Political economy offers the only opportunity to do so in a way that potentially avoids reductionism and economism, without offering any such guarantees. To avoid political economy in deference to a strategy of educating mainstream economists in the virtues of social theory is at best to postpone the reckoning, at worst to put it off altogether.

Part II

2   The enigma and fluidity of capital[1]

Introduction

This chapter has two main purposes. It seeks to a limited extent to lay out how I understand capital and capitalism, at least in its social structures, relations and processes. This provides some theoretical background to the book as a whole. Within this chapter, though, it furnishes a perspective from which some understanding is offered on why social capital should prove to be such an appealing concept despite or even because of its definitional and conceptual conundrums. The second section begins by arguing that social capital is simply an oxymoron. To be otherwise, there would have to be some sort of capital that is not social relative to which social capital has the potential to be distinctive. As capital, especially as embedded within capitalism, is profoundly social and historical in content, this is not possible.

The third section draws upon the analysis in the previous section. For capital will be shown to be social in particular ways as it goes about its business, successively adopting the forms of money, means of production, and commodities; being attached to particular economic and social structures; and incorporating specific types of power and control. Such complexity surrounding both capital and capitalism has the effect of inducing capital to be seen in anything and in any instance that in some way mimics any single part of its various aspects. In particular, whether explicitly as in mainstream economics or implicitly for other social sciences, if the economy is perceived to be non-social, especially when associated with the market, then it is possible to construct social capital out of what is presumed to be non-economic aspects of capital. In short, the third section seeks to show that the fluidity of capital in practice gives rise to equally fluid notions of what it is, with false and/or partial understandings ultimately paving a path for the notion of social capital. In the concluding remarks, the notion of social capital is understood as a particularly intense form of commodity fetishism. For, by it, capital is understood as asocial, so that the social can be brought back in having been arbitrarily excluded in the first place.

Patience is a virtue – but is it capital?[2]

One of the merits and motives for the use of social capital as a conceptual tool is that it seeks to integrate economic with non-economic analysis or at least for the two to complement one another. Its use is an acknowledgement that the economy is dependent upon and is affected by the non-economic. As a consequence, once the term is unbundled, the social and the capital tend to stand, respectively, for one or more aspects of the non-economic and the economic. But the correspondence is not perfect for social capital can be used in contexts without what might be construed as a directly economic content. Possession of social capital, for example, is deemed to enable individuals to accomplish higher achievement in many walks of life – not just to become wealthy but to be healthy and less liable to a life of crime.

Leaving aside this last qualification until later, the notion of social capital necessarily incorporates an opposition between the social and the capital. Here is social, and here is capital. They are separate, so let them be brought together. At the very least, there is an implication that there is some capital that is not social, otherwise the distinction of social from other types of capital becomes meaningless. I do not want to enter into semantics here and argue over whether social is being applied to capital purely for convenience, and possibly as a clumsy or inappropriate adjective. For, to a greater or lesser extent in practice, whether recognised or not, a key aspect of social capital is that it counterposes the social with capital. There must be at least some part of capital that is not social, or asocial, in order to create room for that part which is social.

In this regard, mainstream economists do have a degree of empty logic on their side. For, whilst predominantly unconscious of the deeper issues involved, there is an explicit understanding that capital is first and foremost to be understood as asocial, as the broadly defined physical (productive) properties of available resources and, ultimately, their capacity to provide an equally asocial contribution to utility. Consequently, it does make sense to extend the notion of capital to social capital to include those comparable economic effects that derive from non-physical features of society. Social capital is an explicit recognition of adding society to an otherwise asocial economy.

Social scientists other than economists tend to be less precise about what they mean by capital. For them, it might be social. If so, for social capital, it must be social in some different economic sense that is not usually elaborated. When it is, uncritical faith is placed in the standard terminology of mainstream economics – natural, physical, financial, and human capital – from which a point of departure in the form of social capital is desired. In short, use of the notion of social capital requires a non-trivial understanding, possibly overlapping, both of the social and of capital, which presumes that there can be some sort of capital that is not social in some distinctive sense.

My point in this somewhat pedantic discussion is extremely simple. It is to deny the veracity of an opposition between social and capital, from which the distinctiveness of social capital must inevitably be drawn. The reason is that the presumption that capital is asocial is wrong. Of course, it might be argued that this depends upon how we define social and how we define capital. Capital, for example, could be understood as resources in general and the social as the use to which those resources are put, equally in the broadest sense. Even this definition and distinction involve a fudge if they are to have any analytical rather than descriptive purchase. For they presuppose that we know what are to count as resources before they are put to use, and this is questionable. Indeed, it could be argued that one of the achievements of the social capital literature is to demonstrate that there are resources out there in society which are not generally recognised as such because they do not directly take some sort of commercial form. Much of this literature has also drawn upon a more subtle point. There is more to resources than a list of available objects and their attributes, with more or less of these being deemed to qualify as resource-defined capital. What is useful will also depend upon what is perceived to be useful. This, in turn, in the broadest sense will not rest exclusively upon available objects but upon beliefs and ideologies surrounding those objects, even the language with which they are expressed. These are necessarily subject to social determinants.[3]

These observations will appear facile to any with the slightest acquaintance with postmodernism and the (older) notion that the content and meaning of objects are subject to shifting social construction. Even to deploy a neutral term such as resources to get at a definition of capital without initial social content is doomed to fail. A particularly appropriate example is provided by the notion of natural capital which, along with physical and human (and sometimes financial) capital, is now supposed to fill out the space prior to allowance for social capital. For there can be little doubt that the term has arisen in the wake of the higher profile of environmental considerations in recent years. This in itself does not invalidate an asocial understanding of capital. It could be argued that we have simply more explicitly and broadly recognised a form of capital that always existed but was inappropriately taken for granted as a free good, as in the depletion of the ozone layer. Yet, there can be little doubt that environmental concerns have not only shifted our awareness of the environment but also how we perceive the world of capital. We want to know something about how goods are made, what content they have – are they the products of environmentally sustainable capital, etc.? Throughout history the same has applied to other forms of capital, as with concern for the terms and conditions under which workers have produced goods (and campaigns against child labour today).[4] These examples show that capital is not natural, not even natural capital, but that the meanings and hence uses attached to it are subject to considerable contest and conflict. Corporations spend considerable funds in public relations exercises in order to do much more than advertise their products. They also seek to persuade us of their credibility as capitals.[5] Further, this has a knock-on effect in the resources that are available and how they can be used – are they environmentally and ethically acceptable or presentable as such, for example?

Essentially, the question of the viability of an asocial capital has now been turned on its head. It would no longer appear to be possible to consider capital, or anything else at all, except in its social context. As will be seen throughout this book, the theoretical literature on social capital has been particularly careless in its consideration of the historical and social contexts in which its object of study has been located. It is, then, scarcely surprising that it should be equally careless at the outset in investigating the social content of the capital from which social capital takes its point of departure.

This is the substantive issue to be taken up in this chapter. A constructive or even a critical approach to social capital appears to depend upon defining "social" and "capital" and bringing them together to provide for a distinctive social capital. The tack adopted here is different. It is to lay out some of the ways in which capital is social, the rationale for which has already been provided above. One of the problems in doing so is that, apart from specifying what is meant by capital, which is done, it is also necessary to define social. This is not done explicitly, not least because what is social is itself extremely slippery in content and subject, varying in the literature over a variety of what are often self-serving purposes. When Mrs Thatcher says there is no such thing as society, not even her academic supporters would take her seriously.[6] Rather, she is expressing something about the virtues of the market, the ideology of self-reliance and the role of the state. Each of these is a social construct! For current purposes, it suffices to understand the social as something distinct from, and not confined to, the individual.

The first way in which capital can be taken to be social is in a historical sense. It might have taken two or more hundred years but there can be little doubt that one of the reasons why academics are discussing social capital at the end of the twentieth century is that they are living in a capitalist society. Capital in its fullest sense is confined to a particular period of history. Consequently, theoretical understanding of capital should also be confined to those historically delimited social circumstances that provide its preconditions. The failure to specify these conditions allows capital to be understood ahistorically and in a much more wide-ranging fashion than is suggested by capitalism itself.

Indeed, there is something specific about capitalist society that has induced misplaced interest in social capital, especially towards the end of the twentieth century. For capitalism does create what is perceived to be a division between economy and society, or market and non-market. This is bridged to a large extent by the state. But, when the role of the state is questioned along with that of the market, attention turns to alternative forms of non-economic life, broadly providing a rationale for the notion of social capital. In this, admittedly crude, fashion, social capital can be seen to be an intellectual product of the crisis of faith in both the capitalist state and the capitalist market in late-twentieth-century capitalism. It represents a desire in both analytical and policy terms to find alternatives to the neo-liberal agenda of market versus state.

Ironically, however, whilst a creature of the turn of the millennium, attempts have been made to trace back first use of the term "social capital" to earlier times. Its first use in the English language has been credited to Hanifan (1916). But, for a number of reasons that are made apparent in Chapter 7, the idea of social capital is to be found in substance, but not in name, wherever the prospector cares to look. The basic reason that social capital is perceived to have been so unconsciously popular through the ages is because it is being projected backwards from present theory and conditions, but in the absence of a developed let alone a proper understanding of capital. Unless capital is specified historically, social capital is bound to be found whenever economic and non-economic issues are considered together. In contrast, the sense in which capital is social in a broad historical sense is that it is attached to a specific socio-economic system, namely, capitalism.

In short, whenever we refer to capital and social capital, with an important reservation to be taken up later concerning embryonic forms of capital, we ought to be conscious that we are taking capitalism as our point of historical, and hence, analytical, departure. For capital and capitalism are like a wedding and marriage, respectively, one being set irreducibly within the context of the other. This moves the investigation to a focus on what is social about capitalism in a way that distinguishes it from the social content of previous periods of history, such as those based on feudalism. In this respect, there is an embarrassment of riches from which to choose for there are so many ways in which capitalism is so obviously differentiated from what went before. A perverse way in which this has been recognised, for example, is in current policies towards the formerly centrally planned economies of eastern Europe. It had been felt that introduction of the market and private property would suffice to usher in a period of prosperous capitalism. Experience has delivered a rude shattering of such illusions, although social and economic decline might be taken as indicative of the presence or introduction, not the absence, of capitalism. Capitalism, and hence capital, requires a lot more by way of the social than private property and the market.

What it does depend upon is wage labour, able and willing to produce a surplus for capital. By implication, the social attached to capital takes the form of class relations. For Marxist theory, class relations in general are fundamental in distinguishing between modes of production, such as feudalism and capitalism, and, as a corollary, between different periods of history. Capital and labour confront one another as classes with the capitalist class monopolising the means of production or access to livelihood through work.[7] Consequently, workers can only survive by selling their capacity to work for a wage that represents less in terms of labour time than is performed for the capitalist. The surplus labour performed over and above that necessary to provide the wage gives rise to what Marx termed exploitation, and provides for the profits of the capitalists.

Now, almost every element of the account in the previous paragraph has been subject to dispute, especially where it has been tied to the labour theory of value. Marx and Marxists are deemed to have placed too much emphasis on production and on class, with an associated reductionism, or collapsing, of the significance of other economic and social phenomena to the dictates of capitalist production and the balance of conflict between capital and labour. To a large extent, this involves a misreading of Marxism in the sense of failing to recognise the extent to which the analysis of capital is perceived as central as opposed to all-powerful and all-consuming. On the other hand, such considerations within or against Marxism do reflect genuine, if not always fully explored, differences over the extent to which developments within capitalism are independent of economic and class forces. Social theory has always emphasised forms of stratification other than by economic class alone, and the role played by them in economic and non-economic conflicts. This is most apparent by reference to the new social movements, and the emphasis placed on race, gender, and the environment, for example.

For immediate purposes, it is not necessary to address such disputes over the significance of class and capitalist production in economic and other outcomes. It suffices merely to acknowledge that capital and capitalism are based at least in part on class relations in which the production of a surplus is imperative. The social character of capital in this sense is at most understood differently to the extent that its importance is diluted by other factors that can even be argued to add to, rather than to detract from, the social content of capital. Feminists, for example, might also understand capitalism as being inevitably patriarchal, which is to add to the complexity of, not to deny, the social character of capital. In short, the social character of capital is reinforced and not denied by understanding capitalism in terms of the new social movements, irrespective of the way in which these are themselves understood.

Apart from incorporating the social as class relations, capital is also attached to a definite economic structure, not least because it is primarily based upon the production and sale of commodities. It is, in other words, a market system although, for Marxists, it is a market that is unavoidably attached to the system of capitalist production and exploitation. Thus, there is a fundamental structural division between the spheres of production and exchange. This has been explicitly recognised in transaction costs economics which investigates in its own way the issue of why firms exist outside the market with their own internal forms of organisation, such as hierarchies, that are separate from market relations. For such an approach, the firm is a more efficient internal, possibly informal, way of doing business than contracting through the market.

Here, though, there is a contrast with the Marxist approach, in which the firm is the institution which concretises in specific instances the more general relations of exploitation between classes. The sphere of production is where capital and labour directly confront one another over how much work will be done, with what quality and intensity, and subject to what wages and conditions. This is not to suggest that the outcomes of such detailed struggles are determined within the firm, or at the place of production, alone. They are heavily influenced by the rich and complex context within which those struggles are situated, factors such as the strength and solidarity of the trade union movement and the legislative environment attached to industrial relations. But, from a Marxist perspective, these do ultimately lead to a question of how much labour under what wages and conditions. The institution of the capitalist firm is not concerned exclusively with greater or lesser efficiency in the making of contracts between capital and labour, it is a site on which power is exercised and conflicts are played out.[8] Power and conflict are not unique to capitalism but their attachment to wage labour in this fashion is so. Accordingly, they are part and parcel of the social content of capital.

There is, as a result, another separate, but closely related, contrast between the Marxist approach and the institutional economics referred to previously. For the latter's theory of the relationship between firm and market is completely general. It might have nothing to do with the capital or the capitalist firm at all. Indeed, the theory has been applied to a range of other instances in which the market is perceived to be excluded in deference to the greater efficacy of other forms of making transactions – as in the new household economics or in explaining the need for a state. This demonstrates that the transaction costs approach has nothing as such to do with capitalism and capital although it can be applied to them by appealing to particular types of costs and benefits attached to the capitalist firm, most notably what is known as asset-specificity for which desirable attributes are not readily transferred between uses. In effect, this approach does draw a distinction between the market and the non-market, with each representing different ways of making contracts or exchanges. The new institutional economics, then, simply reads off history as the shifting balance between the two, according to the costs and benefits of transacting through the market or not.

In contrast, the Marxist approach deals specifically with the separation between production and exchange that is uniquely attached to capitalism. It does so in a number of ways. One is by relating the structural separation between the spheres of production and exchange to the ebb and flow of capital between them. Left at this level of generality, such movement between the two spheres makes no reference to capital at all, as previously observed of the cost and benefit logic of transaction costs economics. Marx, however, develops an understanding of the movement between production and exchange that is both more refined and specific to capital. In particular, he defines an industrial circuit of capital, for which, irrespective of what is produced, capital successively moves through three different forms, those of money, productive, and commodity capital. Initially, capital is advanced as money capital in order to purchase means of production, raw materials, capital equipment and labour power. Upon doing so, the circuit departs the sphere of exchange for the sphere of production where productive capital is engaged in the manufacture of commodities. The commodity capital that results can then be sold, or "realised" to use the vernacular, re-entering the sphere of exchange to retrieve the money form of capital. The purpose in engaging in the circuit is that the money realised should exceed the money advanced, thereby producing a profit. Whilst the acts of exchange, in initiating and closing the circuit as described above, are essential, the source of profit lies in the surplus labour performed in the sphere of production. As capital moves through its circuit, it is social in different ways. As money capital, it is attached to the power of purchase, not in general, but in the context of the general availability of a labour market and with the motive of generating a monetary profit. The social nature of productive capital has already been discussed above, as signifying a system of class exploitation. Commodity capital is social in terms of needing to serve needs, again not in some general sense, but through being able to attract purchase at a price that allows for profit.

What, if in different ways, both Marxist political economy and the new institutional economics share in common is a recognition that, under capitalism, the market does constitute itself as an arena of economic relations which are structurally distinct from non-market relations. In Marxist political economy, however, the primary distinction is not between market and non-market. Rather, it is based on the distinction between the aggregate circulation of industrial capital, just described, which includes the non-market relations attached to the *production* of a surplus but not other non-market relations, and the broader social environment upon which such economic reproduction depends. In other words, capital is social in being associated with a structural division between economic and what is termed "social reproduction". Interpreted on very narrow terms, social reproduction includes the processes necessary for the reproduction of the workforce, both biologically and as compliant wage-labourers. More generally, social reproduction is concerned with how society as a whole is reproduced and transformed over time.

On its own, this is an innocuous definition of social reproduction. It gains a much more critical content once it is attached to another social property unique to the capital of capitalism – its imperative for profitability. In most mainstream economics, this has the effect of driving the economy to equilibrium for which social reproduction is either set aside in deference to a system of supply and demand alone or, as in much of the new institutional economics, social and economic reproduction are mutually harmonious. For Marxist political economy, the social nature of capital is understood entirely differently.

First, tensions are created within the circuits of capital themselves over and above those already covered. These include distributional struggle between capital and labour, for example, as well as the competitive processes across different capitals. Mainstream economics tends to emphasise one form of competition alone, market competition in sale and purchase. But, as can be readily seen from the circuit of industrial capital, competition between capitals also depends upon the productivity with which productive capital is deployed, itself dependent upon the extent to which capitalists have access to money capital. For Marx, this is a result of what is generally the greater competitiveness of ever larger capitals that tend to beat out their smaller rivals. Consequently, the imperative for profit is also associated with an imperative to accumulate capital, both for individual capitals and for the capitalist system as a whole.

Second, these imperatives are associated with definite tendencies and tensions within the evolving economy, not least monopolisation or the concentration of capital and what is known as combined and uneven development whereby some capitals and their associated locations experience rapid growth whilst others fall behind and decay. Within capitalism, such tendencies are broadly recognised across the social sciences, most recently for example in contemporary attention to globalisation. But there are other social outcomes and influences as well such as urbanisation. Consequently, capital is social in driving particular tendencies. Moreover, these are not simply economic but are influenced by, and give rise to, tensions both within social and economic reproduction and between them.

Third, as a corollary of the very last point, capital is a highly invasive form of production. It tends to subordinate non-capitalist forms of economic activity and incorporate them into its domain, thereby redrawing the boundaries between economic and social reproduction. Elsewhere, I have argued at length, in different contexts, that this is not a one-way traffic of what is known as commodification or commoditisation. There can also be decommodification, as in the taking of activities out of the private commercial sphere and assigning them, for example, to the welfare state.[9] To some extent, this language is confusing or ambiguous. For commodification or commercialisation more generally are much broader than dependence upon capital for which they are a necessary but not a sufficient condition. Non-capitalist producers, for example, can be drawn into selling on the market without thereby becoming capitalists. Nonetheless, one of the social properties of capital is to penetrate non-capitalist arenas of activity and to impose upon them one or more aspects of its forms of economic reproduction, whether it be commodification or debt dependence, for example.

In short, throughout this section, I have attempted to show how capital is social and, hence, as a consequence can only be inappropriately placed in opposition to the social. Capital is embroiled in social relations, social structures, in social reproduction involving social power and conflict, and is attached to definite economic and social tendencies. In one sense it is not surprising that one or usually many of these aspects of capital tend to be overlooked by those who engage in the use of social capital as an important analytical category. For, to recognise them, even in these very general terms, would be to undermine the validity of the notion of social capital. On the other hand, it might be expected that such striking aspects of capital's sociability would be thrust to prominence once addressing the social aspects of capital through social capital. In general, this has not been the case except by way of critical literature on social capital. The following section seeks to explain why this has been so by reference to the nature of capital itself, which tends to conceal or disguise its sociability even as it fully draws upon it.

Capital is social

The preceding section has sought to establish that capital, as part of capitalism, is social in an extremely complex and varied set of ways, and the coverage has by no means been exhaustive. There has, for example, been no direct reference to the way in which such capital is associated with particular types of labour processes and a corresponding division of labour within enterprises. There are also established particular hierarchies of skills and tasks, between enterprises as commodity production is vertically integrated or disintegrated, and internationally as particular countries do or do not specialise in the production of particular commodities. As implied, those with the inclination to deploy the term social capital are liable to detach their understanding of capital from this complex sociability, if in part to restore one or more aspects in specifying what is distinctively social about social capital. In a sense, capital is itself responsible for this state of affairs. At a very general level, for example, as most notable in Mrs Thatcher's denial of (capitalist) society, there is an inclination to perceive capitalism as primarily a bundle of economically and politically free individuals, more or less harmoniously coordinated through the market and democracy, respectively. As Marx (1965, p. 176) famously puts it, once outside production, there is "a very Eden of the innate rights of man":

> There alone rule Freedom, Equality, Property and Bentham. Freedom, because both buyer and seller of a commodity ... are constrained only by their free will ... Equality, because each enters into relation with the other ... Property, because each disposes only of what is his own. And Bentham, because each looks only to himself.

It only takes the slightest reaction against such laissez-faire ideology to recognise the sociability of capital and to open the world of social capital.[10] Capitalism is so much based upon both property and the private that it is readily ideologically stripped of its social and systemic features, only for them to be restored piecemeal by a more considered social theory.

In this light, consider first what might be termed the fluidity of capital, that it characteristically moves between different forms as it follows the previously described circuit of industrial capital. As observed, it successively and repetitively moves from being money capital, to productive capital, to commodity capital and back again. Associated with each of these forms of capital, taken in isolation from one another, is induced a particular understanding of capital. Thus, in the case of money capital, money in and of itself is seen as capital. This is further consolidated by two other features. On the one hand, money capital does not remain confined to the simple form that has been adopted earlier for exposi-tional purposes in specifying the circuit of capital. It becomes embroiled in an extremely complex financial system with a whole variety of different types of money capital as well as with a credit system that may or may not involve capital at all. For the latter, note that we might talk of our capital even when we make a personal loan to friend or relative without the expectation of charging interest. On the other hand, where money is genuinely deployed purely as capital, it does seek out the highest form of return, typically in the form of interest, and so mimics the movement of the industrial circuit but without the trouble of going through the phases of producing and selling commodities. That money capital is not completely capital on its own, despite these powers of short circuiting, is abruptly revealed whenever a crash follows a speculative boom.

In case of productive capital, capital is perceived merely to be the instruments of production which allow for the provision of (surplus) output. Sometimes, as in the notorious production function of mainstream economics, which is supposed to capture and limit production to technological possibilities, capital is contrasted to labour as input and is generally understood as machinery (with a correspond-ing neglect of other inputs such as raw materials). Production is entirely detached from the other economic and social conditions that are its precondition. In case of human capital, however, even the distinction between capital and labour is set aside, and workers simply become another form of capital. In short, capital in its productive form induces a notion of capital as anything that can contribute directly as an input to the production process, especially if it can be bought and sold for that purpose.

Commodity capital, like productive capital, associates capital with its physical properties. But, unlike productive capital which is attached to production and is set apart from the sphere of exchange, commodity capital is understood as capital only in its connection with exchange. Indeed, it induces a disconnection from production in the same way that money capital does itself when commanding a surplus within the financial system alone. As a result, commodity capital induces the notion that anything that can be sold is capital, even if not in pursuit of a surplus but for whatever purpose. It is most notable in the question "what are your realisable assets?", which becomes another way of asking, "what is your capital?".

In short, with each of the forms of industrial capital, there is associated a particular corresponding understanding of capital – as finance, as instrument of production, or as an asset that can command purchasing power. In each case, whatever the analytical purpose and meaning involved, capital tends to be construed not only in isolation from its other forms but also apart from the social relations upon which it is based.[11] The crucial point that follows is that the failure fully to recognise and specify the fluidity of capital appropriately leads, paradoxically, to an even greater fluidity in its definition. This is because any recurrence of any one of its forms in any context – whether attached to capitalism or not, and not necessarily in a logical relation to its other forms – is potentially open to misconstrual as capital. Whenever money, resources for production, or resources for whatever other use arise, they are liable to be interpreted as capital.

Nor is this the end of the matter. For, the movement of capital through its circuits does presuppose the presence of, and interaction with, the general economic and social conditions that are its prerequisites, arising out of the structural separation between the reproduction of capital and the reproduction of capitalist society more broadly. Obviously, irrespective of the extent of mutual determination, the general socio-economic environment can be more or less conducive to the functioning of capital whether this be due to the scope and efficiency of the financial system, say, as part of economic reproduction, or the educational or policing systems, let alone the role of the state more generally, as representatives of social reproduction. Consequently, the fluidity of capital in that it needs to move through its various forms, leads to a conflation between capital itself and the conditions that are necessary for it, or beneficial to it.[12]

The leading example is simply provided by time itself for this is essential to the movement of capital except in the ideal and timeless worlds of general equilibrium beloved of economists. Thus, the long-standing notion derives – even from before the marginalist revolution establishing modern economics –

that capital is nothing other than the productivity of time. More generally, anything that can contribute to productivity or efficiency can be understood as capital, whether it be a physical factor – a country has more capital because of a better climate – or, equally significant in the context of social capital, one that is socially constructed – an efficient civil service, free from corruption, for example.

A further aspect in the fluidity of capital needs to be emphasised over and above its movement through various forms in definite socio-economic conditions. Capital is also fluid in the tendency to extend its scope of operations to new activities, as in commercialisation or commodification. Because of its invasive tendencies, the boundaries between what is and what is not capitalist production are constantly shifting – most notably, for example, in contemporary patterns of privatisation as opposed to many earlier forms of public provision that removed profitability as an operative criterion of production. Such fluidity between capitalist and non-capitalist production allows each to be understood as capital. A different illustration is provided by household consumption, which has become increasingly dependent upon commodities as opposed to domestic production. Because the household is perceived to compete with the commercial sector and for them to be substitutes for one another, the household itself is perceived to be in possession of "capital goods", those that it can use over a period of time.[13] Such fluidity in forms of provision reinforces the ambiguity attached to the notions of capital that have already been highlighted.

Whilst capital can be understood by projection of its properties or one or another aspect to arenas of capitalist society which are quite distinct from capital as such, the same sorts of projection can equally be made to non-capitalist societies. Money, commodities, and production all precede capitalism historically. As a result, pre-capitalist societies can be interpreted as deploying capital whenever these factors are considered in isolation from the broader social relations to which capital is attached under capitalism. Slaves, for example, are purchased with the slave owners' capital. The potential for confusion is compounded by the presence not only of money and commodities but also of various forms of the capital associated with them even before capitalism proper is established. Thus, both commercial and interest-bearing capital precede capitalism, along with merchants and bankers, reinforcing the idea that capital has no attachment to capitalism as such and to the class relations and exploitation attached to capitalist production.

A final way in which capital is fluid is, in a sense, the sum of all of the other aspects and, as such, more than the individual parts. Just as money can buy anything, so it can buy everything and is a general power to purchase. So, capital in money form is a general power to command, and serves as a symbol of class and of exploitation. Similarly, productive capital can be understood in a socially neutral way as the command over nature or, with a greater social content, as the power over labour. Possession of commodity capital is a generalised symbol of power over wealth and consumption. In a word, capital becomes synonymous with power in general and also with stratification according to access to money, occupation, or wealth. Capital becomes associated with capitalism, its functioning within the economy extrapolated more generally to society as a whole, and even to pre-capitalist societies.

Concluding remarks

In short, that capital is fluid in reality – in its own movement, the conditions to which it is attached, the boundaries within which it moves, and the broader powers that it confers and exerts – is conducive to highly fluid interpretations of what constitutes capital. Broadly, two contradictory intellectual and even popular responses are evident, usually in combination in some way with one another. On the one hand, capital can become understood as almost anything according to the different forms, conditions and scope of activity with which it is embroiled, as is evident in the notions of personal and social capital, used by Becker as discussed in the next chapter. This indiscriminate application of the notion of capital to any activity has become so pervasive that Baron and Hannan (1994, pp. 1122–24), in their now dated review of the impact of economics on the new sociology, already despairingly refer to the recent emergence of a "plethora of capitals". Sociologists, they lament, "have begun referring to virtually every feature of life as a form of capital". By the same token, by virtue of categori-cism, there is a tendency to label any differentiation, by race or gender for example, as social, thereby providing a cast iron explanation for outcomes in terms of social structure, say, which yields little more than tautology.[14] In this light, social capital would appear to be a dream, if vacuous, ticket in addressing any aspect of social theory. On the other hand, just as capital has the capacity to be understood as almost anything, so it can become fixed as such as something specific as one or other of its aspects is perceived to be decisive. For example, in neoclassical economics, capital is routinely understood as the quantity of physical (fixed) capital that gives rise to output through a technically fixed production function. In general, neither of these extremes is all that is involved since, however much recognised, at least the fluidity of capital through its various forms is an object of analysis. How do resources, or the various forms of capital, give rise to consequences such as generating output and utility, for example?

Once recognising the fluidity of capital between its different forms, there is also a presumption of economic and social structures, not least between production and exchange and between the economic and the non-economic.[15] The necessity of these structures, however, is a consequence of the class relations, between capital and labour, which are reducible to neither the economic nor the non-economic. Without corresponding property, political, and cultural relations, the economic relations could not be sustained. Nonetheless, the structures associated with capitalism induce analyses in which the economic and the non-economic are initially separated out and perceived to be independ-ent from, or interdependent with, one another. In this way, the economic and the non-economic are counterposed, need to be brought back together and, thereby, providing a rationale for setting the social (rather than labour) against capital. In addition, there is a potential for a more general blossoming of structuralism. For, wherever difference or inequality is to be found, it is theoretically embraced as a structure of independent components, whether this be through stratification such as that attached to the new social movements, by gender and race, etc., public versus private, and so on. In short, capitalism is highly conducive to the suggestion that it is social in ways that are independent of or cut across what is presumed to be the asocial economic.

Consequently, the social sciences are replete with the economic and the non-economic examined separately from one another, with each subsequently extended to consider the other. This is most apparent in the notion of social capital. However understood, capital and social are broadly associated with the economic and the non-economic, respectively. Having been artificially separated, they are brought back together in this all-encompassing term. By contrast, capital is only appropriately understood as social from the outset in the economic relations that it encompasses. Any use of the term social capital is an implicit acceptance of the stance of mainstream economics, in which capital is first and foremost a set of asocial endowments possessed by individuals rather than, for example, an exploitative relation between classes and the broader social relations that sustain them. The social can only be applied to capital because it has been forcibly and artificially torn away in the first instance.

Once going down this false path, the candidates for the social partner for capital are legion, not least because of the enigmatic fluidity of capital itself. These observations can be approached in a different fashion. In his analysis of commodity fetishism, Marx is very clear that the world of commodities creates illusions, apparently concealing the underlying social relations involved by expressing them in the fetishised form of a relationship between things. Two coats are equivalent to three chairs.[16] For Marx (1965, p. 72):

> A definite social relation between men, that assumes, in their eyes, the fantastic form of a relationship between things … the Fetishism which attaches itself to the products of labour, so soon as they are produced as commodities.

Marx is at pains to observe that such illusions are not trickery or simple fantasy in the sense of commodities presenting themselves as something that they are not. Commodity exchange really is a relationship between things whereas, certainly from the perspective of an atheist or non-believer, religious fetishism entails a false, non-existent relationship between god and worshippers or believers.

Such is the perspective in which social capital can also be understood. There can be no doubt of the genuine analytical, empirical, and humane concerns of those who deploy the notion. It does, indeed, correspond to very real processes within capitalism – although these are deliberately designated as social rather than physical as in commodity fetishism. Yet, the weakness of the notion of social capital is not in what it does present but in what it does not. As a result, it is subject to both capital and to social, rather than to simple commodity, fetishism. If social capital seeks to bring the social back in to enrich the under-standing of capitalism, it does so only because it has impoverished the understanding of capital by taking it out of its social and historical context.

3   Bringing the social back in[1]

Introduction

For neoclassical economics, capital, at least in the first instance, is particularly solid. It is any physical object that aids in the production process, most notably formally and technically indicated by the notion of a production function in which output depends positively in a fixed fashion upon quantities of capital and labour. The more capital you have, the more output you get. But, from this solid foundation, capital becomes more ephemeral as such a physical grounding is perceived to be a special case of more general considerations. Capital is the productivity of time, getting more by taking longer to produce goods not least through delaying immediate gratification by using time to make machines rather than consumption goods. Financial assets become capital as they grow in worth over time through interest or dividend payments. They represent deferral of consumption and the presumption that someone is taking the savings made and putting them to productive use to provide for more in the future. Ultimately, capital is anything that provides for an enhanced stream of utility over time. Human capital, for example, representing the improved skills of the workforce through resources devoted to education and training, is embodied in the worker. More can be produced with more human capital, thereby enhancing utility. In this respect, capital is not physical but rests in the mind or in experience and skills. Less recognised except in passing, is that human capital can be used to increase our enjoyment of consumption directly without necessarily raising productivity, simply by enjoying more by knowing more.

From such considerations, it is immediate that capital has very little to do with capitalism as a socially and historically specific form of economic organisation. Indeed, capital is something that belongs to individuals, and neoclassical economics even prides itself on introducing students to an understanding of capital, or the market economy, by reference to the decisions to consume or to save that would be made by Robinson Crusoe. Such an understanding of the (market) economy can also be extended to non-market or social relations, with the latter treated as if a market. Whether I study or watch television is a choice to invest or to consume that parallels the decision whether to use my income to spend or to save. At the forefront of such an understanding of society as if a market, ground out from atomised individual decision making, has been Gary Becker. In this respect, the results of his early endeavours are presented in the next section. He is shown to have obsessively sought to explain as many economic and social phenomena as possible on the basis of such methods.

For this, he has drawn the scorn of fellow economists who consider that he applies the principle of rationality too far, both in its range or application and in its exclusion of other principles of action. Yet, remarkably, despite being the most unlikely candidate for this role, the third section shows that Becker has also been in the vanguard in deploying the notion of social capital. Why is this? The answer is that social capital allows Becker to accommodate an even wider range of economic and social phenomena whilst retaining a continuing commitment to methodological individualism or economic rationality. In effect, social capital becomes a catch-all for anything that improves life but that has not already been covered by those elements of personal capital that provide the starting point for understanding capital. As discussed in the closing section, Becker's precocious adoption of social capital allows him implicitly to have outflanked his erstwhile opponents, incorporating and generalising their critiques of his earlier work. By the same token, the use of social capital by Becker, the anti-social, and the social as economic, economist par excellence, reveals with sharp intensity how the notion of social capital depends upon bringing the social back in, having previously taken it out of the economy.

Taking the social out

With the benefit of hindsight, as the logic of his position has been elaborated, Becker's use of what he himself terms "the economic approach" is remarkably simple. Assume that all individuals are the same and that they are motivated exclusively by the wish to maximise their own welfare or utility. On this basis and with externally given constraints, explain as many social phenomena as possible without being confined by traditional interdisciplinary boundaries. As Becker (1996, p. 1) puts it in his Nobel Prize acceptance speech in 1992: "My research uses the economic approach to analyze social issues that range beyond those usually conceived by economists."

This appears in a book that ranges in coverage far beyond the topics for which Becker is best known – such as human capital theory and the new household economics (Becker 1993), although these are touched upon in passing. Indeed, within a few pages of his introductory chapter, Becker delivers notice of the putative power of the economic approach, purporting to be able to use it to shed light on issues as diverse as smoking, addiction, churchgoing, playing tennis, child abuse, divorce, jogging, violence, lying, sexual abuse, psychotherapy, patriotism, and government propaganda. Early notice is thereby served of the distant horizons encompassed by the economic approach. As observed by Febrero and Schwartz (eds) (1995) in an edited volume of Becker's articles, sanctioned by Becker to mark his sixty-fifth birthday and designed to capture his "essence" (Febrero and Schwartz 1995, pp. xx–xxi):[2]

Many activities thought to be noneconomic in nature ... are actually economic problems. Economic theory can thus help explain phenomena traditionally located outside the scope of economics, in the areas of law,
sociology, biology, political science, and anthropology ... The development
of this *economic imperialism* ... is another significant contribution that Becker
has made to modern economics.

Nothing could illustrate better the imperialistic designs of economics. But
matters are not so simple. For, if the economic approach is such a jack, and
master, of all analytical trades, applicable across all of the social sciences without
distinction, why is it to be dubbed the *economic* approach. The most obvious
answer is that it should not be and its name is an accident of its historical origins
within economics, as discussed below. More suitable, then, might be the
disciplinarily neutral term "rational choice" that is familiar outside economics. It
represents a conscious choice of methodology in other social sciences that is
usually taken for granted within economics. There is, however, an important
reason why rational and economic should have been considered synonymous
rather than complementary as in the notion of the rational economic agent. For
the latter is generally considered to be entirely a construct of economists applied,
with whatever validity, to an analytical domain confined to the market, the world
of supply and demand.

In this light, whilst Becker's economic approach claims universal applicability,
both its name and its content, despite disclaimers to the contrary, betray their
origins within mainstream neoclassical economics. As Becker (1996, pp. 25–26)
unwittingly confirms his concern is the universal projection of the market
model:[3]

The economist continues to search for differences in prices or incomes to
explain any differences or changes in behavior ... one searches, often long
and frustratingly, for the subtle form that prices and incomes take in explaining differences among men and periods.

In short, Becker's economic approach seeks not only to deploy reductionism in a
particular form of methodological individualism. He is also concerned to treat as
much as possible as an as if market, as if life was a virtual world with individual
choices being made in the context in which everything else is or is equivalent to a
price or income. As a result, the market is analytically privileged and unques-
tioned. It is always there to be used as a prism for understanding any social
phenomenon.

A remarkable, if paradoxical, illustration of the faith in the market model in
Becker's work is the more or less complete absence of money or monetary
theory in his considerations. Whilst money is generally thought of as a means by
which to enhance the efficacy of the market, and even on occasion to be neutral
in its effects, it is also strongly associated with dysfunction, especially where
speculative activity and financial crises are concerned but also for Keynesian

unemployment. For Becker, however, not only can the economic approach apparently eschew the social in general in deference to the individual, it can also set aside money, the most social and symbolic aspect of the market itself. Indicative is that the index of his articles collated by Febrero and Schwartz (eds) (1995) contains no entry for "money" and, in over 659 pages, just one article deals with money in any way whatsoever. This was published in 1952.[4] There is an equal lack of attention to unemployment. Essentially, Becker takes the neutral and frictionless use of money as given, together with a full-employment equilibrium. It can scarcely be claimed to be a realistic starting point for understanding a market economy, let alone the basis on which to extend such an understanding to the non-market. This all, however, reflects Becker's own analytical preferences. It is not logically necessary that money, or unemployment, be precluded from the economic approach. For it is possible to examine the conditions under which individuals eschew barter and accept the efficacy of a monetary system, reducing something as social as money to a matter of rational choice.[5] Similarly, unemployment could be considered a voluntary choice in given circumstances.[6] Becker prefers to engage with the world from a starting point both of methodological individualism and the presumption of essentially money-less, full employment, harmonious equilibrium. Only if this proves incapable of delivering the analytical goods should different assumptions be made.

One reason why he might be committed to efficient equilibrium as starting point is revealed in an early contribution (Becker 1958), concerning the application of the economic approach to democracy. There, he argues in typical style that, at least in principle, the economic and political systems are similar in content (Becker 1958, pp. 105–6):

> An ideal democracy is very similar to an ideal free enterprise system in the market place. That is political decisions would be determined by the values of the electorate and the political sector would be run very efficiently.

They are also potentially similar in outcomes if, for simplicity, "assuming that all voters have the same preferences" (Becker 1958, p. 107):[7]

> If the party in office did not adopt the policies preferred by the electorate, another party could gain more popular support by offering a platform closer to those preferences. Consequently, the only equilibrium platform would be one that perfectly satisfied these preferences ... The ultimate aim of each party may be to acquire political power, but in equilibrium no one, including those "in power", has any political power.

Consequently, because of ignorance, costs of large-scale political organisation, and lack of continuous elections, political imperfections are arguably worse than market imperfections so that, in closing conclusion, the state should not be encouraged to correct the latter (p. 109):[8]

I am inclined to believe that monopoly and other imperfections are at least as important, and perhaps substantially more so, in the political sector as in the market place. If this belief is even approximately correct ... it may be preferable not to regulate economic monopolies and to suffer their bad effects, rather than to regulate them and suffer the effects of political imperfections.

In this light, it is a simple, if false, step, to prefer to treat the society as if it were a perfect market because it would be better off if it were.[9]

In brief, with such beliefs on board, Becker's economics has three elements. First, he is driven by reductionist logic. Second this is attached to personal idiosyncrasies reflecting his role as economist with perfectly competitive (money- and unemployment-less) economy as starting point. Third, this logic and starting point provide the basis, only touched upon so far, for pushing out the boundaries of the economic approach by making endogenous, or variable and to be analysed, what was previously exogenous, not least in subsuming the social within the economic approach. With no apparent sense of irony given the extent of his reductionism, Becker considers that economists have been unduly concerned with technical formalities within their own discipline at the expense of addressing the concerns of others (p. 194):[10]

From a methodological viewpoint, the aim ... is to show how [what] is considered important in the sociological and anthropological literature can be usefully analyzed when incorporated into the framework provided by economic theory. Probably the main explanation for the neglect of social interactions by economists is neither analytical intractability nor a preoccupation with more important concepts, but excessive attention to formal developments during the last 70 years. As a consequence, even concepts considered to be important by earlier economists, such as social interactions, have been shunted aside.

In his later work, a crucial aspect of the third point, the expanding scope of endogeneity, is that it is inward looking in character. It is concerned with the preferences of individuals that are taken as given for the purposes of maximising utility. It is one thing to be rational in this sense but from where do the preferences arise, especially if the presumptions of social theory are to be rejected with their notions of social norms and the like? This is a particularly challenging issue for Becker since he wishes to deploy a representative optimising individual not only over that individual's lifetime but also across all individuals as a whole and throughout history: "The establishment of the proposition that one may usefully treat tastes as stable over time and similar among people is the central task" (p. 25).

The assumption of given preferences across all individuals is attractive to Becker since he wants to explain why different choices are made across generations of households – in fertility and female labour market participation for example – without relying on changed preferences which would border on tautology (p. 49):[11]

> No significant behavior has been illuminated by assumption of differences in tastes ... [which] along with assumptions of unstable tastes, have been a convenient crutch to lean on ... ad hoc arguments that disguise analytical failures.

The distaste for assuming that preferences differ across individuals ultimately leads to the idea that they are biologically rather than socially determined. Finally, with a breath-taking and unjustified leap of faith, we are informed that the economic approach extends not only to the other social sciences but to the natural sciences also (p. 9):

> I believe the main reason habitual behavior permeates most aspects of life is that habits have an advantage in the biological evolution of human traits. For as long as habits are not too powerful they have social as well as personal advantages.

Nor is this a latter day presumption of socio-economic Darwinianism. For, as argued in a much earlier contribution co-authored by Becker in 1973 and cited in Febrero and Schwartz (1995, p. xliii):[12]

> If genetical natural selection and rational behavior reinforce each other in providing speedier and more efficient responses to changes in environment, perhaps that common preference function has evolved over time by natural selection and rational choice as that preference function best adopted to human society.

But if natural selection homogenises preferences across individuals as history evolves, how do we explain the apparent instability of the preferences of a single individual over a lifetime,[13] let alone across different individuals? Ultimately, Becker (1996) addresses this problem in very general terms and purports to deal with it. He continues to insist that, subject to gender differences,[14] we all have the same *underlying* preferences, stable over an individual's lifetime, but that these are derived from what he terms an "extended utility function". This is a normal utility function from an economist's perspective, drawing positively from goods consumed. But is supplemented by the additional variables of accumulated experience and consumption over a life so far lived, whether the latter be chosen consciously or not as a result of being outside personal control or choice. In formal terms, a person's utility is given by $U(g_1, g_2, ...; X_1, X_2, ...)$ where the g_i are normal consumption goods, and the X_i are any other of a set of factors that influence preferences over time (Becker 1996, p. 126): "Each person is born perhaps not as a *tabula rasa* – an empty slate – but with limited experiences that get filled in by childhood and later experiences."

Consequently, whilst preferences seem to change over time, this is an illusion. For the apparent change in preferences is explained by changes in the X_i. An example is readily supplied by addiction in which there is an apparent enhanced preference for a drug or like, signifying a shift in tastes. Not so argues Becker. Given cost and availability of drugs, individuals might deliberately choose to become addicts if the pleasures of present consumption are perceived to outweigh the heavily discounted costs of future pains attached to withdrawal symptoms, loss of earnings or whatever.

At this point, Becker is being driven out onto an analytical limb, not only from the perspective of other social sciences but from within economics itself. Surely, the assumptions and methods that he uses are directly contradicted by the most readily available empirical evidence. Different individuals identically placed in terms of prices and incomes behave very differently, whether preferences have evolved through natural and market selection over time or not. More generally, such extreme assumptions are not required if the scope of the economic approach is less modest. Becker takes his reliance on methodological individualism and his antipathy to the social too far. Consider the commentary of his fellow economists at the end of the 1980s. It displays considerable hostility to, even contempt for, Becker although this tends to be tempered by admiration for his technical virtuosity.[15] Most significant is the stance of George Akerlof. He is an acknowledged pioneer in the revolutionary new micro-foundations of economics[16] and in using it to colonise the other social sciences, although the colonisation can be presented as being in the opposite direction.[17] Akerlof (1990, p. 73) sees himself as always doing "the opposite of what Becker does" as the latter is perceived to rely too much on market-clearing, rationality, etc., rather than "why the economy is not working" (p. 72). As Elster (1990, p. 238) observes:[18]

> Becker and Akerlof ... represent two different trends. There is the imperialist trend of economics, which I would say just ignores sociological theory in its attacks on sociological problems. And then there is the trend that Akerlof represents, which takes sociological theory seriously and uses it to study economic problems.

More sarcastic is Akerlof's (1990, p. 73) commentary on Becker-type analysis by reference to the jibe made at Milton Friedman by Paul Samuelson, that he learnt how to spell "banana" but did not know where to stop.[19]

Nor is this critique of Becker confined to a few individuals. Sen (1990, p. 264) observes that, "Becker's tools have been chosen on the ground of their alleged success in economics, but they are too narrow and do not have much predictive and explanatory power even in economics." Schelling (1990, pp. 193–94) admits:

> I myself don't find Becker's work so helpful ... he is completely satisfied with the traditional economic model of rational behaviour ... what annoys me

about Becker, and maybe your term, "imperialism", somewhat catches it, is that he doesn't think there is anything to learn from outside economics.

And for Solow (1990, p. 276), "my nagging feeling is that what he gets ... oscillates between the obvious and the false".

From personal to social capital

Significantly, these criticisms derive from Swedberg's edited volume, *Economics and Sociology, Redefining Their Boundaries: Conversations with Economists and Sociologists* published in 1990. It comes at the time when the new micro-foundations of economics are gaining ground, not only within economics itself but also by extension to other social sciences, not least the new economic sociology. Becker is possibly perceived to be an obstacle in these endeavours because of his peculiar insistence upon the denial of the social in deference to the individual. Not that methodological individualism for economic analysis is at stake. For, as Solow – one of his harshest critics – puts it elsewhere (Hahn and Solow 1995, p. vii), in criticising the new classical economics, a particularly extreme form of monetarism:

> We also both regarded ourselves as neoclassical economists in the sense that we required theories of the economy to be firmly based on the rationality of agents and on decentralised modes of economic communication among them.

The difference with Becker then seems to derive not from methodology but from scope of application and undue emphasis upon the timeless, as opposed to the socially and historically formed, individual. Interestingly, in his conversation recorded with Swedberg on 13 April 1988, Becker (1990, p. 33) is sufficiently circumspect to have claimed to have anticipated much of the economic approach to political science.[20] Yet, nowhere in the interview covering the shifting relationship between economics and sociology is there any mention of the most important and most recent facilitating device within economics: the information-theoretic approach to micro-foundations. One possible reason for this is that the new approach, by then well over a decade old, was far from compatible with Becker's work to that point, especially given its two most favoured areas of application. On the one hand, it was orthogonal to his work insofar as it focused upon finance, neglected by Becker, and its informationally-asymmetric markets for borrowing and lending. On the other hand, more damagingly unacceptable, was the application to labour markets, especially the notion of efficiency wages. For the idea that wages might be determined by informationally-based market imperfections more or less completely undermined the practical relevance of human capital theory, especially in its empirical derivation of rates of return to education. For Blaug (1987), one of the most ardent popularisers of human capital theory and its application to the economics of education, these new developments within the economics of labour markets were sufficient to invalidate the whole approach and to convert him from a "True Believer" in human capital theory.[21]

In this light, it is hardly surprising that Becker should be slow, if not hesitant, to embrace the new micro-foundations. Nevertheless, within a few years, Becker has implicitly responded, even conceded in this respect, to his critics by embracing the new approach to incorporate the social. In a formal sense, the extended utility function is allowed to include social variables amongst the X_i. Thus (p. 4):

> This book retains the assumption that individuals behave so as to maximize utility while extending the definition of individual preferences to include personal habits and addictions, peer pressure, parental influences on the tastes of children, advertising, love and sympathy, and other neglected behavior.

In case of peer pressure in the context of addiction, influence is exerted by the norm set by others and not just straightforwardly by own internally generated pleasure and pain. More generally, social norms are accepted by Becker: "Norms are those common values of a group which influence an individual's behavior through being internalized as preferences" (p. 225). In other words, the social makes the individual, an inversion of Becker's guiding methodology.

Of course, this leaves open the question of why an optimising being should internalise social norms, especially where the result is an apparent divergence from otherwise rational behaviour. Are the principles of adopting social norms and pursuing utility maximisation inconsistent with one another? The answer is no, with a rationale provided by restoring the second principle to primacy by subsuming the first. Consider the illustration provided in terms of a seemingly inexplicable group preference for one of two otherwise identical restaurants even though the unpopular may be forced to lower prices for lack of custom. There is a presumption, however, that the long queues at one restaurant reflect greater knowledge of its qualities on the part of its customers which, whether correct or not, serve as a signal to others. This leads to rationally emulative behaviour, reinforcing the message that the trendy restaurant is superior.[22] In face of ignorance, use the knowledge that is possibly being revealed by others. In other words, social norms and the like are a rational response to limited knowledge and experience. Indeed, those who are older know better which norms or groups to trust, just as they accumulate more sophisticated tastes from consumption already enjoyed, a sort of learning by consumption in parallel with the learning by doing in production that forms part of human capital.

It is now apparent that a very different analytical procedure is being developed by Becker to expand the scope of the endogenous. It derives from outside, rather than from within, the individual. It is social rather than individualistic. It runs against the grain of all of Becker's personal and previous analytical idiosyncrasies. In part, this might explain why such factors emerge only at such a late point in his intellectual life. Seeking to colonise disciplines and subject matter other than economic, there are plenty of raw materials upon which parasitically to exercise the as if a perfect market paradigm – taste for discrimination, the household, human capital, fertility decisions, etc. Yet, despite considerable ingenuity to sustain his old ways, Becker appears to have the intellectual integrity, or opportunism, to admit defeat. However hard he tries, at some point, he must confess that there are forms of empirically observable behaviour that are not reducible to straightforward individual optimisation in an as if perfect market world. The social is essential to complement the biological.

Not surprisingly, though, the social constructed by Becker is trimmed to the barest minimum. It exists outside individuals and is internalised by them but, as a result, must lead to forms of behaviour that reproduce the social. This is not liable to be the case over the long run for an expensive restaurant in vogue as consumers learn as such. Nonetheless, an opening has been made for Becker to incorporate traditional variables from social theory at will: "Men and women want respect, recognition, prestige, acceptance, and power from their family, friends, peers, and others" (p. 12).

As a result of Becker's conversion to the merits of the social, there is a most remarkable turnabout relative to his fellow economists. The one most fanatically attached to the as if market model is, nonetheless, ahead of the field in embracing the notion of social capital. Indeed, the Becker (1996) volume to which I have already extensively referred can almost be interpreted as rewriting his previous work in the light of the need to incorporate the social and, in particular, social capital. It is called *Accounting for Tastes* and, as the title suggests, is designed to explain how tastes only appear to change in light of the underlying and unchanging role of the extended utility function.[23] The book brings together articles that had appeared over a twenty-year period, but also adding new contributions, especially more circumspect reflection on his methodology and its implications. The work for which Becker is renowned, on human capital for example, only figures in passing. Its analytical underpinnings are, however, covered in Part I of the two parts of the book. This is entitled "Personal Capital", denoted formally by P. This is a generalisation of human capital, the freely chosen accrual of productive capacities. It represents the other individually chosen experiences, etc., that allow for greater or lesser individual capacity in generating utility over and above items consumed. Those who have been to an opera previously, for example, can enjoy a second visit more than those who have never been before, and are, *ceteris paribus*, more likely to go again. Hence, individuals who differ in their levels of personal capital will appear, wrongly, to have different underlying utility functions.

In Part II of the book, however, personal gives way to social capital from which the part takes its subtitle. Social is distinguished from personal capital in that it is dependent upon factors outside the choice or control of the individual but which, as variables, S, in the extended utility function, affect both welfare and choices. In short: "The effects of the social milieu, an individual's stock of social capital depends not primarily on his own choices, but on the choices of peers in the relevant network of interactions" (p. 12). Some social capital lies entirely outside the individual's control, as in various aspects of parenting (although these can still be examined in terms of the rational choices of parents). More centrally, social capital depends upon the choices made by others with little or no effect on own social capital but with significant spill-over effects when aggregated over all individuals. Not surprisingly, Becker explicitly uses the analogy of externalities (p. 12). More generally, social capital both allows for a fuller scope of explanation on the basis of given extended utility function and, thereby, theoretically justifies the latter concept (p. 5):

> The utility function itself is independent of time, so that it is a stable func-
> tion over time of the goods consumed and also of the (personal and social)
> capital goods ... the extended utility function ... is stable only because it
> includes measures of past experience and social forces.

In broad brush, if not in detail, Becker has constructed a full account of social capital – not least its attachment to externalities, networks, norms, interactions, and even social forces. He has also gone through a progression from physical and natural, if not financial,[24] capital to human capital, from human to personal capital, and from personal to social capital. As more capitals are added,[25] so are the boundaries of explanatory scope, with social capital serving as residual to tidy up what is otherwise inexplicable. At last, the economic approach delivers the analytical goods fully (p. 6):

> We were impressed by how little has been achieved by the many discussions
> in economics, sociology, history, and other fields that postulate almost arbi-
> trary variations in preferences and values when confronted by puzzling
> behavior ... personal and social capital are crucial not only for understand-
> ing addictions ... but also for most other behaviour in the modern world,
> and probably in the distant past as well.

Economics simply reigns supreme (p. 25): "We assert that this traditional approach of the economist offers guidance in tackling these problems – and that no other approach of remotely comparable generality and power is available."

Whilst Becker's personal inclination has been to look within the individual for evolving preferences, ultimately resting upon biological determinants, he has been driven outwards to acknowledge the role of the social as captured by the notion of social capital. Having taken the social out of the understanding of society, it is a simple matter to bring it back in again and to claim to be able to explain everything from addiction to the distant past. But it is a social that is very limited in scope, being relational only in the sense of summing individual interactions other than through the market although, as will be seen in later chapters, these can be thought of as incorporating or leading to institutions, norms, and values. From the kernel of the individual and rational choice can grow or evolve the entire economic and social firmament.

Concluding remarks

That Becker, as economist, should have so readily, and early, in its short life so far, embraced the notion of social capital, despite his long-standing antipathy to anything social other than the as if market, derives from three important factors, each of which has significant implications. First, so far unremarked, Becker has had a close working relationship with his sociologist colleague at the University of Chicago, James Coleman. Indeed, Becker has held a joint appointment in the economics and in the sociology departments there.[26] Coleman is generally credited with having secured a place for social capital within sociology from the late 1980s. He provided a continuity with social exchange theory, shifting its emphasis from psychology to economics in forming social capital, whilst consolidating the role of rational choice. This is the briefest of summaries of Chapter 5. For the moment, it suffices to observe that Becker's adoption of social capital is in part fortuitous to the extent that it depends on this collaboration with Coleman, although this is itself by no means purely accidental given their mutual commitment to rational choice. More significant, though, is the ready marriage of convenience between economics and sociology, to form a new economic sociology, with social capital officiating at the ceremony.

Second, Becker's intellectual integrity is to be admired. His own preference is to deny the social and to confine himself to the aggregated outcome of atomised individual behaviour. Despite this inclination to eschew the social, he has found it indispensable as an explanatory device in order to widen his explanatory range. Once, having done so, a whole new world, if not the universe, is opened up for the economic approach. Now anything seems to be open to explanation since, by definition, the "social" exhausts all that is not already "personal". The only, unobserved, omission is the construction of meaning itself. Significantly, in this respect, language is for Becker primarily a matter of who chooses to speak which language, with majority driving out minority languages in view of the positive externalities of the greater numbers of speakers of a common language (Becker 1990, p. 41). Language as the most basic social construct – an evolving and contradictory reflection of a cascade of social relations, structures and processes – is simply set aside. Without such esoterica, it follows that social capital is far from being incompatible with the most extreme forms of methodological individualism. By contrast, it is its culminating triumph.

Third is the issue of where this leaves those neoclassical economists, Becker's erstwhile critics, who would distance themselves from what they have taken to be his extreme stance. A decade ago, their contempt for his "bananalysis" seemed to be well founded by comparison with their more well-grounded moderation. Now, however, they have been outflanked since Becker has done no more than to generalise his social theory, through the notion of social capital, by use of the very principles that they would use to attack him. Effectively, common ground outside the discipline has been occupied from two opposite directions within economics – from Becker's as if market and from Akerlof's as if market (as informational) imperfections. As a result, social capital gains what social theory loses.

4   Bourdieu's social capital: from distinction to extinction[1]

Introduction

In the early social capital literature, it was commonplace to find the French social theorist, Pierre Bourdieu, acknowledged as one of its founders. As the literature has evolved, his presence has been observed more in the breach and has at most been token, reference in deference to superficial scholarly standards – conferring a sort of symbolic academic capital upon both authors and their articles. Paradoxically, Bourdieu remains important in other areas of social theory. His most famous book, *Distinction*, is an acknowledged classic, seeking to establish how cultural distinctions are created, deployed, and related to stratification.[2] Further, social capital is just one of the types of non-economic capital utilised by Bourdieu. Amongst others, he has also promoted the notions of cultural and symbolic capital for which he is more fully recognised although, other than in specialised areas of study, these have not prospered to the same extent as social capital for reasons discussed in the concluding section of this chapter.

There are a number of reasons why Bourdieu should have fallen from favour around a notion that he himself did much to initiate. These are worth rehearsing in their own right since he is deservedly an inspirational figure. The discussion will also provide some background to his treatment of social capital. First, Bourdieu is inclined to rely upon the heavy abstraction that is traditionally characteristic of French social theory. This is undoubtedly a deterrent to the more empirically minded Anglo-Saxon traditions, especially where social capital is concerned. In particular, Bourdieu has been a point of reference for examining the empirical relationship between social stratification and cultural activity rather than their meanings and significance.[3] This, no doubt, has been encouraged by his own case studies along these lines, which investigated the correlates of success in attaining educational qualifications. But, as Lamont and Lareau (1988, p. 161) observe in surveying the US literature, with cultural being a counterpart to social capital:[4]

> In general, American researchers have abstracted the concept of cultural capital from the macro-political framework in which it was originally em-bedded. From a tool for studying the process of class reproduction, the concept became a tool for examining the process of status attainment.

In short, cultural (and social) capital becomes a property of individuals even if it is shared in common by socio-economic groups, and Bourdieu is first bowdlerised and then ditched.

Second, as already apparent, Bourdieu is heavily engaged in issues associated with culture, whether high or low brow, and what makes them such. Consequently, a reading of his work is more than otherwise demanding in requiring knowledge of the field of cultural studies. This is often beyond both reach and aim of many of those who would deploy the notion of social capital.

Third, as a cultural theorist, Bourdieu is exceptionally determined to traverse a path between what is perceived to be a dogmatic Marxism, with its class and productionist determinism, and the flights of fancy associated with the extreme subjectivity of postmodernism. Thus, on the one hand, he is convinced of the presence of economic and social relations, structures and tendencies.[5] These provide the context that constrains, but does not determine, the way in which particular activities are constructed in substance and meaning. Bourdieu's commitment to the realities of everyday life is sharply revealed by his scathing attacks on Jean Baudrillard, the dandy of postmodernism, subjecting him to a scarcely undeserved ridiculing (Bourdieu and Haacke 1995, p. 39):[6]

> You probably remember how, in January of 1991, the prophet of the simulacrum announced in *Liberation*: "There will be no Gulf War". A few months later, the great dissimulator offered us a collection of his analyses under the title *The Gulf War Did Not Take Place*. Such an escape from reality looks ... more and more like a mental disorder. But there is also an occasional sign which demonstrates that Baudrillard has, in fact, not left the world of real exchanges. When *Der Spiegel* asked him whether he would accept an invitation to visit the battlefield in Iraq, he answered: "I make my living with the virtual."

On the other hand, in displaying an unflinching solidarity to working people, Bourdieu is equally contemptuous of those intellectuals who, in contrast to Baudrillard, have insisted upon abeyance to the supposedly unyielding dictates of economic realities. For they have done so by succumbing to, and even promoting, the postulates of neo-liberalism. Bourdieu (1998a) considers them to have abandoned the integrity required of scholars as well as their broader responsibilities.[7]

At the end of the day, these factors do not account for the limited extent to which Bourdieu has been acceptable to the social capital movement. At most, they might explain why he has not been so much discarded as ignored. In brief, if to anticipate, despite founding the social capital enterprise, Bourdieu has not been endowed with sufficient cultural capital and distinction, at least of the right type, to sustain his presence. It is a striking illustration of the inverse relationship between quality and sophistication of scholarship and its status. For, whilst Bourdieu's approach to social capital is itself fundamentally flawed and might even in some respects be judged to have supported the path taken by the vast majority of the literature that abandoned him, his own theory has sufficient critical content to have scuttled what social capital has become.

In the next section, a critical assessment is made of Bourdieu's concept, or should it be concepts, of capital. Essentially, it is shown how he has fallen victim to capital's enigmatic fluidity, as laid out in Chapter 2, with his presumption that capital is to be found in its various forms in every walk of capitalist life and also through the course of pre-capitalist history. However, despite an apparent parallel with mainstream economics in this respect, as discussed in the third section, Bourdieu deliberately draws an unbridgeable distinction between himself and the dismal science. This is because his notions of capital, although ranging widely across society and history, are heavily imbued with a social and historical content derived from the activities and periods under consideration. Capital is understood as a social construct, not least in its meanings as well as in its effects. As discussed in the concluding remarks, irrespective of his unsatisfactory understanding of capital that tends to go unobserved, Bourdieu's commitment to the socially-specific has effectively reinforced his exclusion from the "mature" social capital literature. For this prospers by reinforcing an equally if differently inappropriate understanding of capital with an almost total lack of recognition of, let alone sensitivity to, the social and historical realities attached to capitalism.

Bourdieu's multifarious capitals

Against this background, consider how Bourdieu uses the term capital. First, he divides it into a number of broad categories – economic, cultural, and symbolic – with each of these open to disaggregation in the light of particular activities, as in academic, professional, literary, scientific, legal-economic, philosophical, political, informational, and educational capital. At times, economic capital is simply seen as resources (Bourdieu 1996a, pp. 83–84), of which the ideal type would be those most readily convertible into money.[8] Cultural capital, which itself has three broad forms – embodied, objectified, and institutionalised (Bourdieu 1986b, p. 243) – is typically marked by socially but differentially recognised and constructed qualifications, not least those formally given by education but also other forms of social attainment to which rank might be attached. Symbolic capital is represented by prestige, as in honour.

The place reserved for social capital is one focused on the extent of social connections or networks (Bourdieu 1996a, pp. 361 and 368; and 1986b, p. 248). A favoured example is provided by the family (Bourdieu 1996b, p. 292): "Thus, a network of family relations can be the locus of an unofficial circulation of capital." This can give rise to "an extraordinary concentration of symbolic capital" (Bourdieu 1996b, p. 79), not least in the marriage potential of children (Bourdieu 1996b, p. 280). Further, the family serves as a parallel for the social capital embodied within large-scale corporations (Bourdieu 1996b, p. 286), or in the presumed shift in power from industry to finance (Bourdieu 1996b, p. 327). In short, for Bourdieu (1987, p. 4):

In a social universe like French society, and no doubt in the American society of today, these fundamental social powers are, according to my empirical investigations, firstly, *economic* capital, in various kinds: secondly, *cultural* capital or better, informational capital, again in various kinds; and thirdly two forms of capital that are very strongly correlated, *social* capital, which consists of resources based on connections and group membership, and *symbolic* capital, which is the form the different types of capital take once they are perceived and recognized as legitimate.

Second, as the notion of capital is consciously and deliberately spread across what are not directly economic categories, so it takes on a broader analytical content, and is specifically attached to the notion of power. Indeed, capital and power almost become synonymous, with reference to "the different types of capital (or power, which amounts to the same thing)" (Bourdieu 1986b, p. 243).[9] As Postone et al. (1993, p. 4) observe: "Bourdieu's notion of *capital*, which is neither Marxian nor formal economic, entails the capacity to exercise control over one's own future and that of others. As such, it is a form of power." Further, the concentration of such powers is seen to reside within the state (Bourdieu and Wacquant 1992, p. 114) in "a specific capital, *properly statist capital*", confirming the identification of capital and generalised power with one another. Indeed, for Bourdieu (1998b, p. 41):

> The state is the *culmination of a process of concentration of different species of capital*: capital of physical force or instruments of coercion (army, police), economic capital, cultural or (better) informational capital, and symbolic capital ... [and] leads indeed to the *emergence* of a specific, properly statist capital ... which enables the state to exercise power over the different fields and over the different particular species of capital, and especially over the rates of conversion between them.

Here is revealed a particularly fluid application of the notion of capital across the various activities that are embraced by the state, with fungibility between them. The metaphor is even extended to the state as a central bank, a sort of lender of last resort for society, with the state's total sum of capitals comprising more than its individual parts.[10]

Third, then, capital is not only power in general, it follows that it is power of any type in particular even if subject to classification as economic, cultural, social, or symbolic. Moreover, capital in its economic form is freely used as a metaphor, and its language and notions are readily deployed.[11] Indeed, capitals are not only more or less fungible, so is the language of commerce. The various types of capital can be understood as assets. They are subject to cycles, generate returns, are distributed, acquired and inherited. Equally, there is accumulation, preservation (or depreciation), and transformation of the different types of capital (Bourdieu 1987, p. 4):

> Thus, agents are distributed in the overall social space, in the first dimension

according to the global *volume* of capital they possess, in the second dimension according to the *composition* of their capital, that is, according to the relative weight in their overall capital of the various forms of capital, especially economic and cultural, and in the third dimension according to the evolution in time of the volume and composition of their capital, that is, according to their *trajectory* in social space.

Fourth, however, because power is relative and not absolute and resources in general are available to all, capital readily becomes identifiable with socio-economic groups or even with each and every individual.[12] This is despite Bourdieu's concern to elaborate a theory of classes on the basis of distinction by volume and composition in overall possession of the different forms of capital, especially Bourdieu (1987). Thus, there is the issue of the amount of social capital of an agent dependent upon, "the size of the network of connections he can effectively mobilize and on the volume of the capital ... possessed in his own right by each of those to whom he is connected" (Bourdieu 1986b, p. 249), with "position in the field of power (defined by the structure of a person's capital)" (Bourdieu 1996b, p. 162). Capital is distributed across all students (Bourdieu 1996b). Individuals invest time in accumulating cultural capital (Bourdieu 1986b, p. 253), as in self-improvement (Bourdieu 1986b, p. 244). The linguistic capital of blacks in the form of their own vernacular is devalued by their subordinate social position (Bourdieu and Wacquant 1992, p. 143).[13] Women are seen as inferior across modes of production because "men are the *subjects* of matrimonial strategies through which they work to maintain or to increase their symbolic capital" (Bourdieu and Wacquant 1992, p. 173).[14] Most clearly, the individualistic basis of Bourdieu's notion of capital emerges in making comparison between those with different portfolios of endowments: "Two individuals endowed with an equivalent overall capital can differ ... in that one holds a lot of economic capital and little cultural capital while the other has little economic capital and large cultural assets" (Bourdieu and Wacquant 1992, p. 99).[15]

More generally, there is perceived to be a hierarchy both of cultural and of economic capital which is liable to be symmetrically but inversely distributed (Bourdieu 1986a, p. 120 and 1996b, p. 158). Thus, diverse forms of capital are not detached from their social context but they are possessed by individuals like private property and economic capital in particular.

Fifth, the attachment of capital to metaphor, individuals, resources, and power is also conducive to transhistorical use. Thus, for example, aristocratic status deriving from pre-capitalist relations is perceived as a form of social capital: "The title of nobility is the form *par excellence* of the institutionalized social capital which guarantees a particular form of social relationship in a lasting way" (Bourdieu 1986b, p. 251).[16] Bourdieu (1993, p. 272) himself acknowledges that his notion of capital originates in, and is transcribed from, pre-capitalist concerns, with symbolic capital originally derived to explain honour in such societies.[17] Bourdieu (1981, p. 314) also refers to capital to construct a general theory of the power that bureaucrats derive from the institutions that they inhabit:

> Such agents perform their oblation all the more easily because they have less capital outside the institution and therefore less freedom *vis-à-vis* the institution and the specific capital and profits that it provides ... He is predisposed to defend the institution, with total conviction, against the heretical deviations of those whose externally acquired capital allows and inclines them to take liberties with internal beliefs and hierarchies.

Sixth, Bourdieu is concerned with the relationship between the various types of capital, in part as being in conflict with one another, as fractions or within and between different types of agents, but also in terms of how one can be converted into another (Bourdieu 1986a, pp. 132 and 137; and 1986b, pp. 243 and 252).[18] The motivation for this concern is various – how does the artist or aesthetic appreciation retain autonomy (cultural capital) whilst dependent upon material resources (economic capital),[19] what are the relative merits of the forms of capital in gaining employment in public and private management, how does the distribution of cultural and symbolic capital give rise to the reproduction of a hierarchy of tastes and socio-economic positions? Despite these common concerns, and use of capital, across these various activities, Bourdieu sustains a clear logical and structural distinction between them, not least in the meanings that are attached to them. Most sharp is the example provided by the household and the sentiments attached to domesticity. For, the household cannot become the commercial economy just as love itself is negated if it is commercialised (although both the household and love can comprise a shifting range of activities and meanings) (Bourdieu 1998b, p. 106):[20]

> With the constitution of the economy and the generalization of monetary exchanges and the spirit of calculation, the domestic economy ceases to furnish the model of all other economic relations. Threatened in its specific logic by the market economy, it increasingly tends to affirm its specific logic, that of love ... one can thus oppose the logic of domestic sexual exchanges, which have no price, and the logic of the market sexual relations, which have an explicit market price and are sanctioned by monetary exchanges.

A similar point is made about the Church which, whilst an economic enterprise, if treated solely in terms of supply and demand, would lead to uproar, disbelief, and "the laughter of the bishops" (p. 112).[21]

In this light, the economy creates "anti-economic sub-universes", devoid of, or in opposition to, the world of economic capital (p. 113). By the same token, money is the fluid material by which intergenerational obligations are fulfilled but it cannot explain such familial commitment attached to the corresponding presence of a gift economy despite its monetary form. Nor why it is based on devotion and excludes not only interest payments but also the sharply defined terms and conditions associated with the commercial world (p. 109). Ultimately, however, the language of quantification is employed by Bourdieu with an exact analogy with the conversion of one form of economic value to another, as in the " 'exchange rate' (or 'conversion rate') among the different forms of capital" and "the determination of the relative value and magnitude of the different forms of power" (Bourdieu 1996b, p. 265).[22]

These characteristics of Bourdieu's use of capital represent a clear extension of the scope of the concept in response to the fluidity of capital outlined in Chapter 2. Significantly, for example, where Marx views the display of wealth as a necessary condition for the functioning capitalist, an expenditure of revenue distinct from capital, Bourdieu (1986a, p. 287) considers it as a form of symbolic capital itself, apparently drawing upon Marx for analytical support (capital?):

> The members of the professions ... find in smart sports and games, in receptions, cocktails and other society gatherings not only intrinsic satisfaction and edification but also the select society in which they can make and keep up their "connections" and accumulate the capital of honourability they need in order to carry on their profession. This is only one of the cases in which luxury, "a conventional degree of prodigality", becomes, as Marx observed, "a business necessity" and "enters into capital's expenses of representation" as "an exhibition of wealth and consequently as a source of credit".

In effect, there is a double fluidity in Bourdieu's notion of capital that is quite independent of the fluidity of capital itself as an economic category.[23] On the one hand, the notion of *economic* capital lacks depth, precision and rigour. Thus, Beasley-Murray (1999) points to Bourdieu's refusal to address the economic and cleverly observes that he tends to understand (economic) capital exclusively in terms of exchange value (monetary value) but the other forms of (non-economic) capital in terms of use (value). Economic capital is scarcely examined at all in sharp contrast to the extent to which it is projected onto other putative forms of capital. On the other hand, then, this inadequate concept of economic capital is extrapolated to the other forms of capital even though these are endowed with a distinctive content of their own.[24]

Bourdieu versus Becker

The previous section has established that Bourdieu has fallen victim to social capital fetishism. This leans almost entirely on the capital fetishism side, for Bourdieu is otherwise acutely conscious of the mysteries of the social. As a result, it is worth examining how Bourdieu's approach to, and notion of, capital differs from that offered by others, especially mainstream economics. Because of his work on educational attainment, he is aware of the parallels that might be drawn with human capital. But he is unsparingly critical of its intellectual pretensions and ideological role. In commenting generally on mainstream economics, it is perceived as both unrealistic and ideologically driven (Bourdieu 1998a, pp. 94–96):

> This tutelary theory is a pure mathematical fiction … performed in the name of a strict and narrow rationality, identified with individual rationality … [it] consists in bracketing off the economic and social conditions of rational dispositions … and of the economic and social structures which are the condition of their exercise, or, more precisely, of the production and reproduction of those dispositions and those structures … this initially desocialized and dehistoricized "theory" has … the means of *making itself true* … an immense *political operation* is being pursued … aimed at creating the conditions for realizing and operating of the "theory"; a *programme of methodical destruction of collectives* (neoclassical economics recognizes only individuals, whether it is dealing with companies, trade unions or families).

And, further (p. 101):

> Cut off by their whole existence and above all by their generally purely abstract and theoretical intellectual training from the real economic and social world, they are … inclined to take the things of logic for the logic of things … [t]rusting in models that they have practically never had the occasion to subject to experimental verification, tending to look down on high on the conclusions of the other historical sciences, in which they recognize only the purity and crystalline transparency of their mathematical games and whose real necessity and deep complexity they are most often unable to comprehend.

More specifically, in addressing human capital directly, although recognising that economics is a diverse field, he considers that it displays "all kinds of reductionisms, beginning with economism, which recognizes nothing but material interest and the deliberate search for the maximization of monetary profit" (Bourdieu and Wacquant 1992, p. 118). Hence, he considers, "the only thing I share with economic orthodoxy … are a number of words".

For the new household economics, a simple critique and dismissal is offered (Bourdieu 1998b, 106):

> We see that, contrary to economistic reductionism à la Gary Becker, who reduces to economic calculation that which by definition denies and defies calculation, the domestic unit manages to perpetuate at its core a quite particular economic logic.

This logic has been mentioned previously as "anti-economic" and based on sentiment, obligation and love. It is further connected, across different societies, to social reproduction that, in the case of commerce as a corrosive force, requires a countervailing force of cohesion that is simultaneously undermined (p. 107):

The family is subject to two contradictory systems of forces: on the one hand the forces of the economy which introduce the tensions, contradictions and conflicts I have evoked, but which, in certain contexts, also impose the maintenance of a certain cohesion, and, on the other hand, the forces of cohesion which are in part linked to the fact that the reproduction of capital in its different forms depends, to a large degree, on the reproduction of the family unit.

However, this and other direct commentary on Becker, as in Bourdieu (1996b, pp. 275–76 and 1986b, p. 255), show that Bourdieu has not kept abreast with the developments in Becker's own thinking let alone with those neoclassical economists who are more adept at, and more inclined towards, constructing a theory of social structures and strategies on the basis of methodological individualism. For Bourdieu – although, to be fair, writing much closer to its peak of influence – it is as if the world of economists is exclusively occupied by those with a theoretical stance that is totally committed to perfect competition and laissez-faire. It even appears that Bourdieu adopts a stance in which reference to the social alone is sufficient to separate him from the reductionism and economism of human capital theory. This is a consequence of his notion that the reproduction and inheritance of social, cultural, and symbolic capital is obscured by the processes that take place, for example, within the family.[25] Indeed, it is an irony in Bourdieu's work that his fluid and ambiguous extension of the concept of capital to the non-economic arena leads him to consider that the presence of such capital has been hidden, only to be revealed by his own account – the invention of fetishised, even non-existent, capitals is inevitably compatible with a theory of their invisibility! But, as seen in Chapter 3, the factors to which Bourdieu points have proved highly visible to Becker in his theories of personal and social capital.[26]

Whilst appropriately condemning the reductionism of mainstream economics, Bourdieu is more favourably inclined to the new economic sociology in which considerable emphasis is placed upon the social as networks.[27] As Wacquant observes, with copious references: "There exist obvious and large zones of overlap and convergence between Bourdieu's older and newer work … and the concerns of the 'New Economic Sociology' " (Bourdieu and Wacquant 1992, p. 118). Quite apart from how acceptable this might be to mainstream economists such as Becker, the following definition of social capital fits extremely comfortably within the framework offered by Granovetter (1985) and his network theory followers, discussed in Chapter 7 (Bourdieu 1986b, pp. 248–49):

Social capital is the aggregate of the actual or potential resources which are linked to possession of a durable network … The volume of the social capital possessed by a given agent thus depends on the size of the network of connections he can effectively mobilize and on the volume of the capital … possessed by a given agent, or even by the whole set of agents to whom he is connected.

This is not to suggest that Bourdieu's work is reducible to such network theory. His methodology sets him apart in two closely related ways. First, he is conscious of the need to define the meaning of the social in its historically specific context. It is not sufficient to establish the presence of a network but also to examine its content in practice. Such is the basis on which those such as Zelizer (1988) and DiMaggio (1990) have criticised the new economics sociology for its failure to interrogate the cultural content of the objects of study rather than taking this as self-evident by virtue of the interactions that are consolidated and even congealed. It is an accusation that cannot be levelled against Bourdieu.[28]

Second, Bourdieu adopts a particular stance towards empirical work. Whilst he uses statistical techniques to establish connections between the various forms of capital, the various correlations involved are considered meaningless in the absence of an understanding of the meanings of the correlates themselves (Bourdieu 1986a, p. 18). His methodology involves the use of categories that are investigative in intent and only become systematic with use. Tracing the intellectual genealogy of such concepts is considered to be pointless as each proves to be a "temporary construct which takes shape for and by empirical work" (Bourdieu and Wacquant 1992, p. 161).[29] This contrasts with the use of (mathematical) models with what are taken to be well-defined components whose meaning and interactions can be fully explored or tested empirically on this basis, with little or no reference to context.

Concluding remarks

Bourdieu's methodology, then, attempts to strike a balance between economism – by which is meant the treatment of non-economic forms of capital as if they were purely equivalent to the economic – and retaining a hold on the specificity of non-economic forms of capital without ignoring the "brutal fact of universal reducibility to economics" (Bourdieu 1986b, pp. 252–53). In this way, the fluidity of capital – its convertibility – poses a central methodological conundrum (Bourdieu 1986b, pp. 252–53):[30]

> The real logic of the functioning of capital, the conversions from one type to another, and the law of conservation which governs them cannot be understood unless two opposing but equally partial views are superseded: on the one hand, economism, which, on the grounds that every type of capital is reducible in the last analysis to economic capital, ignores what makes the specific efficacy of the other types of capital, and on the other hand, semiologism ... which reduces social exchanges to phenomena of communication.

As McLennan (1998) has sharply clarified Bourdieu's motivation in positing different types of capital – and the *fields* they create and the *habitus* that is brought to them – is to avoid crude determinism in social theory, both in what is caused and how. To have attempted to do so by appeal to different forms of capital is, however, symbolic of failure in two respects. On the one hand, there is the creation of a chaotic concept of capital itself and, on the other hand, a metaphorical slippage into reductionism to the economic (as "capital"). At least such tensions remain in Bourdieu's work,[31] in contrast to what has followed within the realm of social capital, where, along with Bourdieu himself, they are scarcely recognised let alone addressed.

To a large extent, this furnishes a logical explanation for Bourdieu being dropped from the domain of social capital whilst he continues to prosper in the intellectual worlds around other forms of capital, such as the cultural and the symbolic.[32] These forms of capital have also been marginalised into specific, if locally prominent applications, usually within cultural theory or analysis. For illustrative purposes, consider the relationship between economics and geography, with the former always having found a more or less comfortable role within the latter, whether in mainstream neoclassical versions or as the political economy of space. In this respect, what sets geography apart from economics is that it has been profoundly influenced by postmodernism. As Zukin (1996) has observed, this has given rise to two schools of thought on the built environment. The traditional focuses on the political economy of land use, whereas the more recent addresses the symbolic economy, visual representation, and inclusion/exclusion in the production of space.[33] In bringing the two schools together, it is hardly surprising that the influence of the fluidity of capital should be felt, with notions of cultural and even social capital being deployed freely and flexibly, further encouraged by the resonances between capital as wealth and as city itself.[34] For Kearns (1993, p. 50) cultural capital is tied up in historic sites and images, Crilley (1993, p. 234) views buildings as functioning as "symbolic capital", Philo and Kearns (1993, p. 16) consider property ownership and fancy possessions as the surface badges of cultural capital, and Goodwin (1993, p. 146) argues, in an inversion of the truth, that "urban capital is in the end valorised like any other form of capital".[35]

In short, as demonstrated by the early appearance of such notions relative to the short life of social capital, Bourdieu's influence, in this case in geography, is central. Yet, from social capital having been one type of capital within Bourdieu's work, it has become universalised across all non-economic aspects. The same step has allowed its social, historical, and cultural content to be set aside. In other words, social capital has become broader in scope but so much shallower in depth relative to Bourdieu. Further, as Bourdieu is abandoned in reconstructing social capital within the literature, so it becomes a general category where, previously for him, it was specific. As such, the literature proceeds by perpetrating an irony at Bourdieu's expense. It takes the now generalised notion of social capital and disaggregates it once more into specific types. Thus, Castle (1998) offers the notion of "rural capital" as a form of social capital in the countryside.[36] By the same token, it can stride freely across all social sciences, whereas Bourdieu's other capitals have become much less wide-ranging in interdisciplinary scope. For, even their names would suffice to sustain a more rounded connection to social and historical specificity.[37] It is surely tempting to conclude, in gentle irony, that "social capital" is itself a form of social capital, and of the other types of capital, in the sense of Bourdieu. It has created a "field" of endeavour and a "habitus" for its participants, the social capitalists.

5 Bringing rational choice back in

Introduction

From the previous chapter, three particular features of Bourdieu's work on social capital should be highlighted. First, he pursues a highly fluid notion of capital; second, it remains highly socially and historically contextual; and, third, his work – not least in light of the previous aspect – has been discarded as the social capital literature has evolved. The contribution made to social capital by James Coleman shares none of these features. His work draws upon a notion of social capital that is analytically fixed as the capacity to deal with public goods or market imperfections. Otherwise, it is profoundly asocial and ahistorical (it is historically fixed insofar as there is a presumption of both market and non-market relations), and it remains acknowledged as the source of the social capital literature to follow. What is so different about Coleman and why should he prove so inspirational for social capital and social capital theory?

This chapter seeks to answer these questions. It begins with an account of social exchange theory. Scarcely acknowledged as such in the social capital literature, this field of sociology prospered from the 1960s until it gave way to social capital theory. It was not simply superseded, however, for it proved to be the analytical precursor to its successor with marked continuities and some discontinuities between the two. I cannot claim to have discovered this connection between the two theories. For Astone et al. (1999, p. 1) see social capital as extremely popular, "a concept that originated in sociology and is being widely incorporated into much current social science. The social capital concept is an extension of social exchange theory." Yet, it was through this citation alone – rather than others that simply are not to be found elsewhere – that I stumbled upon the connection between social exchange and social capital. This may reflect my poor background in social science, or an equally poor scholarship and vision, but I doubt it. The article by Astone et al. is also significant for belonging to the field of demography where social exchange was used as a factor in explaining fertility choice. Demography has only received limited attention from social capital theory, although it has become used as the residual explanatory factor in fertility choice.

It will be shown in the second section that social exchange theory addressed many of the same problems as social capital theory. Not least of these are how to relate micro to macro theory and how to relate economic to non-economic factors. At root, however, it has been a project to foist methodological individualism upon social theory. As such, it simply failed under the contradictions of the task that it set for itself of constructing the social out of the individual. Coleman was a major contributor to the social exchange literature, something usually overlooked, but he occupied a particular approach that distinguished him from others in two closely related respects. On the one hand, he was committed to a particularly narrow version of methodological individualism, a utilitarianism based on simple pursuit of self-interest. On the other hand, he placed much greater emphasis on economic as opposed to psychological factors. In effect, Coleman uniquely combined, within sociology, social exchange theory and an economic orientation. It allowed him to give birth to social capital. This will be demonstrated in the third section.

But Coleman's contribution has, in the event, gone much further than this. As remarked, the social exchange literature, including that of Coleman himself, was organised around methodological individualism and, as such, proved both incapable of satisfactorily addressing the social and generally unpalatable to social scientists other than economists. Subsequently, methodological individualism has enjoyed something of a revival, in the wake of neo-liberalism, not least in the form of rational choice theory. But Coleman, and the transition from social exchange to social capital, has benefited from a much more powerful antidote to the antipathy to methodological individualism. It has disguised its ultimate dependence upon this approach by cloaking itself in the traditional concepts of social theory. As the final section observes, this has been aided and abetted by a loss of memory over the association between social exchange and social capital. With the simultaneous shift towards an economic emphasis, the transition from social exchange to capital has been completed. It simply required a band of ready social capitalists for it to flourish. The social sciences have not been found wanting.

From social exchange ...

In retrospect, it is much easier to see what social exchange theory has been and how it has developed. It emerged to prominence in the early 1960s and enjoyed a period of intense activity for a couple of decades before passing away or, more exactly, being superseded by social capital theory. My discussion of its short life will be organised around three major contributors: Homans, Emerson and Blau, and their followers and interpreters.[1] The literature has been organised around two fundamental issues.[2] First, how are social relations, structures, norms, institutions, or whatever to be understood in the light of individual behaviour?[3] Second, what are the appropriate types of individual behaviour or motivation on which to focus in order to address the previous issue? In short, the social exchange project has always been about methodological individualism – how to understand society on the basis of the aggregated behaviour of individuals. Its reference to social is readily to be understood in this vein; in addition, the reference to exchange is a consequence of its pre-occupation with how individuals relate to one another.

At the outset, then, as a theory of individual interaction, it draws upon a generalised understanding of exchange of which, for example, market relations are of a special type. They are both impersonal and readily quantifiable whereas other forms of exchange are personal and qualitative. Fine and Lapavitsas (2000) have argued that such an approach to both sorts of exchange is inappropriate.[4] Market and non-market exchanges do not mutually belong to, and exhaust, a common category. For both are based on, and so exchange is a concrete form of, specific social relations that are quite different from one another. In particular, capitalist commodity production is distinct both from more general exchange relations within capitalism as well as other forms of exchange derived from non-capitalist societies. As a result, the social exchange literature is generally marked by a lack of sensitivity to the historical and social scope or specificity of the concepts that they employ. The social tends to be derived from the asocial, ahistorical, and – what are presumed to be – universal characteristics of individuals as they go about relating to, or exchanging with, one another. Significantly, this could only be possible by a total disregard for that core component of anthropology which addresses exactly the same issues – albeit normally under a different name, the study of the gift.[5]

Initially, then, in the work of Homans (1961), it is hardly surprising that social exchange theory should draw upon behavioural psychology for its point of departure, and that social psychology should be reduced to its barest flesh and bones, almost literally.[6] As Ekeh (1974) carefully documents, Homans ultimately degenerates to Skinnerian behavioural psychology in which "men as men" are studied as belonging to the human as opposed to other animal species and, despite being socialised as such,[7] all psychology is itself reducible to behavioural psychology (p. 91). Indeed:[8] "Homans is pre-eminently Skinnerian in his belief that human behavior can, perhaps should, be reduced to principles of animal psychology in order to be fully understood" (p. 95).

What accounts for this extraordinary "reductionism" on the part of Homans, a term explicitly used by Ekeh (1974) and to which Chadwick-Jones (1976) devotes an entire chapter in appraising social exchange theory?[9] The answer is in his obsession to discard any form of collectivist sociology or functionalism, wherever it might be found, from Lévi-Strauss to Durkheim. For, as Ekeh (1974, p. 88) cites Homans, the latter is committed to "the notion that the nature of individuals determined finally the nature of society", with a corresponding rejection of "Durkheim's assertion that society was an entity *sui generis* and that sociology was not a corollary of psychology" (p. 89).[10]

Whatever the motives and rationale for Homans' reductionism, the latter rapidly proved unsustainable against the weight of alternative modes of thought even within limited horizons. Homans had taken so much out of social theory in constructing his theory of social exchange that he had provided an open invitation to restore as little or as much as took a critic's fancy. Indeed, Homans himself was prepared to move beyond the psychological to the economic animal, and to append an elementary calculus of pleasure and pain and provide a marriage of psychological behaviourism and utilitarian economics.[11] This is immediately to yield on the first issue outlined above, the factors underlying human behaviour. It is also to raise a different aspect in the evolution of social exchange theory, its relationship to economics. It has a number of components.

First, as in much of the literature on the gift where the latter is seen in opposition to the commodity, the economic and the market are taken as synonymous with one another, and social exchange is seen as separate from, and different to, market exchange. Consequently, social exchange requires distinct principles for investigation. Emerson (1987, pp. 11–12) puts it particularly clearly:

> At its core, neoclassical economic theory views the actor (a person or a firm) as dealing not with other actors but with a *market*. In economic theory, decisions are made by actors not in response to, or in anticipation of, the decision of another party but in response to environmental parameters such as market price ... By contrast, in the various forms of social exchange theory, the longitudinal *exchange relation* between two specific actors is the central concept around which theory is organized ... Thus, while social and economic theories of exchange might be seen as growing toward each other, they remain radically different in their conceptual core. Social exchange theory studies person–environment relations.

In short, economics studies individuals in the context of market parameters, social exchange studies them in their social relations.

Second, social exchange theory has been remarkably uncritical of economics, possibly less surprising in view of its own reductionist roots in methodological individualism. Mainstream neoclassical economics is generally taken as uncontroversial within its appropriate area of application. Otherwise, as observed, other principles are required for social exchange. By the same token, the extent to which the economic itself is broached and understood is extremely limited. Generally, at best, the perfectly competitive economy and associated optimising conditions in terms of marginal utilities are acknowledged, not least because the only concern is with the motivational or behavioural aspects of individuals as the basis for understanding society.

Third, knowledge of economics as a discipline is revealed to be superficial even within the bounds of mainstream neoclassical economics, let alone heterodoxies or political economy which are more inclined to address precisely issues concerning the relationship between social exchange and the economy. As a further consequence, even taking account of this being a retrospective reading, the knowledge of mainstream economics revealed by social exchange theorist is embarrassingly simplistic, often wrong, and hopelessly out of date. This possibly reflects ignorance of readers and writers alike and intimidation of the one by the other, respectively, transposing the formal apparatus and jargon of one discipline to others. As a result, the social exchange literature is hardly liable to keep abreast of developments taking place within economics, even as the latter is itself evolving. This enables it to see itself as occupying an analytical vacuum that economics leaves unfilled because of its inability to address power, justice, exploitation, distribution, interpersonal comparisons, institutions, etc. In short, social exchange theory damagingly suffers a triple displacement. It understands the economy through the eyes of economics as a separate discipline; it understands economics as neoclassical economics; and it understands neoclassical economics in its most elementary and, at times, mistaken forms.

From the perspective of the second major issue of social exchange theory – how to derive the social from the individual – this commentary is literally academic. For it is only of (considerable) relevance to the intellectual concerns that were to be passed on to its successor under the rubric of social capital theory. Neither adding economic motives or others for human behaviour is capable of explaining the social. For, the social exchange theory literature has ultimately had the intellectual integrity to develop in opposition to Homans, to recognise that the social cannot be derived from the individual. The anatomy of society is not to be found in the human anatomy, unless impressed by outside stimuli that would then themselves need to be explained. Consequently, an alternative route must be taken although it might be supported by a more or less rounded account of human behaviour, with the incorporation of psychological, economic, and other elements.

The first step is to construct a mini-society, exchange between two individuals and what is termed dyadic exchange. It is simply an issue of whether the whole is the greater than the sum of the individual parts. Can we understand society on the basis of an aggregated collection of dyads? In general, again in opposition to Homans, the social exchange literature delivers a resoundingly negative response. In Mitchell's (1978, p. 25) view: "The substance of Homans' position is that societal forms and structures are nothing more than composition effects of the sum of individuals pursuing self-interest." The problem is that Homans would be unable to explain collective forms of behaviour. Indeed, he borders on the presumption that they do not exist other than as cumulative individual interaction. How does social exchange theory move beyond this impasse?

Essentially, there are three different routes. The first is to generalise from dyads to interpersonal networks of interactions. Further, such networks can then be endowed with a social or structural content of their own. Institutions or customs, for example, come to command a social presence independent of the specific individuals that occupy or observe them, respectively. This clearly anticipates the network theory that forms part of social capital theory. The second route, essentially a corollary once removed from the first, is to focus much more upon the value systems, in the ideological or cultural sense, that are attached to individuals. This strategy is most closely associated with Blau (1964) who is less reductionist than Homans and more inclusive in his sources of analytical content. As Mitchell (1978) observes, he seeks to explain the emergence of power, conflict and institutions out of accumulated social exchanges, not least in the form of a value system that flows free from its origins within exchange and stands in lieu of individuals in the exchange. In short, "his theoretical offerings reflect a willingness for intellectual eclecticism ... utilizing the best aspects of severally mutually exclusive perspectives" (p. 74).[12] Similarly, for Emerson (1987), as observed above, the problem is one of moving beyond person–market relations to an understanding of person–environment relations, thereby incorporating issues of equity, justice, power, and exploitation.[13] He even purportedly constructs a multidimensional value system for this purpose.[14] In this respect, once again to anticipate, there is a truly remarkable parallel with social capital theory with its apparent capacity to incorporate any theory and to address any problem despite its own limited analytical foundations.

Thus, as evidenced by contributions in Cook (ed) (1987) for example,[15] social exchange theory had the option of constructing the social out of the individual by reference either to networks, to values, or to both.[16] Before considering the third route taken, however, it is worth reporting on Blau's (1987) contribution to this volume since he has undergone a conversion for reasons that are most revealing, especially for the prospective social capital theory. He concludes that "I changed my mind since I wrote the book on exchange and power, in which I suggested that macrosociological theory should be built on the basis of microsociological theory" (p. 99). The reason is that the gap between the micro of social exchanges cannot be satisfactorily filled out to social relations or whatever. Indeed (p. 87):

> An important issue in constructing macrosociological theory is the linkage with microsociological theory. One approach is to start with microsociological principles and use these as the foundation for building macrosociological theory. The alternative approach rests on the assumption that the different perspectives and conceptual frameworks are necessary for micro and macro theories ... I have come to the conclusion that the second approach is the only viable one, at least at this stage of sociological theory.

Essentially, the prospect of micro/macro is not denied in principle, only at that stage of our knowledge. Most interesting, however, are the parallels that are drawn with economics. For, the micro and macro of each are seen to correspond, "One might say, speaking metaphorically, that exchange theory examines the social relations from within whereas macrostructural theory examines them from without ... it is a micro but a general theory, like microeconomics" (p. 96). And exactly the same unresolved problem exists for economic as for social theory (p. 99):

> The ultimate aim, to be sure, is to develop a unified sociological theory that encompasses explanations of the significance of both macrostructure and microprocesses for social life. But the day we can achieve this is still far off,

just as microeconomics and macroeconomics have not yet been able to develop a rigorous theory.

If only Blau had recognised what was going on around him! Not only were the new micro-foundations of macroeconomics being established but also the very same principles would be extended by economists to address problems of social as well as of economic theory, as outlined in Chapter 1.[17]

Nonetheless, Blau's stance does not command universal acceptance amongst social exchange theorists because of the third route to resolve its conundrums. The latter derive from the need to take as given the social context, within which individuals, their values and their networks interact. Hence, a major part of the social is left unexplained even if more of its territory is appropriated through broader understandings of individuals and the form (networks) and content (values) of their interaction. Consequently, critical literature has referred to the low level of explanation, and even of tautology, within social exchange theory, a potential weakness recognised by Emerson (1976) for example. The solution lies in the simple expedient of allowing society itself, and not just values and networks, to be the dependent/independent consequence of individual exchanges, providing the context for social exchanges which themselves re-produce, or even transform, the broader social context. As Cook (1991) argues, social structures need to be built out of exchange relations and exchange networks. She purports to reject reductionism to individuals as not satisfying the necessary criterion for viable social theory, for "the theory cannot remain at the [unexplained] macro level, and, when it descends to the individual level, it cannot return to the macro level through simple aggregation" (p. 39), the concern being with "how these patterns of interaction are reproduced and replicated over time and space" (p. 41).[18] Consequently, Cook (1987, pp. 218–19) explicitly disagrees with the renegade Blau (1987), discussed above, who is seen "to hold to an old dichotomy between individuals and aggregates that is counterproductive", since "social structures are, after all, structures composed of the social relations among actors, whether these actors are individual or collective (acting through agents)".[19]

My account of social exchange theory has now reached its conclusion with the maturity of the theory itself. It seemed it could go no further. It had failed in its project to provide social theory with (individualistic) micro-foundations that could complement economic theory. It had also reflected three persistent and inter-related oppositions in the literature: is economics being taken to sociology or vice versa; is analysis based on the individual or the social; and what is the analytical status of the historically or socially given factors if taken independent of rational choice?[20] Yet, closely related, if separate, developments were about to transform the intellectual scene and, in a way, to resolve these oppositions. By shift of emphasis and terminology, as shown in the next section, Coleman launched social capital on what was to become a willing audience. Meanwhile, the new micro-foundations (of macroeconomics or otherwise) were gathering momentum within economics, simultaneously offering both to resolve the macro/micro dilemma within economics and to extend optimising principles to non-economic applications.

... to social capital

In work on social capital, Coleman is almost always referenced as an initiating contributor and, unlike Bourdieu, has commanded at least token acknowledgement as the literature has evolved and expanded.[21] Whilst there has been some effort to trace earlier uses of the term social capital and, to a limited extent, its earlier use other than in name, surprisingly little care has been taken to comprehend how Coleman became one of, if not the, first social capitalists of the modern period. Most interest in his work focuses on his *American Journal of Sociology* article of 1988 and his book of 1990, although Coleman's (1987b) article appears to mark his first use of the term.[22] Consequently, it is almost as if social capital was suddenly inspirationally invented, and Coleman is usually perceived to have derived and generalised his theory of social capital out of the wish to explain differential school performance on the basis of differences in familial and environmental circumstances. Those from "better" [Catholic] families or neighbourhoods do better at school. Social capital is a source of human capital over and above the resources invested in the latter by the individual, the employer, or the state.

Significantly, however, Coleman et al. (1966) were already concerned with such issues at least twenty years earlier.[23] Further, it is not any new insight into the problems that had occurred over the intervening period, merely a change in language and intellectual climate, which allowed social capital to emerge. In particular, at the end of the 1980s, Coleman is in a unique position to seek a particular synthesis of his own whilst engaging in the emerging confrontation or compromise between economics and sociology.[24] On the one hand, his new stance is based on a barely acknowledged social exchange theory,[25] which had exhausted its limited horizons. On the other hand, he retains his long-standing methodological stance based upon rational choice.[26] Consider each of these in turn.

Although deliberately left temporarily to one side in the previous section, Coleman was a major contributor to the social exchange debate. At the very least, his use of social capital should be examined for its representing continuity with this earlier work on social exchange (Coleman 1972, 1973, and 1975). In this respect, Coleman certainly lies within the core problematic posed by social exchange theory: how to derive the social from the individual. Indeed, he agrees that all social science other than psychology can be reduced to rational choice, the exception being psychology as a result of its depending upon a biological as opposed to a social system (Coleman 1990b, p. 53). In this respect, he lies at the opposite extreme to Homans for whom social exchange theory begins with behavioural psychology.[27] Nonetheless, Coleman (1990b, p. 51) is fundamentally concerned, not so much with individual behaviour, as with how it leads to systemic behaviour:

One of the things that I have always been distressed by is the fact that most quantitative work is work in which it is the behavior of individuals which is taken as the thing to be explained. We therefore are not really explaining the functioning of the system but just the behavior of individuals. One of the things I have gotten very excited about just in the last couple of months is the way in which one can begin to use quantitative data to explain not the functioning of individuals, but the functioning of the system.

Presumably, this is a veiled reference to social capital. For, in his crowning magnus opus, Coleman (1990a, pp. 305–06) raises exactly the same issue explicitly in the context of social capital, albeit with at least uncertain expectations of its likely worth:

Whether social capital will come to be as useful a quantitative concept in social science as are the concepts of financial capital, physical capital, and human capital remains to be seen; its current value lies primarily in its usefulness for qualitative analyses of social systems and for those quantitative analyses that employ qualitative indicators.

The methodology involved, however, has already been laid out in Coleman (1986) and corresponds exactly to the third route, outlined in the previous section, for resolving the problems of social exchange theory by identifying the social with consistent aggregation of, and extrapolation from, individual interactions.

For, in laying out the appropriate domain of social theory, he begins by suggesting that it must focus on society as a whole and individuals (with allowance for intermediate categories). As a result, there are four possible types of theory depending on whether society and individuals are related to one another causally: society–society, society–individual, individual–society and individual–individual. He concludes that "the central theoretical problem in sociology is the transition from the level of the individual to a macro level – the problem that economists call … 'aggregation', although the term is a misleading one" (p. 347). As is already apparent, the economist's mode of theory is perceived to be attractive. Indeed:

Despite the misnomer, "aggregation", that economists have given to the problem of moving from individual to macro level, economists may have made the most progress in addressing it. Their principal tool is the conception of rational action carried out in a competitive market.

Economists are only seen as deficient for not having shown that aggregate outcomes in terms of the social are consistent with individual optimisation, "because it is insufficient to aggregate; it is also necessary to show how aggregation is consistent with reproduction of social structures in which individuals act" (p. 360).[28] Further:

> Social norms ... give a sense of the problem ... the correspondence between social reality and the existing or potential social theory. What is necessary for reality is to have *social institutions* ... which translate individual tastes and endowments into a set of prices and a distribution of goods or into a collective decision. What is necessary for social theory is to have conceptual devices to describe that translation.

It is already more than apparent that Coleman has entirely shifted the emphasis in social exchange theory towards a dialogue with economics rather than psychology and, thereby, endowed it with a much stronger economic content. In this second element in his background, that of his stance on the new economic sociology, he was again uniquely placed by virtue of being Professor of Sociology at the University of Chicago and, as such, the counterpart to Becker as economist with whom he jointly ran a bi-weekly rational choice seminar for many years to promote the application of the "economic approach" to the other social sciences. Out of his two articles and book (Coleman 1987b, 1988, and 1990a, respectively, the latter running to a thousand pages), the notion of social capital emerges with disarming simplicity, especially for an economist. It merely represents the extent to which an appropriate solution has been found to the problem of public goods (from which all can consume without cost but none has an incentive to provide unless charging an inefficiently high cost) and externalities (where the actions of individuals have direct repercussions for others). The capacity to deal with these issues reflects a balance between satisfying individual interests and exercising control over them (to prevent free-riding). Once such arrangements are internalised by individuals, they represent norms of behaviour. Coleman (1987b, p. 153) appears to consider that putting these elementary insights together constitutes a dramatic discovery both for economics and for sociology:

> But just as neoclassical economics was slow in recognizing the fundamental differences introduced by externalities and public goods, those who use "exchange theory" in sociology have been slow in recognizing that many social actions and transactions generate externalities or have the character of public goods or bads. This has meant that exchange theory in sociology has been incorrectly individualistic, failing to recognize that externalities create an interest in exercising control ... It is in this sense that social norms constitute social capital.

Coleman's understanding of social capital will be considered more closely shortly. For the moment, it is worth observing that his argument is remarkable in two respects. First, his understanding of economics is hopelessly ill informed. It is as if his colleague, Gary Becker, in adopting, at least initially, an analytical stance of the economy (and society) as if a perfect market is the only economics available. This is certainly not true of mainstream economics, which has been extensively concerned with market imperfections for well over a century, being most prominent in the work of Alfred Marshall.[29] Given our account of social exchange theory in the previous section, it is also incomprehensible how Coleman could be unaware that it is precisely its individualistic basis that is a central concern in generating social outcomes that might diverge from simple aggregation. It can only be presumed that Coleman either has gone about rediscovering the wheel in shifting social exchange to social capital or that he has deliberately set aside the previous literature in bringing his sociology to an audience of economists.[30]

The second, as yet unobserved, aspect of Coleman's argument is his treatment of history. Implicit in his theory, as will be seen, is the use of universal, asocial, and ahistorical concepts such as resources, power, and control, quite apart from interests, externalities, public goods, etc. Nonetheless, he does have a sharp and simple understanding of historical change based on the idea that a watershed exists at some point in the past before which non-market exchange predominates. Subsequently, the more impersonal forms of market exchange have come to the fore and have undermined the social capital upon which society previously depended. Thus, having ahistorically constructed the notions of social as opposed to different types of economic capital, these categories are then superimposed upon the historical record to allow an extraordinary inventiveness even relative to casual evidence. For Coleman (1991) suggests that there were no constructed social organisations prior to the thirteenth century (p. 4),[31] and that a shift occurred, "in the past century from subsistence economies of households" (p. 11).

Such crudity and falsehoods are a consequence of the great transformation that is perceived to have shifted society in "a progression from a 'natural' or 'primordial' physical environment to a 'constructed' physical environment" (Coleman 1993). Consequently, social scientists are advised:

> We make a mistake, both in society and in sociology. The mistake is simple and correctable: We fail to recognize that the social capital on which primordial social organization depends is vanishing; we fail to recognize that societies of the future will be constructed, and that we should direct our attention to designing those social structures.

Most social scientists might be astonished both at this accusation and the terms in which it is expressed. For Coleman (1993), reverting to his theme of how education is undermined by broken homes, illustrates his approach by neatly combining his conservative family values[32] with his commitment to rational choice. He suggests that those who do not bring up their children properly impose an externality upon society not least in wasting their minds but also in creating a prospective future of crime and drugs. Perceiving schools as incapable of meeting the parental task, he suggests that parents be rewarded for building the social capital of their children through a system of payment by results, with higher rewards for those handling more difficult children.[33] Irrespective of the practicalities of such a scheme, with horrendous moral hazard problems as parents have an incentive to exaggerate, more than as a dinner-table banter, how difficult are their children, the result is a scarcely concealed social engineering through an as if market, for (p. 14):[34]

> The opportunities lie in a future in which social control no longer depends principally on coercion, constraint, and negative sanctions, under the oppressive blanket of closed communities, but instead depends principally on positive incentives and rewards performance.

In short, brave new world meets the market place!

This is scary stuff and a salutary lesson to would-be social capitalists. Whilst a digression, it does, however, provide some insight into Coleman's worldview and how social capital fits into it. More specifically, for him, social capital is simply the extension of economics to address the handling of market imperfections and public goods/bads. It is the extension of the theory of the individual in social exchange theory to deal with market imperfections, etc.[35] From such humble beginnings, and leaving social capital aside for the moment, Coleman's work has appealed to rational choice to explain the whole of social science (Coleman 1990b, p. 53).[36] The social system can be built up out of an agglomeration of relations between individuals in which control and interest are fundamental categories, readily deployed in problems involving fallacy of composition, principal agents, etc.

The parallels with developments in economics, especially the new micro-foundations, are striking. They have not gone unnoticed so that there has been discussion of the differences between Coleman and Becker and, hence implicitly, the corresponding relationship between economics and sociology. Swedberg (1990, p. 6) puts it as follows:

> Becker ... is mainly concerned with how the neoclassical analysis can be extended to areas outside the economy. Coleman, on the other hand, is trying to recast sociology on the basis of rational choice. Therefore he is more concerned with maintaining certain traditional sociological features in the analysis than Becker.

As Frank (1992) observes, these traditional features lie mainly in Coleman's willingness to eschew reliance upon representative individuals and allow that intermediate agencies be taken as given (on the presumption that some separate rational choice argument will justify this; see below). More important, whilst Becker starts from the equilibrium exchange models of neoclassical economics and extends them to situations without monetary exchange,[37] the reverse is the case for Coleman. He is concerned with the variety of social exchanges that take place in the absence of money, and which are treated as a variety of barters with social capital serving, by way of analogy, as a form of credit on which individuals can draw so long as the mechanisms exist for them to pay back and reproduce the social capital systemically.

However, these differences can only be exaggerated since they reflect a difference in starting point rather than content, and their common commitment to rational choice must be emphasised.[38] For economists, the starting point is a perfectly working market, which is then reconstructed with a social content in light of market imperfections. This content has to be shown to be consistent with economic rationality in light of informational imperfections. Sociologists, on the other hand, start from the social as defined by their disciplinary traditions and seek to reconstruct it on the basis of rational choice.[39]

Finally, in general discussion, in considering its relationship to sociology, Coleman makes explicit that his divorce from economics could readily become a marriage of convenience, for "the appropriate paradigm for sociology ... is derivative from Walrasian general equilibrium theory, though one which deviates from that theory ... in part because of social structure, which a Walrasian system ignores" (Coleman et al. 1986, p. 364). The only other part that Coleman mentions as deficient within the Walrasian system is the absence of market imperfections. In short, the new micro-foundations, in using market imperfections to explain the social on the basis of methodological individualism, have attained Coleman's goal for social theory.[40] In this light, his assessment that he would rather and does see sociology as taking over economics rather than vice versa, and that sociology is not a "scout for economics", is scarcely credible (Coleman 1990b, pp. 56–57). Yet, Coleman (1990a, p. 300) considers himself so much in the vanguard of social theory – despite his own commitment to methodological individualism – that, with no apparent sense of irony, he warns against neglecting the social in focusing upon the individual:

> There is a broadly perpetrated fiction in modern society ... that society consists of a set of independent individuals, each of whom acts to achieve goals that are independently arrived at, and that the functioning of the social system consists of the combination of these actions of independent individuals.

Such self-elevation to occupation of the scholarly high ground in terms of others' neglect of the social is only explicable if rational choice is taken for granted as the only legitimate approach which, of course, it is for Coleman. In this light, it is also possible to understand why he should see himself as bringing sociology to economics. If, as starting point, the social is drawn out of the individual, and the economic is substituted for the psychological, it is hardly surprising that the lamb going to slaughter should see itself as feeding the lion! Coleman's sociology is so much penetrated by the postures of mainstream neoclassical economics that it is understandable that his professional commitment to address the social should appear to be sufficient for him to claim that he is nourishing economics rather than being devoured by it.[41]

More specifically, for social capital, Coleman is generally and correctly acknowledged in subsequent literature to have understood the notion functionally with respect to the goals and actions of individual agents. For social capital "is defined by its function ... a variety of entities having two characteristics in common ... some aspect of a social structure, and they facilitate certain actions of individuals who are within the structure" (Coleman 1990a, p. 302). Social capital changes when social relations change in ways that facilitate action (p. 304). Further, social capital is neither physical nor human capital in this respect. Social capital "inheres in the structure of relations between persons and among persons ... lodged neither in individuals nor in physical implements of production" (p. 302).

On this basis, the notion of social capital, which effectively appears only after 300 pages of his book have already been covered, is perceived to have limited added value, remarkable in view of the literature that it has spawned: "Using the concept of social capital will uncover no processes that are different in fundamental ways from those discussed in other chapters" (p. 304). Rather, social capital provides a terminological umbrella for grouping together an extraordinarily diverse range of casually constructed illustrations – from revolutionary action to rotating credit associations.[42] Further, the accompanying notions that have become standard within the social capital literature are also rounded together, having been explicitly employed without need for social capital. Appeal is made to authority, trust, norms, obligations, expectations, information, sanctions, public goods, externalities, and so on.

Essentially, analytically, two broad themes inform Coleman's understanding of social capital and social theory more generally. Each is derived from the problematic of rational choice theory raised to the level of the social. First, he is concerned with the duality between free-riding and zealotry, with each leading, respectively, to under- or over-provision of certain functions. Outcomes depend in part upon the extent to which economic and political or other resources are capable of being deployed in pursuit of individual or collective aims, for better or for worse for all concerned. When such capacity has been built in practice, so that varieties of powers can be used to attain varieties of interests, then we have created social capital – in contrast to other types of individual capital or resources that we can use on our own without prior creation of collective organisation or whatever. In effect the economic model of market (im)perfections is extended to the non-market, which may or may not be capable of overcoming divergence between individually pursued interests and collective outcomes. In effect (the analytically challenging part of) the systemic in social theory is understood as the persistent unintended outcomes of collected individual actions for which collective, non-market action can be an appropriate response.[43]

Second, then, the more general framework within which this understanding of social capital is situated is clarified by Coleman's (1990a) discussion of the "perfect system". Ideally, he would like the world to be organised as a perfectly working Walrasian system, or general, market-based, economic equilibrium, for the market system most closely approximates a perfect system. The reason for this is that, in principle, in the market, everything is convertible into money or fungible (a term deployed by Coleman; 1990a, p. 720). Resources can be applied wherever required. Unfortunately, the monetisation of all aspects of society is impossible, not least because it is socially proscribed in certain instances, as in not allowing money to be used to buy votes in a democracy, for example. This represents a lack of fungibility across resources and powers in pursuit of interests – a void that can be filled by social capital. Indeed, "if social capital is deficient in the system, this means that the assumption of generalized, or systemic, power is invalid" (p. 816). It seems as if lack of fungibility (and social capital) can impede total dominance by those with an overwhelming possession of resources, and hence power.[44]

In short, the perfect social system could be a Walrasian economic system if it comprised the totality of society. But it does not and cannot, so social capital is needed to provide for an *as if* market society to the extent that it allows resources and powers to function smoothly in attaining goals in disparate arenas – just as money is capable of buying most things. As is apparent, however, from rent seeking and zealotry, the imperfections or incompleteness of monetary exchanges can only be complemented by social capital in principle. Quite apart from the ready destruction of social capital through abuse or disuse, there is no guarantee that its functionally substituting for economic fungibility will lead to all, or all the right, things being done.

Concluding remarks

In a nutshell, and by way of parody of Marx's theory of the transition to capitalism, Coleman has turned simple social exchange theory into social capital theory by the primitive appropriation of economics. Whether he has, whatever his intentions, done more to bring economics to sociology, or vice versa,[45] is neither here nor there. He has, however, opened the way for a disguised, and hence more palatable, form for rational choice to thrive and prosper. As mentioned, at times, if only for convenience, it is permissible to take collective agencies as given but not in fundamental theory (Coleman 1990b, pp. 51–52):

> One can, I think, take corporate actors as given ... for certain kinds of theoretical purposes. At the same time, for other purposes, one has to take them as problematic. In other words, I say that methodological individualism can work at more than one level. True methodological individualism takes natural persons ... as the only starting point ... [But] the micro-to-macro framework is a *relative* framework. At whatever level one finds actors acting purposively, one can take that as a micro level and examine the functioning of the system of those actors. But, as I say, for the fundamental explanation, one also wants to take those actors as problematic.

Yet, he is also acutely conscious of how simplistic his approach will appear to other social theorists as a result of the facile generalisation of neoclassical microeconomics with a degree of fudginess and reductionism. Indeed, he confesses to (p. 52):

An extraordinarily simple system at the micro level … [with] two kinds of elements: actors on the one hand, and something I call "events" and sometimes "resources" and sometimes call "goods" on the other hand. So there is a little bit of slipperiness there with respect to that. The two things that connect them are "interest" and "control".

Further, "the principle of action depends … on maximization of utility … but I like to think of it in terms of interest because … interest corresponds more nearly to the natural way in which we think about persons' orientations to action" (p. 52). In short, economic rationality is rendered more presentable by attaching it to collective agencies and the terminology of interests. Control, on the other hand, depends upon alienable resources or social constraints, such as norms – for non-smoking for example – and power is understood as the interpersonal distribution of non-economics resources (pp. 56–57). Again, the parallel, if not the identity, with economic analysis is striking as is the wider scope of application through the simultaneous adoption of the language of social theory. In short, for Coleman (1990b, p. 56), "if it were applied to economics – power and wealth are equivalent":

But when you deal not just with economic resources but also with other resources (including things involving collective actions), then it can be better interpreted as "power" rather than as wealth. So that is a very fundamental difference that I have with the neoclassical economists.

In other words, power is simply economic wealth by other, non-market, means for which social capital can provide an analytical umbrella.

This is nothing other than a self-confessed mish-mash of unswerving devotion to rational choice and shadow-boxing at the otherwise precluded notions that are traditional to social theory. As Tilly (1998, p. 19) so perceptively observes:[46]

James Coleman feinted repeatedly toward relational accounts of norms, commitments, and similar phenomena but pulled his punches as they approached the target. Although his verbal accounts mentioned many agents, monitors, and authorities who influenced individual actions, his mathematical formulations tellingly portrayed a single actor's computations rather than interactions among persons.

The absence of the genuinely social in Coleman's social capital has not rendered it irresistible to those who have sought to restore the social in one way or another by deploying or refining the concept. By doing so, they have failed to be mindful of the rational choice framework within social exchange theory from which they unwittingly take their point of departure as well as the concept of capital derived from mainstream neoclassical economics.[47] Social capital represents a remarkable triumph within social theory both for methodological individualism and for economics which – despite concessions that conceal more than they concede – would have been unthinkable a decade or so ago.[48]

6 Making the benchmark work for social theory

Introduction

In the early 1980s, a new round of literature appeared examining the causes of mass unemployment in the 1930s in the UK. It had been prompted by the contribution of Benjamin and Kochin (1979),[1] hereafter B&K. They argued that the unemployment had been voluntary, a consequence of too high a level of unemployment benefit relative to wages, the so-called benefit–wage ratio. The unemployed chose to be so on the basis of the price signals and, hence, (dis)incentives that they faced. Not surprisingly, this appalling article in almost every respect was subject to the full counterweight of academic opinion against it, ranging over theoretical and empirical grounds, incorporating more variables, disaggregating by region, age, sex, refining the data, and so on. In the event, however, although Benjamin and Kochin can hardly be held responsible, nor given exclusive credit for this, the idea that higher benefits results in higher unemployment has persisted, although it is perceived to be tempered, and even swamped, by other factors.[2]

What is the relevance of this to social capital? Well, absolutely nothing, except I am going to give a name to the academic scholarship of the sort that arose out of the B&K affair. I will call it a "benchkin". Characteristically, a benchkin begins with a contribution, or a number of contributions, which are not necessarily novel in thinking, if possibly so in application; recall the New Poor Law, for example. What is lacking in originality, however, is made up for both in dramatically denying conventional wisdom (surely the unemployed wanted jobs) and in straddling both academia and popular consciousness (the unemployed are work shy and burdens on an over-generous welfare state). Further, a benchkin is marked by being fundamentally flawed, whether by theory or fact. Finally, and most important, benchkins generate a voluminous literature that prospers by devastatingly criticising the initial contributions as point of departure. Paradoxically, far from the initial contribution then thereby being dismissed and vanishing without trace, it survives by incorporating the criticism, not always successfully or coherently, and evolving in ways that remain influenced to a greater or lesser extent by the (false) starting point.

This chapter establishes that Robert Putnam's work on social capital is a benchkin. Of course, this is just a metaphor for the vague processes and outcomes outlined in the previous paragraphs, using the illustration provided by B&K. No one benchkin exactly replicates another; their paths differ by virtue of their wider environment, as does their content in view of context. Initially, observe just how important Putnam is to social capital. Newton (1999a, p. 3) credits him as being, "the creator and main exponent of social capital theory", although Coleman is mentioned later. By contrast, in the edited volume to which this contribution belongs, Bourdieu does not warrant an index entry, although he is referred to three times in total throughout the collection.[3] More or less no contribution to the literature is made without at least passing reference to Putnam's work. This is not just within his own discipline of political science but, like a bridging network, pertains across the social sciences as a whole, including history. For the latter, a double special issue of the *Journal of Interdisciplinary History* has been devoted to social capital, with Putnam as point of reference and contributor (Gamm and Putnam 1999).[4] It is edited by Rotberg (1999) in an introductory essay entitled "Social Capital and Political Culture in Africa, America, Australasia, and Europe" that, together with the chronological span of the articles, indicates the putative geographical as well as historical scope of the notion.[5] Further, lest social capital be considered merely of academic interest, the journal *Housing Policy Debate* has followed the precedent set by its historical counterpart, albeit with a single special issue of articles, opened by Putnam (1998), and incorporates social capital as a factor in housing provision. As Keman (1999, p. xv) puts it in the foreword to van Deth et al. (eds) (1999), social capital brings academic political science down from the ivory towers whilst retaining the traditions established in the past by writers such as de Tocqueville and John Stuart Mill.

It is much easier to establish and convince of the positive side of Putnam's launching of a benchkin, its popularity and prominence, than it is to address the negative side, the spurious and contested scholarship. For the former, Putnam's (1993a) work on Italy – in which he first mooted the notion of social capital – has been pronounced by the editor of the mainstream *Quarterly Journal of Economics* as the most cited contribution across the social sciences in the 1990s. As Lemann (1996) observes, such prominence was only attained by this work after Putnam re-imported social capital to the United States, having taken it to Italy by way of Coleman. As a result of confronting the putative decline of US civil society, Putnam gained a status bordering on stardom, being invited to Camp David for an audience with Bill Clinton, and featuring in popular magazines, ever the acid test of public exposure. Nor has this been at the expense of his scholarly status, with his delivering the prestigious Marshall Lectures in Cambridge in 1999.

As Lemann observes, Putnam's reception was markedly different from that suffered by Banfield (1958 and 1970) whose work also travelled from southern Italy to the United States and its inner-city ghettos. Banfield suggested that both locations exhibited an amoral familism leading to neglect of the community's common long-term good in the taking of individualised short-term gains. Banfield required police protection in order to purvey his views about the sources of black disadvantage. Putnam, on the other hand, has been warmly received amongst community activists being promoted, for example, by the *National Civic Review*.[6] His understanding of social capital appears to have qualified him to air his views on similar matters as Banfield, and to provide him with an appropriate frame of reference for doing so. For, as reported in Wallis et al. (1998), he reveals himself as in favour of bussing black children to white schools in order to build bridging social capital between communities (what others might call racial integration). This is not just, then, to better education for blacks. On the other hand, he sees the effect of bussing as undermining the social capital of the local black community, termed non-bridging capital. Thus, "the tragedy in the bussing controversy was that both of us were right." A moment's reflection suggests this is all about social capital and has nothing to say about bussing and racism other than a very little of what is known to all.

This is, however, already to move to the downside of social capital as a benchkin. More substantively, we begin in the second section by questioning the Italian case study that prompted Putnam's own primitive accumulation of social capital. His first offering has been subject to a devastating assault on theoretical, historical, methodological, empirical, and conceptual grounds. To my knowledge, Putnam has never responded to these criticisms. Indeed, they are unanswerable. Instead, from such humble, even humiliating, beginnings, Putnam had the extraordinary acumen to transpose his notion of social capital back to the United States from which he had appropriated it in the first instance from Coleman. Putnam has bemoaned the decline of civil society in the United States, the loss of a virtue first remarked by de Tocqueville in observing its citizens' predilection for forming and belonging to associations. Putnam has also thrown in, not anticipated by de Tocqueville, the rise of television as the villainous cause of couch potatoes at the expense of socially active individuals, providing an undoubted appeal to the thinking, as opposed to the viewing, person's sensibilities. Putnam has launched his own programme of research and popularisation that has subsequently been dwarfed in breadth and depth by the activity of those who have seized and marched forward with it under the banner of social capital.[7]

In the third section, however, it is shown that Putnam's US venture has been received no more favourably than his Italian study by those academics willing and able to retain their critical faculties in opposition to, or in advance of, the seductive powers of academic fashions. Before social capital rapidly established itself as a new conventional wisdom across the social sciences, its shaky and shallow foundations had already been revealed if to no avail. And, as that old adage (of social capital, in retrospect) goes, "if you can't beat it, join it". Far from departing the academic stage under the weight of the critical points levelled against it, the latter have been incorporated to sustain social capital's continuing momentum. In addition, as suggested in the concluding section, the Putnamesque odyssey from Italy to the United States has had a further effect on the concept of social capital. For, whilst far from breaking with its dependence on methodological individualism and limited economic content, it has tended to conceal these aspects, imparting a self-reinforcing process as the non-individualistic categories of social theory more generally are brought within the compass of social capital's expanding orbits.

The Italian job

Putnam (1993a) represents his first use of the notion of social capital. He explicitly acknowledges that he was inspired by Coleman's (1988) study of the contribution of individual social capital to educational attainment. Putnam, however, shifts from education to politics and from the United States to Italy. His goal is apparently simple enough – why has the north of Italy's record of development proved superior to that of the south of Italy? His answer is equally simple – because it has enjoyed superior levels of social capital. More specifically, social capital is identified with the formation of associations within civil society, in the interstices between government and the economy. Such civic, so-called horizontal, associations prospered, along with democracy and growth, in the north as opposed to the south. In other words, social capital makes both the government, and hence the economy, work better.

The association between such civil society and economic and political performance is explained by two processes, one internal and the other external to association membership and its induced civicness. Internally, members of associations formed for one purpose will become familiar with, and trust one another, with positive spill-over effects for other areas of activity. Externally, social capital induces a more general ethos of trust so that the spill-over effects are not confined to association members alone. Further, the conditions for such generalised trust to prevail were laid down almost a millennium previously, before being slowly and variably built up and consolidated, or not, over time across Italy; social capital can take a long time to create but it is easy to destroy if trust proves misplaced. Whilst social capital can hold out a helping hand in economic and political development, its absence is a dead hand. Societies are liable to be divided between two equilibria, of which the north and south of Italy are, respectively, archetypes, according to whether they have or have not been endowed with high levels of social capital. Thus, Putnam (1993a, p. 177):

> Stocks of social capital, such as trust, norms, and networks, tend to be self-reinforcing and cumulative. Virtuous circles result in social equilibria with high levels of cooperation, trust, reciprocity civic engagement, and collective well-being ... Defection, distrust, shirking, exploitation, isolation, disorder, and stagnation intensify one another in a suffocating miasma of vicious circles. This argument suggests that there may be at least *two* broad equilibria toward which all societies that face problems of collective action (that is *all* societies) tend to evolve and which, once attained, tend to be self-reinforcing.

Putnam's argument is made empirically by examining levels of social capital, associational activity, in twentieth-century Italy and, subsequently, reading off the historical account briefly outlined above in light of the evidence of the north's advantage in social capital. As such, it has been subject to a number of what can only be described as devastating critiques, not least from scholars of Italian history.[8] Tarrow (1996) is both early and in the forefront of these. He bends over backwards to praise Putnam for what he has achieved, not least in attempting to combine quantitative and qualitative evidence, to straddle disciplines, and to address the relationship between civil society and economic and political performance with particular emphasis on the differential impact of otherwise similar institutions when located in different historical contexts. Yet, in fewer than ten pages, Tarrow effectively slices the case study into pieces from which it should never have been able to be put back together again, let alone provide the stock from which the social capital vine has subsequently grown and spread.[9] I can only encourage a careful reading of Tarrow's piece by any of those attracted to social capital and admit to plundering it myself in what follows for its incisive insights (and gentle humour) whilst incorporating, by comparison, some pedestrian and heavy-handed commentary of my own.

Tarrow begins by observing the impact of Putnam's work as "one of the most acclaimed recent works in the field ... which has caused a sensation outside academic circles ... a rare linkage between scientific effort and popular success" (p. 389). What seems to have made this possible is less the result of new research, since the work of Putnam and his associates had been available for more than a decade in other publications,[10] and more the growing scope of its implications – from the "modest claims" around institutional success to "nothing less than the correlates of democracy". Social capital has been the externally appropriated notion that has made this possible. Indeed, Putnam (1993a) concludes with a chapter on social capital without it ever having been mentioned in the text before, let alone in the publications from the decade-long research programme that preceded it. In short, social capital is a theoretical afterthought to a long-standing study for which it previously did not appear to be necessary – unless it allowed a bridge to other bigger, if not better, things.

Tarrow's critical commentary can be viewed as being made up of two broad types. First, putting it in formal terms, which is not entirely appropriate although Putnam does run simple regressions, there are the questions of how variables are measured, omitted variables, model specification (how the variables interact with one another), relating cross-section with time-series analysis (can we understand development within regions over time by studying their differences at one point of time?), and the relationship between correlation and causation. In less formal terms, and more specifically, this can all be summed up by reference to the way in which social capital in the form of associational life had been disassociated by Putnam from the broader context in which it is supposed to be both created and have effects. Most notably absent is the role of the central state. Tarrow puts it bluntly: "the lack of state agency in the book is one of the major flaws of his explanatory model" (p. 395). One aspect of this is the extent to which the north did itself subjugate the south, following a long history of foreign domination (p. 394):

> Every regime that governed southern Italy from the Norman establishment of a centralized monarchy in the twelfth century to the unified government which took over there in 1861 was foreign and governed with a logic of colonial exploitation.

In short, democracy, governance, policy and associational activity itself are hardly liable to be independent of such factors. More generally, Putnam paints an entirely unsatisfactory picture of political life, and its determinants, by focusing upon social capital.[11]

Nor is this simply a matter of delving into the historical past and painting too rosy and too uniform a picture of the good governance of the north relative to the south. Putnam's analysis was being undermined even as it was being published by the wave of corruption being revealed in the north.[12] Is it possible that eight hundred years could be undone in a few years? Tarrow rhetorically asks (p. 392):

> What would Putnam make of the successive explosions in northern Italian public life ... of corruption scandals on top of separatism; of mafia infestations on top of years of terrorism and political kidnappings; of the collapse of the Marxist and Catholic subcultures with their panoply of mass organizations, giving way to a party system whose capillary structures have all but disappeared?

Tarrow also points to the recent flourishing of associational activity in some areas of the south, a point made most forcibly by Goldberg (1996) who charges Putnam with having addressed differential development between the north and south without having explained differences within the two regions. In this respect, a totally destructive, if simple, criticism is provided by Grote (1997) who effectively suggests that, whatever else its merits, Putnam's historical reading of the impact of social capital is an artefact of too little data too late. For Putnam's account of the south's historical inertia depends upon a difference between north and south in associational activity, as measured in 1982. Later data, for 1982 to 1990, show homogenisation of associational activity across Italy, with the south catching up with the north, but without any corresponding catch-up in economic development. With modern associational activity coming to the south more slowly than the north over the most recent period, this all may have nothing to do with a longer history of broader economic and political development, other than in reversing causality. Grote reasonably concludes that the later data "undermine much, if not all, the civicness argument" (p. 5),[13] and suggests that the role of the state and governance are of much more importance. This is a recurring theme across critical commentary, although it is the source of an avenue through which social capital has been more constructively seen by providing context and vertical, as opposed to horizontal, interaction as elements in the study of social capital.[14]

Tarrow's critique concludes by pointing to an alternative which structurally incorporates the factors that Putnam omits and reverses the direction of causation that he hypothesises (p. 396):

> If the absence of civic-capacity is the by-product of politics, state-building, and social structure, then the causes of the malaise in U.S. cities or in Third World agriculture are more likely to be found in such structural factors as the flight of real capital, in the first instance, and the instability of commodity prices, in the second. In north Philadelphia and the Sahel, as in southern Italy, while the indicators of malaise may be civic, the causes are structural. If my critique of Putnam in southern Italy can be extended as far as his theory, then policy makers who attack the lack of social capital by encouraging associations would be attacking the symptoms and not the causes of the problem.

This is a very early and apt warning for social capitalists, highlighting theoretical lacunae and policy misdiagnoses within Putnam's use of social capital even where confined to Italy and setting aside the blundering through the historical and contemporary record.[15] A second broad, if more implicit, critique of Putnam, however, lies less in questioning his model of development and more in his understanding of the concepts attached to such models. As is apparent, whether dubbed as social capital or not, the variables concerned, not least those associated with civicness, trust and so on, are being applied without differentiation across eight hundred years of Italian history. As Tarrow puts it (p. 396):

> History is not a neutral reservoir of facts out of which viable generalizations are drawn ... how can a concept that is derived from contemporary democratic politics be transposed to other periods of history and to other political systems?

Along the same lines, in discussing Napoleonic influence on Italian development, Grew (1999) differs with Putnam not only in methodology and chronology but also in concept of politics, referring to a notion of political culture which should not be confined to institutions at the expense of traditions and memories, the exercise of power, and the generation of sharp discontinuities.

In sum, although it can hardly have been intended with malice aforethought, given that it represented the culmination of his work on Italy, it is as if the case study simply served the purpose of highlighting equilibria of vicious and virtuous circles around social capital. To complete the Italian job required a considerable degree of rough justice – to the state, to the historical record, to contemporary evidence, and to the basic concepts attached to politics and civil society. With such a bundle of analytical sins accommodated at the outset, fully exposed by the commentary of regional and historical experts, it is hardly surprising that social capital should move to pastures new. Only by neglect and ignorance of such critical literature has Putnam's promotion of social capital become even more celebrated with an equally strongly negative reaction to accompany it.

Bowling in the alley

Both in time and place, it might be thought that it is a long distance between the presumed social capital laid down in Italy over the past millennium and the corresponding situation in the contemporary United States. But the scholarly, let alone the popular, application of ideas moves with a speed and facility that shames the current globalisation of communications. For having moved from Coleman to Putnam, social capital moved with the latter from Italy to the United States. In doing so, the focus on horizontal civic associations remains, bordering on self-parody as reference is made to the decline in congeniality attached to ten-pin bowling clubs (Putnam 1993b, 1995, and 1996a).[16] Yet something has been lost and something has been gained in social capital's transatlantic voyage. What has been lost is the deep pessimism attached to the Italian study: with differential development laid down hundreds of years before in the long-term making of social capital, there is not much that can be done in the short run. For the USA, and elsewhere in the world, such pessimism is ditched, and it is a matter of being much more upbeat about what can be achieved by paying attention to, and building up, social capital. As Jackman and Miller (1998) observe of Putnam:

> He attributes [for Italy] the superior performance of northern regional governments and the lacklustre performance of those in the south to cultural differences in civic engagement. These differences are cast as enduring, and indeed Putnam traces them back to the Middle Ages ... In stark contrast, in his equally well-known "bowling alone" thesis, offered as an elaboration of the argument from the Italian case, "Civic America" is said to have evaporated in just two decades!

What has been gained, possibly in response to criticism,[17] is a recognition of the role of the state. In short, for Putnam (1993b, p. 42):

> *Social capital is not a substitute for effective public policy but rather a prerequisite for it and, in part, a consequence of it. Social capital ... works through and within states and markets, not in place of them ...* The social capital approach promises to uncover new ways of combining social infrastructure with public policies that work, and, in turn, of using wise public policies to revitalize America's stock of social capital.

Of course, however they might relate to effective public policy, bowling clubs are simply a metaphor for the more general ways in which US citizens can participate in civil society and spin off externalities to one another. But it is a metaphor that has been noticed to be full of ironies. As Levi (1996) points out, Timothy McVeigh and other conspirators in the Oklahoma bombing were members of a bowling league. My preferred example, though, is the bowling fraternity portrayed in the film, *The Great Lebowski*, which includes numbers of individual and collective dysfunctionals. The other factor that Putnam deploys to mark the decline of US social capital is the rise of television,[18] since this is perceived to have crowded out other activity outside the home.

Not surprisingly, the position occupied by these symbols of the decline of US social capital has been contested in a number of different ways – by denying their decline, the effect of their decline, the simplicity of the mechanisms through which they supposedly have an effect, and the suggestion of compensating increases of social capital in other forms. Thus, Greeley (1997a and 1997b) and Wood (1997) emphasise the continuing importance of the church in encouraging social values and activity. The purely negative role of television is contested by Norris (1996), for example, who recommends watching the news to create social capital.[19] Valelly (1996) also argues that political apathy is a consequence of the form taken by present-day politics, in which television plays a significant role, and does not necessarily imply decline of social capital as such, a result supported by Moy et al. (1999).[20] Some see the internet as the positive counterpart to television (Kern 1997).[21] For Stubbs (1998), the internet is a source of social capital deployed to create virtual wars around the Yugoslav ethnic conflicts.[22] Schudson (1996) questions Putnam's measurement of decline of civic life in light of commercialisation of leisure activities as gym membership, for example, takes over from the YMCA and YWCA. He also welcomes new forms of politicisation such as those for women's equality and the ability to take legislative class action. Further, if decline in social capital has occurred relative to the generation of 1910–40, then it must have been built up previously, possibly born of the politics of just wars and the New Deal.

Most dismissive of Putnam, however, are Jackman and Miller (1998), especially in questioning the decline of US social capital by a quarter in the twenty years to 1994. Putnam's evidence is seen as selective and his inferences flawed. They cite Ladd (1996) who concludes on a wide array of evidence from a variety of sources that "I was entirely unprepared for the extent of the increase [in social capital] the data in fact show. Not even one set of systematic data support the thesis of 'Bowling Alone'."[23] Membership of charities and the like increased by as much as 50 per cent, for example, and growth in environmental associations has been fivefold, in which supposedly couch-potato youth has been particularly prominent. Indeed, the data used by Putnam excluded new types of groups formed after 1967 such as those around civil rights, the environment, and consumerism! Those infamous 1960s might just as well have been a mirage.

Even those supportive of the notion of social capital have been highly critical of Putnam, as in the collection of van Deth et al. (eds) (1999) and their comparative accounts of the incidence and effect of social capital across Europe. The study of volunteering in the Netherlands by de Hart and Dekker (1999) points to the possibility of private services crowding out a public ethos for volunteering, denies as implausible, "that a simple exchange has taken place between TV and volunteering" (p. 101), and suggests a closer link to the intensity of consumer society and increasing turnover of fashions, not least as "political parties are out, environment and refugees are still OK, being a buddy for a terminal AIDS patient past its peak" (p. 102). Maloney (1999) suggests that political participation through membership may have given way to the cheque book, not necessarily a signal of less commitment,[24] a point put by Whiteley (1999) in assessing the psychological formation of social capital in the absence of social interaction through, for example, personal morality and imagined communities.[25] Eastis (1998), drawing on an ethnographic study of a music group, advises that associations are complex and diverse and not reducible to size of membership alone.[26] Torcal and Montero (1999) point to low but growing levels of trust in Spain, as a consequence of the continuing influence of the Franco era. Siisiäinen (1999) finds no decline of membership in voluntary organisations in Finland whereas Selle (1999) finds that there is for Norway but emphasises the important, and shifting, role played by government (and trade unions) in fostering them. Stolle and Rochon (1999) use the World Values Survey to suggest that social capital in the form of political activity and trust are related to association membership but unevenly so across Germany, Sweden, and the USA.[27] Smidt (1999) finds social capital depends upon type of religion and not just affiliation as such.[28] Kaufman and Tepper (1999) argue for the importance of availability of public space for the social capital of informal associations rather than formal groups.

What all of these studies do is to highlight the extremely narrow framework within which Putnam has understood social capital, not least in excluding the role of the state, political parties and culture, and so on. In many different, usually unrecognised, ways, with different incidence, the variables being charted will, for example, have been influenced by the rise and fall of campaigns such as those around the Vietnam War, nuclear disarmament, and the anti-apartheid movement. More substantive and wide-ranging criticism has emanated from those who have given consideration to Putnam's work in a wider analytical framework than his own.[29] It is not just a matter of adding missing variables and connections between them to sustain the notion of social capital, but of thinking about the issues in a different way. Nonetheless, the most important omission remains the role of government – as emphasised by Levi (1996) and Tendler (1997) – and that of more traditional political forms (parties and trade unions) in promoting horizontal associations and their own or corresponding activity (Kenworthy 1997). Foley and Edwards (1996) suggest that Putnam overlooks the importance of the role of political organisations in creating the associations on which he relies and that he also neglects other forms of civic engagement in the United States to the extent that politics as such tends to be left out altogether.[30] They observe that associational activity can either work in support of good government or as a means of resistance to an oppressive state.[31] From here, it is but a short step to the widespread questioning of whether social capital is necessarily a good thing. For the notion that social capital may be used negatively has also been heavily emphasised. Portes and Landolt (1996) require that, like any other resource, social capital be defined independently of the use to which it is put. As it can be put to bad uses, the world of the perverse side, or whatever, of social capital immediately arises, and outcomes depend on context. In this vein, Rubio (1997) coined the expression "perverse" social capital; others have preferred the expression of a "downside" to social capital to refer to the mafia,[32] drug-dealing, corruption, etc. Attention can also be drawn to the role of the National Riflemen's Association and the Ku Klux Klan, in the United States, quite apart from fascism in Italy and Nazism in Germany. As a corollary of the negative aspects of social capital, it follows that it is liable to be inequitable – positive for some, and negative for others whether by exclusion or not – and consequences will depend on wider context. For some associations generate inequality merely by exclusion of others from membership. Others are more far-reaching by virtue of the way in which the spin-off effects accrue. Only if a positive sum game is being played, and if social capital is all inclusive, are there no distributive or other effects related to power and control, notions that tend to be absent from the social capital vernacular as opposed to cooperation and benefits. As Edwards and Foley (1997, p. 672) succinctly put it:

> The context dependency of social capital gives rise to at least two conse-quences not adequately specified in the recent debate. First, access to social capital is not evenly distributed ... and, second, the value of social capital is inextricably linked to the fate of the social sectors in which it is nested.

This all implies a dark side to social capital (Putzel 1997),[33] and that it, or its consequences, be a potential source of conflict. Social capital, or its decline, may reflect the entrenched interests of the elite, as suggested by Portes (1998), Heying (1997), and Levi (1996) in finding that corporate delocalisation of affiliates is damaging to local community life.[34] This signifies, in a sense, a matter of blaming the collective as opposed to the individual victim. When companies decamp, they leave individuals behind, apparently the work-shy unemployed; they also abandon communities, supposedly in decline for being deficient in social capital!

To a large extent, much of this criticism derives from the failure of Putnam to offer an appropriate economic analysis.[35] For, whilst much effort has gone into examining the indices of social capital in both qualitative and quantitative terms, much less attention has been devoted to the mechanisms by which such measures of social capital lead to discernible differences at the economic level. Does more social capital, for example, lead to a higher growth rate or merely to a different growth path or the same growth rate on a higher base? This is to enter the world of endogenous growth theory and its incorporation of social capital (on which see Chapter 7). Otherwise such questions are generally left unaddressed in the social capital literature. But, as Levi (1996, p. 46) appropriately questions at a more mundane level, what are the "mechanisms by which membership in such groups as bird-watching societies and soccer clubs leads to high level of civic engagement, democratic politics, and high quality government performance", with the same applying to other outcomes, such as economic growth?

In some respects, the neglect of economics is surprising. For there is a ready-made economic theory for Putnam to have embraced – that of flexible specialisation, initially associated with Piore and Sabel (1984). Yet, this only merits a passing reference towards the end of Putnam's (1993a) book. In many respects, the theory of flec-spec is the economic counterpart to, even in anticipation and in advance of, Putnam's political science – that small-scale industry can both survive and outcompete in an increasingly redundant large-scale industry as long as it is housed within appropriate cooperative local industrial districts and communities. In addition, "Third Italy" is the most favoured and even clichéd, if contested, illustration of the flec-spec approach.[36] Ironically, Bazan and Schmitz (1997) provide a relatively rare application of flec-spec to social capital, observing for themselves as well as for Putnam's Italy that this is a retrospective application of theory to their research. They conclude by suggesting that social capital is useful if it is essential for their story of industrial history to be told. Right or wrong, as it has been told many times before, not least by themselves, the answer is clear.[37] The retelling for Italy in terms of social capital only serves the purpose of generalising from Italy to the United States, and from the United States to whatever, wherever and whenever, a truly flexible concept.[38]

However, if trust and horizontal and civic associations are the political mirror images of economic flexibility, what both approaches have in common is a profound weakness in economic theory, matched by limited assessment of overall economic significance.[39] To some extent, this might be excused in the case of the flec-spec approach which argues that we are only now entering the second divide, with flexibility at the cutting edge. But for Putnam and his followers, the entire history of comparative economic performance is potentially at stake. Not surprisingly – given they do not have the tools to deal with this – they do not do so except in the most brash and superficial terms.[40] Neatly combining the lack of economics and the omission of the state, as recognised by Edwards and Foley (1997, p. 674):[41]

> What is striking in recent accounts of the decline of social capital and the sources of citizen disenchantment in the United States and elsewhere is the glaring omission of reference to two of the most far-reaching changes in late twentieth century life, both in the United States and worldwide – namely, the twin phenomena of economic restructuring and dismantling of the welfare state.

Nonetheless, at the opposite extreme to economic critiques of Putnam are those that are more culturally inclined. Putnam and his followers are extremely easy and legitimate targets for postmodernist critique, although deconstruction à la mode has been relatively rare. The Putnamesque raw materials, such as community, association, civil society, and trust, can only be endowed with meaning in particular historical and social contexts. They are favoured and long-standing objects of deconstruction. Yet, it is precisely such considerations that tend to be absent from the theory of social capital, if necessarily implicitly present in empirical studies. In short, how can we assess the nature, let alone the significance, of networks or associations until we know the content of what flows along them and how it is constructed? This is not only contextual and dependent upon subjective interpretations of participants, but such content is itself contested, chaotic, and contradictory as in all belief and knowledge systems. As Edwards and Foley (1997, pp. 670–71) precisely put it:[42]

> Social capital cannot be conceived in purely structural terms because even in its structural sense it carries a cultural freight ("expectations", "obliga-tions", "trust") that is nested in structure but not simply reducible to struc-ture. Second, what is equally clear about the cultural component of social capital is that it is appropriated by individuals but is not simply an attribute of individuals ... It is precisely this sociocultural component of social capital that provides the context with which it acquires meaning and becomes available to individuals or groups in a way that can facilitate an individual or collective action not otherwise possible.

Nor is it necessary to confine such critique of Putnam for limited contextual content to the realm of political culture in the sense of ideas and meaning; for politics is lived and experienced. Consequently, Törnquist (1998, p. 124), in undertaking a comparative study of democratisation across Kerala, the Philippines, and Indonesia, concludes that "the *politics* of democratisation is more decisive than a vibrant society with social capital", advising against the "inconclusive promotion of civil society and social capital [and a shift] to the specific support of genuine actors in real processes of democratization" (p. 138). His argument is based on a comprehensive critique of Putnam, consolidating many of the points already covered: Putnam's neglect of power and the unequal distribution of, and access to, social capital; his reliance upon a questionable distinction between politics and civil society as a basis for examining the impact of social capital; his limited economic analysis; failure to recognise the weak relationship between social capital and democracy in light of fascism in particular and authoritarianism, etc., in general; neglect of power, not least in view of the importance of colonisation and its heritage; and, from an analytical perspective, the effect of social capital is understood deterministically, not least in omitting intermediate variables (for assessing, for example, the relationships between economic performance and democracy, and democracy and social capital).

Concluding remarks

If Putnam acknowledges a debt to Coleman in his discovery and use of social capital, the next generation of social capitalists has repaid the compliment to Putnam many times over. This is despite the devastating criticism that has been levelled at Putnam for each of his case studies, Italy and the United States, as well as for his methodology and theoretical framework. As a benchkin, however, the response to Putnam's work has characteristically been both to undermine and to strengthen it, thereby taking it as a benchmark for social theory. The underlying foundations are demonstrably unsound. To continue the metaphor, the building could be demolished. Instead, missing fundamentals are chaotically attached to the ungainly edifice, seeking and providing scholarly accommodation for all and sundry. Social capital becomes the academic equivalent of the Third Way in politics. You can have whatever you want, although we would prefer to draw a hard line against certain factors – such as class, power, conflict, and control (social capital without the capitalist system in other words) – and a discernible but softer one against the role of the (central) state and major agencies in economic and political life – such as ruling elites, trade unions, and major political parties and movements.

As Skocpol (1996) has observed, quite apart from his being wedded to a romanticism around local voluntarism and associations, Putnam exhibits a reliance upon atomistic concepts and data. As the social capital literature has prospered, few of its contributors have acknowledged this dependence or even shown themselves to be aware of it. As a result, the passages both from social exchange to social capital, and from Coleman to Putnam, complete the process of making methodological individualism and limited economic content respectable. Paradoxically, it does so frequently and to a large extent both by concealing its origins and by widening their scope of application, as will be seen in Chapter 7.

To these general observations, however, there are exceptions that prove the rule. Jordana (1999, pp. 49–50) explicitly addresses, and welcomes, the methodological and theoretical underpinnings of Putnam's work, if not tracing them back through Coleman to social exchange theory.[43] Although Putnam is perceived to be ambiguous, technically informal and conducive to confusion, "which allows a reconstruction of the concept" of social capital, "an important element in explaining the success enjoyed by Robert Putnam's book over recent years is that it manages to provide a certain connection, albeit somewhat strained, between the comparative politics perspective and the rational choice approach". He is perceived to have sought to connect the macro to micro through the key variable of trust, never properly defined, and to have proven popular, despite heavy criticism, because of the analytical promise offered in the wake of the failure of grand theoretical models of the 1980s.[44] Much of my own assessment appears to be replicated. This is because Jordana adopts a stance from within methodological individualism itself, with the critique leading to discussion of appropriate game theory through which to resolve Putnam's stimulating conundrums. Yet, Putnam and his followers cannot survive and prosper on such a basis, for they are dependent upon methodological individual-ism and associated formal methods only insofar as they are veiled and, thereby, allowed to be incoherently attached to the social and informal.

7 The expanding universe of social capital

Introduction

Chapters 3 and 4 furnished two extremes in approaches to social capital. In one corner stands Gary Becker, obsessive proponent of rational choice and society as if a perfectly working market – if reluctantly accepting an imperfect market if necessary. In the other corner, Pierre Bourdieu seeks socially and historically specific constructs of different types of capital and how they interact with one another in social reproduction. It would be a mistake to see other social capitalists as lying on a continuum between these two extremes – there are too many differences in methodology, theory and concepts despite similarities in language and, at times, mechanisms. But what the other two chapters in this part demonstrate is that both Coleman and Putnam share a much closer affinity with Becker than with Bourdieu. Putnam is distinctive in his emphasis upon horizontally formed social capital, especially through civic associations and its impact upon government performance. In this respect, he takes one small step in what has subsequently become the forward march of social capital. For the process of excising Bourdieu from social capital has had the effect of endowing social capital with an unlimited scope of application both in terms of what it is and in what effects it has. With such a wide range of coverage of social theory, it is hardly surprising that the literature has become chaotic and frequently confesses to ambiguity in what is social capital. As discussed in the third section, this is reflected in reliance upon explicit reference to social capital through anecdote and metaphor and as heuristic device. A further effect, as discussed in the second section, is that Bourdieu's concerns are being restored to the literature, usually unwittingly, in a piecemeal fashion. With an accumulation of case studies, those prepared to take a circumspect view are almost bound to accept, in one way or another, that social capital is highly contextual as generalisation proves invalid.

The question is what is to be meant by contextual. For economists, as revealed in the fifth section, the issue might just as well be non-existent. Social capital simply represents the non-market means by which market imperfections are (mis)handled. At most they are more historically grounded only by reference to contingent initial conditions or random shocks. Network theory, addressed in the fourth section, can be equally oblivious to context, focusing more on organisational forms. But, here, once again, context forces itself to be heard as networks are nothing in the absence of the content of what flows through them and of the motivation of participants. This is especially so more generally for social capital once it is recognised to be attached to the distribution and exercise of power and the resolution or suppression of conflict, as discussed in the fifth section.

In short, social capital can only survive and prosper by expanding its scope of application. It is in a sense the mirror image of an imperialistic economics. It seeks to colonise every aspect of social theory (other than the economic). And the more it does so, the more chaotic and all embracing it becomes as is revealed in the closing section of this chapter. It reviews a late attempt to define social capital that simply offers a shambles. Yet, there remains a major difference between the imperialism of social capital and that of economics. For the latter truly accepts no bounds whereas social capital never, despite its name, enters the world of capital and never challenges the economic. Indeed, it is fundamentally based upon the social as the imperfect, and hence absent, market that is the starting point for economics' colonisation of the social sciences.

Bringing Bourdieu back in

In the first paper I wrote examining the World Bank's approach to social capital in detail, I used the subtitle, "A Critical Skinning". In personal communication, this drew offence from a leading social capitalist at the World Bank because of its alleged overtones of flaying. But this had not been the original intent, despite the admittedly heavily critical content and tone.[1] Rather, the resonance was intended to be with the many different ways of skinning a cat. Indeed, in a mixed and self-referential metaphor, the World Bank's venture into social capital was itself seen as social capital in view of its different components networks and the like, not least in the more general projection of itself as a knowledge bank. The problem was one of choosing how to unpick the World Bank's social capital because of the many different ways in which it could be done.

The same applies, possibly more so, to the literature on social capital more generally, not least because the literature has grown explosively over less than a decade both in volume of contributions and in scope across the social sciences. Evidence for this is the emergence of a whole series of survey articles and special issues devoted to social capital (Foley and Edwards 1997, Harriss and de Renzio 1997, Edwards and Foley (eds) 1998, Lang and Hornburg 1998, Portes 1998, Wall et al. 1998,[2] Woolcock 1998, Morales et al. 1999, van Deth et al. (eds) 1999, and Mondak (ed) 1998). Significantly, Woolcock (1998) for example, points to seven or more different areas of application – economic and social development, (dys)functional families, performance in schooling, community life, (work) organisation, democracy and governance, and collective action.[3] Social capital has ranged over the needs of informal Mexican street traders (Pena 1999), through the need for integrity and trust in political leadership (Renshon 2000),[4] to become a tool of top management (Snell 1999), small innovating enterprises

(Cooke and Wills 1999), and an accepted part of management studies more generally.[5] As is already apparent from the other contributions cited, and as will be confirmed in what follows, such is an unduly modest account of the analytical domain of social capital. As will also emerge, social capital has attracted its own counter-literature, but critics and cynics tend to find themselves in a fight with a pillow, their devastating blows simply being absorbed with little more than a dull effect.

Such growth, as will be seen, is not without its own logic and dynamic but, reinforcing the difficulties of organising an overview, is the chaotic character of the literature. Without exaggeration, currently, a typical contribution to the literature might well begin with its own definition to suit its own purpose, observing that there are many competing definitions from which to choose and none has been settled upon. From Chapter 2, this can hardly come as a surprise. For, social capital essentially reflects the imprecision with which the dual notions of "social" and "capital" have been used and combined. The social takes as its point of departure anything that is not reducible to individualistic exchange relations and, correspondingly, social capital is anything other than tangible assets. As Harriss and de Renzio (1997, p. 921) observe in quoting Narayan and Pritchett (1996, p. 2) in what is probably an understatement: "Social capital, while not all things to all people, is many things to many people."

Both the ambiguity and scope attached to social capital, however, are strikingly illustrated by the attempts to trace back its intellectual origins, a task that testifies to the speed and depth with which the notion has already been established.[6] At one extreme, Hyden (1997) locates the concept within the different approaches to the relationship between the state and civil society as development proceeds, dating first explicit references to the mid-nineteenth century, albeit in Italian. In this context, social capital is concerned with grand theory and systemic analysis from whatever perspective. As a result, social capital offers an open invitation to social theory without intellectual responsibility. Woolcock (1998, p. 155) bemoans:

> It now assumes a wide variety of meanings and has been cited in a rapidly increasing number of social, political, and economic studies, but – as so often happens with promising new terms in social science – with limited critical attention being given to its intellectual history or its conceptual and ontological status.

I return to such highbrow issues later. At a more mundane level, betraying social capital's more recent origins and inspiration, our typical social capital contribution article might be less concerned with social theory other than as a more or less seriously treated setting for an empirical case study. The template is derived roughly from Coleman's initial concerns with the relationship between social capital as family background and its impact upon educational attainment. Here, the model is strikingly simple. Define (familial) social capital in some way or other. Define educational outcome in some way or other. Find a correlation between the two and interpret it as causation due to social capital. Of course, the opportunity exists for greater scholarly sophistication in the discussion of the data and the robustness of the statistical techniques and inferences.[6] For it cannot be emphasised how crude is Coleman's own empirical work because of failure to consider omitted variables, reverse causation, and the like. For Nauck (1999, p. 215):[7]

> There is an astonishing contrast between the richness of Coleman's explanation ... and his application of it to the empirical analysis of familial social capital.

His appreciation for Coleman's explanation is explained by his own closing comment, indicating an apparent commitment to Colemanesque rational choice (p. 236):

> The principles of the New Home Economy have to be reformulated within the framework of a general individualistic-structural theoretical model.

Crudely appealing to Bourdieu, he throws in as many as ten interactive variables. He concludes, for Germany, that "the influence of social capital on the educational success of children was rather low, when compared to the influence of cultural and economic capital" (p. 235), suggesting this might be due to its low level of ethnic diversity and strongly performing institutions, undermining the need for, and effects of, social capital relative to the United States. Similarly, Neal (1997), although almost apologising for not modelling residential choice himself (for which minorities are likely to be unable to afford superior schooling areas), shows that for wages and graduation, "these results do not indicate that Catholic schools are superior to public schools in general. Rather, they suggest that Catholic schools are similar in quality to suburban public schools, slightly better than the urban public schools that white students usually attend, and much better than the urban public schools that many minorities attend" (p. 121). Thus, schooling performance has much to do with broader socio-economic environment and levels of funding. Further, Pribesh and Downey (1999) point to the neglect of distinguishing between house moves that do or do not involve changes in schools (moving is supposed to reduce social capital) and vice-versa. They find that the socio-economic characteristics of movers is more likely to explain school performance than moving itself. See also Morgan and Sørensen (1999a and b), and the debate with Carbonaro (1999) and Hallinan and Kubitschek (1999) for the idea that the (intergenerational) social closure associated with Catholic schools leads to underperformance (in mathematics).[8]

Yet, this is little more than ornate, even obfuscating, trimmings from an analytical point of view. Much more important for the initial evolution of social capital is that the empirical work completes, or complements, the theoretical task accomplished by Coleman, as discussed in Chapter 5. For, whilst there is token acknowledgement of Bourdieu from time to time, the substance of such studies is to excise the contribution he has to make other than in examining (educational) status attainment as an unproblematic property of individuals (Lamont and Lareau 1988, p. 161).

From such humble beginnings, it is not difficult to see how the social capital literature would evolve once given a free rein. First, simple correlations between dependent and independent variables need to be strengthened by the addition of more independent variables to correct for spurious results due to omitted variables. There are after all many different ways to carve up the family in terms of its composition and socio-economic characteristics, although some of these can themselves be understood as social capital and can be incorporated as such, rather than used to level the playing field between families. Second, the dependent variable can be changed. There is no reason to confine the influence of social capital to educational attainment. Indeed, with respect to Coleman's functional understanding of social capital, it can be deployed in the study of achieving any outcome in any area of application. Consequently, cultural or social capital can be attached by proxy to individuals and correlated with the incidence of other variables. Finally, the relationship between variables can be rendered multivariate, structured, lagged, or reciprocal.

In this vein, Coleman has inspired a range of empirical studies, mainly for the United States, that seek to demonstrate how individual attainment is affected by family or other aspects of the micro-social environment, readily interpreted as (individual possession of) social capital. Whether parents are separated, mothers work or not, families belong to particular ethnic or cultural communities, are new or long-established migrants, move frequently, communicate with their children, watch TV, and so on, are the variables that make up positive or negative social capital. These factors are used to interrogate, statistically or otherwise, success at school or college, including drop-outs, and correlation with criminality, delinquency, and political extremism.[9] Thus, Ramsay and Clark (1990, p. 188) exhort the family to raise social capital by suggesting they "take piano lessons, tennis lessons, university classes – whatever – but do it and share it with the family".[10] Schneider et al. (1997) perceive parental choice over schooling as inducing them to build up social capital through more active involvement in their schools. Sun (1998) rounds up Becker, Bourdieu, and Coleman to construct an investment model for school success in maths and science, finding that East Asians, despite less extra-familial social capital, invest more, especially in view of fewer siblings and more stable families.[11] Parcel and Menaghan (1993 and 1994) relate children's behaviour to internalisation of acceptable social norms that depend in part on work norms attached to their parents. Hirabayashi (1993) treats migrant networks as a form of social capital, with Wilson (1998) suggesting five different principles through which they operate.[12] Zhou and Bankston (1994) argue that ethnic assimilation depends upon extent of initial financial and human capital and whether advantage lies more in relying upon own community. Flora (1998) and Flora et al. (1997) are concerned with social capital as a determinant of entrepreneurship.[13] Kelly

(1994) studies the incidence of Afro-American pregnancy in West Baltimore by reference to the distribution of social (and cultural) capital, a notion, it is argued, that was reclaimed from classical sociology by Bourdieu in the 1970s and Coleman in the 1980s. Labour market analysis offers an excellent avenue for bringing together the different notions of capital in view of sociological and economic traditions, with credentialism and social closure complementing human capital, respectively, as observed by Brown (1995).[14] Similarly, Sanders and Nee (1996) perceive social capital of immigrants to the USA in terms of their human capital, family networks, and access to finance whether from their country of origin or newly found credit associations.[15] Swartz (1996) examines the cultural capital attached to religion. Astone et al. (1999, p. 2), noting that social capital suffers from "fuzziness and inconsistency", still deploy it as a residual explanation in fertility choice.

But there is in principle and practice a mass of studies to be had. In short, it is a matter of whether A is correlated to B, with A interpreted as social capital and as causing B. As already remarked, such statistical reasoning confuses correlation with causation. Possibly B caused A, or both were caused by something else altogether. This raises a third route for the social capital literature to prosper, quite apart from statistically unscrambling correlation and causation. For, what such statistical analysis does not do is to address the mechanisms or social processes by which A causes B or whatever, although these can be hypothesised. Here, there are two different aspects. On the one hand, in the immediate and narrow sense, there is how the presumed deficiency in social capital leads to a specific outcome – broken home means poor education. Here, the underlying rationale tends to be provided, however implicitly, by the notion of capital as a productive input, like other types of capital, only social. Lack of possession of the latter does not allow outcomes to be achieved. Literature on social capital, then, has been concerned with how A is translated into B.[16]

On the other hand, this raises a broader concern. For in the previous paragraph, the discussion dealt with the individual relating to society, not how society itself functions as a system. Recall that this precisely reflects Coleman's rational choice pre-occupation and hopes for social capital, both as theoretical and empirical category (Chapter 5). In this respect, the leap from micro- to macro-functioning is illegitimate. What may be true for individuals might not be true for society as a whole. Not everyone can become a Nobel Prize winner, although I daresay that social capital might help. Nor is the issue resolved by substituting macro- for micro-data as if there were representative individuals with crime rates, for example, explained by levels of unemployment, mobility, and marriage as in MacMillan (1995).[17] Such studies have the explicit aim of leaping from the individual to the social by the use of macro-structural indicators and statistics to avoid both conceptual issues and the causal mechanisms and processes by which the social is reproduced or, it must be added, transformed. For, whilst social capital is presumed to be the source of an outcome, that outcome is itself presumably the basis on which society, and its individuals, continue to proceed unless perceived to be in an unchanging equilibrium.

In an unsatisfactory way, these conundrums have been reflected to some extent by a particular concern within the literature that echoes, but is not reducible to the problems associated with, the ambiguities in the definitions of social capital. Along with many others, Portes and Landolt (1996) emphasise the need to distinguish between what social capital is and the uses to which it is put. This distinction appears in part to be motivated by the wish to avoid tautology in deriving cause from effect. For, for example, if social capital is defined as something that allows you to perform better at school, it is hardly surprising that it fulfils that role. In addition, the wish to distinguish the definition of social capital from its effects is a consequence of the recognition that it can be used in a number of different ways that are not pre-determined, with a particular eye on the perverse, negative, or downside of social capital to which I return below.[18]

These are excellent reasons but they are used to draw an absurd conclusion, even though widely accepted within the literature. To be pedantic, can we understand a hammer simply as a piece of wood and metal, independently of the uses to which it is put? By the same token, without degenerating into tautology or determinism, social capital cannot be understood in isolation from its use. To attempt to do so is to degenerate into the notion that social capital is akin to a thing, by analogy with the physical notion of capital itself (of which a hammer may or may not be an element depending upon the social and economic relations within which it is situated and the use to which it is put!). In a rare exception to the current of wishing to separate out what social capital is from what it does, Falk and Kilpatrick (1999) suggest that social capital is only defined by its use, their focus being upon interactive learning in rural communities in Australia. Like trust, social capital is situated at micro-, meso-, and macro-levels, and depends upon opportunities as well as past, present and future, based on (anticipated) skills, knowledge, and values.[19]

The fact that the definition of social capital cannot be independent of its use is in part a consequence of its being context dependent. Paradoxically, though, equally prominent in the literature to the wish for an outcome-neutral definition of social capital is the critique that social capital has been insufficiently understood as context dependent. At the forefront in this regard have been Foley and Edwards (1999). In their survey of forty-five empirical studies dating from 1995 onwards that employ social capital,[20] they draw the distinction between approaches based on social capital as attitudes such as trust, generally drawn from politics, economics, and psychology,[21] and those associated with sociology that perceive the social in terms of networks and associations. The first approach is judged to be a cul de sac because of its inability to address macro-outcomes in view of the absence of the broader context within which attitudes are situated and determined.[22] For social capital depends upon how it is produced as well as how it is used, and its incidence varies across time, space, and class, as well as varying in extent of "excess capacity" and "portability". In short, it depends upon the context of the when, the whom, and the how. In this respect, they explicitly declare that they "favor a view more in keeping with that of Bourdieu". To be more precise:[23]

Neither resources in general, attitudes and norms such as trust and reciprocity, nor social infrastructures such as networks and associations can be understood as social capital by themselves ... the key to understanding how social relations facilitate individual and collective actions lies in a conception of social capital that recognizes the dependence of its "use value" and "liquidity" on the specific social contexts in which it is found. The context-dependent nature of social capital, moreover, means that access to social resources is neither brokered equitably nor distributed evenly, as Bourdieu's conception, alone among those canvassed here, explicitly recognizes. The access required to convert social resources (the "raw materials" of social capital) into social capital has two distinct, but necessary, components – the perception that a specific resource exists and some form of social relationship that brokers individual or group access to those particular social resources ... The specific social context in which social capital is embedded not only influences its "use value"; it also shapes the means by which access to specific social resources is distributed and managed.

Here, then, is the strongest possible statement that social capital is context contingent.[24] However, there are two different meanings to be associated with context. One – and it is heavily present in the earlier work of Edwards and Foley – is an understanding that the very meaning of social capital itself is dependent upon the social and historical circumstances in which it is located. Indeed, such is the inescapable content of social and other forms of capital to be derived from any serious reading of Bourdieu. Whilst there may be presumed to be fungibility or liquidity between different types of capital in given circumstances, as one form can be converted into another, what those capitals are is determined by the circumstances themselves – just as a hammer can be tool, weapon, or archaeological artefact depending upon situation. In this light, the other meaning of context is differently oriented and is considerably weaker for it considers that meaning (of social capital) as unproblematic but that its use, distribution, or whatever depends upon a whole range of accompanying conditions and circumstances that need to be specified. It is essentially equivalent to the theoretical and statistical issue of ensuring that a model is properly specified (all relevant interactions between variables are incorporated) and that there is no omission of relevant variables. In short, the weaker form of context is to treat the social and the historical as having evolved to provide for the initial conditions which allow for difference in outcomes for otherwise identical levels and incidence of social capital.

Such a weaker understanding of context is entirely acceptable to the vast majority of social theory that remains untouched by postmodernism or, it should be added, earlier theory that is more self-conscious of its own social and historical specificity in the stronger sense.[25] It is unfortunate that Edwards and Foley should appear to have slipped from the stronger to the weaker form of context and, as a consequence, found themselves able to provide their own definition of social capital which, in an unwitting self-parody, is itself context free as well as a general synthesis of such approaches:

Social capital is best conceived as access (networks) plus resources.

Despite such problems, Foley and Edwards (1999), again unconsciously, tease out two crucial characteristics of the empirical literature. The first is to bring into question the significance of the case studies themselves, either for comparative or for policy purposes. For, if social capital is context dependent – and context is highly variable by how, when and whom – then any conclusions are themselves illegitimate as the basis for generalisation to other circumstances. A hammer is a tool in one hand, a weapon in another.

The second aspect revealed by Foley and Edwards, a direct consequence of their relatively rare continuing reference and commitment to Bourdieu, is the extent to which the evolving literature is effectively based upon bringing Bourdieu back in on a piecemeal basis, having taken him out in the transition to and from Coleman. Essentially this is a more specific, dare I say, contextual reflection of the more general process of bringing the social back in through the instrument of social capital. For, not surprisingly, as this amorphous category has been applied across a variety of case studies, so each of these has sought to refine it, to contextualise it, to bring out those theoretical and empirical absences that mark its character irrespective of its dodgy methodological and theoretical content. However, with very few exceptions, to which I return later, Bourdieu's stronger form of context remains elusive in the social capital literature.

The anecdotal, metaphorical, and heuristic

From the previous section, it follows that one way of skinning the evolving social capital literature is by charting how it has re-introduced the context that it has previously omitted, either by widening or refining the definition of social capital itself or by differentiating the effects of a given definition on the basis of different circumstances or the addition of other variables. Broadly, as already observed, and accepted within much of the literature, social capital can be almost anything. Consequently, two broad and mirror image processes mark its analytical evolution. On the one hand, as evident from the discussion in the previous section, an abstract definition can be narrowed down by focusing on particular social interactions in the context of a particular case study. The result is that new factors and variables can be incorporated, reflecting the specificity of such case studies. Such is the example set by Putnam's initial endeavours, as social capital is teased out of Italian civic society before moving on to US bowling clubs. The same applies to Coleman before him in identifying social capital with familial conditions conducive to educational attainment. Two opposing aspects are involved, as social capital is first reduced to one of its empirical manifestations. But social capital is liable then to be infused with a broader content as the details of the case study or whatever proves suggestive of the need to incorporate further effects.

A remarkable illustration, even parody, of the case study approach in specifying social capital is provided by the use of anecdote as starting point, a reflection in part in scholarly literature of ambiguity in definition and meaning. Thus, Coleman (1993) begins his contribution with, "a canoe trip down the Wisconsin River and a portion of the Mississippi … in a setting much like that experienced by Indians". Woolcock's (1998) comprehensive survey occupies the first few pages of his article by reflecting on the difference in standards between airports in Madras and Singapore. Raiser (1997) speculates on the significance of how cars are driven in Rome as opposed to Helsinki! From anecdote, it is but a short step to metaphor in elaborating social capital.[26] This is extraordinarily popular within the literature, and is permissive of considerable latitude, allowing a stance along the lines of "social capital is like this for the purposes of exposition but it is also different or otherwise as necessary in what follows".[27] A most apt example is provided by Robison and Siles (1998) who seek to widen the range of social interactions encompassed by social capital by focusing on whether one individual relates to another through hug, carrot, or stick. They suggest for organisational networks (p. 13):

> Thus, changes between adjacent nodes are more likely than changes between non-adjacent nodes. Thus, we might move from hug–hug to carrot–carrot relationships, but it would not be likely to move from hug–hug to stick–stick in one step.

A most favoured metaphor for social capital, and it applies to economic and social development and change more generally, is that of health. Societies without social capital are sick and will not function successfully unless they obtain more of it and use it appropriately. Further, in a marvellous inversion, and to an extent that is not yet proportionately represented in the literature, health practitioners themselves have rapidly begun to use the metaphor of social capital to explain morbidity.[28] Individuals or various social strata are differentially ill because of their lack of social capital. This idea reflects well-established evidence that the incidence of ill health is heavily conditioned by both absolute *and* relative standards of living. Inequality – in particular, income inequality – is, for example, bad for the health of the poor because of relative deprivation. One, if not the, leading practitioner in this field of endeavour has explicitly attached his long-standing research to the cause or, more exactly, the consequences of social capital, most notably Wilkinson (1996). Characteristic of such work is empirical evidence in search of a theory for ill-health.[29] It is a consequence of guilt by association, analytically begging for a mechanism that relates cause and effect – just as we want physiological evidence for the relationship between smoking and cancer and not just statistics. Not surprisingly, such mechanisms can certainly be provided in terms of the psychological stress attached to social inequality.[30] Yet, it is a huge, and unjustified, analytical step to move from such mechanisms to draw broader conclusions concerning the grand variables of social theory, with the same guilt by association being elevated from the concrete to the abstract variables, and from the micro to the macro.[31] Such is evident in Wilkinson's (1996) superficial use of social theory. It effectively mirrors Coleman's notion of a lost world of social cohesion with the emergence of commerce, with the significant difference, justified by reference to the sociability of chimps, that pursuit of self-interest has been correspondingly and far from naturally engendered.[32]

The way in which Wilkinson has exploited social theory in the attempt to provide an underlying explanation for his empirical results is as unfortunate as his rounding up residual explanation for poor health under the rubric of social capital.[33] He displays nostalgia for the gift economy of the past,[34] a view of differentiation as increasingly based upon access to money, and distaste for the market economy as a source of disintegration as opposed to social cohesion. It would, however, take a long discourse to lay out his use and abuse of social theory in addressing the gift and the commodity, and the nature and rise of commercial society. Fortunately, this is not necessary for what is involved is brought out very clearly in a single diagram in Kawachi et al. (1999a). This contribution is significant, not only in bringing together the leading US and UK researchers in the field, Wilkinson being a co-author, but also for extrapolating from causes of ill-health to the causes of crime, presumably another form of sickness.[35] Their figure 1 effectively has five blocks to lay out their conceptual framework. With block content, other than heading, where it is given being indicated within brackets, these blocks have the following headings: relative deprivation (containing income inequality and anomie); social cohesion (social capital, collective efficacy, social disorganisation); absolute deprivation (poverty, unemployment, low education); violent crime and property crime (mutually conditioning one another); and poor health. The first three blocks are perceived to cause the fourth (with the first also influencing the second); all blocks other than the first directly affect the last.

Now, as Muntaner and Lynch (1999, p. 67) observe in a rare critique of the approach, "most of the aspects of social cohesion discussed by Wilkinson pertain to individual psychological attributes (such as emotions, stress, attributions, helplessness, motivation, self-perception, disrespect) rather than indicators of relations per se". The shift from such considerations to those of social relations and analysis is simply not legitimate, especially where policy conclusions are concerned, however desirable these might be in principle – as in the reduction of inequality and the increase in social cohesion.[36] In going from the individual to the social, systemic analysis is essential.[37] This is notably absent or weak in the health literature, for which social capital is a token panacea. For Muntaner and Lynch emphasise too much focus is placed upon the receipt of income, not on how it is generated: "The 'starting fact' for Wilkinson's model is that by some process (which he does not discuss) income is distributed unevenly and that this has consequences for health" (p. 64).

In short, the conclusion drawn is that there is a need to probe much deeper into the class relations, powers, and conflicts attached to contemporary capitalist society and how these generate both inequalities in income and in health. Otherwise, by unfair analogy, we are left with an analysis suggesting that, once correcting over and above for income differences, educational levels, etc., slavery is bad for the slaves and owners alike because of the stress induced by inequality and lack of social cohesion![38] In addition, how do we know that the implied policy conclusions in favour of greater income equality, if such could be achieved, would not yield an even greater fragmentation and loss of social capital – in the form of a sub-strata of welfare dependents as those on the right would argue?[39]

So far in this section, the evolution of social capital from case study has shifted from anecdote to metaphor. It completes its literary journey by moving from metaphor to heuristic device, another popular peg for the concept. For example, Portes (1998) understands social capital as a heuristic device, but one that loses its worth if used too broadly without being grounded in a specific application. For Foley and Edwards (1999), it is a heuristic device for addressing how social resources are distributed across individuals and groups, with some capacity for examining their effects.[40] In short, social capital as heuristic instrument undoubtedly allows for investigative research, but this does not endow it with analytical legitimacy for other purposes.[41] As Morrow (1999, p. 760) puts it, favouring Bourdieu's capital over those of Coleman and Putnam, in the context of children's health problems:[42]

> The concept remains a descriptive construct rather than an explanatory model ... best construed as a useful heuristic device ... There is a danger that "social capital" will become part of what might be termed "deficit theory syndrome", yet another "thing" or "resource" that unsuccessful individuals, families, communities and neighbourhoods lack.

As revealed by this important insight, the examination of how social capital has evolved needs to recognise how the concept has begun to shift from generalising out of case study to its mirror image of taking social capital as social interaction in general. It can then begin its journey at the most abstract level and be more or less gradually disaggregated whether theoretically or empirically.

The network connection

Interestingly, such a procedure can also begin with an anecdote. Becker's work in general, for example, is often based on abstract speculation around life's simple incidents such as the fashion for particular restaurants (Chapter 3).[43] More usually, abstract approaches to social capital draw upon existing theories or concepts. Thus, for Portes and Sensenbrenner (1993), there are four types of social capital as value introjection, reciprocity, bounded solidarity, and sanctioned obligations. This abstract conceptual work is complemented by the formal consideration of networks, as in the use of organograms or network modelling.

Davern (1997) suggests the networks underlying social capital comprise four components – the structural, the resources, the normative, and the dynamic. Straddling the conceptual and the formal are other contributions questioning whether networks should be dense, with many connections as for Fox (1996), or not, as new information flows across "thin" networks until they "thicken" as for Burt (1992 and 1997a).[44]

Burt's work is particularly revealing for two reasons. One derives from the idiosyncrasy already mentioned. He perceives the worth of a network to an individual to be greater the more unique is the flow across the network whether by virtue of the individual's contribution or the capacity to make that contribution, human, and social capital, respectively. Thus, Burt (1997a, p. 359):

> With respect to consequences, social capital is the contextual complement to human capital. Social capital predicts that returns to intelligence, education, and seniority depend in some part on a person's location in the social structure of a market or hierarchy. While human capital refers to individual ability, social capital refers to opportunity.

Basically, as a manager, you are better off in having fewer peers and suffering limited career pressure to conform so that you are better able to innovate and create or fill "structural holes". Essentially, this is an unwitting argument by analogy with the economic theory of comparative advantage. The more you differ from your trading partners, the better you do in trade (if they want what you have). It contrasts with the alternative that parallels the notion of economies of scale – the more the same within the network the better, as for language as opposed to translation! Of course, the two forms of networking can be complementary rather than competitive, like economies of scale and scope, and have become referred to within the social capital literature as bonding and bridging.[45] But, in short, for Burt (1997b, p. 7): "Structural hole theory gives concrete meaning to the social capital metaphor. The theory describes how social capital is a function of the brokerage opportunities in a network." Significantly, though, in testing his theory empirically, Burt sets about correcting for individual differences that might explain differences in outcome. As a result, it is inevitable that he will find a structural hole as residual explanation! It is not clear how his approach could be shown to be wrong.

This is true of the last study cited which purports to explain why women with equal qualifications as men appear to gain promotion more quickly. Not surprisingly, his answer, once correcting for qualifications, etc., is that women seek out promotion by different routes than men, reflecting and deploying their networking qualities. Whatever its empirical validity and worth, however, this highlights a second and crucial aspect of Burt's work – the more or less complete absence of the content and context of the networks involved (other than for empirical purposes). In particular, despite dealing with the relative success of men and women in management, there is otherwise no discussion of gender or gender relations whatsoever![46]

These are the consequences of formal network theory with its heavy dependence upon diagrammatic imagery or mathematical modelling. In their survey, Emirbayer and Goodwin (1994) note that such analysis has been negligent of structure, culture, and agency in understanding the formation, reproduction, and transformation of networks, let alone their effects.[47] They point to the failure to criticise fundamental theoretical presuppositions and how abstruse terminology and state-of-the-art mathematics have deterred outsiders. Further, there has been. a lack of dialogue between analysts, social theorists, and historical sociologists.

In less formal terms, the same weaknesses in terms of context and content have been noted with the emergence of the new economic sociology. Rational choice aside, this has not taken the optimising agent as starting point. In general, Baron and Hannan (1994, p. 1117) set up the problem as follows:

> First, motivations, preferences and behaviours are molded (and thus must be understood) in social context. Second, individualism, rationality as an approved standard of behavior and the infrastructure supporting markets (e.g. property rights) are themselves *social and historical products*, not timeless abstractions.

For sociologists such as Granovetter (1985), most closely associated with a more rounded sociological approach to networks, emphasis is placed on the social and historical, as networks of interpersonal relations become congealed or embedded and, consequently, more important than the antediluvian individualism that might be construed as having created them at some point in the distant past. Thus, more or less as an analytical manifesto, Granovetter (1990a, pp. 95–96) asserts:

(1) action is always socially situated and cannot be explained by reference to individual motives alone; and
(2) social institutions do not arise automatically in some inevitable form but rather are "socially constructed".

So the social can be taken as the historically given basis for examining the individual, as in the notion that "The general principle may be that the actor whose network reaches into the largest number of relevant institutional realms will have an enormous advantage" (Granovetter 1992, p. 10). Consequently, those such as Becker are perceived to adopt too simple an approach and as "very narrow" for neglecting the "particular history in a relationship" which is "embedded in networks" (Granovetter 1990b, p. 100). Yet, it is a moot point whether Granovetter has embedded the contextual in anything other than the socially and historically weak form outlined in the previous section (Zelizer 1988 and DiMaggio 1990).[48]

Even so, Granovetter does appear to have been sufficiently discerning never to have used the term social capital himself (Astone et al. 1999). Indeed, in their survey of network analysis, Podolny and Page (1998) make no reference to social capital at all, although their piece appears in the same issue of the *Annual Review of Sociology* as the social capital review of Portes (1998)! Nonetheless, Granovetter does not escape from being rounded up within the social capital network. The most comprehensive and wide-ranging synthesis in this regard is provided by Adler and Kwon (1999). Starting from a position within organisation studies, they observe, "social capital within organization has long been studied under the label 'informal organization' ". With corresponding sets of references, many of which pre-date, and so do not use, social capital explicitly, they offer three sets of interactive themes: between individuals and firms (career success, executive compensation, and workers finding jobs); within and between subunits (inter-unit resource exchange and product innovation, the creation of human capital, relative turnover rates of labour, and cross-functional team effectiveness); and within and between firms (organisation dissolution and start-ups, supplier relations, regional production networks, and inter-firm learning). They reasonably conclude that "the growing interest in social capital has not, however, been matched by a corresponding degree of theoretical clarity" and proceed to provide their own definition:

> *Social capital is a resource for individual and collective actors located in the network of their more or less durable social relations.*

They pass quickly over the "social", noting that "much recent network theory and some other schools of sociological theory are committed to methodological individualism in theory-building, and are therefore skeptical of the explanatory as distinct from descriptive value of socio-centric analysis". A more considered account of "capital" essentially reduces to treating it as one of a "broad and heterogeneous family of resources", leading them explicitly to reject the complaint of Baron and Hannan (1994) that social theory has been capitalising on everything.[49] Indeed, "such a proliferation is to be welcomed".

This is standard, if comprehensive, fare for social capital. But what sets Adler and Kwon apart is a recognition of the scope of what needs to be included to make their definition legitimate even on the basis of an organisation theory that is generally perceived to be underdeveloped in relation to social theory. On the one hand, both internal and external aspects of organisation (theory) must be included, in order to address the relevant networks and their content at each end of whatever interactions are involved. On the other hand, these are wedded to the values or the ethos of individuals or agencies at each end of the network, for outcomes (or value of social capital) depend upon the ability, motivation and opportunity, and the risks and benefits attached to interaction.[50] In short, although there is a notable absence of power and conflict, the result is to throw everything into a gently bubbling analytical cauldron and expect social capital to result as accommodating synthesis. As will be seen for others, social capital is seen both to define and resolve social theory, despite its impoverished starting points in both the social and capital.[51]

The notion of embeddedness, prominent in the contextual location of networks, does, however, figure prominently in the evolution of social capital in another way. For, whilst social capital is understood as distinct from other forms of capital, it is perceived to be both dependent upon and interactive with them and within the economy and society more generally. In this light, social capital is understood "vertically", not least in mediating the public–private divide in an era of privatisation or otherwise and addressing the role of the state. Pointing to a remarkable and acknowledged synergy between the political and the sociological involved in networks and embeddedness, Evans (1996a, p. 1033) observes:[52]

> By labelling such norms and networks "social capital" contemporary theorists ... project primary ties as potentially valuable economic assets ... The language echoes Granovetter's classic work on the embeddedness of market relations.

Such vertical analysis has not been prominent in the literature. One reason is that the more social capital is situated vertically, the more it is seen to be of lesser relevance. As Evans (1996b, p. 1124) concludes for the studies in the collection that he has edited:

> The cases analyzed here suggest that prior endowments of social capital are not the key constraining factor. The limits seem to be set less by the initial density of trust and ties at the micro level and more by the difficulties involved in "scaling up" micro-level social capital to generate solidarity ties and social action on a scale that is politically and economically efficacious.

Moreover, it is not simply a matter of seeking to set the vertical aside analytically but also to do so in reality by promoting the private at the expense of, even if in conjunction with, the public. Ostrom (1996), in particular, suggests that more attention be devoted to coproduction between the public and private sectors.[53] Somewhat simplistically, she posits coproduction as a production function, with isoquants containing citizen and government inputs. It follows that efficient production requires a mix of the public and private sectors.[54] Social capital is, however, only mentioned in passing – "The experience of success of coproduction also encourages citizens to develop other horizontal relationships and social capital" (Putnam 1993a, p. 1083). Her greater emphasis analytically is upon the neglect of such coproduction because of the allocation of academic specialisms to the public and private sectors. In principle, she is pressing for greater interaction between public and private sectors. In practice, however, her point seems to shift the balance between private and public sectors in favour of the former (p. 1083):

> Let me be more radical than Peter Evans expects and suggest that coproduction of many goods and services normally considered to be public goods by government agencies and citizens organized into polycentric systems is

crucial for achieving higher levels of welfare in developing countries, particularly for those who are poor.

Harriss and de Renzio (1997, p. 919) are considerably less confident of the approach, let alone its conclusions:[55]

> Policy arguments which pose civil society against the state, or which rest on the view that rich endowment in "social capital" is a precondition for "good government", are almost certainly misconceived.

Further, as Champlin (1997) has perceptively observed, the idea of social capital has proved an instrument for ideologically supporting privatisation, especially through its construction of community as private rather than as public. In this light, it is hardly surprising that policy analysis should match analytical prejudices in leaving out the vertical. Such ideological leanings are, to some extent, veiled by their being couched within the language of vertical, embeddedness, public–private, etc., with rational choice and methodological individualism nowhere to be seen. In conceptual terms, however, they are made explicit by Boix and Posner (1998, p. 686) who, seeking to harden up hypotheses in political science around Putnam, recall the conundrum set by Coleman:[56]

> Cooperation sometime *does* take place in contexts where, according to theory, actors should have little incentive to engage in it. To account for such behaviour, theorists have developed the concept of social capital.

They suggest an equilibrium analysis of how social capital is reproduced and used, and how the micro- is translated into better macro-government performance. They offer five processes: sophisticated voters make the elected more representative and accountable; norms and an ethos of compliance reduce government enforcement costs; civic virtue displaces short-term gains by long-term prosperity; there is a virtuous circle of intra-, inter-, and extra-bureaucratic performance; and there is a tempering of destructive antagonisms between elites.

In contrast to vertical are "horizontal" accounts of social capital. These proceed as if the vertical has already been safely disposed of, other than as distant environment with which there is limited interaction. On this basis, it is a simple if huge extrapolation to the whole of "civil society" from that microcosmic part made up by the family.[57] In this way, social capital is understood as ranging horizontally across society, filling out any of those areas not occupied by the state, formal politics, trade unions, or the economy. Thus, Hyden (1997) interprets social capital as civil society, Woolcock (1998, p. 153) praises it for restoring civil society to social theory, and Bain and Hicks (1998) see it as the source of social inclusion and exclusion. The result is effectively to declare open season on any variable that might be thought to be important in social or cultural life, and to endow it singly, or in conjunction with others, as significant for economic or other performance.[58] As Edwards (1999) loftily and anecdotally observes from his own experience,[59] civil society is a slippery notion at the best of times, and social capital even worse in this respect, quite apart, then, from drawing a distinction between them. He has found himself using the two interchangeably although, on reflection, concludes that social capital is broader than civil society since it is capable of being drawn from outside it, as is apparent from its also being vertically situated as just discussed. Of course, civil society has long been recognised to be contentious in meaning and validity.[60]

Consequently, following Putnam, such niceties have been pushed aside, leading to studies that are heavily empirical, drawing upon a notion of civil society in terms either of attitudes on trust or the like or of associational membership.[61] For this, Putnam has been heavily criticised by Edwards and Foley (1998), for having unduly narrowed the meaning of social capital to norms and associations, and for neglecting its embeddedness within social structure characteristic of the intent set down by Coleman and Bourdieu. They perceive the result in terms of having "added little new to the analytical repertoire ... Furthermore, the opportunistic operationalisation of social capital in extant survey data, treating it primarily as a social-psychological characteristic of individuals, has led the social capital argument back to something rather old – the richly appointed and populous analytic cul-de-sac of the empirical democratic theory of the 1950s." In particular, Edwards and Foley perceive the heuristic potential, mentioned previously, of social capital as having thereby been wasted, along with the equally problematic and heuristic notion of civil society, both of which are capable of serving as antidotes to economism:

> In different, but parallel, ways, the concepts of civil society and social capital each address the perceived failings of the predominant economic models for explaining the social and political behavior of individuals and groups within contemporary societies.

What Edwards and Foley appear to fail to recognise is that such embeddedness has become part and parcel of the economic model, including its notions of both social capital and civil society.

Economists rush in ...

For, where some academics tread carefully, pretentious popularisers are quick to follow. In his article entitled "Social Capital and the Global Economy", Fukuyama (1995, p. 103) typically paints a future in terms which have long since become fashionable:

> The most important distinctions between nations are no longer institutional but cultural ... culture will be the key axis of international differentiation – though not necessarily an axis of conflict. The traditional argument be-tween left and right over the appropriate role of the state, reflected in the

debate between the neomercantilists and neoclassical economists, misses the key issue concerning civil society. The left is wrong to think that the state can embody or promote meaningful social solidarity. Libertarian conservatives, for their part, are wrong to think that strong social structures will spontaneously regenerate once the state is subtracted from the equation. The character of civil society and its intermediate associations, rooted as it is in nonrational factors like culture, religion, tradition and other premodern sources, will be key to the success of modern societies in a global economy.

As social theory falls under the spell of economics, the opposite illusion emerges spontaneously as if use of terms such as social capital were the denial of the new economics rather than its perfection. But it is hardly surprising that the end of history should seamlessly give way to the triumph of economics. And, just as economics confidently confronts the non-economic from a position of ignorance, so non-economists return the compliment. For Fukuyama (1996, p. 13):[62]

> Over the past generation, economic thought has been dominated by neo-classical or free market economists, associated with names like Milton Friedman, Gary Becker, and George Stigler. The rise of the neoclassical perspective constitutes a vast improvement from earlier decades in this [the twentieth] century, when Marxists and Keynesians held sway. We can think of neoclassical economics as being, say, eighty percent correct: it has uncovered important truths about the nature of money and markets because its fundamental model of rational, self-interested human behavior is correct about eighty percent of the time. But there is a missing twenty percent of human behavior about which neoclassical economics can give only a poor account. As Adam Smith well understood, economic life is deeply embedded in social life, and it cannot be understood apart from the customs, morals, and habits of the society in which it occurs. In short, it cannot be divorced from culture.

Fukuyama's crude and speculative exercise in growth accounting does, however, have its counterpart in the genuine article. For, as if by coincidence, and as part of the colonisation of other social sciences by economics, new or endogenous growth theory has shot to prominence within economics in parallel with the rise of social capital theory. It is worth dwelling on this development.[63] Traditionally, in the old or exogenous growth theory, mainstream economics has relied upon the estimation of what is termed total factor productivity to measure the contributions to economic growth. This involves a method of calculating the contributions to an increase in output that are warranted by an increase in inputs, such as capital and labour. In effect, if inputs rise by 2 per cent and outputs by 5 per cent, then there is what is termed a residual 3 per cent contribution to growth that remains unexplained. It has been put down to unexamined technical progress, for example, and is otherwise dubbed the change in total factor (or input) productivity.

Two crucial points need to be made about this empirical approach to growth. First, it has long been known to be fundamentally flawed as a result of what is known as the Cambridge critique of capital theory. Essentially, the model's measurements are only legitimate in a world of just one good for both consumption and production – hardly plausible – since, otherwise, relative price changes in factor inputs may reflect changes in prices or income distribution rather than changes in productivity.[64] Second, quite apart from the realism of the assumptions on which it is based (and these include perfect competition and full employment of all resources as well as the requirement of a single good), the residual or total factor productivity is appropriately understood as unexplained. It is the extent of our ignorance in understanding the contributions to growth. In order to fill out an explanation, attempts were initially made to include previously omitted inputs in the calculations, especially those that increased disproportionately. Thus, the inclusion of human capital – that labour inputs were becoming more skilled – added to the empirical explanation or, more exactly, reduced the extent of the residual.[65]

Until the last decade or so, despite its deficiencies, measurement of total factor productivity had remained the main means by which economists have assessed growth whether of individual economies or sectors of the economy. Now, however, it has primarily given way to what is known as endogenous or new growth theory. For a further problem with the old, exogenous growth theory was that it implied that per capita growth rates would converge across countries given relatively free flow of capital and technology. As this appears to be refuted by the empirical evidence, with the persistence of the undeveloped world, theories have been sought to explain why growth rates differ, especially through the rates of productivity increase. Simplifying enormously, an answer has been found in theories of productivity increase in which market imperfections are translated into differences in growth rates and not just into differences in the level of output around which growth rates converge. The literature, theoretical and/or empirical, has itself witnessed explosive growth with a thousand or more academic contributions since the mid-1980s. It has done so because there is a wide range of market imperfections upon which the theory can be based – around technology, saving, education, finance, economies of scale, externalities, intergenerational transfers, level of inequality, etc., and even non-economic variables such as political regime. In addition, like regressions that use social capital as an independent variable, attention tends only to focus upon cause and effect and not the mechanisms that connect them.

Typically, empirical work has been based upon what are termed Barro-type regressions in which country or other cross-sectional growth rates are estimated on initial levels of output, increases in factor inputs as previously, and any number of variables that might reflect market imperfections.[66] Such efforts are bedevilled by a range of theoretical and empirical problems. The Barro-type regressions do not really test the theory. For, as soon as you include even one variable in an endogenous growth model, the dynamics can become horren- dously complicated with multiple equilibria and complex paths of adjustment to or around them. Any particular observation of growth might reflect movement towards, away, or around one or more growth paths. The Barro-type regressions cannot disentangle such effects. In addition, many of the variables thrown into the regression will themselves be related to one another and should be theorised as such. This is, however, impossible because the models become technically too complicated. In addition, the significance of different variables can change substantially or change in sign according to the other variables included in the regression. This has long been recognised in the literature on growth theory. As Temple (2000) concludes:[67]

> The fundamental problem here is that the most general model, which in principle would allow us to discriminate easily between the competing hypotheses, has already become too large to be informative.

What is the relevance of all of this to the economic approach to social capital? The answer is straightforward. There is a close overlap between the new growth theory and the economic approach to social capital.[68] Both are based on market imperfections and incorporate non-economic variables. The difference is that the growth theory tends to be more firmly rooted within the discipline of economics, and social capital theory originates from and wanders outside more. Even so, it follows that the weaknesses in the empirical methods attached to the new growth theory carry over to social capital. Those that claim to have explained differences in growth rates in terms of differences in social capital must be treated with considerable scepticism. Their theoretical and empirical methods will inevitably have failed to take account of the complicated dynamics and estimation problems associated with such an exercise.[69]

Such studies are limited in number but include Knack and Keefer (1997), Moesen (1998), Temple (1998) and Temple and Johnson (1998). Significantly, the method of throwing non-economic variables into growth regressions or whatever is neither new nor only inspired by recent fashions within economics.[70] The same sort of analysis derives from the broad notion, as already revealed in case of Fukuyama, that culture is important to economic performance. The idea dates back to Weber's reliance on the Protestant ethic as the reason for the geography and chronology of the rise of capitalism. It has been a long journey from there to growth regressions but it is well illustrated by the debate between Granato et al. (1996a and 1996b), Jackman and Miller (1996a and 1996b), and Swank (1996) in a special issue of the *American Journal of Political Science*. Here, from crude beginnings to use of more sophisticated techniques and readily available data sets, is revealed a continuing attempt to explain as far as possible the world history of differential growth on the basis of cultural and/or political differences. Whilst contributions to the literature on social capital and growth are liable to be a little less ambitious in practice, the approach is the same in content and in scope in principle – ahistorical, asocial, and mechanistic application of formal models to available data. As Jackman and Miller (1996a, p. 654) conclude, and reiterate (Jackman and Miller 1996b, p. 712), "further attempts to refine and test the case for political culture along the[se] lines ... seem unlikely to be productive."[71]

Elsewhere, in a survey of the use of social capital in politics, Jackman and Miller (1998) draw a division of the literature in a way that is in part comparable to that of Foley and Edwards (1999), by trust, etc., as opposed to social structure. For them, the two approaches are incompatible since the first, for which they have little sympathy, takes trust as long-standing and, hence, exogenous and from which outcomes for government and economic performance follow. This is the method deployed by Putnam for Italy as well as by the new growth theories both analytically and empirically.[72] By contrast, the tradition associated with Coleman perceives such outcomes in the norms of trust as endogenous, and to be explained on the basis of historically evolved rational choice. In this respect Putnam's work is representative as such, and is mutually inconsistent by allowing US norms to change so rapidly once social capital migrates there. In short, the durability of core values as one form of social capital and group formation, or dissolution, in associations as another are seen as incompatible approaches.

Such niceties do not tend to bother economists unduly who move smoothly and unthinkingly as a matter of course between exogenous and endogenous, and short and long runs, with effortless ease. Nor, however, has economists' use of social capital been confined to considerations of growth. Indeed, the latter is just one opportune example of the discipline's more general contribution to the evolving literature. For, in economists' hands, the simplest extensions can be made to existing analytical principles – because they have purportedly known about social capital in the past without realising it.[73] As revealed in Chapter 3, for economists, social capital is perceived as social in contrast to prior reliance upon the isolated individual. In other words, it is where individuals engage in interaction with one another. Of course, this is already done through the market that is thereby set aside. So social capital is a consequence of the collection of non-market individual interactions. This provides a necessary but not a sufficient condition, for interaction alone does not necessarily give rise to capital. In addition, the social interactions must yield a (positive) and persistent impact upon output – like a natural resource, a machine or more highly skilled labour for physical capital.

Now, of course, the presumption within mainstream economics is that the market works perfectly unless there are market imperfections (who could disagree?). Consequently, social capital depends upon the presence of market imperfections, otherwise it could not provide for a (persistent) improvement in economic performance. Having constructed this general analysis of social capital, it simply becomes a matter of filling out the details of what social interactions are to be addressed as social capital, other than those entered through the market mechanism, and what market imperfections they affect and which, hopefully, are to be corrected.[74]

Before proceeding along this route, it is worth dwelling upon the two separate ways through which economics constructs social capital, although neither is liable to be found in its pure form. The first is in a sense introspective and speculative in simply seeking to extend the scope of the model of the market-coordinated optimising individuals to non-market situations. It is typical of Gary Becker, although he often needs the non-economic to define his object of enquiry. The second is more typical of the more recent literature in which the analysis of social capital by other disciplines is appropriated and reinterpreted within the given economic framework. In this way, whatever the intentions and content of the initial non-economic understandings, they are reduced to the non-market handling of market imperfections through individualised social interaction.

These observations can be illustrated by a number of examples from the literature. In an early contribution, Schiff (1992) simply suggests that there are positive externalities across groups of people formed over time. Consequently, when an individual leaves one group to migrate to another in pursuit of higher economic gains, a negative externality is imposed upon the abandoned community whose productivity would suffer.[75] This can all be modelled in a simple way. Schiff goes on to suggest that this is the way that the dissolution of native communities in Brazil should be understood as a consequence of the arrival of a highway. Far from investigating the power and economic interests underlying the penetration of the rainforests, the highway is seen as undermining the social capital of indigenous tribes by easing the constraint on individuals being able to leave them. This example is as close to purely speculative as you can get. It proceeds simply by extending neoclassical economics on a logical basis without regard to the realities of the object of study.[76]

Less fanciful is the study of Robison and Siles (1997), despite their later work attaching social capital to hugs, carrots, and sticks. It suggests that social capital allows for higher levels of income within communities and for greater trade between them.[77] The economic analysis is standard fare:

> The effects of changes in social capital on income distributions have been deduced using two different approaches. The first approach used production models to show how social capital internalised externalities and increased the level and reduced the disparity of income. The second approach emphasised how social capital organized trade among social rich groups.

Apart from these interpreted qualitative results, however, social capital bears no relationship to the statistical work which seeks to show that the rise of female-headed households with children is a source of lower income and increased dispersion of income across states in the United States. This is an important result but its attachment to notions of social capital has the disturbing effect of more or less excising any reference to gendered relations and their mutual and cumulative impact through the wide range of socio-economic factors that make up social capital.

Trust as a component of social capital has been addressed by Dasgupta (2000). He emphasises seven points on trust: there is a need for incentives; there is a need for the threat of punishment to be credible (i.e. the presence of an enforcement agency); there is an interaction between individual and agency trust; talk is not enough, the need to take account of and estimate one another's perspectives; the value of trust is measurable; and "correct expectations about the *actions* of other people ... have a bearing on one's own choice of action when that action must be chosen before one can *monitor* the actions of those others". This gives rise to the need for reputation and credibility, for analysis of asymmetric information and how it is used. The untrustworthy can be trusted if the incentives are set correctly, for it is all a matter of playing the game from a technical point of view, especially formulating strategy backwards from final outcomes, and even taking account of predictable shifts in preferences. In short, social capital as trust is simply reduced to the pre-existing perspectives furnished by the new micro-foundations of economics. Trust is a matter of predicting behaviour of others on the basis of imperfect information. There is no account taken, except by way of departure, of the variety of meanings of trust and their contextual content. Not surprisingly, Dasgupta confesses that his paper was written[78] "to connect the ideas I developed in Dasgupta (1993) with those of Putnam (1993a), to see if the concept of social capital has potency for our understanding of the kinds of institutions that are most likely to protect and promote human well-being in poor countries". Consequently, the article reproduces analysis from the earlier work, merely adding · a social capital interpretation. It is also notable, despite use of emotions, culture, context, beliefs, norms, trust, etc., for relying exclusively on given meanings and seeking to reduce social capital to game theory and even production functions.

Collier's (1998) contribution to social capital as an economist appears in the first instance to be more derivative of existing non-economic literature which he sees as disparate, ranging across many disciplines, and needing to settle down in agreed definitions. But, he seeks to provide the latter "from basic economic theory".[79] In other words, it is a matter of taking the non-economic literature and incorporating it within economics as it is. He begins with the social:

> Social capital is "social" because it involves some non-market process which nevertheless has economic effects. The economic effects are consequently not "internalised" into the decision calculus of each agent by the prices faced in markets. In the language of economics, they are "externalities". ·

On the other hand, social capital is capital if it has the economic effect of sustaining a stream of income. On this basis, the notion of social capital is further refined according to "the forms of social interaction, the particular type of externality which is being internalised, and the mechanisms of internalisation". More specifically, "The building blocks of the analysis are thus the three externalities, the four types of social interaction, and the six mechanisms of internalisation." These blocks are, respectively, the externalities of knowledge of others' behaviour, knowledge of the non-behavioural environment, and collective action; social interaction in the form of hierarchies, clubs, networks, and observation; and internalisation of knowledge through pooling and copying it, of opportunism through trust gained by repeat transactions or reputation built on gossip, and of free-riding through norms and rules.

No doubt this list could be extended with some reference to network and organisation theory, or even personnel management. In a less harmonious vein, notions of power and violence could also be added. As it stands, Collier's contribution represents a compromise between the new microeconomics, which is essentially concerned with more efficient contracting through non-market mechanisms, and the non-economic social capital literature with its concerns over social organisation and behaviour. He does, however, lean heavily on the side of pure speculation rooted in received, mainstream economic theory. The extent of use and evidence of knowledge of social theory is particularly limited. Thus, whilst Collier's paper is considerably more sophisticated than Schiff's, essentially in its degree of disaggregation, both share two fundamental features. The first is that the social, as capital, can only be introduced because it has already been left out in the first place in considering the economy. Second, the latter is non-social because capital (and other assets) are conceived of in the first instance as both physical (even where natural or human) and attached to individuals. This is, of course, entirely unacceptable since capital can only exist on the basis of the "glue" of the social relations in which it is embodied. These can be added as an afterthought, as a corrective to their omission at the outset, although perceived as an innovative insight and extension.

In a sense, economics has explicitly provided some clarity to the broader literature, even if at the expense of rendering it less acceptable. For I suspect that many non-economists would reject Collier's reductionist representation of the economy and its implications for social capital in conceiving both as being constructed out of individual behaviour. Yet, he has shown, language, tradition and intent to the contrary, that much of the social capital literature is consistent with his approach as a consequence of appending social to capital. Whilst Collier has a particular view of the economy, drawn from mainstream economics, which makes the relationship between capital and social capital clear in his approach, the absence of an understanding of capital is a licence for ambiguity in the non-economic literature.

Paradoxically, Collier inadvertently verges on an acceptance of this point in his own discussion of social capital. He uses the example of a choir (or club more generally), arguing, quite correctly, that the notion is social in content since an individual cannot constitute a choir even if singing solo. But, by the same token, an individual cannot generate capital since it depends upon exchange activity with other individuals. The only refuge for Collier is the physical notion of capital. It is, however, fundamentally flawed since, for example, it would imply that non-human species engage in the use of capital in storing food or whatever. They even incorporate social capital in the behaviour that reproduces their gene pool. It would also follow that we have no way of demarcating capitalism. These are, of course, long-standing criticisms of neoclassical economics. They are, however, especially salient in the context of social capital where the social is explicitly being *re*-introduced. But even here, Collier's contribution fails totally.

For, as even casual scrutiny of his thirteen factors comprising externalities, interaction, and internalisation reveals, they are without social and historical content – except insofar as the market is taken as an invisible point of departure.[80]

On this basis, Collier's contribution moves from simple augmented growth regressions to consider poverty. As seen above, social capital has also been attached to consideration of a wide range of outcomes for different agents, whether individuals or some form of grouping. Once again, there tend to be major problems with these endeavours. For the models are liable to be too complicated if they include too many factors, so they tend to be estimated in the form of a standard model – which has already proved deficient – supplemented by a social capital variable or two. I suspect that in most cases such analyses are liable to miss the wood for the trees, at best marginally shifting the explanation, for the incidence of poverty, for example. Whilst anything that alleviates poverty is scarcely to be sniffed at, addressing the issues in terms of Collier's thirteen factors is another matter. We know that poverty has to do with the power relations around gender, class, and race for example. Surely, these need to be confronted directly rather than as the consequences of pooling, networking and opportunism? As Collier concludes:

> The distributional consequences of civil society capital are likely to be mixed. Copying will tend to be progressive, except for barriers of social segmentation; pooling, repeat transactions and reputation will tend to be regressive; and norms and rules will tend to be progressive, except where the concentration of leadership among the higher income groups has the effect of marginalising the interests and participation of the poor.

Obfuscating vernacular aside, did we not know it all already?[81]

Whilst social capital applied to growth confronts the workings of the economy as a whole, albeit on an aggregated individualistic basis from the theoretical point of view, the social capital and poverty literature is microeconomic, generally being pitched at the level of the household. It seeks to fill out previous, inadequate explanations for poverty by adding previously excluded variables. In this respect, there is a close parallel with the total factor productivity as residual approach. Social capital is the residual explanation for poverty after everything else has been taken into account, and the same can apply to the incidence of any other socio-economic or socio-cultural outcome, from schooling, through teenage pregnancy to criminalisation. As has been seen in the labour market discrimination literature, the extent of discrimination is gradually whittled away as wage or employment differentials are putatively explained by the incremental inclusion of ever more variables.[82] By this device, social capital becomes an alternative explanation for discrimination and its results, just as human capital has done so previously. At best, even if inequality in human and social capital is acknowledged, gender and race become the residual explanatory factors after these have been taken into account.[83]

Conflict and power

Not surprisingly, economists tend to view social capital positively, as a means both to understand the response to market imperfections and to correct them. This is a reflection of the absence in economics of concepts that are standard in social theory, such as conflict and power. Consequently, whilst proponents of social capital have often understood it in terms of a positive sum game in which all can potentially gain, the more circumspect of social theorists have sought to re-introduce more troublesome considerations. The simplest economics, however, suffices to make the same point – as Adam Smith observed, producers meet and require trust to operate a cartel. There is not necessarily anything positive or pre-determined about the impact of social capital, until both its intrinsic and extrinsic content is examined. That social capital is unevenly distributed and (dis)advantageously used by some at the expense of others has been brought to the fore in the study of international law, for example. Dezalay and Garth (1997) argue that through the functioning of international law, large US law firms and law schools comprise legal and social capital (political connections) that lead to the Americanisation of laws to the advantage of US economic and, it should be added, political power.[84] Closer to home and more generally, Seron and Ferris (1995) argue that men gain in professional occupations, over and above the networks in which they engage, because they enjoy the gendered social capital that requires that their private lives are secondary and taken care of by others, presumed to be their wives.[85]

The study by Beall (1997, p. 960) of waste-collection services draws analogous conclusions concerning the neutrality of social capital in power and conflict:[86]

> Synergy across the public–private divide … between representatives of communities and governments were seen to reinforce and cement relationships founded on patronage and clientelism rather than to foster more inclusive forms of civic engagement … As with Bangalore so in Faisalabad, power relations and existing structures of inequality have to be understood because in both cases, investment in social capital in waste proved to be a solid investment, but for some far more than others.

Most notable in this respect, however, is Heller's (1996) admirable study of the way in which the mobilisation of industrial workers in Kerala has allowed progressive policies to be adopted despite the hostility of the national state. Is it fortunate or unfortunate that analysis of such mobilisation, and its explicit reference to class formations and class conflict, should be attached to notions of social capital? For, as Evans (1996b, p. 1127) unremarkably deduces in summarising the analytical conclusions from a number of other such case studies: "If a community is riven by conflicting interests, the nature and meaning of social capital becomes more complicated." The inevitable implication from this conclusion is that if conflict undermines the notion of social capital, then why not take conflict and its theoretical underpinnings as a starting point rather than a social capital that has been rendered both ambiguous and redundant?

Thus, in confronting social capital with inequality, power, and conflict, the choice is posed either of dealing with these directly or of incorporating them, bringing them back in as part of the social or contextual. Once recognising that social capital is good for some but not for others – in view of power, etc. – then it follows that it can be adjudged as bad in practice, as was recognised early and, subsequently, extremely widely in the literature in terms of negative, perverse, downside, or dark social capital (Portes and Landolt 1996).[87] Rubio (1997) studies Colombian criminal drug activity, which is associated with strong networks, as perverse social capital, an illustration frequently attached to the mafia, Italian or otherwise, this proving only slightly more popular than fascism as a product, in part, of social capital through common ethos and association. Most topically, Foley and Edwards (1999) note that dense networks have been a prominent feature of society in Rwanda.[88] On the other hand, it is the relative absence of the right sort of social capital that is emphasised for east European countries. Any consideration of ethnicity and migration is liable to confront the two faces of social capital in terms of the benefits of inclusion and the costs of exclusion (Portes and Itzigsohn 1997, Massey and Espinosa 1997).[89] In short, as soon as social capital is perceived to have effects, especially if they can be negative, it raises questions of power and conflict over outcomes that ought to be the starting point for analysis in the context of other sources of power. In the case of rural development, having taken note of the neglected radical tradition attached to Bourdieu, Shucksmith (2000, p. 216) concludes:

> The Putnamian view, of cultural and civic institutions as positive elements, conflicts with the Gramscian view that these are instruments of class domination which must be overthrown in order to establish a more equal society. Social capital may be relevant in both senses, on the one hand as a form of social control and on the other through the existence of tight networks dedicated to the violation of these rules.

As such, a neat link is provided both with the earlier theme of modifying social capital to bring Bourdieu back in and the one, to be taken up in the closing chapter, that social capital can incorporate anything and everything.

Concluding remarks

The previous sections have been at pains to try and establish some order over the big bang that has been characteristic of social capital's appropriation of social theory. It has moved horizontally across civil society and vertically across the public–private divide. It knows no historical and geographical bounds. It has been multi- and interdisciplinary. It has depended upon anecdote and metaphor and has served as a heuristic device, revealing its bright as well as its dark sides, extrapolating from case studies to abstract principles and vice versa. Its analytical, empirical, and policy scope knows no bounds. No earlier contribution to social theory is safe from re-interpretation within its expanding and accommodating framework.

None of these ways of increasing the scope of social capital is surprising given what can only be described as its gargantuan analytical appetite matched by its being a truly magical pudding. With few exceptions, however, the feast falls short of including any course with an ingredient reflecting what I have termed the stronger form of contextual content. Its absence has been frequently remarked upon. This is in part a consequence of its own ambition. For, apart from those recognising that the values, ethos, or whatever brought to social capital are socially constructed, those working more within the cultural field are liable to seize upon social capital as a convenient peg on which to be more worldly, even though their primary concern is with cultural content rather than more efficient outcomes in whatever field of endeavour.[90] For serious and conscientious scholars within the social capital milieu, such considerations cannot be legitimately set aside. Accordingly, if rarely, it is necessary for the most sophisticated understandings of social capital literature to bring socially constructed culture back in as well as all the other elements as well. The work of Bebbington (Bebbington 1997 and 1999, and Bebbington and Perreault 1999) provides a leading illustration. He goes as far as possible with the notion – listing it together with four different types of capital including the cultural in order to incorporate meaning (as well as produced, human, and natural). He also throws in conflict and power, linking these to sustainability, access, and livelihoods, and raising questions of how to build appropriate social capital.[91] Alternatively, as suggested by Schuller and Field (1998, p. 234), making explicit what others have simply done, social capital can be seen as a further step from the unacceptable human capital, requiring a trade-off, "between specific and focus on the one hand, and contextualisation and scope on the other", especially given the "overinclusive vagueness of social capital".

No wonder social capital has become all-embracing. Indeed, the latter is confirmed by the database of abstracts of hundreds of contributions to social capital being compiled by the University of Michigan on behalf of the World Bank.[92] It reveals that the vast bulk of social theory and policy is being incorporated under the umbrella of social capital for it covers a bewildering array of topics. Of the order of two-thirds of the articles make no reference to social capital at all. Many predate its emergence. A number of the abstracts, admitted to be written without original authors' approval of the texts, contain phrases such as "social capital is not discussed in this article per se". I select two abstracts to illustrate the rewriting of social theory through the use of the social capital. One, derived from the *Annual Review of Sociology* of fifteen years ago (Roy 1984), claims that the works of E.P. Thompson, Barrington Moore and Charles Tilly "contain ample evidence of social capital, although this term was not in use at the time". I suspect that each of these distinguished authors would disagree with the first of these assertions and agree with the second![93] The second abstract is from the *Sociological Quarterly* (Berger 1995). It is an account of the life histories of two Polish and Jewish brothers who survived the Holocaust and, presumably, drew upon and developed their social capital by doing so. In short, across these two abstracts alone, social capital encompasses class action and historical change as well as social agency and structure in the very specialised context of Holocaust survivor research!

The chaos that accompanies such endeavours is illustrated by the endeavours of the University of Maryland. Presumably, its Social Capital Interest Group would be in an ideal position to establish some order over the concept that it has been so long and active in promoting. Consider its "Social Capital: A Position Paper" of 24 August 1999 (Social Capital Interest Group 1999).[94] First, social relations (and their potential benefits) are defined as:

> *The attitudes persons develop toward each other or groups of other persons because of their interactions* ... the potential for benefits from preferential treatment resulting from feelings of sympathy and obligation is the essence of social capital.

The understanding of social relations as self-reflecting individual attitudes is possibly a reflection of the recognition that much of the social capital literature has omitted individual values as contextually determined, but this is only speculation on my part. It leads, however, to the idea that

> Social relations and other cultural norms establish an *idealized self.*

Consequently,[95] in view of the rolling momentum that it has gathered, social capital is defined in a most bizarre fashion as

> The potential benefits, advantages, and preferential treatment resulting from one person or group's sympathy and sense of obligation toward another person or group. Social capital also includes the potential benefits, advantages, and preferential treatment that originate from one person's sympathy and sense of obligation toward his or her idealized self.

Having defined the social in social capital as the benefits derived from the individual's idealized self, with reference to the importance of icons, the capital is simply treated as something durable. As a result, it provides services that alter the terms and level of trade, incorporate externalities, facilitate investment in public goods, direct migration patterns, alter educational achievement, provide access to legal, public, educational, employment, and welfare services, alter the cost of contracting, support provision of emotional services, distribute resources more widely, and decrease the likelihood of criminality. There is even lengthy reference to icons and the like as sources of cultural capital. Finally, a request is made for further research "under the general heading of social capital", including: families and behaviour of youth; educational achievements; the global firm; global inequalities; community development; migration; nonprofit firms; collective action; efficiency in the work place; and a host of other topics.

The conceptual confusion, chaos, and, yet, ambition surrounding social capital is not usually so transparent, nor is the substitution of the individual for the social. Nonetheless, it is far from concealed. Why then should social capital prove so popular? One answer is provided by Harriss and de Renzio (1997, p. 921) who ask rhetorically of social capital: "Does the fact that it means so many different things reflect the fact that it is an idea that serves as a convenient peg for different agendas?" Because it is so flexible, social capital has provided an outstanding opportunity for old contributions and debates to be re-opened and relived, often with an explicit recognition that exactly the same thing is being said again in new terminology. Indeed, it is hardly surprising that it is often less than before that is the outcome, as is apparent in the reduction of social theory to social capital theory. Where there is new added value, it is the fruit of the weaknesses attached to the origins of social capital as laid out in previous chapters. Further, whilst social capital has the capacity to be all things to all comers, by the same token, it is open to capture and subject to particular content and dynamics, as will be shown in the next part of the book.

Part III

8 Making the post-Washington consensus[1]

Introduction

Part II charts the general rise of social capital across the social sciences. This part of the book is concerned with its specific burst to prominence within and through the World Bank, although there has been considerable overlap and synergy between the general and the specific. This chapter outlines the broad context within which social capital has become so important to the World Bank. The second to fourth sections chart a shift in the World Bank's economic stance from Washington to post-Washington consensus, or from neo-liberalism to more state-friendly and interventionist positions. It is shown that the post-Washington consensus is exactly the new information-theoretic micro-foundations of economics applied to development economics and development studies more generally. The fifth section presents the limitations of this approach to development in terms of both economic analysis and policy making. Essentially, the post-Washington consensus reduces the problems of development to those of dealing with market imperfections.

However, like the more general project of the colonising of social sciences by economics, the post-Washington consensus does not confine itself to economic issues alone. It is both capable of and willing to extend economic to non-economic analysis and policy making in the context of development through its new-found ability to comprehend the social as the non-market response to market imperfections. As a result, unlike the Washington consensus which proceeded as if the non-economic did not exist and its economic influences should be minimised where it did, the post-Washington consensus celebrates the social on its own terms. Within the World Bank itself, this has opened an opportunity for the heavily outnumbered and subordinate social theorists to elevate their status and influence. The sixth section examines how they have sought to have themselves taken seriously by economists in the more general context of the role that research plays in the operations of the World Bank, both internally and externally. It is argued that its impact is uneven across the various issues of education, trade and social policy, for example. This is a result of the complex interaction between external and internal influences as well as the substance of the issues themselves and how they are understood and addressed across the social sciences.

However, certain general factors have been crucial. These include the continuing need for the World Bank to justify its business of making loans, to present itself in response to recent criticism as more state friendly and people friendly in its policies and, at a more academic level, to accommodate social theory whilst economics remains in command. As is concluded in this chapter, the winter of discontent of the Washington consensus is made glorious summer for the post-Washington consensus through the instrument of social capital.

The Washington consensus: from modernisation to neo-liberalism

The Washington consensus emerged rapidly in the early 1980s to dominate the policy stances of the World Bank and the IMF. The term itself was coined by John Williamson (1990) who, in reviewing Latin American experience of policy reform in the 1980s, explained that (p. 1):

> For these purposes, "Washington" meant primarily the International Monetary Fund (IMF), the World Bank, and the US Executive branch, although the term was intended to cover also at least the Inter-American Development Bank (IDB), those members of Congress who take an interest in Latin America, and the think tanks concerned with economic policy. It seemed to me that one could identify 9 or 10 policy areas in which "Washington" could muster something like a consensus on what countries ought to be doing, and so I labeled this program the "Washington consensus" or the "Washington agenda". A summary description of the content of this Washington agenda is macroeconomic prudence, outward orientation, and domestic liberalization.

Significantly, from the outset, the Washington consensus has been seen both as a set of policies (and ideas) and as a set of (Washington) institutions that pursue them. A decade later, Williamson (1997, pp. 60–61) explicitly laid out the policy measures that had become associated with the Washington consensus. These are:

- increase saving by (inter alia) maintaining fiscal discipline;
- reorient public expenditure toward (inter alia) well-directed social expenditure;
- reform the tax system by (inter alia) introducing eco-sensitive land tax;
- strengthen bank supervision;
- maintain a competitive exchange rate, abandoning both floating and the use of the exchange rate as a nominal anchor;
- pursue interregional trade liberalization;
- build a competitive market economy by (inter alia) privatizing and deregulating (including the labor market);
- make well-defined property rights available to all;
- build key institutions such as independent central banks, strong budget

offices, independent and incorruptible judiciaries, and agencies to sponsor productivity missions;
- increase educational spending and redirect it toward primary and secondary levels.

The policies involve both macroeconomic and microeconomic elements. The macroeconomic policies are supposed to guarantee short-run stabilisation of inflation, balance of payments, and budget deficits. This is often referred to as stabilisation. On the other hand, the microeconomic policies are geared towards longer-term economic efficiency, and thereby intended to raise long-term growth rates. This is known as structural adjustment. Initially, the neat division between stabilisation and structural adjustment was supposed to correspond to the respective responsibilities of the IMF and the World Bank, one addressing short-run stabilisation and the other long-term structural adjustment and growth. But, during the 1980s, the policy interests and the loans offered by the two institutions increasingly overlapped. Accordingly, despite a less than sharp institutional division of responsibilities between the two, (the Washington) consensus was reached over both stabilisation and structural adjustment.

One good way of understanding the Washington consensus is by comparison with what it replaced. For it marked a distinct break with the previous approach to development under what is known as the McNamara era at the World Bank. The latter is best understood as incorporating an overlapping combination of Keynesianism, welfarism, and modernisation. Three fundamental analytical features are involved. First, markets do not work perfectly, especially in underdeveloped economies. Consequently, it is appropriate for the state to intervene to correct market distortions both at the microeconomic and at the macroeconomic levels.

Second, development should be understood as the passage to the conditions experienced in already developed countries. As a result, the policy goal can be defined to become developed. This itself can be broken down into two broad components. On the one hand, there is a need for structural change. Developing economies need to change their composition of output, with a greater share to be accounted for by industry in place of agriculture. This is, however, only indicative of much broader changes in socio-economic structure which, on the other hand, are associated with the processes of development – industrialisation, urbanisation, proletarianisation, welfarism, and so on.

Third, a dual projection from the developed to the developing countries is involved. Not only should the developing become like the developed countries but also the economic theory of the latter could be applied to issues of development. However, the lack of perfect empirical regularities across countries that had developed and the heterogeneity of the developing countries themselves did give rise to specifically development-oriented innovations and applications of economic theory, ranging over issues such as balanced versus unbalanced growth and the surplus labour economy. In this light, policy becomes a matter of the state intervening to bring about or to facilitate the structural changes and processes associated with development – as in the provision of infrastructure, guaranteeing sufficient resources for investment, and preserving domestic markets for infant industries through, for example, import-substituting industrialisation.

The Washington consensus can be understood as a severe reaction against the rationale for such extensive interventionism. Its broad starting point is that markets work well if left to themselves. Where they do not work well, there is no guarantee that allowing or encouraging the state to intervene will lead to an improvement. The state may not have the capacity to improve upon the poorly performing market. Nor might it have the will, not least because it can be captured by those who use its interventions to benefit themselves at the expense of even greater market imperfections. The indirect may be worse than the direct effects of such rent-seeking, as resources are devoted in pursuit of more favourable discretionary policies. Standing (1999) gives a succinct account of the various elements of the Washington consensus and an important sense of its having evolved to embrace further components:

> As the new thinking and policy action crystallised in the 1980s, the "Washington consensus" evolved to offer a model consisting of eleven main elements, with more being added as its "success" spread. Briefly, they are trade liberalisation, financial liberalisation, privatisation, "deregulation", foreign capital liberalisation (elimination of barriers to FDI [foreign direct investment]), secure property rights, unified and competitive exchange rates, diminished public spending (fiscal discipline), public expenditure switching (to health, schooling and infrastructure), tax reform (broadening the tax base, cutting marginal tax rates, less progressive tax), and a "social safety net" (selective state transfers for the needy). A twelfth element, expressed in World Bank and IMF (and OECD) reports, is labour market flexibility, by which is meant decentralised labour relations coupled with cutbacks in protective and pro-collective regulations.

The Washington consensus has played a central role in informing the structural adjustment and stabilisation programmes that have been attached to loans from the World Bank and the IMF to developing countries. Paradoxically, the Washington consensus has been associated with more and more intensive conditionality albeit with the rationale of ensuring greater reliance upon market forces. Toye (1994, pp. 29–30), for example, lists the following nine chief elements of structural adjustment loans (with percentage of times imposed in brackets): remove import quotas (57 per cent), improve export incentives (76 per cent), reform the fiscal system (70 per cent), improve financial performance of public enterprises (73 per cent), revise agricultural pricing (73 per cent), shift public investment (59 per cent), revise industrial incentives (68 per cent), increase public enterprise efficiency (57 per cent), and improve marketing and other support for agriculture (57 per cent).

The concern here, however, despite its importance, is less with the content and impact of World Bank and IMF policies and more with its approach to, and influence upon, development economics and debate. In its approach, in rejecting interventionism and relying upon the market, the Washington consensus has necessarily become characterised by two features. First, as is immediate, it has no need to put forward policies to achieve development since it has one policy to attain this goal, namely to have no policies and to rely upon the market as fully as possible. Second, and less observed, the notion of development itself could fall off the analytical agenda. There is no need to define or characterise development – it's what the market brings if left to its own devices!

By pushing reliance upon market forces and the withdrawal of state intervention as a means of achieving development, what the latter constituted could to a large extent fall off their analytical agenda. In short, the means – market forces – become an end in themselves. With an antipathy to the state other than in providing the socio-economic basis for the market to flourish in the long run, there was otherwise no need to define policy goals other than in the short run, as in macroeconomic targets, and the relationship between policy and development as long-term transformation simply evaporated.

The impact of the Washington consensus upon debate over development has also been significant. For, it has not only heavily pushed a particular stance with some success, it has also defined the alternative or its own opposition. As discussed next, the Washington consensus set an analytical agenda of market versus the state, even if itself falling heavily upon one side in the ensuing debate. The alternative to the consensus predominantly set itself the task of demonstrating, both theoretically and from the comparative and historical experience, that state intervention is necessary to achieve development. The dissenting literature, much of it ignored by proponents of the Washington consensus, has ranged over many issues and countries. It also has been highly critical of the results of structural adjustment and stabilisation.[2] Towards the end of the 1980s, the opposition to such policies had been gathering strength through observing how they had neglected the consequences for what has become known as "adjustment with a human face". Issues of poverty, the environment, and of women's relative position, for example, had been overlooked, drawing criticism over both the desirability and the efficacy of adjustment policies. In addition, the success of the east Asian newly industrialised countries (NICs) placed a very large question mark over the presumption that state intervention, especially in industrial and trade policy, is inimical to manufacturing competitiveness and (export) growth. By the mid-1990s, the Washington consensus also came under assault from within, as will be seen in the fourth section.

The developmental agenda – state versus market

As has been seen, the Washington consensus not only set policy prescriptions in terms of requiring greater reliance upon market forces, it also induced an analytical agenda focusing on state versus the market. Paradoxically, the effect of its stance in favour of neo-liberalism was to reinvigorate interest in the role of the state not least amongst those who have sought to favour interventionism both in understanding the past and in prescribing for the future. In order to address the challenge posed by the Washington consensus, interest focused on what has become known as the developmental state. Simplifying, two broad questions have come to the fore. What are the appropriate economic policies for the state to adopt in order to promote development? And what are the conditions which allow or induce the state to do so?

Fine and Rustomjee (1997, Chapter 3) address these questions in the more general terms of what they call linkages and agencies. Linkages focus on where one action has knock-on effects whether intended or not. Externalities are an obvious example of technological spill-over effects that are now considered to be important in raising productivity. Further, the development of one industry can provide supply of inputs for other industries or demand for them. Agencies, on the other hand, constitute those who undertake actions whether it be individuals, institutions, or classes. They are what make linkages happen, although potential linkages may bring forth an appropriate agency. Clearly, economic development requires an interaction between agencies and linkages to bring about economic growth and social transformation. By the same token, different economic theories focus on different agencies and linkages and place different emphasis on one or the other, as prime mover for example. Now the developmental state literature can be interpreted in these terms for its concern is with the relations between the state and the market – how do they perform as agencies and what linkages to they promote? The Washington consensus adopts the purist view that the state, in contrast to the market, is liable to reflect the economic interests of inappropriate agents in pursuit of inappropriate linkages. By contrast, the developmental state literature takes a different view of the relative merits of the state and the market. In doing so, it accepts the state versus market framework. It also tends to divide neatly into two sorts, corresponding to the linkage–agency distinction as well as the two questions highlighted at the end of the last paragraph. Fine and Rustomjee suggest that the economic school uses the notion of developmental state to ask what policies the state should adopt, whereas the political school asks whether it is capable of adopting the right policies.

The economic school pinpoints a role for the developmental state by identifying any number of market imperfections, potentially drawing upon standard economic theory and a role for the state in, for example, protecting infant industries, accruing economies of scale and scope, and taking account of externalities. In addition, the economic school identifies dynamic factors in the development process concerning the sources of productivity increase and spill-over effects from one industry to another. Whether in formal models, informal theory, or by reference to historical experience, the economic school argues for the necessity of state economic intervention in order to achieve development. In case of industrialisation, for example, considerable emphasis has been placed on the need for the state not so much to pick winners as to create them. For the Washington consensus, stress is placed on the capacity of the market mechanism to exploit given comparative advantage, with business better at picking winners and having the incentive to do so. In contrast, the developmental state literature locates industrialisation, and continuing manufacturing competitiveness, in the capacity to create comparative advantage where it did not exist previously and even, to coin a phrase, deliberately getting prices wrong and bucking the free market logic of allowing international prices to prevail.

Not surprisingly, especially for industrialisation, the economic school has taken the east Asian NICs as the key illustration of their approach, pointing to the extensive role of the state in South Korea, for example, in restricting imports, allocating finance for investment and designing, implementing and monitoring industrial policy more generally. In part, the case against the Washington consensus became so strong that a huge World Bank study was specially commissioned to re-examine the issue and was published in 1993 just as the consensus was about to come under assault from within. It came to the controversial conclusion that intervention was essentially market-friendly, market-conforming, or even otherwise negative in its impact. In other words, to the extent that it promoted development, the state merely did what the market would have done had it been working perfectly. Further, it was argued that the implications for other developing countries were extremely limited, and the experience of the east Asian NICs could not be replicated.

Whatever the outcome of this debate, the economic school tends to take for granted that its victory in principle means a victory in policy practice. But the Washington consensus has already questioned such a presumption since it emphasises that even if there is a case for state intervention because of some market imperfection, there is no guarantee that appropriate policies will be adopted. Rather, the state may have neither the capacity nor the inclination to be developmental, not least because government failure and inefficiencies might be considerably more serious than those of the market, especially in view of non-market rent-seeking through the political process. Such issues are the point of departure for the political school's approach to the developmental state, and the two schools complement one another. One – the economic school – asks what are the right economic policies in view of market imperfections, presuming they will be implemented once identified. The other – the political school – is exclusively focused on whether the state has the capacity to implement appropriate policies more or less irrespective of what they might be!

To some extent the political school was influenced initially by the need to respond to the challenge posed by the deadweight of rent-seeking. How could a state be developmental if it merely served as a market mechanism by alternative distorted means, with politics being used for pursuit of self-interest without the discipline of the market? An answer can be given in terms of the state being autonomous to a sufficient degree from the economic interests that seek to act upon it. In this respect, stylised comparison is made between the authoritarian and developmentally successful states of the east Asian NICs and the populist and unsuccessful states of Latin America.

Such simplistic conclusions are, however, readily contradicted by differences within these broad groups of countries as well as by consideration of a wider range of examples. If a state is both autonomous and strong, why would it not become a "vampire" state with those in command drawing upon its power for the accumulation of personal wealth and patronage? In this light, the state has to be autonomous and strong but not too autonomous nor too strong. Rather, it must be embedded within the economy and society in such a way that it is positively influenced but not captured. In this vein, the political school has been drawn into specifying a growing basket of conditions, and corresponding terminology, in establishing regularities over whether a state is liable to be developmental or not. Given the heterogeneity of African states and perform-ance, it is hardly surprising that the continent has not attracted as much attention as east Asia and Latin America. Even so, as Fine and Stoneman (1996, p. 16) observe:

> Thus, autonomy has become redefined as relative, bounded, or embedded, and the conditions for the state to achieve this autonomy extend from strength to geopolitical position, independence from earlier regimes, the sequencing of democratisation and national independence, the degree of cultural unity and governance, etc., with corresponding qualifications in the meanings of strong, weak, soft, hard, autonomous as applied to the state.

They go on to argue that this conceptual reinvention and refinement in chasing the increasingly heterogeneous empirical evidence from case studies, and the division of analytical labour between the two schools, with little by way of synthesis, are both a consequence of the prior acceptance of the developmental agenda set by the Washington consensus of state versus market. Instead, they suggest that there is a case for returning to the classical or Marxist tradition in which both the state and the market are the consequences of underlying economic and political interests and relations, most notably those attached to classes or fractions of classes such as those comprised from finance, industry, agriculture, or even particular families and "cronies" or beneficiaries by patronage.

Thus, the developmental state literature accepted the state versus market approach even if rejecting the neo-liberal stance of the Washington consensus in favour of the market. It did so by supporting appropriate state interventionism, enabled by appropriate political conditions. By the same token, in offering an alternative to the Washington consensus, attention has been shifted away from class relations, their underlying economic and political interests, and the corresponding role of conflict and power. These are not absent from the developmental state literature, especially for the political school, but they tend to be addressed in terms of conflict within rather than through the state.

From Washington to post-Washington consensus

The Washington consensus was experiencing growing difficulties from the late 1980s onwards in face of mounting criticisms along a number of lines; the need to take account of adjustment with a human face; how to account for the east Asian miracles; and the apparent failings of adjustment policies to deliver significant differences in performance let alone development. The post-Washington consensus has seemingly resolved these problems, at least at the analytical and rhetorical levels. It is most closely associated with its leading proponent, Joe Stiglitz, Senior Vice President and Chief Economist to the World Bank over the last years of the 1990s. In a sense, he explicitly launched the manifesto of the new consensus in early 1998. First, he distances himself from the old consensus (Stiglitz 1998a, p. 1):

> [The Washington consensus] held that good economic performance required liberalized trade, macroeconomic stability, and getting prices right. Once the government handled these issues – essentially once the government "got out of the way" – private markets would produce efficient allocations and growth … But the policies advanced by the Washington consensus are hardly complete and sometimes misguided. Making markets work requires more than just low inflation, it requires sound financial regulation, competition policy, and policies to facilitate the transfer of technology, to name some fundamental issues neglected by the Washington consensus.

Then, after his own constructed critical dialogue with the Washington consensus, he puts forward his alternative by way of contrast (p. 25):

> Trying to get government better focused on the fundamentals – economic policies, basic education, health, roads, law and order, environmental protection – is a vital step. But focusing on the fundamentals is not a recipe for a minimalist government. The state has an important role to play in appropriate regulation, industrial policy, social protection and welfare. But the choice is not whether the state should or should not be involved. Instead, it is often a matter of how it gets involved. More importantly, we should not see the state and markets as substitutes … the government should see itself as a complement to markets, undertaking those actions that make markets fulfil their functions better.

A number of features of the post-Washington consensus stand out. First, it is sharply critical of the Washington consensus and seeks an alternative in which state intervention is greater in depth and breadth. Second, it rejects the analytical agenda of state versus market, arguing that the two are complements and can work together and not against one another. Third, if less explicit, it poses an alternative agenda for development economics and policy debate, seeking to establish the appropriate role of the state in view of market imperfections. Fourth, it also brings the social back into the analysis as the means of addressing, and potentially correcting, market imperfections – rather than simply creating them as for the Washington consensus for which the world would be a better place if it were made more and more, if not completely, like the market.[3]

None of this is surprising given the analytical principles upon which the post-Washington consensus is based. Here, Stiglitz's own career as an academic economist is instructive. By coincidence, as he himself observes at the height of the crisis of confidence of the Washington consensus (Stiglitz 1994, p. 5):

> During the past fifteen years, a new paradigm, sometimes referred to as the information-theoretic approach to economics ... has developed ... This paradigm has already provided us with insights into development economics and macroeconomics. It has provided us with a new welfare economics, a new theory of the firm, and a new understanding of the role and function-ing of financial markets.

This new paradigm has already been laid out in Chapter 1. It is the (new imperfect information) theory of market imperfections applied to development economics and, by extension, to development studies more generally. Stiglitz himself is renowned for his theory of share-cropping, for example, as an institutional response to asymmetric information across landlord and tenant as well, particularly, for work on credit and financial markets.[4]

Significantly, the analytical principles just covered are not specific to, nor in general did they originate with, the problems of development. After all, the presence of market imperfections, how to handle them, and the relationship between market and non-market activity are as central to advanced as they are to developing economies. So in what respect does the post-Washington consensus understand the latter as distinctive? The answer is disarmingly simple. On the one hand, developing economies are perceived to be particularly burdened by the presence of market imperfections within and across their various markets and, in addition, to be underdeveloped in the non-market institutions and capabilities for dealing with them. On the other hand, developing economies are seen as structurally marked apart by their composition of output, with a particularly low share of manufacturing and high share of primary, especially, agricultural production.[5] On this basis, Stiglitz had already completed the intellectual programme of establishing the new development economics, first comprehensively broached over a decade earlier, with development analysis reduced to the incidence and impact of market imperfections (Stiglitz 1989). This has been refined and extended in scope over the intervening period, with the old neoclassical model of perfect competition taken as point of departure (Stiglitz and Hoff 1999):

> In leaving out history, institutions, and distributional considerations, neoclas-sical economics was leaving out the heart of development economics. Mod-ern economic theory argues that the fundamentals [resources, technology, and preferences] are not the only ... determinants of economic outcomes ... even without government failures, market failures are pervasive, espe-cially in less developed countries.

Further, with casual reference to the Black Death, as an illustrative accident of history, and multiple equilibria, an explanation is provided for the fundamental problem of why "developed and less developed countries are on different production functions":

> We emphasize that accidents of history matter ... partly because of pervasive complementarities among agents ... and partly because even a set of dysfunctional institutions and behaviors in the past can constitute a Nash equilibrium from which an economy need not be inevitably dislodged.

Not surprisingly, on this basis, Yusuf and Stiglitz (1999) feel able to divide development issues into those that are resolved and those that are not. These seem unwittingly to fall into the theoretical as opposed to the policy, respectively, not least because the analysis is one of market imperfections but the policy will depend upon their incidence in practice.

What are the policy implications of the new consensus? At least in principle, they are relatively straightforward. It is a matter of making better choices than the market, incorporating divergence between social and private returns into decision making, and rectifying the past through addressing market imperfections and inappropriate customs and institutions. This is all very well in theory but, in practice, matters are much more complicated. For, as should be apparent, because the post-Washington consensus is based on microeconomic principles, and these are extended to non-market influences as well, there are any number of imperfections to be identified and rectified. Moreover, from a theoretical perspective, one or two imperfections are more than enough to allow either for favourable of for unfavourable patterns of (endogenous) growth, vicious or virtuous circles, low or high equilibria. Models and estimates of the economy which properly incorporate more than a few factors become too complicated to be useful. It becomes a matter of focusing upon a few factors that are privileged by being chosen as the key to promoting development. These can range from human capital to stance on trade policy, although it is also possible to be much more heterodox and argue that variables such as levels of equality, trust, or political stability can be of importance.

So much for the policy principles upon which the new consensus is based. There is another way of looking at this. How does it compare, not with the Washington consensus that it sees itself as displacing, but to the developmental framework that preceded that consensus? How does the post-Washington consensus compare with the Keynesian–welfarist–modernisation approach to development?

As we have seen, the analytical basis for the post-Washington consensus is the optimising individual in a world of market imperfections and historically evolved non-market institutions and customs whose persistence and effects can be explained by aggregating over economic agents taken as a whole. Growth paths, and success or otherwise in development, are understood as movements to or around one or more equilibria. At most, socio-economic structures are an exogenously given starting point laid down by history or accident or are an outcome of aggregation over optimising individuals. We do not need to visit development to make these points. The information-theoretic approach to macroeconomics, for example, understands Keynesian unemployment for developed countries in terms of market imperfections in which optimising employers might not reduce the money wage even though there are workers offering themselves for work at lower wages (because of efficiency wages, or the willingness to pay a wage premium to attract a skilled and compliant workforce). Similar considerations can apply in money and other markets. So, just as the post-Washington consensus comprehends Keynesian unemployment on the basis of a wide definition of market imperfections to include informational asymmetries, so it incorporates welfarism and modernisation on the same terms. Welfarism is needed in order to correct for market imperfections in the provision of health, education, and social and economic infrastructure more generally. Modernisation, at least in its non-economic aspects, can be disaggregated into a number of components broadly comprising the creation of good governance, on the one hand, and the beneficial aspects of civil society, on the other hand. In other words, modernisation within the post-Washington consensus is the increasingly effective non-market means for handling market imperfections, even though these are presumed to lessen, if not to disappear, with development.

In light of the previous paragraph, it would appear that the post-Washington consensus not only breaks with, and generalises from, the Washington consensus by allowing for market imperfections, but it also incorporates insights from the development economics that preceded the Washington consensus. Indeed, at times explicitly, the post-Washington consensus has taken traditional contributions from the earlier developmental literature and reinterpreted them within its own framework, thereby claiming to place them on sound microeconomic foundations. But does it lose anything by doing so? The answer can only be in the affirmative to the extent that analysis constructed on the basis of aggregation over optimising individuals is rejected. In other words, the post-Washington consensus depends upon a notion of development in which socio-economic change is the outcome of individual actions rather than vice versa. Much of the earlier development economics does not sit comfortably within such a framework since it has been concerned with broad structural features of the economy and the broad processes of development, and how the two interact with one another. Industrialisation, for example, stands for a complex shift in composition of output as well as a transition from a predominantly rural self-sufficient, surplus labour economy to one that is urbanised and proletarianised. The key issue posed by the post-Washington consensus is whether such transitions are reducible to the evolving interaction of market and non-market imperfections as individuals go optimally about their business.

Now consider the policy implications of the post-Washington consensus – again less by virtue of its more state-friendly stance by comparison with the old consensus and more in relation to the policy perspectives of the previous period. Once again, the new consensus is able to claim that it is capable of incorporating all policy options previously posited in view of its correspondingly wide range of analytical coverage. Yet, as many of its critics have already observed, the policy stance of the post-Washington consensus, and its commitment to interventionism in practice, does not diverge enormously from the previous consensus. In other words, it is a much paler version of the earlier Keynesian–welfarism–modernisation perspective.

Why is this? There are two reasons. First, the earlier commitment to interventionism is based upon a view of development in which the state is required to bring about major structural change and to facilitate socio-economic processes. Support for state-ownership of utilities, for example, is significant. The post-Washington consensus is much more cautious across the range of potential interventions. These can only be justified on microeconomic grounds in which there are significant market imperfections which can be corrected. Second, then, the state cure must be preferable to the free market (or non-market) symptoms. The pre-Washington consensus view of the state as a benign force for development has been lost in the transition to the post-Washington consensus which has adopted from the Washington consensus an understanding of the state as being subject to capture by rent-seeking agents. Consequently, whilst not accepting that the potential for rent-seeking undermines the rationale for any state intervention, the post-Washington consensus is mindful of the need to ensure that correction of market imperfections is not nullified by non-market imperfections. Interventionism should be limited to the capacity for good governance which itself becomes an object of policy.

Beyond the post-Washington consensus?

Although the post-Washington consensus only emerged at the end of the 1990s, it has already attracted both critical support and rejection. Less favourable responses have been prompted by disquiet from a number of different perspectives with the way in which development is understood within the new consensus as well as with its analytical principles. A number of issues have been to the fore, focusing on the following question: What are the continuing *limitations* of the post-Washington consensus from other analytical and policy perspectives rather than its strengths in breaking with the Washington consensus?

First, the post-Washington consensus is firmly based on methodological individualism by which is meant an understanding of society from the perspective of aggregating over the behaviour of individuals. Moreover, such methodological individualism is of a special type, that identified with mainstream economics, in which individual motivation is confined to utility maximisation rather than other behavioural rules and/or motivations. Whilst the information-theoretic approach to economics, and rational choice as it is known when applied to other disciplines, does now account for individual and collective behaviour which appears to violate utility maximisation, this is only because of a deeper understanding of the latter in the context of market, non-market and informational imperfections. In a sense, methodologically, the post-Washington consensus reduces individuals and society to their barest elements of selfish pleasure seeking. Altruism, for example, can only be cynically regarded as a strategy for self-advantage!

Second, the post-Washington consensus is heavily oriented around the notion that certain things are exogenous and certain things are endogenous, leading to definite outcomes on the basis of the exogenous determinants. Relative to the traditions of mainstream economics, more factors have become endogenous. Nonetheless, this is more by way of shifting the boundary between exogenous and endogenous rather than challenging this way of proceeding. Whilst there is some scope for variation in outcome because of random shocks, multiple equilibria and path dependence, underlying axiomatic model-building implies that outcomes are heavily predetermined.

Third, the post-Washington consensus is perceived to rely unduly on generalised principles and concepts without sufficient sensitivity to socially and historically specific conditions, whether bound to particular countries or stages of development. In this sense, it is an extension of mainstream economics with its understanding of economies in terms of the allocation of scarce resources between competing ends with these, in turn, determined by given production functions, preferences, and factor endowments. To these considerations, the post-Washington consensus adds market and informational imperfections.

Fourth, bringing the previous points together, the post-Washington consensus can be considered to be "reductionist" by which is meant that the complexity and social and historical content of issues tends to be ·stripped away and restricted within the narrow analytical principles attached to rational choice in an imperfectly informed world. In short, there is no such thing as society other than as a historical accident or inheritance, and individuals are pretty much one-dimensional as well! The social theory derived from other disciplines is thereby reduced to a calculus of individuals optimising across market and non-market, with each of the latter evolving as a result.

Fifth, the post-Washington consensus is accused of reinventing the wheel only with fewer spokes! In many ways, its results are well known – that there are market imperfections, that institutions and social customs matter, that the state can play a role in promoting development where the market and private institutions fail, that initial conditions matter, and so on. Such insights can be recycled by attaching them to the information-theoretic approach, but much analytical content is lost by doing so.

Sixth, this is a consequence of the extreme discomfort that the post-Washington consensus experiences in dealing with social variables and processes that are traditional within other approaches outside mainstream economics. There are issues of power and conflict, concepts attached to social structure such as class relations, and transformations in society associated with factors such as globalisation which both analytically and historically do not readily reduce to the optimising behaviour of individuals.

Seventh, the post-Washington consensus is treated with suspicion because of its origins within the World Bank. The Washington consensus was previously under considerable strain and was no longer serving adequately two important functions – providing, paradoxically, a rhetoric to justify considerable and growing economic and social interventionism in adjusting countries as well as the public relations exercise of being perceived as successfully promoting development in practice. The post-Washington consensus has neatly reintroduced a more favourable stance towards the state and wider social considerations as well as rationalising discretionary economic and social intervention on a piecemeal basis. In addition, Japan had emerged to prominence as a, if not the, leading donor of aid. Compared to the United States, its stance is more favourable to the state in promoting development. For this reflects both its own historical experience in achieving late industrialisation, as well as the need for interventionism to guarantee success in host countries in the Asia–Pacific Rim which are in receipt of its direct foreign investment. In short, the post-Washington consensus has emerged primarily in response to shifting pressures on the World Bank rather than, as it presents itself, as a careful internal reconsideration of the Washington consensus from the perspective of the new information-theoretic micro-foundations. Even the weight of critical academic literature that the previous consensus attracted predominantly continues to be overlooked by proponents of the new consensus. This does not imply that developments within the Bank are unimportant and this issue is considered next.

Taking the social half-seriously

The central aim of this part of the book is to examine critically the treatment of "social capital" in the work of the World Bank. As such, it is primarily an intellectual exercise. But is it merely academic? In the broader context of assessing the operational impact of the World Bank, the question arises of the relationship between its own research and its own policies as well as the more general influence it exerts on the research and policy environment, and vice versa. At an even more general level is the issue of the relationship between (academic) research and policy outcomes, especially in view of the esoteric nature of much economic (and social) theory. Is it totally irrelevant? Is it otherwise forced to conform to policy dictates and interests that prevail over it? Or does it make a genuine difference? To answer these questions requires a full account both of how such knowledge is produced and circulated and how it is received and used. This is beyond my abilities and ambitions although I would place emphasis on the complexity and diversity of the impact of research or ideology more generally.[6]

More narrowly, in the context of the World Bank, there are two opposite stereotypical views on such issues. On the one hand, the World Bank's research can be seen as irrelevant to the loans made and how they perform, with such research and operations functioning, to whatever individual effect, in essentially different worlds. This approach tends to be informed by two very different stances on the source of the independence between research and policy. Either those directly responsible for making loans within the World Bank proceed oblivious to any intellectual turmoil that surrounds them, not least because they are practical and steeped in local knowledge and experience; or, on a grander scale, policy is seen as determined by external economic and political conditions, with research at most rationalising (or even contradicting) what is done in practice. In other words, is the World Bank's research merely presentational froth, a conduit for predetermined policies, a sideline with little or no impact upon operational outcomes? Ranis (1997, p. 79), for example, identifies two "circulatory systems", one around the President's office, the research wing, and the chief economist, the other around operating departments concerned with "being polite but getting on with the lending".

On the other hand, research is seen as highly influential in setting policy perspectives and priorities, trickling down to affect if not to determine internal operations. Such research can also have a seepage effect on operational activity outside the World Bank. In this light, the World Bank can be perceived to exercise an influence far beyond the conditions attached to the loans that it makes itself (whatever the role of research in determining these) as both an educational and, most recently, as a self-styled knowledge bank. With a research budget in the region of $25 million, Ranis (1997, p. 75) also observes of the World Bank that[7]

> Its dissemination efforts, especially in the Third World, are prodigious and overwhelming. At the same time the Bank has paid relatively little attention to the output of other national and international organizations ... Indeed even much relevant output by academia is largely ignored.

Such a luxury – or is it disdain? – follows from the sheer weight of research, backed up with the power to lend (Stern and Ferreira 1997, p. 524):

> In analyzing the Bank's influence on development economics it must be recognized that the Bank's size gives it a unique position. The Bank employs around 800 professional economists ... These resources dwarf those of any university department or research institution working on development economics. There are more than 3,000 additional professionals in the Bank. The size of the Bank's lending program (of the order of $15 billion to $20 billion a year) allows it to exert considerable influence on the thinking and policies of borrowing countries. The weight of the number of development economists, the research budget, and the leverage from lending means that the Bank's potential influence is profound, and that the Bank cannot be seen as just one of a number of fairly equal actors in the world of development economics.

Further, the World Bank has sought to incorporate governments into the formulation of adjustment policies in order that they be indigenously owned. Whilst presented as a means of democratising and enhancing policy formulation by local participation, it is a moot point whether this is more accurately perceived as a form of repressive tolerance and a more sophisticated means of ensuring implementation. Helleiner (1994, pp. 10–11) puts it most delicately:

> The World Bank now says that it is encouraging local programme owner-ship, "insisting that the materials we use as the basis for ... lending decisions be the product of Africans", hiring local African consultants rather than foreigners wherever possible, and attempting ... to develop professional and analytical skills in public policy in Africa. These efforts are overdue, and they are probably biased in their orientations (toward orthodox Bank perspec-tives), but they have been welcomed in Africa.

A more blunt assessment is given by Harberger (1992, p. 93). Having pointed to the low weight of the World Bank loans relative to other flows and what is needed, he observes:[8]

> The Bank must recognize that ultimately its role is that of a teaching insti-tution. It teaches developing countries lessons they have to learn about economic policy. In part it does so by training young people from developing countries ... In part it does so through what people from developing coun-tries learn when they occupy staff jobs. In part it does so through Bank missions going to developing countries and working with the ministers and their staffs.

Consequently, loans and operations can be seen as supplying a token demonstra-tion effect to allow World Bank policy (and research) to prosper by other educational means. In particular, the World Bank played its part in not only promoting the neo-liberal Washington consensus, but the latter also set the analytical agenda for development studies, as the market versus the state, whilst heavily leaning on the market side. Even so, this might have been driven by the dictates of Reaganism and the like. As Ranis (1997, p. 74) puts it more generally, in the warmer climes of adjustment with a human face:

> The Bank has shown a tendency not to innovate but to take over quickly the leadership on any given theme ... More current examples include the envi-ronment, women in development, military expenditures and governance. Subjects accepted as topical from either a functional or political point of view are quickly incorporated into Bank language ... become part of the Bank's research and analysis agenda, and sometimes even of its stated lending criteria.

An intermediate position is adopted here between these two extremes of whether World Bank research has an effect or not; indeed, it is useful to view the World Bank's research as both cause and effect. It does have an impact on its own and the broader policy environment as well as being a response to its dictates. Consider the conclusion of Edwards (1997, p. 47) for trade policy, for example:[9]

The Bank has contributed somewhat (but not a whole lot) to these policies ... ideas have had a role in the recent reform movement. And, over the years, the Bank has made a contribution to the intellectual debate on the consequences of alternative trade regimes. Although the quality of Bank research has not always been very high, and although no memorable pieces have been produced, I believe that the Bank has been able to accumulate an impressive body of evidence that points toward the benefits of liberalization policies.

Further, Krueger (1997, p. 19) suggests that the associated research work was of practical significance:

High marks must go to the analytical research that pointed to measurement techniques such as effective protection and cost benefit, which enabled policy makers and their analysts to obtain empirical quantification, however rough, of the relevant magnitudes.

Another area in which the World Bank has been particularly prominent is in the human capital approach to the economics of education, which has been attached over the last decade or more to the promotion of primary schooling, especially for girls.[10] As early as Psacharopoulos (1981, p. 141), the World Bank's 1980 Policy Paper on education is described in these terms: "It might not be an exaggeration to treat this Paper as a modern Bible on educational development." As Jones (1992, p. 229) accepts:

There can be no doubt as to the quality of much of the Bank's research output in the 1980s, evidenced by the number of articles by Bank staff gaining acceptance in leading academic journals.

However, he heavily qualifies this praise by pointing to the over-generalisation of the research from the results of a few country studies, the failure to develop and draw upon indigenous research capacity, and the wish to reduce educational provision to a flow of financial costs and benefits. Indeed, he adds (p. 227):[11]

It would be facile to criticise Psacharopoulos' research leadership as too focused, too bound to Bank requirements, insufficiently open-ended and insufficiently free-ranging, as it would be to criticise the highly repetitive nature of his publications.

And he ultimately sees the educational research as being driven by other imperatives (p. 220):[12]

The most powerful force for change in policy has been the desire to keep the Bank functioning as a bank. Its borrowers need to be confronted with new reasons for borrowing, whether on commercial or concessional terms. It is simply not in the scheme of things for the Bank officers to promote a fresh view about education and development if it did not have possibilities for opening up new patterns of lending ... In their daily work, loan officers are driven by (and to an extent their careers are dependent upon) their success in negotiating large numbers of sizeable loans and in encouraging quick disbursements for each stage of projects. This latter aspect, encouraging as it does superficial evaluation so as not to slow down the rate of disbursements during a project, helps explain the relative lack of interest displayed by the Bank in matters of educational detail, especially in the classroom. Loan officers, but also research and policy analysts in education, display – as a group – a certain naivety about process matters in education, not least the practical dimensions of teaching and learning, policy formulation, the management of educational change, and community motivation and participation.

In contrast to the case of trade theory and policy, in which the World Bank research is generally considered to be influential and accepted, this explains what has been described as an ignorance, rejection and/or manipulation of human capital theory for advocacy purposes by World Bank educational operatives. The theory is more or less irrelevant to them once loans have been agreed. Unlike trade policy which tells you, however well and however legitimately, what to do with tariffs, calculating rates of return on educational expenditure does not help to put an education project in place other than in principle.

Privatisation provides a sharp contrast to education and trade by way of illustration of World Bank research, both in level of academic sophistication and in influence on outcomes. Whilst consistently and aggressively pursued as a policy measure, the World Bank's research has remained impoverished at best and apologetic at its worst. Analytically, it has fallen far short of the content of the approach that dominates the orthodoxy – with its conclusion that ownership as such does not matter relative to the conditions of competition and regulation.[13] Its empirical work has simply and primarily been self-serving. If the lessons from existing literature had been learnt and followed in advance, policies would have been very different, particularly in terms of the desirability as well as the sequencing and integration of privatisation, or public sector reform, with other policies.[14] I suspect that even its authors would not claim that research on privatisation at the World Bank is at the intellectual frontier, let alone pushing it outward.

So, as privatisation shows, even if education and trade are areas in which the World Bank has been highly active in the wider academic environment, and through which it has yielded some influence,[15] this is not so in all other areas. Even for education and trade, there is some doubt over quality as already indicated by reference to Jones and Edwards, respectively. Even the generally favourable de Vries (1996, p. 240) is light in his praise:

Nevertheless one can say that the Bank is only to a limited extent a creator of new ideas. It absorbs ideas from many other places, integrates them in its

operations practices, tests their practicality, and provides a forum for inter-
change among academics and government officials.

And even where policy is research-led, the research in the lead has become both
internationalised and Americanised, with the two more or less synonymous
around mainstream neoclassical economics.[16] This leads Kapur et al. (1997, p. 4)
to cast some doubt on the independence of the World Bank economists:

> Economics would become the Bank's hallmark scholarly discipline, and the
> economists who heavily shaped Bank operations as well as its research were
> recruited from a wide array of countries. To a large degree, however, they
> were the product of the graduate economics departments' English-speaking,
> but especially American, universities. This fact, as it played into the Bank's
> consulting, research, technical assistance, and agenda setting, would enhance
> the US role in the institution beyond the apparatus of formal governance.

Initially, then, it can be concluded that the role of research in the World Bank
is complex, uneven and shifting, depending upon the issue concerned as well as
the internal and external environments, both intellectual and political.[17] Even so
a number of weaknesses can be identified: poor quality, poor engagement with
alternatives (Americanisation), excessive dissemination at the expense of
independent research capacity building (ditto), poor coherence and integration
in how research is used in choice, design, monitoring and assessment of
activities, overgeneralisation in order to rationalise loans and leave room for
discretion despite need for country and issue specificity, and limited engagement
in self-criticism, and assessment even when there are sea-changes in approach.
Further, the gaps between World Bank and high quality academic research and
between research of whatever quality and practice seem to be wider the more
microeconomic or project-based is the issue concerned as opposed to macroeconomic or programme-based.[18]

So far, however, consideration has only been given to research *within* economics. Now consider the relationship between economics and the other social
sciences. A view is now prevalent that a long battle has been waged in order to
have social factors taken seriously by World Bank economists.[19] Cernea (1991a,
p. 6) regrets the absence of cultural factors in the thinking of (World Bank)
economists, who, "as the professional body presiding most often over the rites of
project making, have done little to incorporate cultural variables into project
models." Further, he continues, "the neglect of social dimensions in intervention-
caused development always takes revenge on the outcome." This is one reason
why social science knowledge ultimately becomes incorporated into projects, as
the latter fail, or otherwise can be enhanced by studied participation rather than
relying on dubious trickle-down effects. The imbalances that social science must
seek to redress are those of the "econocentric", "technocentric", and "commo-
docentric" in-house cultures at the World Bank, that is undue emphasis on
getting prices and technology right and neglect of social actors, respectively

(Cernea 1996, pp. 15–16). There appears to be a heavy criticism of economists. It is not so much that they are wrong as that they are one-sided, primarily as a consequence of their university training (Cernea 1996, p. 17):

> Many of the former students in economics ... brought to the Bank – or to governments and the private sector elsewhere – biased, one-sided conceptual models ... Can we correct afterwards what the university has not done well at the right time?

At times, particularly in earlier work, it is a question of making given policies work better, "how can sociology and anthropology help improve resettlement?" (Cernea 1991b, p. 198). Yet it is but a short step to a position in which social science must inform policy making in something more than a limited way (Cernea 1996, p. 10):[20]

> For all these reasons – economic, social, moral, financial – social analysis is not only *instrumental* but ... indispensable. It directly increases the successes of programs ... [It] *is not a luxury or a marginal add-on* to inducing development, but is as necessary *as the economic analysis is* for designing and ascertaining the feasibility and adequate goal-directedness of development programs.

From painfully late beginnings, the presence of social theory has gained momentum and presence. Cernea (1996) observes the first anthropologist was appointed to the World Bank only in 1974, compared to 1950 for the World Health Organisation.[21] Subsequently, however, Cernea (1996, p. 4) notes:[22]

> The group assembled during these twenty years is today the world's *largest group of this kind working in one place* – about 50–60 social scientists, who actually practice development anthropology and sociology. In addition, hundreds of social scientists from developing and developed countries are employed each year as short term consultants, largely due to the demand for social analysis *legitimized by the core in-house group.* (emphasis added)

In retrospect, such growth and influence looks like a successful assault upon the narrow and narrow-minded hegemony exercised by World Bank economists. Especially in view of the increasing prominence of adjustment with a human face, social science has also been promoted by external influence. As Cernea (1991a, p. 36) observes, under the slogan of putting people first, the opportunities for social science are unlimited:

> The range of entrance points for sociological knowledge and skills should be expanded to all segments of development planning, from policymaking to execution and evaluation, and from theorizing to social engineering.

Looking forward, however, the achievements of the social scientists are considerably less impressive. From the perspective of the post-Washington consensus, there is nothing at all troublesome in the positions adopted by the non-economists. Emphasis on market imperfections are positively embraced, as is the co-existence of economic and non-economic factors. In addition, four distinct but closely related features of the work of the social scientists are particularly disturbing. First, there is an acceptance of the division between the economic and the social. Second, this division carries the implication that the economic is non-social. Third, the economic analysis of the World Bank is accepted uncritically other than its omission of the social. Fourth, even if pursued aggressively, the social serves primarily as an add-on to the economic. In a sense, in its interaction with economic engineering, the social engineering has been pushed to its logical conclusion. For projects to be chosen, for them to be of higher quality, for implementation to be successful, and to clear up at the end, it is as well to incorporate what is involved at the outset.

In this light, it is hardly surprising that the non-economists should have accepted their marginal position if only to press for it to be less marginal. This is illustrated by what is possibly their most active area of engagement – involuntary resettlement. The issue itself is already one of self-marginalisation – dealing with the consequences of projects that might otherwise be overlooked but for putting impediments in their way. Paradoxically, that the economic is social emerges in the (economic) areas explicitly addressed by the poverty-induced resettlement literature, with Cernea (1991b, pp. 195–96) listing them as landlessness, homelessness, joblessness, marginalisation, food insecurity, increased morbidity and mortality, and social disarticulation.[23]

Most of these issues are often at the core of development economics. If they are social, so is the economic in general. How can social sciences deal with these by relying on what might be termed non-economics alone? How can they do so without challenging the economics itself? Significantly, Cernea seems to offer only limited criticism of economics other than in its oversights. Indeed, Guggenheim and Cernea (1993) praise Schuh (1993) for emphasising the role of family and household even though the article concerned is entirely couched in the terms of mainstream economics with reliance upon the new household economics and human capital theory. As has been seen, the introduction of the non-economic to the economic has become entirely acceptable to mainstream economics without challenging, even reinforcing, its underlying methodology. One of the ways of papering over the fundamental schism between a non-social economics and a social non-economics has been to invent and/or to deploy the notion of social capital which World Bank non-economists have heavily promoted. As will be shown, it does not challenge the economics and economists of the World Bank and can have the effect of strengthening their position and scope. In this respect, heirs to Cernea (1996, p. 16) should heed his advice, for social capital does not assert new ideas, it merely consolidates the old: "For applied social scientists, quibbling only for improving practical fixes is never enough. Asserting innovative ideas does require intellectual wrestling and theoretical engagement."

It appears, then, as if the World Bank contains two worlds, one of economists and one of non-economists. Social capital holds out the prospect of bringing these two worlds together, although it is a meeting, even a confrontation, that is based on entirely different intellectual backgrounds and dynamics. How it turns out is the subject of the next chapter.

Concluding remarks

I hope enough has been said to convince the most hard-boiled and academically cynical of both NGO (non-governmental organisations) activists and World Bank operators in the field that World Bank research does matter. It does so in a number of ways and through a number of aspects, at least as rhetoric and possibly more substantively. First, the research tends to be organised under an umbrella of the most general kind. This has the advantage of opening avenues for the business of the Bank as bank – a rationale by which to lend to its customers. Under the Washington consensus, the commitment to laissez-faire paradoxically provided considerable scope for discretionary intervention. Just a casual glance at World Bank and IMF programmes from this perspective suffices to perceive how these institutions interfere in adjusting countries. With the post-Washington consensus, the scope for intervention and the rationale for it are both widened and deepened. Policies can be designed to be either market-strengthening or market-correcting. Avenues for investments are unlimited. In addition, they leave considerable room for discretion and for more extensive intervention in "civil society", for non-market responses to market imperfections are fair game for improvement.

Second, in setting analytical agendas, research can have the effect of dictating the terms under which opposition is posed. In this respect, the World Bank has moved from an opposition between market and state. Now, in the wake of the post-Washington consensus, we are all to be channelled into a dialogue of corrections of market imperfections and building of social capital. When set against the Washington consensus, this seems to have the potential advantage both of skirting criticism, for being austere and dogmatic, and of incorporating critics – for neglect of the poor, women, popular participation, the environment, etc.

Third, however, this continues to reflect a sharp dichotomy between the economic and the non-economic which has only been reinforced, if veiled, by the emergence of the post-Washington consensus. Indeed, this can be understood as an initiative to smooth the way for otherwise only marginally changed economic policies to be implemented without challenging their efficacy and desirability. Where previously the Washington consensus painted a picture of the economy as unduly obstructed by the intrusion of the non-economic, the post-Washington consensus construes the market and non-market as inextricably attached to one another through greater or lesser efficacy in handling market imperfections. However, the result is one in which the social remains extraneous non-economic facilitator to the economy.

Fourth, the World Bank has considerable impact in steering research for both internal and external purposes. This has clearly been much more important in some areas than others, especially trade policy and the economics of education, and the World Bank has never been able to dictate or determine either research or policy directions without opposition. Nevertheless, its influence is arguably excessive, setting the terms of debate in conformity with its own phases of modernisation (emulative stages of growth or different patterns of development), Washington consensus (market versus state), and post-Washington consensus (development as non-market responses to market imperfections).

By now, it should be apparent why social capital should prove so attractive to the World Bank in moving from Washington to post-Washington consensus. Analytically, it allows for market imperfections and for these to be understood as inducing non-market responses. Policy-wise, discretionary intervention is justified and its scope extended. Rhetorically, both the state – but especially the social other than the state, trade unions, and traditional politics – are more warmly received. And, intellectually, the social and its theorists are taken seriously by economists without questioning their economics.

9 World banking on social capital

Introduction

From the previous part of the book, an overall conclusion to be drawn is that social capital is a totally chaotic, ambiguous, and general category that can be used as a notional umbrella for almost any purpose. Its evolution is, however, marked both by "path-dependence" and continuing intellectual context. The general literature on social capital has a dynamic that purportedly promotes interdisciplinarity, particularly between economics and the other social sciences. It is a moot point whether economics is colonising the other social sciences or vice versa. In this chapter, such judgements are applied to the position occupied by social capital in the research and, to a limited extent, the practice, of the World Bank, drawing upon the context laid out in the previous chapter. As established in the following sections, as far as economists are concerned, the economic principles underlying the post-Washington consensus (market imperfections, particularly those based on imperfect and asymmetric information) are being applied to the non-economic or to less traditional areas of application, such as the role of civil society or the conditions conducive to the emergence of a developmental state. In this respect, in part through social capital, economists are gaining a leverage over the subject matter of other disciplines whilst their own economic principles remain unchallenged. On the other hand, it can appear to non-economists that the issues, especially the social, with which they have long been engaged, and which have been so studiously ignored by economists in the past as unimportant or exogenous, are at last being taken seriously.

Within the World Bank, the notion of social capital has its own idiosyncrasies. It is, as suggested, being used by non-economists as an instrument to have themselves taken seriously by economists. In a nutshell, adjustment with a human face, which has been the response in various dimensions to the criticisms of stabilisation and structural adjustment, is being extended from the realm of policy targets to policy analysis. Social capital is good in itself and (can be) good for the economy. This has not, however, led to critical reassessment of the economic policies and analyses themselves beyond those which are already attached to the post-Washington consensus. On the other hand, economists within the World Bank are deploying social capital to complement, not fundamentally to reassess, existing economic prognoses. At the level of policy analysis, greater interventionism in "civil society" is thereby being justified, although this consolidates existing trends in World Bank thinking – get policies implemented by working with and/or around the state.

It would be a serious mistake, however, to overlook the contradictions and tensions involved in the evolution of World Bank thinking around social capital. These include, first, the opposition between the Washington consensus and post-Washington consensus. The latter has opened up a window of opportunity for economists and non-economists alike in challenging the principles and practices of the former consensus. They have not been timid to exploit it. Yet, within the World Bank, there should be no lingering doubts about the hegemony of economics (and the market) and economists over the social and social theorists, respectively. In short, the post-Washington consensus and social capital opens up the limitations attached to mainstream economic thinking only to leave them unresolved. Second, then, there is a tension between economists and non-economists, reflecting potential differences in how the relationship between the economy and society should be understood both analytically and for policy purposes. Third, as already revealed at length in the previous part, social capital is itself a notion riddled with contradictions.

The key (readings) to the missing link?

That the notion of social capital has shot to prominence in the research of the World Bank is reflected in its rise within five years from nowhere to the opening up in late 1998 of a dedicated website, http://worldbank.org/poverty/scapital. It is primarily organised around two themes.[1] One is to specify sources of social capital – families, communities, civil society, public sector, ethnicity, and gender; the other theme is by topic – crime and violence, economics, trade and migration, education, environment, finance, health, nutrition and population, information technology, poverty and economic development, urban development, water supply, and sanitation. Each of these topics is subdivided with a page or two of text, usually including one or more key readings and propositions. That social capital may have a downside is explicitly recognised in many but not all of these accounts. For example, the possibility of pressure towards use of child labour is seen as a consequence of globalisation in the section on economics, trade, and migration but it does not warrant mention in the section on the family (which does, however, view familial obligations as a potential obstacle to freedom of action).

More generally, these pages share the following characteristics. First, they are simplistic and reductionist. Thus, the entry under conflict begins by suggesting that "conflict is the struggle over scarce resources arising over competing goals between two or more parties". The family is seen as the "first building block in the generation of social capital for the larger society". Ethnicity is seen in terms of diversity and difference for which inner organisation and bridging spin-offs have to be set against the potential for conflict. The crucial point is that each of the areas covered under each of the two themes has long, contested, and rich intellectual traditions. These are effectively sacrificed in order to import social capital as an organising concept. It is particularly disturbing, in the context of social capital as elsewhere in World Bank literature, how ethnicity has become reduced to a range of stereotypes.[2]

Second, social capital tends to be seen in terms of two broad effects, each with a positive and a negative side. Intrinsically, it is good but it can be bad if it is improperly used or is exclusive. Extrinsically, it can complement the market but it can also obstruct it. Essentially, social capital is nepotism – you have to use the ones you know but at least you know them! Thus, ethnic entrepreneurs benefit from their close-knit relations of trust but if they breach norms for sound commercial reasons, such as doing business outside the community, they may be punished. Such an analytical framework, of course, has the benefits of a dual either/or content, with the positive or downside effects of social capital, in or out of the market, allowing for both flexibility and balance (or is it discretion?) in analysis and policy advice.

Third, whilst rarely embracing explicitly reactionary positions, the two previous characteristics are highly conducive to romanticised views of the objects of study. The entry under "Social capital can prevent crime and violence" condones disorder by warmly acknowledging that "social capital is a crucial security system. It is not uncommon to witness a parading mass of cheering people who have apprehended a thief. In some cases, they will beat him or her before turning the culprit over to the authorities." In general, the romanticised views of the family, civil society or whatever are positive but they can be negative where corruption and clientelism are concerned. Even more important, though, is what is excluded. The public sector is about good governance based on collaboration with, and decentralisation to, the private sector and civil society. Otherwise politics, trade unions, big business organisations, etc., might just as well not exist.

Fourth, there is nothing in analytical nor policy terms to rock World Bank thinking and practice, especially in light of the post-Washington consensus. There is even a hint of critique of stabilisation and structural adjustment:

> Macroeconomists are recognizing that while open trade can yield many economic benefits to nations, those benefits are not evenly distributed among the populace. The danger is that growth which benefits only a small minority of the population increases inequality and can lead to social disintegration … This in turn ultimately affects the standard of living in a society.

Taken together, however, it is not so much the limited and biased content of these entries that is significant as the scope of intended coverage. Such is confirmed, as previously revealed in Chapter 7, by the database of abstracts of articles that have been provided by the World Bank through its website. The range covered by social capital – by discipline, content, method, etc. – is vast.[3]

According to the World Bank's own definition, often reproduced in different, at times, abbreviated forms:[4]

> The traditional composition of natural capital, physical or produced capital, and human capital needs to be broadened to include social capital. Social capital refers to the internal social and cultural coherence of society, the norms and values that govern interactions among people and the institutions in which they are embedded. Social capital is the glue that holds societies together and without which there can be no economic growth or human well-being. Without social capital, society at large will collapse, and today's world presents some very sad examples of this.

In one important respect, this is already to accept an approach grounded in mainstream economics, for social capital is the ultimate destination for a progression which begins with natural capital and travels via physical and human capital (Grootaert 1997).[5] For the latter, and others that follow, it is the *missing link* (and not an obstructive link) in explaining economic development. This can be understood in two different ways. First, conceptually, the role of capital in economic growth, say, is already presumed to be understood as far as its natural, physical and human components are concerned. They are stocks which aid production and which can either be added to or depleted. Easily overlooked but equally, in a sense, emphasised by the addition of social capital to the analysis, is the presumption that capital in these other senses is non-social. This is a consequence of the physicalist notion of capital that is employed in each of the three non-social variants in the sense that they are perceived in terms of their physical productive properties alone. Insofar as capital, dare I say capitalism, depends upon social relations, these are now separately assigned to the component of social capital. Further, it is even recognised that some sort of social arrangements are essential for the other capitals to be able to function in practice, outside the world of Robinson Crusoe, so that social capital is perceived as the "glue that holds societies together", another favoured World Bank metaphor.

In short, social capital fills out everything that is not already taken care of in terms of standard economic analysis.[6] In principle, it could be anything.[7] For Dixon and Hamilton (1997, p. 3), in the introduction to the volume to which Grootaert has contributed, it is the

> extra element that defines how individuals and societies interact, organize themselves, and share responsibilities and rewards. It is now recognized that social capital is a critical explanatory variable in explaining the success of certain countries and the lack of progress of others. Although there are a number of definitions of social capital available, and a variety of indicators are proposed that can be used to identify and track changes over time, we unfortunately know less about how it is created and how to invest in its development.

Grootaert's article is just one amongst fifteen recommended by the website as "key readings on social capital", listed in alphabetical order. Presumably, these indicate elite ideas and thinkers within the social capital being established. A substantial minority of the authors are or have been employees of the World Bank, and this becomes a substantial majority if fellow travellers of various sorts are added. Further, such association with the World Bank has strengthened over the course of social capital's short life, with few remaining unembroiled in its promotion of the concept. Economists are well represented by Schiff (1992), Knack and Keefer (1997), Robison and Siles (1997), Collier (1998) and Temple (1998), all of which have been discussed in Chapter 7. They treat social capital as an outcome of market imperfections. The core of Grootaert's (1997) article – a chapter in a volume dedicated to indicators of sustainable development (is social capital as social environment being eroded alongside the natural environment?) – is devoted to the economic approach.[8] It can explain, indeed it may need to be measured by, its contribution to the residual in growth accounting. Social capital is understood as like human capital in that it is both input and output but it is attached to groups not individuals. This gives it the flavour of a public good with its dual features of externality and underinvestment, since social exceed private returns. Ultimately, Grootaert offers an extremely wide definition of social capital, adding to the largely informal, local, horizontal, and vertical networks, "the more formalised institutional relationships and structures, such as government, the political regime, the rule of law, the court system, and civil and political liberties", thereby drawing in the conservative economic historian, Douglass North, and political scientist, Mancur Olson, to the analysis of economic development. A number of case studies are also included: the East Asian miracle as institutional arrangements and cooperation; Putnam's study of the role of voluntary associations; the role of a Somalian local warlord in the port city of Boosaaso in 1991 for allowing trade to flourish due to support of clan elders and local people; how the Gujurat conflict between local people and government officials over forest management caused stagnation until communities were mobilised; information sharing through the Grameen bank (and mutual credit for poverty alleviation); Russia as an hour-glass society with many local activities but total distrust of higher level bureaucracy; diamond merchants and the mafia, and so on.

Each of these illustrations is open to dispute, especially whether the application of social capital at best expresses what is already known and at worst conceals it. The more important point, however, is to observe the wide range of applications that are read off from the notion of social capital. Indeed, Grootaert (1997, p. 78) widens the definition of social capital to capture "social structures at large, as well as the ensemble of norms governing interpersonal behavior". In this light, social capital can float free of economic considerations, as is essentially the case for the group of key readings in the Putnamesque vein, including Coleman (1988), Putnam (1993b), Fukuyama (1995), and Portes and Landolt (1996). The last is rare in casting some doubt on the careless use of social capital but that it might be a source of conflict is less well-represented in the key readings.

The economic and non-economic approaches to social capital are brought together in the more or less simple statistical methods used to investigate the impact of social capital, most notably represented in the key reading provided by Narayan and Pritchett (1996).[9] Their study of income differences in Tanzanian villages is based upon a Participatory Poverty Assessment (PPA) of 6,000 people in eighty-seven villages. Data are collected on associations – do you belong to a burial society? for example – and cultural attitudes such as compassion, altruism, respect, and tolerance. These are the elements of social capital and are perceived to be a potential source of higher income for individuals who possess it but, even more important, for inhabitants of villages which possess it irrespective of its individual incidence within the village. If it has a well-supported burial society, everyone benefits – even those who do not belong.

PPAs are the World Bank's way of undertaking surveys so that the poor can supposedly define for themselves what are the key factors in identifying who are the poor and what causes their poverty. This is to be welcomed in principle. But there is one glaring contradiction in the relationship between researcher and the poor in this respect. It is impossible for the researcher not to bring analytical preconceptions to the sample survey, and also to its interpretation. I suspect that none of the poor, in Tanzania or elsewhere, has ever identified the condition to be a consequence of inadequate social capital!

In the event, the study is quite measured in its conclusions. It suggests that there are five mechanisms by which social capital can increase income: horizontal connections inducing more efficient government through better monitoring; cooperation for local problem solving; diffusion of innovations; less imperfect information and lower transaction costs; and informal insurance. It is accepted that these may only affect the level of income and not the growth rate (indicating no formal model relating social capital to income). However, the study only focuses on social capital that is embodied in individuals, leaving aside affiliation to national associations, more general institutional capacity, and cultural attitudes. In addition, some care is taken to establish that the relationship between social capital and income does run in this rather than the opposite direction (which would occur if those who are richer choose to consume more social capital or associational goods). This is done by choosing an instrumental variable to test for the effect of social capital on income, which requires a variable to be chosen which is correlated to social capital but not to income. The choice made is levels of trust external to the village.

Despite its cautions, the headline for the study, which is designed to trail-blaze publicity for social capital, is dramatic. In the preface, Serageldin (1997, p. vii) claims that[10]

> This study provides quantifiable evidence that village-level social capital – membership in groups with particular characteristics – significantly affects household welfare. In one telling statistic the study finds that one standard increase in village-level social capital increases household income per person by 20 to 30 percent. By comparison, a one standard deviation in schooling –

nearly three additional years of education per person – increases incomes by only 4.8 percent.

There are, however, a number of problems with these conclusions which are liable to be characteristic of other studies irrespective of their individual merits, quality of data, etc. First, the results are derived from cross-section analysis alone, by comparing villages at one point in time rather than examining the experience of a village over time. To understand why this might be a problem, consider the following hypothetical circumstances. Suppose that the distribution of income across Tanzanian villages is given as a distribution but that the allocation of winners and losers in terms of higher and lower income does indeed depend upon a corresponding distribution of social capital across the villages. The statistical results reported above will follow. *Ceteris paribus*, a village that increases its social capital will also increase its income. But, by assumption, as the distribution of income is given, this can only be at the expense of some other village. In other words, villages will be jockeying for advantage by laying out more and more resources on social capital without any net gain by assumption of zero sum.[11]

Second, the point in the last paragraph is essentially about the need for a systemic analysis of the role of social capital. In a way, for estimation purposes, this is recognised by the use of the instrumental variable and the presumption that it is independent of income. But is this valid? The problem is that nearly all the variables are liable to be related to one another either in simple or in complex ways. This can only be disentangled by a more inclusive analysis both in terms of exploring the relationships between the variables that are present as well as incorporating the variables that are absent (above village level).

Third, social capital is a peculiar variable and it is almost certainly inappropriate to incorporate it in a standard way into statistical analysis. At very low levels of social capital – when the first two individuals get together to form the first association – there is liable to be negligible impact. At very high levels of social capital, the same problem prevails. One more club or member will add nothing. Indeed, it seems reasonable to argue that in terms of the number of individual social interactions, the level of social capital or its impact will take the form of hysteresis – limited to begin with and rising rapidly before tailing off.[12] It follows that the relationships being estimated are not linear, that standard deviations are not likely to be constant, and that the dramatic impact expected of social capital is unlikely to materialise at the bottom of the distribution if aimed at poverty alleviation (quite apart from any systemic effects discussed in the previous paragraph).

Fourth, following on more or less immediately from the previous point, social capital is liable to be subject to threshold effects – both in its creation and in its impact. This is highly conducive to multiple equilibria, especially poverty traps. Consequently, the statistics may be measuring a correlation between income and social capital created by high and low equilibria.[13] As a result, raising social capital by one standard deviation will not have the proportionate effect for the poor of raising it by ten standard deviations. Bringing many of the previous points together, it becomes necessary to explain the distribution of high and low equilibria as well as the mechanisms by which villages become allocated to them. Significantly, it is often claimed that social capital is marked by a long gestation period in building it up but that it can be destroyed relatively rapidly as it relies on trust, etc. Is it not plausible that random events or shocks, such as poor harvest or disease, might not have generated both distributions of income and social capital through assignment to different equilibria?[14]

In short, projecting to the urban context, such studies seem to be sophisticated ways of saying that if only ghettos could capture the features of other neighbourhoods, they need no longer be ghettos and there need no longer be any ghettos. More generally, the price of a house in a neighbourhood could be higher if only all house prices were higher in that neighbourhood.[15] Exploration of such propositions are not without worth. They tell us about the ways in which gentrification can take place. But they do remain of limited value until they are placed in a wider setting, not least how the housing system as a whole functions. Further, the weaknesses discussed above can be addressed to a greater or lesser extent on a piecemeal basis. Taken together, however, they are liable to be intractable. For it is almost certainly more important to address the social and historical specificities of the case studies involved whether, say, of Tanzania as a whole or of individual villages, than it is to refine the estimation techniques in view of model specification, multicollinearity, omitted variables, multiple equilibria, cross-section as representative of time series, etc.

The Tanzanian study has inspired a cottage industry of imitations and improvements. These range across different countries, utilise more sophisticated statistical techniques, and have prompted further surveys and survey designs where existing data sets are not available or considered suitable.[16] Typically, hundreds of variables are incorporated concerning trust, associational behaviour, and the like. Of necessity, irrespective of their intrinsic merits, the studies either avoid contextual content in both weak and strong senses previously outlined in Chapter 7 or, rarely, incorporate it at the expense of pushing social capital into the background as explanatory variable with comparative or policy implications. A striking illustration of personal interest is provided by Maluccio et al. (1999) in their study of the impact of social capital in South Africa between 1993 and 1998, a period bridging the transition from apartheid to formal political democracy. They find that social capital has effects in the later year but not earlier, and suggest this is due to the removal of many of apartheid's restrictions.

Elsewhere, however, I have argued that South Africa's transition has been heavily marked by economic policies that have been widely recognised to conform to the Washington consensus as the World Bank and IMF gained influence over policy makers in that period (Fine 1999f). More controversial is the idea that this reflects the continuing economic interests of highly concentrated South African corporate capital.[17] It has been primarily concerned to globalise its operations with the lifting of sanctions against South Africa. Consequently, it has limited, if uneven, commitment to a programme of government-led economic and social restructuring, preferring policy to be geared towards reduction of government expenditure and intervention and the lifting of exchange controls. Indeed, in Macroeconomic Research Group (1993), ironically and coincidentally entitled *Making Democracy Work*, I argued that the effect would be disastrous for housing, health and schooling delivery of relying upon the market and treating the economy as if it were financially constrained. Rather, the major constraint on provision of such basic needs was the institutional capacity to deliver, primarily by government, and this more than anything needed to be addressed. Against this background, the status of results concerning the creation and use of social capital must be limited in neglecting the major factors governing economic and social performance.[18]

The three remaining key readings stand out from the rest. Two of them, Evans (1996b) and Ostrom (1996), appear in the same issue, and special section, of *World Development*, edited by Evans (1996a) and have been discussed in Chapter 7. They differ from the other readings in directly addressing the role of the state, albeit in the context of synergy between it and the private sector through the mediation of social capital. Significantly, the inclusion of Ostrom's contribution is at the expense of the others in the collection edited by Evans that are considerably more sophisticated and radical in the way in which they understand social forces and their impact upon the state. In general, as taken up later, the role of the state and of the economy are notable for their absence in the World Bank's world of social capital except as a back-drop to be marginally corrected.

Finally, consider the key reading provided by Woolcock (1998). This is on a different plane from the other contributions, containing a considered and wide-ranging review of the literature on social capital.[19] In doing so, it observes many of its weaknesses, not least that it is chaotic in range and application. Yet, as suggested by the critiques that he himself offers, he does not seem to consider, except in passing, the possibility of rejecting the concept altogether. Rather, he proposes a rationale for the notion by attaching it to ever more detailed theoretical and empirical research (p. 159):

> Where do these criticisms of the idea of social capital ... leave us? Short of dismissing the term altogether, one possible resolution of these concerns may be that there are different types, levels or dimensions of social capital, different performance outcomes associated with different combinations of these dimensions, and different sets of conditions that support or weaken favorable combinations. Unraveling and resolving these issues requires a more dynamic than static understanding of social capital; it invites a more detailed examination of the intellectual history of social capital, and the search for lessons from empirical research that embrace a range of many such dimensions, levels, or conditions.

Whilst as an author of this article he is designated as being at Brown University, Providence, Woolcock soon reappears as the moderator for the World Bank's Email Discussion Group on Social Capital.[20] As will be seen, he is a suitable appointment in view of his warm embrace of the notion despite (or is it because of?) its weaknesses in conjunction with what is essentially an avoidance of economic issues, especially as posed by the economists.

Surfers beware the undercurrents

The World Bank's web has a number of satellites attached to it.[21] One of these is the series of Social Capital Initiative Working Papers. Initially, these comprised six papers, two of which have already been discussed (Grootaert 1997 and Collier 1998). Another (Feldman and Assaf 1998) provides an annotated bibliography of social capital, soon doomed to be outdated. The first two papers in the series, however, cover the twelve successful proposals for funding under the initiative (World Bank 1998a and 1998b). These are extremely diverse, add little of novelty in the analytical and policy arenas other than to impose social capital, often uncomfortably, as an organising concept. Indeed, the proposals are marked by a degree of unanimity in being unable to define social capital satisfactorily and needing to operationalise it during the course of their research.[22]

It is worth pausing to consider a couple of these projects briefly. One, for example, is concerned with the decline in health provision in Russia and how social capital networks might be used as a remedy (Rose 1998, itself a working paper). According to the project proposal (World Bank 1998b, p. 22):[23]

> The research findings will be used to design policy recommendations for the formulation of welfare and health promotion policies, especially regarding the ways in which informal social capital networks add value to policies, or substitute for government programs.

Such goals might be thought to be a little modest for a society of 150 million people which, without precedent, has experienced a fall in the male life expectancy between 1989 and 1995 by as much as six years (Field 1995).[24]

Another project addresses the social capital of those whose lives and livelihoods are impaired by the mining operations of Coal India Limited (CIL). I have no expertise in this area but have consulted both the project proposal (World Bank 1998b) and a number of documents from NGOs and local organisations that have long been in dispute both with the World Bank and CIL over rehabilitation. Suffice it to observe that the two sources represent very different worlds. For the project proposal, the building of social capital will enhance the benefits of rehabilitation through community participation. Over its thirteen pages, there is scarcely a hint of the conflict engendered in the past over the desirability of many of the mining projects in the first place, let alone the roughshod ways in which rehabilitation and participation have previously been handled, as revealed by alternative accounts. At best, we are told that

> The notion of consulting project affected people (PAPs), target communities at large, local state authorities, and NGOs on social and environmental

issues is entirely new to CIL. Moreover, previous interface between the key stakeholders in the mining areas – due partially to issues of power, equity, and access to resources – has not always developed under cooperative terms.

From the alternative perspective, this might be considered more than an understatement, misleading and mutually inconsistent (CIL both new to consultation and facing lack of cooperation). As one commentator has put it:

> The problem seems to be that in micro projects (building a village road) the people are encouraged to decide and implement, but in the wider macro context (issues of future livelihood, legal recognition, land and water control), their opinions are ignored. The Bank, government and CIL are selective as to when/on what terms they will give participation. It is they who claim power to decide. Thus, in the context of macro projects (and people's economic dispossession, felt helplessness), the micro-project participation is largely irrelevant. Everybody, from top company management to village simpleton, knows this.

Further, the Berne Declaration (1998) document reports as follows:

> Participants of the March 1995 workshop complained that no representatives of project-affected people were able to attend, and that such consultations must rather take place in the project areas proper. The responsible Bank representative claims that the consultation process was as inclusive as possible, and that no groups were purposely excluded. Affected NGOs do not agree. The report of the March 1995 workshop lists one group which was excluded because it was "too radical". At least three other grassroots groups reported to Northern NGOs that they had never been consulted and that their letters to Coal India and the World Bank had never been answered, although they had worked with people affected by coal mines for many years. Two of them, the Jharkhand Janadhikar Manch (JJM) and the Chotanagpur Adivasi Sewa Simiti (CASS) from Bihar, prepared detailed, state-of-the-art critiques of Coal India's resettlement and rehabilitation policy and of the new Bank projects.

In short, if we are to allow the term, it would appear that there is no shortage of social capital in this sector. The kindest interpretation of the project to promote more and better social capital might be to suggest a wish to wipe a dirty slate clean; the unkindest interpretation would be one of cynical disregard for the past and the wish to promote "social capital" of the right type to filter and minimise opposition to predetermined coal projects. Further, despite its popular rhetoric, social capital can also be seen as a potential means of formalising and institutionalising participation, the better to be able to centralise and control it!

Such conclusions are essentially consistent with those drawn by Pantelic and Pantoja (1999) which have responsibility for assessing the Coal project for the

World Bank. The opportunity is seized to take a broad view. The wide range of application and celebration of social capital is acknowledged and, yet, " 'What is social capital?' has not yet been satisfactorily answered."[25] A pragmatic approach is needed, "on how social capital works, which forms does it take under which circumstances and cultures, and how is it produced". From this point, everything is thrown in,[26] requiring incorporation of power relations as part of social exchange, how social capital is created, destroyed, recreated, dynamic, subject to cycles of conflict, etc., with capacity to implode or explode. The descriptive background to the case study effectively makes no reference to social capital other than for the need of Coal India to address social issues. Social capital embodies a tension between the social and the individual, and must be contextual, relational, and structural rather than universal and ahistorical – hence undermining longitudinal measurement, with explicit reference to Edwards and Foley (1998). Trust is made of many different types, with problems deciphering cause and effect in its relationship to civicness and community, problems of cause and effect, what it is rather than what it does. At the end of the day is the general conclusion that it is necessary to examine social capital in terms of what and for whom. The more specific, and brave, implication is to highlight the conundrum that engendering efficiency in rehabilitation may lead to intra- and inter-community social capital that, quite apart from jockeying for advantage if operations proceed, may oppose a project altogether:

> In fact the notion of building bridges among … and between … villages was perceived by many mine representatives as counterproductive and as a threat for the smooth operations of the mines.

Surely, such a conclusion should be the starting point for uncovering underlying economic and political interests and how they are represented, rather than closing point for an artificially imposed account based on social capital?

By the end of 2000, to return to the working papers, even leaving aside those that have already been discussed above or elsewhere in the book, the twenty or more working papers represent a mixed bunch of contributions, reflecting the scope and chaos surrounding social capital. A sub-group made up of Isham et al. (1999), Kähkönen (1999), and Krishna and Uphoff (1999) address issues concerning water delivery. These, along with Krishna and Shrader (1999), place considerable emphasis on the contextual significance of social capital, ranging over how trust is understood and recognised to the ways of dealing with errant children and common pastures. On the other hand, a number of the other papers use social capital in the narrowest of technical senses – how to overcome contractual or informational problems, as in van Bastelaer (1999) on how social capital can be used to monitor credit to the poor and Fafchamps and Minten (1999) on networks for this as well as the sharing of price information and quality amongst traders.[27] They, along with Paldman and Svendsen (1999), who see social capital metaphorically as an analytical smoke condenser, even deploy social capital as a variable in a production function.[28]

Not quite attaining the status of working papers are "Papers in Progress", most of which have already been discussed. They are complemented by a website for social capital surveys and measurement tools, comprising Narayan (1998), Sudarsky (1999), and Szabo (1999) at time of writing. These together with other studies, such as Krishna and Shrader (1999)[29] and R. Rose (1999), reveal a bewildering array of variables, garnered from household surveys, for the construction of social capital. Sudarsky (1999), for example, deploys ten dimensions and sixty-nine variables for social capital, and Narayan (1998) a questionnaire addressing fourteen types of groups and networks and eighty-seven questions overall. In effect, this is household surveys in search of a theory and vice versa!

Another satellite is the Email Discussion Group on Social Capital. Like any internet discussion forum it contains much that is dross. But it does also include some gems. The overall impression is one of confusion and ambiguity around what social capital is and how it should be measured. As is accepted by the moderator, Michael Woolcock, in the first posting:

> While social capital conforms imperfectly to standard economic forms of capital such as real estate, it nonetheless serves as a very useful *metaphor* for facilitating discussions across disciplinary, sectoral, and regional lines. The idea of "human capital" (education and training) suffers from similar problems, but from shaky beginnings in the early 1960s has become enormously helpful in terms of getting these substantive issues taken into consideration at the highest levels of theory, research and policy. One hopes that social capital, though inherently less concrete, will come to occupy a similar place in "mainstream" discussions somewhere down the line.

In the second issue, Voth comments that the ideas underlying social capital have long been known to sociology but that the current usage is oversimplifying social theory by generalising its application. As Woolcock responds:

> Several critics, not without justification, have voiced their concern that collapsing an entire discipline into a single variable (especially one with such economic overtones) is a travesty, but there are others that are pleased that mainstream sociological ideas are finally being given their due at the highest levels. For them, the term "social capital" is as much good marketing as it is pragmatic theory! I tend to side with those in the latter camp, while endorsing ... that serious students should commit themselves to mastering the broader literature.

In short, analytical integrity can be traded off with influence at the highest levels whatever that might be![30]

In the eighth issue, without moderator response, Legge accepts that social capital is a metaphor but he adds:

> Clearly the metaphor has rhetorical value and this seems to be the main

> reason for its recent ascendancy ... even here the question of usefulness needs to be asked. Opponents of the neo-liberal hegemony seek to use the term "social capital" as a way of exercising leverage in policy debates dominated by neo-liberal frameworks ... There is a discussion to be had here about the politics of the emergence, migration and use of this term.

This issue will be taken up in the concluding remarks and closing chapter. Before that, as discussed in Chapter 7, observe how the notion of social capital as metaphor recurs in view of its scope and ambiguity.[31] Of course, some of the metaphors have been derived to a greater or lesser extent from analytical discourse, as with externalities, trust, and networks, etc. In this respect, the biggest metaphor of all is that of "social" "capital", neither term of which tends to be adequately understood. Further, it must be wondered how a bunch of metaphors can be the key to the missing element in development. It is worth recalling the metaphor of social capital as the source of a healthy society for, within the medical profession, ignorance is veiled or revealed – depending on which way you look at it – by a doctor's diagnosis as idiopathic – we do not know.[32]

Concluding remarks

In brief, what place does social capital occupy and is it likely to occupy in the Catholic post-Washington displacement of the Lutheran Washington consensus?[33] I can begin by confessing two errors of judgement or, more exactly, prediction. Fine (1999b, p. 11) suggests that because mainstream economists depend heavily upon formal models, the vague notions attached to social capital would essentially restrict its use for them to market imperfections and social interaction as individual interactions. This is correct, but I was also of the view, less explicitly stated, that such considerations would discourage Stiglitz himself, as leading post-Washington pioneer, from employing the term. This, in a sense, was an acknowledgement of his intellectual integrity and continuing reliance upon his own instincts as a mathematical economist.[34]

I was shown to be wrong before the mentioned piece could be published. In his Prebisch Lecture, Stiglitz (1998b) devotes a section to social capital that is indistinguishable in use from the vague informalities that are so bountiful in other hands.[35] There are four disturbing implications. First, whatever the merits of Stiglitz's information-theoretic economics, he has headed a critique of the Washington consensus from an independent, analytical perspective. His adoption of social capital is just one piece of evidence amongst much more, that he was being co-opted to be more diplomatic and less wide-ranging in pursuing the implications of his challenge to the old consensus.[36] As discussed below, however, and to his credit, with his early resignation from the World Bank in November 1999, Stiglitz had obviously not moved far and fast enough.

Second, as is evident in Stiglitz's Prebisch speech and other World Bank publications that draw upon the post-Washington consensus, the colonisation of the non-economic by the economists is a severe setback to development studies, with key topics such as industrialisation, gender, and ethnicity being heavily stripped of their empirical and intellectual traditions. As in the World Development Report on knowledge, for example, the procedure is one of economic reductionism to the information-theoretic, and otherwise leaving the non-reducible in a state of chaotic and fragmentary disorganisation.[37]

Third, and as a corollary, the form taken in the post-Washington consensus by the economic colonisation of the social sciences is extremely one-sided. There is an appropriation of the social by the economic but not vice versa. In other words, whilst economic analysis and economists have been granted a broader remit, the relationship is not reciprocated. This perhaps explains what is often disappointment outside the World Bank with, and even suspicion of, Stiglitz's policy perspectives, many of which remain little changed from those of the Washington consensus. On the other hand, the non-economists within the Bank can delude themselves that they are being taken more seriously as the economists encroach upon their territory.

Fourth, during the 1980s, as the deleterious effects of the Washington consensus were recognised in both the economic and social arenas, adjustment with a human face represented the World Bank's response to the iatrogenic consequences of its policies for poverty, gender, the environment, etc. These factors were incorporated, however fully, centrally and genuinely, into the portfolio of policy objectives. With the post-Washington consensus embracing social capital, a further step is taken in that these factors become incorporated analytically, albeit on a limited basis. Social objectives increasingly become an instrument as well as a target in the hands of the economists.[38] In addition, as Budlender and Dube (1998) have recognised, social capital forms part of a broader initiative to humanise the World Bank, incorporating the care economy, national accounts from a gender perspective, intra-household resource allocation, and sustainability, etc.

This all leads to my second error – the presumption that social capital would provide the conceptually limited basis on which the post-Washington consensus would both address issues around the developmental state and side step the existing literature. As is evident from the work of Peter Evans, such an assessment is correct in the wider debate around social capital. But, despite the inclusion of one of his pieces as a key reading, both the economic and the state are being excluded from the World Bank's treatment of social capital.[39] In other words, economists are allowed, under the rubric of social capital, to address issues from which they have previously been excluded but non-economists do not address either the economic or the state. This in sharp contrast to the hopes expressed by Woolcock (1998, p. 186, my emphasis) for social capital:[40]

> The challenge for development theorists and policy-makers alike is to identify the mechanisms that will create, nurture, and sustain the types and combinations of social relationships conducive to building dynamic participatory societies, sustainable equitable economies, and *accountable developmental states*.

What is the evidence for this assessment of exclusion of the developmental state from the orbit of social capital? It is glaringly obvious from the structure and content of the World Bank's social capital website. The programme is situated inside the Division for Environmentally and Socially Sustainable Development.[41] From the perspective of non-economists, social capital has been allowed an almost unlimited free rein as long as not breaching the borders of the economy and the state.[42] The economists' perspective is unambiguously laid out by Collier (1998), staking out a protected traditional territory that belongs to economics, which then both defines what is non-economic, civil society, and how it should be understood – an unintended externality that is not otherwise internalised by selective interactions between government, firm, or household:

> Putnam has an excellent reason to chose [sic] a form of social interaction in which the internalisation of an externality was indeed incidental to the purpose of association. This is because in civil society the vast majority of social interactions which internalise externalities are like this. There are three major exceptions: social interactions which are obviously purpose-designed for internalising externalities. The first of these is government, which can be regarded as an arrangement for overcoming many of the problems of collective action ... The second is the firm: within the firm resources are allocated partly by non-market processes and this permits internalisation of externalities. The third is the household: within the household resources are allocated by non-market processes which internalise externalities. However, it is generally sensible to work with a concept of civil social capital which excludes the activities of government, the internal organisation of the firm, and the internal organisation of the household, partly because we already have a huge corpus of work on them, and partly because they are so different from other social interactions. I will refer to the social interactions which exclude the organisation of government and the internal organisation of the firm and the household as "civil society". Civil society thus includes the interaction of households, the interaction of firms, and the interaction between households and firms.

This is, of course, a remarkable, speculative understanding of civil society – let alone the household, firm and government – based on an uncritical extension of neoclassical economics without reference to a vast literature on the meanings of these terms and whether it is analytically appropriate to construct society and social interaction in this fashion. There is also a presumption of independence between the various issues that are split off for separate consideration.

Not all those contributing from within and around the World Bank have been so rigid and limited in their understanding of social capital as some of its economists. This is especially so with some recognition of the mounting burden the concept has been required to carry with its widening scope of application. Bebbington, in Chapter 7, has already been recognised as deploying social capital as appropriate only when inclusive of all relevant social aspects including conflict and context. Narayan and Woolcock in their various contributions can be seen to have responded by way of compromise, both in the inputs and outputs attached to social capital and in focus of attention.[43]

Thus, Narayan (1999a and 1999b), for example, essentially acknowledges the difficulties in the definition of social capital by accepting that societies are built up from social groups and not individuals, that it is required for social cohesion, stability, and welfare, that it involves (following Sen) tensions between social and individual capabilities, but can lead both to social exclusion and civic engagement. In this vein, social capital is understood as relational, with Portes (1998) quoted to the effect that "to possess social capital, a person must be related to others". Yet, the notion is seen as clarified by the suggestion that "social capital is defined as the norms and social relations embedded in the social structures of society that enable people to co-ordinate action and to achieve desired goals", thus rendering it both relational and functional and residing somewhere between the individual and the social (understood as interactions?)! On this basis, social capital is perceived to have effects on a "broad range of outcomes from education to income, to health, to performance of firms, to collective action at the community level". But outcomes depend upon state embeddedness, autonomy, and community participation. Civil society is also important "as the space that exists between the family and the state", with each apparently constituted independently of another. However, this unmistakable process of throwing almost everything into the social capital net is complemented by the process of recomposition of what has been a previous disaggregation across the multifarious factors concerned to give rise to what might have been acknowledged as middle-range theory.[44] Social capital is perceived to be of two broad types, bonding within groups and bridging between them.[45] This itself presumes well-identified groups for intra- or inter-action and, of course, the different types of social capital might cut across these even if they could be well defined and identified. Bonding by ethnicity might be bridging by gender and so on. The messiness of social capital, as it has evolved, cannot be resolved by such intermediate categorisations.

Social capital is also seen as either broadly complementary to the state, where both are working well or, otherwise, as a substitute for it. In other words, we have good or bad states, good or bad social capital, and four corresponding regimes, with development understood as good state, social capital, and complementarity between the two. In this way, Woolcock and Narayan (2000) take the middle-range approach further, suggesting there have been four broad approaches to social capital: communitarian (focusing horizontally on associations), networks (as horizontal in the form of bridging and bonding, good and bad, and with heavy reliance upon Granovetter), institutional (good governance), and synergy (horizontal and vertical or linking in which the state is important). Their preference is for the latter and they advise that analysis of social capital needs to "identify the nature and extent of the social relationships characterizing a particular community, its formal institutions, and the interaction between them". However, despite such postures, as well as the claim that social capital provides for interdisciplinarity, especially the bridging between economics and sociology, two continuing features stand out. These are the complete neglect of economics and the failure, apart from vague reference to values, to contextualise social capital in the stronger sense outlined in Chapter 7. This is paradoxical given Narayan's long-standing commitment to, and study of, popular participation.[46] Indeed, there is a remarkable slippage in their work as a result of these omissions. On the one hand, the potential for conflict and the potential downside of social capital is fully recognised in abstract definitional discussion. But, this tends to be set aside or to be taken as a policy objective to be tempered. This is to promote development as social capital is defined as the norms and networks that allow people to act collectively, with full and fair participation by all concerned to yield positive interaction. In short, echoing Coleman's search for a perfect society in a world of market imperfections, as discussed in Chapter 5, once departing the definition of social capital, the economic, the contextual, the downside, conflict, and power, their text reads like a libertarian version of (im)perfect market socialism![47]

Where, however, does this leave the concept of social capital? There are those who argue that it, as part of the post-Washington consensus more generally, opens up a more progressive analytical and policy agenda, despite the conceptual shortcomings, many of which are recognised. Such seems to be the position adopted by Woolcock, now within the World Bank, but it is an extremely common position more generally. However, as was raised in the Email Discussion Group on Social Capital, the emergence and evolution of social capital is highly intellectually politicised. A case could be made that it provides a framework for combating economism in the social sciences more generally. I doubt such an outcome will come to fruition unless at the expense of a proper economic analysis within social theory. The prospects for engaging successfully with the World Bank on an agreed analytical terrain of social capital are even more bleak, with co-option rather than criticism the most likely result. Just as economics is colonising the social sciences, so the post-Washington consensus incorporates the dissent against its neo-liberal predecessor, and social capital colonises social theory. Social scientists are struggling for status within the World Bank and believe they have won some through engaging with economists over social capital.[48] Whatever the realism of their sense of achievement, it is not the basis on which to revitalise development studies in the wake of the Washington consensus.

For, returning to the metaphors of "missing link" and "social glue", they do symbolise perfectly the compromise and limited terrain of engagement between economists and social scientists within the World Bank. For both agree that the economics has failed so that they need to supplement the economic with the social. This is the concession of the economists, even if the modus vivendi of the non-economists. Thus, economists seek to incorporate the social, non-economists to have it taken seriously. Nor is this simply an intellectual exercise in coming to terms with one another. For, there is a tacit understanding over policy. Economists despair that their economic engineering, otherwise known as structural adjustment and stabilisation, has faltered because of lack of attention to the social; the non-economists hold out the prospect of social engineering to complement economic policy and interventions. Consequently, the paucity of the World Bank's *economic* analysis remains unchallenged not least because it has opened what is perceived to be an opportunity for non-economists.[49] The latter are scarcely going to offend in light of the door that has been opened to them, although it has arguably been opened by the push from the other side as opposed to their pull. Analytically, it is not the glue and missing link that need to be critically addressed but the economics of the post-Washington consensus itself. Neither economists nor non-economists need enter this highly loaded analytical terrain being established around social capital in the context of the post-Washington consensus. To do so would be to consolidate and legitimise the knowledge bank of the World Bank, whether as the hired mercenaries or unpaid foot soldiers in other people's battles.

The pertinence of this commentary is highlighted, some might even say contested, by the early departure through resignation of Joe Stiglitz as Chief Economist at the World Bank, announced at the turn of the millennium. Press speculation concerned whether he jumped or whether he was pushed. Significantly, there were even suggestions that he was told to keep silent or resign, especially over Russian privatisation and the handling of the East Asian crisis. It was observed that World Bank President, James Wolfensohn, had fully and openly supported him but for one public rebuke a month or so earlier. This had been over Stiglitz's criticism of the IMF for its premature programme of Russian privatisation, not for being wrong but because of the unfair benefits of hindsight. It was rumoured that Wolfensohn's reappointment was dependent upon Stiglitz's de facto dismissal if the latter would not temper his criticisms of the Washington institutions. But there can be no doubt that Stiglitz had no such intention, as was increasingly clear in his speeches and publications and, most recently, in articles in the then latest issues of both the *Oxford Review of Economic Policy* and the *Economic Journal*. He had pressed explicitly and concretely for alternative policies, in advance, especially for East Asia where, for example, traditional IMF stabilisation policy of raising real interest rates was advised correctly to be likely to have the effect of worsening recession.[50]

One plausible implication to draw from this is that the post-Washington consensus has failed, as symbolised by Stiglitz's forced departure. World Bank research is, indeed, simply rhetoric and, if it gets out of hand, is effectively curbed. There is some element of truth in this but the situation is more complicated, even leaving aside whatever new Washington research paradigm, if any, awaits us. First, Stiglitz's integrity in sticking to the implications of the post-Washington consensus as he sees them can only have reinforced its influence in the wider development community. Second, by the same token, irrespective of the fate of the World Bank's social capitalists, the same applies to social capital. There is a sense in which credibility and kudos are obtained simply by virtue of being in opposition to the Washington institutions. Further, a striking aspect of commentary on Stiglitz's departure is that it is almost entirely free of substantive criticism. For it seems impossible in principle for most to disagree that there are market imperfections, that these might be due to informational asymmetries, and that they can have important implications in practice. Such Stiglitz-speak has become part and parcel of the development rhetoric within both Washington institutions.[51] Stiglitz did not have to go because he was theoretically wrong – only that he took his theory too far in criticising his Washington colleagues.[52] As a result, the post-Washington consensus reigns analytically, and it is simply a matter of debating the incidence of market imperfections and whether the state has the capability of improving upon the market.

In short, whether Stiglitz has succeeded in consolidating the post-Washington consensus within the World Bank other than as providing a more user-friendly rhetoric, his brief reign and precipitous departure have done much to strengthen its external appeal and to set the terms of debate over development. But, finally, and most important, if Stiglitz has proven incapable of shifting economic policies on the basis of economic arguments, the same must surely be doubly so of social theorists marching under the banner of social capital. In general, they have only sought to civilise economists by encouraging them to incorporate social factors with results that are liable to consolidate rather than undermine an economic reductionism of the social to market imperfections.

10 Measuring social capital – how long is a missing link?

Introduction

As is already apparent from the last chapter, there has been some focus in the literature on the issue of how to measure social capital. This is due to the vagueness and variety of the ways in which it has been defined, dependence upon qualitative variables, such as degree of trust and civil association and participation, the lack of availability of standard surveys for social capital, and the wish to obtain an aggregate measure for statistical purposes. The purpose of this chapter is to set many of these difficulties aside in order to examine the measurement of social capital as a theoretical object. Without undertaking such an exercise, the what and how of measurement will remain obscure, a weakness that will itself tend to be concealed by the attendant difficulties of operationalising any measurement technique in practice.[1] Although the content of this chapter was conceived prior to consulting the World Bank's Email Discussion Group on Social Capital, it can be seen as a response to the question posed by the Group's then moderator, Michael Woolcock, in issue number 6:[2]

> We need to begin with a conceptual framework that incorporates different dimensions of social capital, and that recognizes that certain dimensions in combination with others may lead to a range of outcomes, from anarchy and violence to cooperation and prosperity. This implies that a single number or index of social capital is highly problematic, especially when applied across different nations. Still, I can't imagine this basic problem is unique to social capital: can an economist share with us how they deal with these issues when measuring other "capitals"?

It seems remarkable that the concept of social capital, and associated empirical studies, should have progressed so far, even if in a short time, without these issues having been satisfactorily addressed. Neglect of previous treatments of measurement problems is startling, especially given the proclivity of the social capital literature to have plundered previous theoretical literature under its new-found terminological banner.

In short, Woolcock is correct in his intuitions that a single index of social capital is liable to be unacceptable and that this result can be retrieved from well-established and well-known literature in economics. Whilst economists have not been shy to contribute to, even to attempt to dominate, the social capital literature, these problems have not been shared with fellow social capitalists. To a large extent, this is because they have been set aside within economics itself despite their devastating implications even on the much narrower analytical and empirical terrain on which it operates. In each of the following three sections, different ways in which economics has handled problems akin to the measurement of social capital are presented and, with the exception of the final illustration, deeply pessimistic conclusions are drawn. On the more positive side, the last example draws conclusions about how social capital can be measured in principle. This, however, and not surprisingly, depends upon setting aside the contextual content of social capital. Consequently, by referring to yet another set of literature – that on consumption in which the meaning of objects has been especially prominent outside of economics – it leads to a penultimate section which questions the entire intellectual enterprise attached to social capital. A final section draws out some wider implications.

Social capital as utility

One of the problems in measuring social capital is that it involves many individuals, in many activities, and many attitudes. Begin by assuming that all individuals are the same and that all individual activities and attitudes are equivalent to one another. Then, measurement is very easy. We simply count up the number of interactions between individuals. It is possible to go a little further by relaxing the underlying assumptions, if only slightly. If designated interactions are always equivalent to one another in some fixed proportion (or in a linear function like conversion of Fahrenheit to centigrade) and such proportions are consistent with one another, then measurement remains unproblematic. Belonging to a bowling club is worth twice trusting your neighbour, is worth three times but opposite to belonging to a criminal gang (negative social capital) which, in turn, is minus one sixth of belonging to the bowling club. The only issue is in what units to measure social capital – in Mafiosi or neighbours? This is, however, simply a matter of scale and origin.

Of course problems arise when we abandon these simple assumptions (which would, presumably, render both analysis and policy extremely simple). Focus on a single individual, r, who has interaction with individual s, and designate this as k_{rs}. Assume now that the intensity of the only available activity can vary and differs according to interactive partner, s.[3] For the individual, the situation is completely described by the vector $k^r = (k_{r1}, k_{r2}, ..., k_{rt})$, where society comprises t people. How do we measure social capital for the rth individual?

This problem is startlingly familiar to economists – the derivation of a measure from a vector space such as that defined by vectors, k. The two most common forms are for utility functions, $u(.)$, which convert the vector k of consumption goods (and even bads such as labour and pollution) to utility, and for production functions, $f(.)$, which convert a vector of productive inputs into output. As social capital is not a well-defined output with its own measure, the appropriate analogy is with utility functions. It works perfectly.

Consider first the problem of measurement for a single, lone individual, $m(k)$. All that is required is an ordering of the vectors, k, incorporating the only property so far available, non-satiation in consumer theory, that more of any (positive) element of social capital means more overall. In general, economics has presumed the existence of utility functions with corresponding indifference curves to represent the ordering of the vectors, k. Indifference curves in the context of social capital would be different combinations of interactions which are equivalent to one another. However, as is well known, such utility or measurement functions, if they exist, are only unique up to monotonic scale. All we can say is that we have more or less social capital; we cannot say how much we have in absolute terms. If $m(k)$ is a measure, so is $n(m(k))$ for any monotonic function $n(.)$. In other words, the measure of social capital can only be ordinal.

There are four further points. First, to go from the measurement function to the individual ordering is the wrong way round. The function represents an ordering of social capitals that is already given. Second, such a representation does not necessarily exist. There is no measure, $m(k)$, if the underlying ordering is not what is known as continuous. Continuity excludes what are known as lexicographical orderings, where indefinitely large connections with one (lowly) individual, b, cannot compensate for lack of the tiniest of connections with elite individual, a.[4] Lexicographical orderings can be justified in the context of (conspicuous, say) consumption, but they are, presumably, to be found commonly in the world of social capital, as social interaction is subject to strict hierarchies and exclusions. Third, both in theoretical and empirical work, it is commonplace to set these issues aside and to presume that the individual's underlying preferences over goods k are, indeed, represented by a single utility function, u. Such is evident from casual glance at both elementary texts and frontier research. This may not matter if the application only depends upon the ordinal measurement implicit in the utility function chosen. But, if the measure is set against any others, it will make a difference since results would be different had the ordinal measure been represented by any one of the infinity of other monotonic measures available. Fourth, it is embarrassing to set out these results to any fellow economist who might be passing by since they are standard textbook stuff at graduate level or below.

These problems arise out of measurement for a single individual. They are worsened for a society of individuals let alone for comparisons across societies. So now throw in a "society" of individuals with interactions.[5] We now require a measure, M, over the vectors of individual social capitals, k^1, k^2, ... k^t. Again the parallel with a well-known problem in economics is immediate. $M(k^1, k^2, ... k^t)$ corresponds to a social welfare function, either on the vectors of goods k^r for all individuals r or, if preferred, by assuming individual social capitals are sufficiently independent of one another, on the vector of individual social capital measurements – for which difficulties have already been highlighted – $M(m_1(k^1), m_2(k^2), ... m_t(k^t))$. Once again, whilst there is a well-established literature on social welfare functions, its implications tend to be set aside as economists simply assume that the state is like an individual with its own welfare function which it pursues on behalf of society. Technically, however, there are two fundamental issues in traversing the path from individual to total social capital. One is how to cardinalise (give a measure to) the individual social capitals in order that they can be set against one another. The other is, having done this, how to make interpersonal comparisons between individuals – how much does my social capital count relative to yours?[6] A slightly different approach to these problems is to be found in a branch of mathematical economics, social choice theory, and its implications will be taken up in the section after next.

In short, there are very serious problems of aggregation and interpersonal comparison in measuring social capital. The total in physical terms – number of associations, etc. – may be measured differently according to what they are, who has them, and how they are distributed. It should be emphasised that these problems arise irrespective of the way in which the measure is to be used. In general, either theoretically or empirically, use is directed towards explaining economic or other outcomes on the basis of some individual, social, or intermediate measure of social capital. Parallels with applied economics, consumer demand in particular, follow immediately in light of the above. For utility functions have been the basis on which to estimate or predict demand. Similarly, social capital interacts with resources to give outcomes. In this area, problems of aggregation are well known – except under very special assumption, demand will depend upon distribution and interpersonal differences. Treating the different components of social capital as if independent of one another requires very special assumptions (as if food demand is to be independent of that for clothing). In addition, whether at the aggregate level or through methods pitched at the household level, theory and estimation techniques have become extremely complex and sophisticated.[7] Whilst social capitalists are providing the survey material to exploit such methods, there seems little awareness of them.

What is social CAPITAL?

In the World Bank's Email Discussion Group on Social Capital (no 5), Professor Varshney offers the following comment:[8]

> While thinking about the measurement of social capital, would it make sense to read the old two-Cambridge debate over how to measure "physical capital"? It was, if I recall correctly, a debate between Joan Robinson and Robert Solow, the former arguing that there was no theoretically defensible way of measuring capital stock, the latter that the problems were serious, but it could still be done. I speak from memory, but at least we have an earlier attempt by two of the formidable minds of political economy, one of whom went on to win the Nobel Prize (Solow) and the other taught Nobel Prize winners (Robinson taught Sen, for example). There may be something

there which may be of great potential use. It might save us from re-inventing the wheel.

This is the moderator's response:

> Indeed. Perhaps one of our readers can give us – or direct us to – a primer on this and other major measurement debates in the social spheres. I'm sure there are multiple "lessons from history" to be drawn here.

There are lessons to be learnt although, once again, it is disturbing that so much attention should have been devoted to social capital before they have been acknowledged.

The Cambridge capital controversy or critique has a number of different elements and purposes whose connections to one another are complex. Both theoretical and empirical issues are involved.[9] In general terms, the problem is one of how valid is a model of the economy in which it is assumed that there is just one good that serves as both capital and consumption. Not surprisingly, the answer is that the results of such a model do not carry over and hold in models with more than one good.[10] More specifically, it becomes impossible to define capital as a physical quantity or, by some other measure, as the basis for determining levels of output or distribution between capital and labour. Even on restrictive assumptions like given technology, given preferences, full employment, and perfect competition, capital cannot legitimately be measured and then used to explain or even measure consequential economic outcomes. Simple results like an inverse relationship between capital-intensity and the rate of profit do not follow, nor even necessarily a positive relationship between output and per capita capital-intensity. The problem is that, once we have more than one good, say even just one for capital and one for consumption, then the measurement of capital for economic purposes (if not physically) depends upon the relative evaluation of the two goods. The economic value of capital depends not only on its physical quantity but how the provision of a stream of consumption over time is evaluated.[11]

What is the relevance of this to the measurement of social capital? First, there is no problem in principle in measuring social capital as long as it is quantifiable in some form or other although – as already discussed and taken up again below – such measurements may not be able to embody all the properties that are desired. Second, the problems almost certainly do arise when that measurement is used to explain economic and social outcomes. It is very easy to see why. Suppose that social capital does require some resources to create or preserve it. Then, presumably, we need to net out those resources prior to measuring the overall level of social capital. To do this we need to evaluate the resources used. Unless they are physically measurable against, or equivalent to, social capital itself, we need to know the economic effects of social capital on that evaluation in order to measure social capital. We are caught in an unbreakable loop. We need to know economic outcomes to measure social capital in order to account for the effects of social capital on economic outcomes that we have already assumed.[12]

Two important implications can be drawn from this debate. First, whilst the results of the Cambridge critique are both well established and well known despite drawing resistance from mainstream economists, they have effectively been ignored to suit pursuit of theoretical and empirical work. Acknowledgement of the critique was at its height in the early 1970s. With the decline of radical political economy, it might just as well not exist today.[13] Indeed, the one area in which the critique is particularly germane, and which inspired its emergence, is that of growth theory (and measurement, etc.). This has blossomed within the mainstream as new (endogenous) growth theory over the last decade or so, more or less oblivious to the destructive implications of the Cambridge critique. In addition, despite being invalid within its own domain, such growth theory has been instinctively extended to be applied to social capital, as in Knack and Keefer (1997) and Temple (1998), for example. In short, whilst lessons are to be learnt from the Cambridge critique of capital theory for the measurement of social capital, the first lesson is that mainstream economics is not likely to be at the forefront of that teaching!

Second, the simple analytical conclusion to draw from the Cambridge critique, irrespective of the method or theory within which it is incorporated, is that social capital, if the notion is to be used, must be understood within a framework of both cause and effect. The factors that are associated with social capital do have economic and social effects. These, in turn, influence the creation of social capital. The two processes are not liable to be independent of one another. How their interaction is to be studied is another matter which is addressed after the following section.[14]

Social capital as social choice[15]

Consider a society of three people, A, B, and C, with three clubs to which they can potentially belong, X, Y, and Z. A ranks the clubs in order of preference, X, Y, Z; B ranks them as Y, Z, X; and C ranks them as Z, X, Y. Now suppose we are comparing states of the world which only have one club. Which of these would incorporate more social capital? Compare X and Y. Both A and C rank X higher than Y. It seems reasonable, other things equal, that social capital with club X is higher than for club Y. However, by the same logic, it follows that social capital for Y is higher than for Z, and social capital for Z is higher than for X!

We are caught in what is known as the voting paradox from which three implications follow. First, measurement of social capital can be constructed as equivalent to social choice theory which commands a substantial literature within economics. Individual social interactions can be construed in terms of their implicit preferences over different states of the world. The measurement or ranking of social capital requires that a social ordering be realised out of the configuration of individual orderings. Second, to some extent in contrast to the approaches in the previous sections, social choice theory proceeds from an axiomatic approach. What properties would we like the ordering of social capital to satisfy – that it should respond positively, for example, to the preferences and/or actions of individuals? Third, with the voting paradox as a special case, the heavy hand of Arrow's Impossibility Theorem hangs over social choice theory.[16] In effect, the failure of majority rule to resolve the voting paradox is representative. Apparently, extremely reasonable conditions on constructing an ordering of alternatives out of the configuration of individual orderings cannot be satisfied. Social choice and, by implication, orderings of social capital are impossible.

Once again, the reaction of economists to such measurement problems is instructive. If acknowledging the problem, most accept that social choice has been shown to be ethically impossible but shrug shoulders and proceed. Unfortunately, a more detailed knowledge of the literature tends to be confined to its participants. In this context, Arrow's Impossibility does not loom so large. Suppose, for example, that the voting paradox is unlikely because rankings of clubs are liable to conform to one another, then the impossibility result can fail.[17] More generally, if the factors attached to social capital tend to be correlated with one another, then a trap may not necessarily lie in wait in its measurement.

More important from the perspective of my own work has been the rejection of the axiom of independence of irrelevant alternatives.[18] In the voting paradox, this axiom allows the comparisons to be made on a pair-wise basis, X with Y irrespective of the placement of Z, followed by Y with Z irrespective of the placement of X, and Z with X ... This leads to the cyclical outcome of the voting paradox. However, casual inspection of the overall configuration of preferences reveals a complete symmetry between individuals, clubs, and their interaction. In the absence of any other criteria concerning the specificity of the clubs or individuals, it is obvious that any measurement of social capital should treat each club as equivalent as social choice or capital.

On this basis, it is possible not only to resolve Arrow's Impossibility but also to embrace other axioms which otherwise remained otiose – those concerned with the impact on social choice of adding more clubs and/or more individuals. To cut a very long story short, with some intuitive modification to deal with the specifics of social capital, the outcome is equivalent to weighting individuals (some may count more than others) and weighting their ranking of clubs or whatever. Social capital is ordered by overall scores accrued under the weighting systems chosen.

Interestingly, such ways of measuring social capital have, on occasion, been adopted in practice even if without any reference to the relevant literature. This is hardly surprising since it is the most natural way to establish commensuration between the otherwise incommensurable whilst allowing for a variable degree of weight across the factors concerned in terms of types of individuals and/or types of association. However, in other work, empirical application of social choice theory has been inadvertently pushed even further in its relevance for social capital measurement.[19] For the elements of social capital often take the form of either/or – you belong to a club or not, or you trust or not, although this can be graded by levels of trust.[20] In this respect, social capital is similar to ownership of consumer durables – you either own them, or a number of them, or not. Just as durables can be ordered socially by such techniques according to the proportion of individual households owning them, so can different types of social capital. Even if individuals order all elements of social capital in principle, in practice only their actual participation will be revealed. For households that do not belong to each of two clubs, or belong to both, we do not know their ranking of them. But we might be able to induce it from the ranking of those who do or do not belong to both. Further, it would be possible to disaggregate by different groups of clubs, etc., and by different groups of individuals.

Social norms and the demise of social capital

In short, it is possible to measure social capital. However, the discussion above, gleaned from a variety of different measurement issues, offers significant lessons and reservations. Only by chance will measures chosen for social capital satisfy the most basic properties even under the most simplifying conditions.[21] Further, three central lessons can be learnt from the above. First, measurement alone will itself depend upon the weightings attached to individuals or groups of individuals and to the various components of social capital or interactions, all taken together. Second, any causal analysis, whether theoretical or empirical, will need to address social capital as both cause and effect in view of its interaction with, for example, the economy. Third, each of these conundrums may be simplified if there are standard patterns of social capital across different socio-economic groups, restricted domain in social choice terms.

The last point provides an entry into the world of social norms, a notion that is heavily associated with the study of social capital since a norm is often understood as a form of social capital (and a potential source of violation of crude, atomised optimisation). Now, in this context, the affinity between social capital and ownership of consumer durables is instructive, for the theory of social choice has been extended to provide empirical investigation of social norms in the ownership of consumer durables. It has been further extended to examine social norms in food consumption (whether, for example, eating habits are healthy or not).[22] In this work – in informal terms supported by technical definitions and empirical application – the notion of a social norm is defined with two components. On the one hand, it is derived axiomatically, as in social choice, as the preferred (revealed) pattern (of ownership in case of durables, and it would be of social interaction in case of social capital). On the other hand, it is equally important to address how well established or common is the norm. What are the patterns of conformity to it across the population?

The importance of the latter point can be established in a number of ways. First, consider the voting paradox above. Essentially, axiomatically, it must be concluded that the norm is one of equality between the various clubs. However, the same would be true if membership of which club was a matter of complete indifference. The norms are the same in measurement but not in conformity. Second, it is important, in this light, to identify absence of a norm and, paradoxically, understand this as a norm itself. In the context of social capital, distrust, lack of civic participation, etc., or random but high patterns of trust and participation may be normal. This would have to be explained as much as the presence of strong and uniform patterns. Third, as is acknowledged in the literature, attention must be given both to the levels and the distribution of social capital. The latter cannot be defined independently of the patterns to which it is attached, as is recognised, for example, in reference to social capital as networks.

So much for the definition of social norms. How do they fit into an account of cause and effect? Here, the more general work on consumption is instructive. Begin by observing that, with the possible exception of the more recent emergence of globalisation, literature on consumption across the social sciences has grown at a greater pace than for any other topic.[23] Everyone agrees on the need to be interdisciplinary, each discipline has its own introverted traditions, and synthesis across the social sciences has not materialised. For these reasons, the literature on consumption offers lessons for the study of social capital. Lest the connection be considered too oblique other than in principle, it is worth emphasising a point that is easily overlooked – that consumption norms are themselves a leading form taken by social capital, not least in the cultures of consumption that in part, for example, define national traditions and modes of public and private behaviour.[24]

By reviewing the literature on consumption,[25] I have argued that the reason why interdisciplinarity has proven so elusive is because what I have termed the horizontal approaches within disciplines have at best been simply stacked up on top of one another. By horizontal is meant analysis that, whilst often induced from specific case studies, is generalised across consumption as a whole. Thus, for example, economics has a theory of demand as utility maximisation which purports to explain consumption across all goods (interestingly in the most formalised way without reference to the nature of goods or individuals), sociology might emphasise emulation and distinction or the formation of identity, and psychology address the range of motives underlying consumption. Consequently, an interdisciplinary theory of consumption is faced with the prospect of combining a set of factors and theories which simply do not overlap with one another.

Moreover, even a cursory glance at the literature on consumption reveals that it is capable of generating almost as many motives for consumption as there are consumption goods. This is typical of contributions from psychology and more interpretative understandings of consumption, for example, especially where these feed into the theory or practice of marketing. It is a reflection of the complexity of human action and the variety of contexts within which it occurs. Yet exactly the same applies, or ought to apply to the raw analytical materials of social capital. Trust, for example, tends to be seen very simply as certainty about what others want to do, although this is complemented by a more nuanced understanding as assurance of others acting in your interest.[26] The latter is, of course, extremely complex, just like consumption with as many dimensions, contexts and, it must be added, contradictions – as is most readily brought forth by the notion of honour amongst thieves. In any relationship, the construction and use of trust may have spill-over effects, but whether it be over money, sexual fidelity or turning up on time, the horizontal interactions may be dominated by the intrinsic conditions surrounding the activity in question as well as its extrinsic circumstances.

To resolve such conundrums around the multiplicity of factors surrounding consumption, it is appropriate to move from a horizontal to a vertical approach, one which recognises that consumption is dependent upon a range of social processes, structures, and relations which connect production to consumption, together with the material cultures attached to that consumption. Further, such an analysis needs to be organised around specific products or groups of products giving rise to what has been termed the systems of provision approach – in which consumption is addressed in the specific context, for example, of the fashion system for clothes, the housing system, the food system, etc. This is not to deny the relevance of horizontal factors, only that they tend to be incorporated into vertically integrated entities in grinding out patterns or norms of consumption. The systems of provision for consumption are quite distinct from one another, not only in being structurally separated but also in the way in which they are internally structured and function themselves.

Exactly the same analytical procedure applies to the subject matter of social capital. At the crudest level of argument by analogy, there is considerable purchase. For, as many have already argued, much of the literature on social capital has been unduly and explicitly horizontal in character – focusing upon civil society and social interactions across it at the expense of the vertically ordered factors to which these are connected. In brief, do not burial societies, housing associations, and bowling clubs have more differentially to do, respectively, with death, building, and entertainment than they do with common elements of trust or whatever? And so the list could run on. The conclusion is that social capital is heavily differentiated according to the vertically integrated connections that it has in specific ways to other specific variables. Only by stripping out the historical, the social, and the specific can the theory of social capital claim its (false) generality. By doing so, out go the baby and bath water, if not the bath as well.

But social capital is not, in general, consumption or as if consumption. Consequently, even if the vertical systems of provision approach to consumption is valid,[27] the study of social capital is more complex since it is possible for the horizontal to prevail over the vertical in the specific creation of norms and institutions – as in general business associations for example.[28] It follows that, at best, social capital will prove a conceptual device for organising, at a greater level of generality, the theory and evidence that is already or prospectively known to us. At worst, it is a recipe for invalid generalisation and the omission of theoretical and historically specific insights according to the more or less arbitrary fashions by which the social capital literature evolves.

Concluding remarks

A very common reaction to criticism of social capital runs along the lines, "Fair enough but have you anything constructive to contribute to the understanding of, and formulation of policy for, the role of the social in development?" To some extent, such a response to criticism is ill-judged. To expose weaknesses and inconsistencies is a constructive contribution in its own right irrespective of whether it is tied to an alternative. But it is also possible to be more constructive in the light of the commentary offered in this chapter.

Consider, for example, that social capital is essentially seeking common patterns of behaviour across social and economic variables. These can be identified descriptively by statistical analysis, as has been attempted by the use of large household survey data sets. Broadly, there are two formal methods of proceeding. One is to use some form of regression analysis underpinned, explicitly or not, by an associated model of cause and effect. Countries grow faster for having more social capital, or households are richer for the same reason. This has the distinct disadvantage of presuming that social and economic life not only unfolds in a deterministic if stochastic fashion but also precludes appropriate consideration of contextual content, other than in the weak sense laid out in Chapter 7 (essentially as path dependence) or through appeal to omitted variables. If the model is valid, after all, it ought to apply universally without distinction by time and place.

An alternative is to use factor analysis, a less familiar procedure, especially to economists. It has been used in the social capital literature.[29] Although, as in all empirical work, there are problems associated with the meaning of the data themselves, factor analysis has the distinct advantage of presuming neither universal nor causal content. It has no pretensions other than to reorganise raw data, although the results can be suggestive in various ways. The classic example is provided by examining results across different pupils and subjects. Factor analysis seeks to identify whether students tend to do well or badly in groups of subjects in order to discover whether ability at maths is associated with ability in sciences and music but not languages, for example. In this way, different types of students can be identified by performance across key combinations of subjects. Similarly, for social capital, factor analysis can identify typologies for network and associational membership, for values, and other socio-economic characteristics.

From factor analysis of examination results, it is immediate that no conclusions can be drawn about why, for example, maths and music tend to go together in sorting out good from bad students. Nor do such results have immediate relevance for other examinations for other students where course content and teaching, and cultural backgrounds, may be entirely different. Consequently, the identification of norms or regularities through factor analysis for social capital and development or whatever, as much as for examination systems, leaves open both causal and contextual questions. This is in contrast to regression analysis that purports to test a model. Presuming norms to have been properly and fully identified through factor analysis, the analysis is at a beginning in exploring their significance within the wider social and economic context.

To return, then, to the question of alternatives to social capital analysis, it is a matter of providing alternative analysis with an appropriate causal and contextual content. In this vein, the constructive criticism offered in this book is to take both the understanding of the social and of capital as point of departure. The extent to which existing household surveys of social capital and empirical analyses remain useful for alternative approaches is an open question, not least because of their insecure analytical foundations and interpretative frameworks. However, interrogation of the potential for empirical and interpretative reconstruction of social capital studies is not attempted here. If it were, there is no reason to believe that the notion would survive the exercise in a recognisable and well-defined way given that social capital is fractured both by the social and by capital.[30]

Part IV

11 Social capital versus political economy

Why social capital

The purpose of this chapter is in part to provide a summary of the conclusions to be drawn from what has gone before. But it also attempts to do more than this by addressing a number of questions that were raised in the introduction. Why has social capital proved so popular with limited effective critical response? And what is the significance of social capital for understanding the way in which social theory is currently being produced and, in particular, for the shifting relationship between economics and the other social sciences as the one seeks to colonise the other? Stripped of their attachment to social capital, these are big questions that have rarely been posed let alone answered. Hopefully, by placing them in the context of social capital, the latest conceptual wunderkind, some light can be shed on them.

First, then, what is striking about social capital is not only the extent of its influence, and the speed with which this has been achieved, but also its ready acceptance as both analytical, empirical, and policy panacea. These features are aptly captured, respectively, by the World Bank's notion of social capital as "missing link", its flush of dedicated household surveys, and its view of social capital as "the glue that holds society together". Social capital explains what is otherwise inexplicable and is the factor that allows society to function success-fully. In limited respects, parallels can be drawn with utility as used by econo-mists. For this is also all-embracing – putatively explaining why we behave the way we do as well as providing us with our welfare. In the case of social capital, however, our sights and ambitions are raised from the level of the individual to the level of society, from the market to the non-market, and from narrowly defined individual motivation to customs, norms, institutions, and rules. In short, social capital is attractive because of the scope application that it provides as well as its capacity to do so whilst not necessarily being critical of what has gone before. It can both generalise (add missing link and glue) and incorporate (reinterpret existing scholarship as an earlier unwitting use).

Second, despite what is already a rush of survey articles, even those who are not using the term for the first time accept that it is difficult to define. The more established social capitalists in an enterprise that is, admittedly, still in its precocious infancy have been forced to compromise with the expanding scope of social capital. More and more variables are included, from the horizontal to the vertical, from the bonding to the bridging to the linking, from social values to networks and associations, and so on. Alternatively, such proliferation of content can be rendered manageable by a re-composition into broad categories to question whether social capital is, for example, complementary with, or a substitute for, "real" capital or the state. The result is to create a field for what has previously been termed middle-range theory (Merton 1957), analysis suspended somewhere between grand systemic theory and mere description. As a result, more recent and less circumspect contributions may acknowledge the ambiguities in the definition of social capital, simply pass on, and choose or add a definition of their own to suit their own purpose. Social capital thereby becomes a sack of analytical potatoes. The notion is simply chaotic as is also reflected in frequent suggestions that it is merely a metaphor or a heuristic device. It is also acknowledged to be difficult to measure (tellingly revealed by World Bank projects that seek to define it by the process of measuring it). What is social capital is readily confused with what it does as if these needed to be conceptually distinct. One reason for thinking so is the early and mounting recognition that social capital is subject to the perverse, dark, negative, and downside so that it can be bad as well as good depending on circumstances. Whilst these features of social capital might be thought to render it unacceptable and subject to collapse under the weight of its own contradictions and inconsistencies, exactly the opposite is the case. Having established a sufficiently weighty presence, it also has the logical capacity to absorb any criticism in the form of refinement by, for example, addition of another variable for consideration.

Third, then, social capital has a gargantuan appetite. On the one hand, it can explain everything from individuals to societies (although global social capital has rarely figured yet, it ought to do so at least to address the international networks and ethos of those running the world)[1] whether the topic be the sick, the poor, the criminal, the corrupt, the (dys)functional family, schooling, community life, work and organisation, democracy and governance, collective action, transitional societies, intangible assets or, indeed, any aspect of social, cultural, and economic performance, and equally across time and place. On the other hand, social capital has been deployed across theories and methodologies as diverse as postmodernist Marxism and mainstream neoclassical economics, addressing the conceptual, empirical, and policy. In this respect, social capital is like other all-encompassing notions that have swept, if not uniformly, across the social sciences, such as flexibility and globalisation. All can participate from their own perspective. Social capital is truly democratic, not only amongst the community of scholars but, as middle-range theory, it is also able to engage (with) the wider community of activists, politicians, and media gurus. This is especially so in terms of its capacity to exploit popular prejudices about the role of television, the family and moral fibre, to touch the nostalgia for a lost world, to address demise and failure that are ever more demanding of attention than success, and so on.

Yet, as already hinted, by reference to globalisation, the emergence of social capital to rapid prominence is a familiar phenomenon in terms of academic fashions. It is most disturbing as evidence of a more general trend towards the popularisation and degradation of scholarship. The pattern is familiar by now. A case study or two leads to the invention of grand concepts and generalisations. These are refined in light of theoretical and empirical critiques that point to omitted theoretical variables and/or case study counterexamples. Existing and new knowledge is run through the evolving framework. Ultimately, the whole edifice becomes too complex and succumbs to the critical heretics or others who have remained or become cynical. It is then time for a new fashion to emerge.

Despite this intellectual cycle, the effects are significant. Quite apart from the waste of scholarly resources, the impact of such fashions over the longer term is not necessarily negligible nor is it even across disciplines and topics. We have yet to see what the long-term effects of social capital will be on the social sciences, although some of the short-term effects are already discernible. Fourth, then, although social capital is unlimited in principle in terms of what it can incorporate and address, and how it does so, the evolution of the literature in practice is far from neutral in its content and direction. It reflects general intellectual fashions, the stimulus of external events, and even the idiosyncrasies of particular participants. What is equally important is what has been left out. As much of the critical literature has observed, contributions to social capital have tended to focus on civil society and its associational forms and ethos. This has been in isolation from, and exclusive of, serious consideration of the economy, formal politics, the role of the nation-state, the exercise of power, and the divisions and conflicts that are endemic to capitalist society although, of course, these can be added to if you want them.[2]

Fifth, more specifically in this intellectual trajectory, although Bourdieu is a (decreasingly) acknowledged initiator of the theory of social capital, the critical aspects of his contributions have been excised in deference to the tamer versions associated with the likes of Coleman and Putnam. In particular, Bourdieu has emphasised the social construction of the content of social capital (what is its meaning and how does this relate to its practices), that it is irreducibly attached to class stratification which, in turn, is associated with the exercise of economic and other forms of exploitation, and the relationship between them. Significantly, the functional approaches to social capital attached to the founding empirical studies of Coleman and Putnam have both been shown to be questionable – respectively, Catholic community as a positive influence on schooling outcomes and the incidence and impact of associational activity on differential regional development in Italy. In other words, false empirical observation has given rise to a theory that has subsequently taken on a life of its own as if both theory and data were mutually supportive. Such are the shaky ("benchkin") foundations for the evolving knowledge attached to social capital. This indicates that the attraction of social capital derives less from the unconsciously scurrilous scholarship of its founders and more from their having tapped the intellectual nerve of social theory at the turn of the millennium. This has a dual aspect.

For, sixth, one particularly important feature of the intellectual environment in which social capital has flourished is the retreat from postmodernism. There is a wish for renewed confrontation with the real. By its very name, despite its conceptual chaos, social capital appears to get to grips with both the social and with capital. Nothing could be further from the truth. For, the very terminology of social capital signifies its weaknesses. That the notion "social" needs to be attached to capital to mark a distinct category is indicative of the failure to understand capital as social in what is taken to be its more mundane economic, putatively non-social, form. What is adopted, however, with use of "capital", especially with the physicalist overtones attached to mainstream economics, is the failure to incorporate the most important insight for social theory to be derived from postmodernism – that concepts need to be historically and socially grounded, if not always subjectively so. In this vein, universal concepts such as social capital would be ruled out of court, and could not be rescued by appeal to historical and social context as path dependence, influence of other factors, initial conditions, or multiple equilibria. These are the long-standing favoured ways of dealing with the social and historical by mainstream economics, at least when the problem is recognised. That social capitalists are forced to adopt, or often willingly embrace, this route has been heavily criticised with little or no effect. It is also indicative of one element in the spreading influence of the postures of economics on other social sciences, to which I return below.

In this respect, the attraction of social capital is its capacity to retreat from postmodernism without having to come to terms with it. Occasionally, more sophisticated and, let's be frank, honest scholars and supporters of social capital have acknowledged the need to incorporate the contextual in what I have termed the strong sense (not just path dependence, etc., but concepts rooted in society under consideration). But, even those that do incorporate the contextual tend to do so by adding one more damned variable without acknowledging that the other elements to which the contextual is added ought to be critically rejected, or reconstructed, as a result. This point is brought home both by the need to design surveys with appropriately attuned questions, in view of the specificity, for example, of the meaning and content of associations, and, polemically, by observing that social capital is in the mind of the observer and not the participant.

Paradoxically, though, work on social capital is replete with variables representing the cultural whether reflecting attitudes, for example, to politicians, governments, or neighbours. It bears repeating that most uses of such variables transcribe them freely across societies, despite criticism for doing so. In particular, as emphasised by DiMaggio (1994), who, interestingly, comes from a critical stance towards Granovetter's network theory that has been incorporated into social capital, culture is cognitive, expressive, and valuative, none of which tends to enter into the meaning of trust, for example, in the approach of social capitalists. Rather, the emphasis is placed on its functional aspects alone, most notably in the economic approach where it concerns access and use of information in market and non-market, "social", interaction between and amongst individuals. Yet, DiMaggio also raises a crucial issue by arguing that economic processes are cultural (and hence, by implication, social) but that to demonstrate that culture has an economic effect is difficult.

Of course, there is no such difficulty for social capitalists because of their simplistic notions of culture and related variables. Either in more or less abstract models or in statistical work, culture, etc., can be shown to have an economic effect, not least in improving growth, equality, or whatever. Presumably, then, DiMaggio has something else in mind, namely the cultural as in the social construction of meaning. To show it has an effect might also mean something else. For, we are so bombarded in our day-to-day lives with culturally embedded attempts to sell us things that it is surely inescapable that the cultural has an impact upon the economic through this and other factors such as the culture of work.[3] Consequently, the problem is not to demonstrate that culture matters but to persuade social theorists to take it seriously, if only in part in deference to the continuing influence of postmodernism. This is a problem because of schisms that have evolved across the social sciences. Where postmodernism has departed the material and objective for the symbolic sign and the subjective, so its alter ego in more traditional social science, rapidly being subsumed under social capital, has hardened in its use of universal analytical categories in order to address what is presumed to be an unproblematic descriptive and statistical reality. In doing so, it demonstrates affinities with long-standing methodological weaknesses within (mainstream) economics, rendering it more readily captured.

This explains the repetitive critical refrain throughout this volume that social capitalists have neglected the social in the contextual sense. But, I suspect that I hold to a different understanding to this than DiMaggio, certainly in terms of the interpretation briefly touched upon above. For, there is an unfortunate tendency to perceive the cultural as something separate and distinct from the non-cultural, even if arguing that it irreducibly needs to be analytically present. Although I have not made it explicit up to this point, however, I understand capital, and certainly capitalism, themselves as cultural. Consequently, the critique of social capital that it depends upon an asocial and ahistorical understanding of capital, and hence of capitalism, is to make both a cultural and an economic critique. Precisely because capitalism, and the capital upon which it depends, are systemically based upon economic and social (including cultural) reproduction in specific historical circumstances – not least those of the last few hundred years – the idea that it is difficult to demonstrate that culture has an economic effect is rendered senseless. Could feudal culture support capitalism?[4]

The point is not, however, to pick an artificial and constructed argument with DiMaggio not least because his work would seem to suggest that he would accept the points being made here. Rather, it is to bring together, and to see as symbiotic, the two critiques that have run separately, if side-by-side, throughout this book – that social capital is ahistorical and asocial and, now as the seventh point about social capital, that it is fundamentally complicit with mainstream economics in the form of its new information-theoretic micro-foundations. As argued in the opening chapter, developments within and around economics on this basis have allowed it to understand both the economic and the non-economic as the consequence of market imperfections. As a result, economics is colonising the other social sciences as never before, with an as if market imperfection world as opposed to the as if market perfection world that previously proved a colonising tool of significant if limited impact. Not surprisingly, social capital has proved attractive to some mainstream economists in such endeavours, with Gary Becker in the forefront. In this light, for economists, social capital is simply everything else after other more traditional forms of capital have been taken into account, with these understood as in the mainstream as physical, natural, financial, or human. Transparently, the effect is to add the social to an otherwise unchallenged economic, albeit of market imperfections. Such a ludicrous posture is at its most extreme in the case of mainstream economics for which capital is a physical or other asset that ultimately provides a stream of utility to individuals, a universal, ahistorical, and asocial thing rather than a definite economic relationship, with associated structures and processes for the generation of profit.[5] This all reflects a profound misunderstanding both of the social and of capital(ism). In a word, economists can bring in the social to complement the individual, only because the social has been omitted in the first instance.

Of equal significance, however, is the response of non-economists both to social capital and to the colonising designs of economics. Here, eighth, a crucial aspect of social capital is the demonstration that its intellectual origins and motivation were provided by a renewed attempt to establish rational choice within social theory (and to swing it towards economic as opposed to psychological reductionism). Significantly, social capital evolved out of a literature (social exchange theory), and was initially designed, to address the relationship between the macro and the micro in the context of the relationship between the social and the individual. To a large extent, if not completely, these origins – and their generally strong affinities with rational choice methodology – have been glossed over in the ready reception granted to social capital as the cure-all for social theory. Thus, whether influenced by a colonising economics or not, the use of social capital across the other social sciences is equally uncritical of the economic. The only, at times insidious, difference is that the same analytical content is disguised and tempered to a greater or lesser extent by more informal types of arguments and by being set together with the more traditional variables of social theory, with the downside, power, and conflict being thrown in if needs be.

Ninth, ironically and perversely, social capitalists from outside economics are attracted by the notion because they perceive it as an assault upon economics. Economists are thought of as being civilised by being forced to take account of the social. In addition, social capital is widely and proudly praised for placing interdisciplinary endeavour upon the agenda. Significantly, however, this is only asserted and never demonstrated. And the only economics on the agenda is that of the mainstream. Essentially, would be civilisers and critics of a colonising mainstream economics are working critically against a model of the discipline that is a hundred years old.[6] They do not recognise the implications of the more recent revolution in and around economics that positively embraces the social by way of extension of the unchanged economic principles (or the economic approach as Becker dubs it). In this light, the role of social capital in social theory's response to a colonising economics is completely clarified. On the one hand, by way of analogy, it can be understood as a form of peripheral colonisation, incorporating all social theory other than economics. On the other hand, it presents itself as the opposition to a colonising economics whereas, at most, it offers feeble resistance because it has no alternative economics of its own – at worst, it prepares social theory for the colonising advance of the economic approach.

Scholarly Third Wayism

So far these nine points have addressed fundamental features of the intellectual climate and academic content of social capital that begin to explain its irresistible rise. These, however, need to be set in a broader ideological and academic context. First is the role played by academic entrepreneurship itself. It is a matter of publish or perish, of obtaining external funding, of increasing disciplinary specialisation despite paper commitment to interdisciplinarity, and of homogeneity of scholarship and teaching apart from the corresponding space created for intellectual niches (of which social capital is one, especially when attached to an existing niche).[7] None of these is, of course, unique to social capital but they do provide some explanation why, when a conceptual fad gathers a foothold, it should gather cumulative momentum at the expense of considered scholarship.[8]

Second, social capital is perceived to pick a way through what is taken to be a dual failure of both socialism and laissez-faire. In tentatively accepting social capital, Bowles (1999) puts this position particularly well:[9]

> The demise of these twin illusions of our century – laissez faire and statism – thus cleared the intellectual and rhetorical stage for social capital's entry. And so, a decade ago, otherwise skeptical intellectuals and jaded policy makers surprised and impressed their friends with the remarkable correlation between choral societies and effective governance in Tuscany, the perils of a nation that bowled alone, and Alexis de Tocqueville on Americans as a nation of joiners. The social capital boom heralded a heightened awareness in policy and academic circles of real peoples values (not the utility functions of *homo economicus*), how people interact in their daily lives (locally, in families and work groups, not just as buyers, sellers, and citizens) and the bankruptcy of the ideologically charged planning *versus* markets debate.

Social capital is acknowledged by Bowles to be attractive to conservatives for having taken the state off the agenda and for putting anything other than it in the role of social provider, if usually at a local level. On the other hand, progressives welcome the ethos of, and commitment to, collective values and actions. More generally, it has been argued that social capital has stolen issues, such as the family and the community, from their traditionally conservative monopoly. Describing it as a slippery concept, Gamarnikow and Green (1999a, pp. 58–9) perceptively observe:[10]

> It is possible to identify a social capital continuum: at the progressive end there is concern with citizenship, empowerment, pluralism and democrati-sation. At the more conservative end social capital is located in commit-ment to traditional family structures and relationships and a collective moral order of "normative" consensus around traditional values, duties and responsibilities.

My concern here, however, is not to draw out the implications for social theory of the perceived failure of socialism in the twentieth century. More pertinent for discussion of social capital is the basis on which it rejects and moves beyond neo-liberalism. There almost seems to be a desperation to find an alternative that is also acceptable to the establishment.[11] As is apparent ana-lytically, so in policy, social capital essentially leaves economic issues alone. It seeks to complement economic with social engineering, and might appropriately be understood as socialism/capitalism rather than social capital. For, as explained in Chapter 9, as social capital becomes ever more all-encompassing and participatory, it resembles a model of socialism at whatever level it applies, with conflict giving way to positive sum outcomes with the single, but crucial, reservation that this socialist nirvana comes to a full halt once it arrives at the portals of the economy, or capitalism.[12]

This is hardly surprising, for the absence of a proper political economy also precludes a proper consideration of how economic powers, structures, and processes impinge upon, constrain, and condition their social counterparts. In this respect, both academically and politically, social capital is a major plank in Third Wayism – you can have anything you like as long as it is compatible with the (market imperfections view of the) economy.[13] Further, as N. Rose (1999) has demonstrated, Third Wayism is heavily embroiled with the ethical concerns of those who are well off. Quite clearly, putting social capital to rights for others to gain economic advance can assume a high priority once your own economic welfare is both secure and secured by doing so. Social capital really is a posture towards the less fortunate of self-help and charity raised from the individual to whatever community level.

Third, all of these preceding observations are given added force, at a qualita-tively higher level, by the adoption of social capital by the World Bank. Recall its wish to move from Washington to post-Washington consensus,[14] to adopt a more people-friendly and state-friendly rhetoric, to retain and expand the scope for discretionary intervention, for its social theorists to be taken seriously by its economists without challenging their economics, and last, but not least, for it to play the role of knowledge bank and, thereby, use its vast research, education, and public relations resources to set the developmental agenda. There surely should be no doubt that the World Bank has imparted considerable momentum to the social capital enterprise, and why it should have done so.

In many ways, these points are all confirmed by a close reading of Edwards (1999) or, more exactly, filling out the spaces in his account. He writes as Director of the Ford Foundation's Governance and Civil Society Unit, having previously been Senior Civil Society Specialist at the World Bank. He effectively accepts that both civil society and social capital are highly ambiguous terms that are often used interchangeably. In a section entitled, "The Rise and Rise of Social Capital", he places much emphasis on the role of Wolfensohn and Stiglitz in having moved beyond the economic to the social that, of course, leaves the economic unchallenged. He then divides responses to social capital into three ideal types: the enthusiasts, the tacticians, and the sceptics. The enthusiasts seem inappropriately to be identified with economists within the World Bank and with work that is primarily reductionist of the social to the economic and is correspondingly statistical in content. The sceptics are portrayed as those who consider that social capital by its terminology and aims alone is conducive to microeconomic reductionism and will lead to the displacement of the study of social development.[15] In other words, they believe that social theory can proceed independently of economics.

The most interesting group, however, is the tacticians. Edwards explicitly cites Bebbington and Woolcock, quoting them to the effect that "social capital offers a way of doing things better, and provides a unifying interdisciplinary discourse in which to discuss a range of otherwise disparate concerns". They are perceived to be more sophisticated than the enthusiasts because of the latter's crudity and neglect of history and context but "they don't want to alienate the economists by rocking the boat too much, so tend to approach disagreements in a spirit of consensus". Last, but by no means least, social capital is perceived by the enthusiasts to be both an umbrella for all social theory and a weapon against economics: "Their hope is that *all* the social sciences will be transformed as the Trojan Horse of social capital makes its way through the citadel of economics."

What is fascinating, especially on a personal level, is that Edwards appears both inadvertently and independently to have arrived at similar conclusions to me. The rise of social capital is being promoted as a second-best strategy to overcome economists, to enhance the position of social theory and social theorists with the World Bank, and is itself colonising social science other than, possibly as well as, economics. What Edwards overlooks, however, is the external, especially the intellectual, environment in which this is occurring not least, leaving aside the World Bank's rhetorical and ideological needs, the wish to charter a course between statism and laissez-faire and the powerful impetus of economics imperialism. In such a context, both the goals of, and the prospects for, the enthusiasts are to be viewed much less favourably than Edwards' compromise position of "sceptical tactician", in which: "We understand social capital as the cumulative capacity to work together for common goals, and civil society as the space where these goals are formed and debated."[16]

What all of this leaves aside is both the absence of any serious economic analysis within the social capital camp other than that emanating from a colonising economics. Most remarkable and profoundly disturbing is the extent to which the tacticians within the World Bank are being replicated outside, not least in view of its influence as "knowledge bank" and all that entails in its new post-Washington consensus role. Social capital is attractive to social theorists for all the reasons previously outlined, and compromises are prepared to be made, both with genuine integrity as well as for professional advancement, in order to gain distance from neo-liberalism, statism, reductionism, Marxism, postmodernism, and all the other isms that have become the fashionably derided symbols of dogmatism and lack of realism. And a more positive case for social capital can be made in terms of its addressing the role to be played in economic and social development by civil society, or whatever, the space occupied between the market and the state.[17]

There is an alternative alternative

In short, opposition to social capital has been limited, neglected, incorporated, or has retreated to the safe havens offered by scepticism, an economicless assessment of the social and, especially, the cultural.[18] Particularly astonishing and disturbing is how critics of the World Bank, in the form of its earlier Washington consensus, have been turned into allies. The major exception is provided by political economists and many, if not all, progressive NGO activists who recognise the encroaching influence of mainstream economics in the post-Washington consensus, the expanding scope for discretionary intervention, limited policy change, and an excellent PR job. Do such factors mean that the tactics of the proponents of social capital are wrong and that what are often worthy aims in analysis and policy will fail? There are strong reasons for believing so.

First, a different way of looking at social capital is in terms of its primarily being confined to the role of an investigative tool, seeking to guarantee that the social, however understood, is analytically incorporated. This is already acknowledged implicitly within the literature as social capital is often addressed in terms of anecdote, metaphor, or heuristic device, as discussed in Chapter 7. Such a rationale for social capital, however, has a number of, arguably destructive, weaknesses, in part in theory and in part in most likely practice. For, social capital is a remarkably neutral term, especially where it comes to power, conflict, the economy, and the role of the state. Unlike other, what I would argue are also primarily investigative categories such as patriarchy and racism,[19] social capital does very little to challenge the status quo and to direct attention to systemic sources of power corresponding disadvantage. Even anodyne terms, such as discrimination, gender, and ethnicity, which are the preferred categories deployed by the World Bank, unlike social capital, point to the systemic and holistic, as well as detailed and specific, practices.

For this reason, second, whilst social capital says you should investigate the social, just as racism and patriarchy do for their concerns, it adds nothing to their understanding other than imposing one or other of the pre-determined analytical frameworks. Third, the idea of building social capital as a development policy borders on the nonsensical. Social capital is so context specific, as now recognised in the literature, especially in view of its pervasive downside, that statements about what it is and what effects it has are either vacuous or non-generalisable from specific instances. Further, to put it polemically, you cannot build development out of a bunch of anecdotes, metaphors, or heuristic devices. Nor is the corresponding social engineering that results liable to take sufficient account of the poor, the powerless, and the economic in view of the analytical slants that have already been attached to social capital. Intellectually, the contextual content – which was originally incorporated, through the work of Bourdieu, by interrogating class stratification and exploitation across the economic, social, cultural, and ideological – has been excised. It has been replaced by rational choice economics, sociology, and political science through Becker, Coleman, and Putnam, albeit heavily disguised and tempered by use of traditional variables drawn from social theory. Last, and by no means least, as already hinted, social capital is a conceptual artefact of the First World (and wealthy), transposed to other Worlds (and the poor) on the basis of two closely related but distinct aspects. On the one hand, it is self-help and cooperation raised from the individual to the communal level at some tier or other. On the other hand, it is the rich and powerful speculating on how to improve the lot of the poor through prompting their self-help and organisation without questioning the sources of their economic disadvantage.

Inescapably, social capital is a cascade of perverse oppositions. Its given name suggests both social and capital. But it is neither – its inescapable origins derive from rational choice and its capital is the all-embracing residual created by a prior physicalist notion of capital as resource. It purports to civilise economists by forcing them to take account of the social and, yet, it opens the way for economists to colonise the other social sciences by appropriating the social in the suggested ways with which it is entirely comfortable. It claims interdiscipinarity whereas it effectively excises the contextual as socially and historically specific and is equally notable for a lack of critical economic content. It imagines itself to be more democratic and participatory whereas it is primarily participation from below imposed from above. And, whilst tactically placing itself in the vanguard in the reaction against neo-liberalism and excessive statism, social capital has parasitically fed upon the processes that have brought these extremes to hiatus. It is better seen, both in analysis and policy, as compromising with established doctrines and with economic and social engineering, whilst simultaneously absorbing and neutralising more radical and coherent alternatives.[20] Thus, as those more favourably inclined towards social capital would have it, social capital is something of a neutral veil that facilitates the exchange and development of ideas. From the evidence presented here, insofar as social capital itself metaphorically adopts the form of money in the market for ideas, it is subject to Gresham's Law! Like bad money, it will drive more appropriate ideas and theories out of circulation, paving the way for its own and for economics' colonisation of social theory. Such an outcome is not inevitable. It can be prevented. Doing so depends upon pursuing alternatives based upon scholarly integrity, genuine interdisciplinarity, and the resuscitation of political economy within and across the social sciences.

Notes

1 Introduction and overview

1 See especially Lee and Harley (1998) but also Hodgson and Rothman (1999).
2 Blaug (1998a, p. 11) observes a flush of recent books providing obituaries for economics. See also Lawson (1997).
3 Blaug (1998a, p. 12) reports from John Hey, previously managing editor of the *Economic Journal*, that there is a 'journal game', based on use of irrelevant material, the stylised facts observed by an author, and designed to demonstrate cleverness rather than address crucial economic problems. Blaug (1998b, p. 45) himself opines:

> I am very pessimistic about whether we can actually pull out of this. I think we have created a locomotive. This is the sociology of the economics profession. We have created a monster that is very difficult to stop.

On the other hand, Krugman (1998) argues that mathematical economics has been in touch with real world and policy but mathematical economists have been negligent in popular elaboration of their ideas. Martin (1999, p. 75) observes, "in his typically self-confident way Krugman has also claimed to have pioneered ... the high-quality, non-technical popular treatise for the intelligent layperson". But also see Ellerman (2000), in the context of Russian privatisation, on how popularisation of their ideas has been carried over into the world of policy:

> As economic theory has become more mathematical, there is now the phenomenon of *wunderkind* professor in economics (e.g. Jeffrey Sachs, Larry Summers, and Andrei Shleifer were all prodigy-profs at Harvard) who are then unleashed (with the compounded arrogance of youth, academic credentials, and elite associations) into the real world as ersatz policy "experts".

As discussed in Chapter 9, however, in case of Joe Stiglitz, such wunderkinds are dispensable if not dispensing the required advice.
4 See King (2000) for a discussion of the prospects for post-Keynesianism as a branch of heterodox economics.
5 Of course, it can reasonably be argued that political economy has, to some extent, been a victim of its own reductionism and narrowness, if not as guilty as mainstream economics. Accordingly, the revival of political economy within the social sciences must be sensitive both to its own deficiencies and the shifts in intellectual and ideological environments.
6 Mondak (1998, p. 433) advises of the social capital literature:

> Disagreement among scholars is to be expected, and the airing of contrary perspectives can be highly fruitful. But the caustic tone found in some works surely

detracts from our common objective of advancing the state of research in this area.

7   See Weintraub (1998) for a recent contribution suggesting that rigour and axiomatics are not the same thing.

8   Hobsbawm (1997) delivers a mixed bag of judgements on economics and economists. On the one hand, he sees the separation of history from economics as deriving from the marginalist revolution, to such an extent that "the arguments and even the existence of the defeated side have largely been forgotten" (p. 99) and, especially for Marx, "survived ... insofar as the arguments ... could be conducted in the analytic mode of neo-classicism" (p. 99). The colonisation of social sciences by economics is dated from the 1970s, so that its addressing "crime, marriage, education, suicide, the environment or whatnot, merely indicates that economics is now regarded as a universal service-discipline" (pp. 106–7). Further, "I have ... had close contact with a discipline which does call for considerable brain-power, or at least nimbleness, namely economics at Cambridge, UK and USA, and I have never forgotten this salutary but depressing experience of trying to keep up with a much cleverer body of people" (p. 58). On the other hand, from his Marshall Lectures of 1980 (p. 95):

> For economics, or rather that part of it which from time to time claims a monopoly of defining the subject, has always been a victim of history. For lengthy periods, when the world economy appears to be rolling on quite happily with or without advice ... proper economics has the floor, improper is tacitly excluded, or consigned to the twilight of past and present heterodoxy, the equivalent of faith-healing or acupuncture in medicine ... However, from time to time history catches economists at their brilliant gymnastics and walks off with their overcoats.

The last twenty years have yet to furnish an example of such a pragmatic historian lest it be Brenner (1998) on which see Fine et al. (1999) and special sections in *Historical Materialism*, nos 4–6, 2000.

9   This is primarily, if not exclusively, to be blamed upon the World Bank. Its prolific output on social capital, regularly arriving or accessible through the internet, strains attempts to keep abreast of developments in downloading and reading, let alone incorporating into this volume and its own corresponding piecemeal evolution.

10 For a more detailed account in the context of labour markets, see Fine (1998a). Over this period, modernisation, or emulating the developed, was the counterpart to Keynesianism for the developing countries.

11 In this vein, Friedman can be considered to have been too left wing in allowing for government to affect the level of employment if only at the expense of ever-accelerating inflation. Reflationary policy, for example, becomes expected to lead to future tax increases or inflation with equal and opposite deflationary effects on economic agents.

12 See Fine (1997a, 1998b, 1999a, 1999c, 1999e, 2000a–2000e) and Fine and Green (2000).

13 For a striking journalistic confirmation of the position adopted here, see the Economist's (1998) anticipation of the economists of the future. It suggests, "the effects of new analytical tools developed in the 1970s spread out from the profession's core like a shockwave". With explicit reference to economic imperialism, it argues that, "unlike the stars of the 1980s, today's impressive young academics are using the tools of economics in fields on or beyond the traditional borders of their discipline" (p. 143). In particular, "these economists take seriously what every layman knows: that people don't always behave in selfish or even rational ways" (p. 146). For a more scholarly appreciation of such developments, but bordering on pastiche of the critique offered here, see Lazear (2000).

14 Over the past five years, even on a casual glance, the *Journal of Economic Literature*, leading publication for surveys, has published articles on economics and the arts, emotions, psychology (twice), religion, preference formation, political science, corruption, sociology (twice), the family, and altruism.

15 See, however, Ingham (1996) and Toye (1996) for similarly harsh conclusions for the new economic sociology and the new institutional economics, respectively. Heilbroner and Milberg (1995, p. 6) refer to an "extraordinary combination of arrogance and innocence" with the "widespread belief that economic analysis can exist as some kind of socially disembodied study".

16 More generally, see Campbell (1993, p. 42):

> The recent fashion for semiotically inspired analyses of both contemporary and past human institutions and practices has served the valuable function of shifting the focus of analytic attention from behaviour to meaning. Unfortunately, it has also served to promote the idea that "meaning" can be the subject of investigation in itself, independent of purposeful conduct of individuals.

17 It is tempting to associate postmodernism with shifting economic conditions as in Stanley (1996, p. 1), quoting from Harvey (1989):

> While simultaneity in the shifting dimensions of time and space is no proof of necessary or causal connection, strong *a priori* grounds can be adduced for the proposition that there is a sole kind of necessary relation between the rise of postmodernist cultural forms, the emergence of more flexible modes of capital accumulation, and a new round of "time-space compression" in the organisation of capitalism.

> Care must be taken, though, in so simply deducing intellectual from material developments, presuming the latter to have been identified correctly. See also a number of the articles collected in Jameson (1998) for the notion that the commercialisation of the image, etc., in late capitalism gives rise to the ideal abstractions attached to postmodernism. Note that, whilst Jameson is acknowledged to be a leading theorist of postmodernism and one who particularly engages with the economy, his analysis of the latter is primarily both superficial and disengaged.

18 For this argument in greater detail, see Fine and Leopold (1993, Chapter 4).

19 Symbolically, the technical apparatus of isoquants and production is identical to that of indifference curves and consumption.

20 For a remarkable recognition of this symbiotic intellectual division of labour between neo-liberal economics and postmodernist theory in the context of the reorientation of the Australian state towards reliance upon the market, see Pusey (1991, pp. 20–21):

> The more balanced model of the modernisation process with its underlying priority of reconciling co-ordination with identity and culture is now under challenge from the practice of an invading economic rationalism, and from the postmodernist high theory within some of our social science disciplines. Both equate rationalisation with co-ordination. Both assume, somewhat prematurely and even "ideologically", that culture and identity no longer have any practical relevance.

21 For critical expositions of post-Fordism, see Mavroudeas (1990), Brenner and Glick (1991), and Fine (1995a), for example. For an account of post-Fordist consumption that unwittingly reveals how limited it is, see T. Smith (1998).

22 See Fine and Leopold (1993) and Fine (2000b) for a more recent assessment for historians in light of the themes presented here.

2 The enigma and fluidity of capital

1 This chapter draws in part upon Fine (1999a).
2 Such virtue will be needed to sustain attention over the pedestrian arguments with which this section opens. For neoclassical economics, especially in dealing with endogenous growth (a norm of) patience could indeed be (social) capital, as it leads to a higher discount rate, higher levels of saving and hence higher productivity!
3 Raising such considerations is far from radical since, in different ways, the new institutional economics of both Douglass North and Oliver Williamson ultimately rests upon the notion that there is something social within which institutions, property rights and individual optimising must be set. For Williamson's (1998, p. 26) approach draws upon social theory as highest level determinant – over and above economising, governance, and property rights – encompassing "embeddedness: informal institutions, customs, traditions, norms, religion". In similar vein, North (1981, pp. 11–12) argues:

> The dilemma of explaining change can be put succinctly ... Why do people obey the rules of society when they could evade them to their benefit? ... Something more than an individualistic calculus of cost–benefit is needed in order to account for change and stability ... Individuals may also obey customs, rules, and laws because of an equally deep-seated conviction that they are legitimate. Change and stability in history require a theory of ideology to account for these deviations from the individualistic rational calculus of neoclassical theory.

For a broader discussion, see Fine (2000d).
4 See Sklar (1998), for example, for discussion of consumer campaigns over wages and working conditions in early twentieth-century United States.
5 See Marchand (1998a and 1998b), Clarke (1999), and Leach (1993) for accounts of corporate "social capital", although they do not use the term. The issues involved in this and the previous footnote are discussed in Fine (2000c) in the context of collective or public consumption. This is the counterpart to, at least for economists, of social capital. For if the purpose of capital (as resources) is to provide utility through consumption, then "social consumption" is liable to mark out a corresponding social capital.
6 Nor does she herself, otherwise she could scarcely ask, "Is [inevitably] he one of *us*?", a reference to the division between "wets" and "dries".
7 For a fuller but elementary account of Marx's theory of capital, see Fine (1989).
8 See Dixon (1986) for the idea, especially through a reading of the work of Shackle, that (informational) uncertainties inevitably lead to, rather than substitute for, questions of power and conflict. See also Slater and Spencer (2000).
9 It should be emphasised that the appropriation by capital of new areas of activity is a complex and contradictory process as opposed to a simple case of shifting but frictional comparative advantage as most usually understood. The productivity increases associated with capitalism which tend to undermine alternative forms of production also have the effect of supporting them through making other sources of income and cheaper inputs available. See Fine (1992), Fine et al. (1996) for discussion in the context of domestic labour and food, respectively. For the former see also Fine (1995b) in debate with Kotz (1994 and 1995).
10 Radin (1996) quotes Marx from his *Economic and Philosophical Manuscripts* of 1844: "Private property has made us so stupid and one-sided that we think a thing is *ours* only when we have it." This is an important feature of social capital with unacknowledged tensions in the literature between its being held in the hands of individuals or society.
11 For a fuller exposition of the circuits of capital, bringing out these implications for ideology and theory, see Fine (1975a, 1980, and 1989). See also Arthur (1998).

12 Although this point is not developed here, it is worth observing the affinities between social capital and Marx's notion of the potential indirectly productive impact of unproductive labour (to which can be added non-wage labour). Note, however, that Marx's account is attached to a systematic understanding of the differences between the different types of labour in their relation to capital.

13 For a debate over analysis of such household appliances, see Bowden and Offer (1994 and 1999) and Fine (1999d).

14 For a discussion in this vein, for example, of patriarchy as an explanation for female oppression, see Fine (1992) following Connell (1987).

15 For a discussion at greater length of the issues that follow, see Fine (1998c) where they are addressed in terms of their relationship to value theory and to more concrete study both theoretically and empirically.

16 With commodities expressed in the monetary form of price, their dependence on social realities becomes almost entirely extinguished.

3 Bringing the social back in

1 This chapter draws on Fine (1998b) but is rewritten around a different theme. The earlier piece examined Becker's treatment of social capital as part of the evolving colonisation of other social sciences by economics, whereas here the emphasis is upon the evolution and position of social capital itself. References are to Becker (1996) unless otherwise indicated.

2 As Becker (1990, p. 39) himself confesses, " 'Economic imperialism' is probably a good description of what I do." It is also worth observing the fulsome praise lavished on Becker (p. xvii):

> By using Occam's razor to cut away ancillary assumptions, he reduces his axioms to one: that all actors in the social game are *homines economici* – economic persons, rational agents who maximize their advantages ... Inductivists would not believe it, but, by placing his models on this minimalist fulcrum, he shifts huge problems that other social scientists found immovable.

3 See also pp. 4, 25, and 49, for example.

4 It is co-authored with Baumol. It is essentially an informal presentation of the implications of Patinkin's denial of the classical dichotomy, with the suggestion that authors in the past were aware of them. The consequences of Patinkin's result are that money is not always neutral, and aggregation over individuals may be misleading in constructing the social. It is hardly surprising that such unpalatable results for Becker, derived from within orthodoxy, should never be taken up again. Interestingly, the style and content of the article are very different from those to follow, with some notable scholarship in the history of economic thought. This may, however, owe more to Baumol's influence, as Becker has rarely shown interest in what those in the past have had to say about a topic unless it has conformed to, or informed, his own approach.

5 Mainstream economists tend to understand the origins and nature of money in terms of a more efficient way of organising barter (or barter as a less efficient way of organising monetary exchange). See Strathern (1992, p. 169):

> It is a curiosity that anthropological attempts to describe non-monetary transactions may well end up concentrating on their monetary aspects ... It [barter] was regarded as a strategy through which people obtained things that they needed, that is, doing in the absence of money what people with money also do. In short, it was understood in "monetary" terms.

Paradoxically, the collection of Humphrey and Hugh-Jones (eds) (1992) in which her article appears also includes a contribution by economists, Anderlini and Sabourian (1992), which falls into this trap. See also Ingham (1999).

6 See the discussion of "benchkin" in Chapter 6. Note that the absence of money and unemployment is a particularly apt symbol of the failure to recognise a crucial characteristic of capitalism – that the labour market is monetised. See Campbell (1998) for a discussion.

7 A footnote compares this theorem with that of economics in which no firm is able to make profits despite being motivated by such. Also note how (political) power is rendered redundant.

8 Becker also begins in similar fashion, setting himself in opposition to Herbert Simon for suggesting that nationalisation might be necessary in a "free society". More generally, Becker's radical conservatism is marked in Becker and Becker (1996), a collection of *Business Week* articles, which include stances against affirmative action, no fault divorce, minimum wages, government expenditure and industrial policy, and stances in favour of vouchers for (third world) schooling and higher penalties for crime.

9 For a remarkable understanding of where such political science leads in the hands of one of his disciples, see Matsusaka (1995, p. 151), who deploys the principle reminiscent of the joke about the economist who will not pick up a bank note from the pavement on the grounds that, if it were genuine, it would already have been pocketed. For, concluding on the economic approach to democracy:

> Consider a policy that would make every single person in the country better off. Clearly there would be some pressure in favor of this policy, no pressure against it, and it would be implemented in short order. It follows that if there are any programs of this sort, they are already in effect.

10 See also: "As greater rigor permeated the theory of consumer demand, variables like distinction, a good name, or benevolence were pushed further and further out of sight" (p. 163).

11 Not surprisingly, Becker is dismissively harsh on psychology, for its reliance upon multiple personalities (p. 12), and cognitive imperfections (p. 22).

12 For a more sophisticated account, referenced by Becker, see Rogers (1994). He comes to conclusions about the evolution of the rate of time preference on grounds such as, "the fact that offspring are imperfect genetic replicas of their parents" (p. 478) in closing his text!

13 See Hargreaves-Heap (1992) for critical discussion of such rationality and from a conventional perspective, Rabin (1998), who observes that behavioural research leads to rejection of the assumptions made by economists about given preferences. There is insufficient learning from mistakes (because of belief perseverance), the presence of multiple-self models, and misperception of own welfare (in adjusting to changed circumstances) as indicated by lottery winners not being as happy as anticipated. The latter has generated a literature amongst economists recently in view of the need to explain the empirical anomaly that long-term sense of well-being does not appear to rise with income. See collection edited by Dixon (1997).

14 These are necessary so that very large differences in the material outcomes for men and women can be explained merely on the basis of the slightest biological differences (p. 151):

> The economic approach to the gender division of labor ... does not try to weight the relative importance of biology and discrimination. Its main contribution is to show how sensitive the division of labor is to *small* differences in either. Since the return from investing in a skill is greater when more time is spent utilizing the skill, a married couple could gain much from a sharp division of labor because the husband would specialize in some types of human capital and the

wife in others. Given such a large gain from specialization within a marriage, only a *little* discrimination against women or *small* biological differences in child-rearing skills would cause the division of labor between household and market tasks to be strongly and systematically related to gender.

15 Note that Solow (1990, p. 276) denies him sympathy on correctly predicting that he would become a Nobel prize-winner. The hostility to Becker has not been confined to economists. He reports (Becker 1990, p. 33), "when I gave my first paper on population, I said I was treating children as 'durable consumer goods'. There was laughter in the audience ... as much from the economists as from sociologists and the demographers." On suggesting in the late 1970s in the sociology department at Chicago that there should be a course on microeconomics for sociologists, "the audience booed me" (p. 34). To some extent, he is deliberately provocative. According to Febrero and Schwartz: "He modeled the family as a multiperson production function, as a 'factory', he says, to shock sociologists" (1995, p. xix).

To shock or not, this is what he does in fact do in the economist's image of a factory. Note that Granovetter (1990b) sees two differences between himself and Becker on relationships. Becker is not specific enough in, for example, suggesting that the utility of the mother enters into that of the child and, in network vein, the whole is greater than the sum of dyadic exchanges. None of this, to anticipate, is incompatible with Becker's subsequent stance.

16 His earliest and most famous contribution is provided by the "market for lemons" (Akerlof 1970), catching the asymmetry of information between buyers and sellers in the second-hand car market and leading to inefficient or even absent markets. Significantly, the paper, dating from 1966, was originally rejected by both the *American Economic Review* and the *Journal of Political Economy* (Akerlof 1990, p. 33). More generally, see Akerlof (1984).

17 Schelling (1990, p. 194) suggests in contrast to Becker that: "George Akerlof is more creative. He has a great curiosity ... [he] is almost the opposite of economic imperialism. He looks into sociology for concepts that he can import into economics."

18 Surprisingly, the mindful Elster (1990, p. 238) refers to Becker in terms of "the mindless application of rational choice theory to everything".

19 Taramasalata is even better. My own preferred parable for Becker's reductionism is that of the child whose first toy is a hammer and who presumes that everything in the world is a nail. Pusey (1991, pp. 203–04) puts it in more scholarly terms:

> This simply points to the much more predatory nature of a new scientism that reappears in an economic reductionism if a very absolutist, cybernetically dynamic and self-referential form. From the moment that humans first began to think critically about the criteria that ought to be applied to the process of thinking itself, it has always been assumed that one test of a good theory is that it should understand its own limits: judged on that criterion neoclassical economic rationalism is, most certainly, not a very good theory.

20 He refers to Becker (1958), discussed above, a shortened version of a graduate paper that, significantly, was rejected by the *Journal of Political Economy* in 1952–53. He expresses regret at how his disappointment led him not to persist elsewhere with the longer version, "nobody paid it much attention ... I was applying economics to politics as early as anyone. But the rejection hurt" (Becker 1990, p. 33).

21 For a fuller account, see Fine (1998a, Chapter 3) and also Fine and Rose (2001).

22 Such herding behaviour, apparently unobserved by Becker, is most sharply typical of financial speculative bubbles.

23 In this light, Becker's pre-occupation with addiction is understandable as it is taken by him to be the epitome of seemingly irrational preferences which can be explained on the basis of the economic approach.

24 Once again, given his lack of consideration of money.

25 Becker (1996) is ultimately a fertile source for a plethora of capitals, the index in his book suggesting for "capital", that the reader "*see specific types*" which are, in the event, not that numerous but do include both addictive and imagination capital. For the latter: "People change the weight they attach to future utilities by spending more time, effort, and goods in creating personal capital that helps them to better imagine the future" (pp. 10–11).

   For this, he is berated by Baron and Hannan (1994, p. 1123) who observe that he has progressed from use of human capital to capital for any type of activity, emphasising that such invention is far from new for sociologists. They refer explicitly to Bourdieu's notions of linguistic and cultural capitals, which are perceived to merge Marxian ideas on class reproduction with economic notions of human capital – Bourdieu is Beckered! See also Calhoun (1993, p. 84) who observes: "Despite his disclaimers Bourdieu does indeed share a great deal with Gary Becker and other rational choice theorists." But see the discussion in Chapter 4.

26 This is despite his modest admission (Becker 1990, p. 29): "After reading Parsons, I decided sociology was just too difficult for me." This is hardly surprising in light of Velthuis' (1999) argument that Parsons viewed economics and sociology as incompatible with one concerned with the theory of the individual and the other with the theory of the social, respectively.

4 Bourdieu's social capital: from distinction to extinction

1 This chapter draws in part on Fine (1999a).

2 In his later work, Bourdieu (1998b) explicitly locates *Distinction* in terms of access to different forms of capital of which social capital is one.

3 For an extreme instance, with technique prevailing over interpretation, see Anheier and Gerhards (1995), who use blockmodelling to examine the social and cultural capital of German writers to explain their elite membership or not.

4 Note that Longhurst and Savage (1996) see Bourdieu has having been appropriated differently by UK and US academic traditions with emphasis, respectively, on active consumerism as opposed to sustaining cultural distinctions.

5 See Bourdieu (1998b) for an elementary account of his approach, with greater emphasis on social relations than social structures. For a sympathetic overview, see McLennan (1998).

6 See also Porter (1993) who associates Baudrillard with hysteria in the context of history and consumption.

7 See especially Bourdieu (1998a, pp. 54–55):

> Everywhere we hear it said ... there is nothing to put forward in opposition to the neo-liberal view, that it has succeeded in presenting itself as self-evident, that there is no alternative. If it is taken for granted ... as a result of a whole labour of symbolic inculcation in which journalists and ordinary citizens participate passively and, above all, a certain number of intellectuals participate actively. Against this permanent, insidious imposition ... researchers have a role to play ... [to] analyse the production and circulation of this discourse ... [and] describe very precisely the procedures whereby this worldview is produced, disseminated and inculcated ... [by] analyses of texts, the journals in which they were published and which have little by little imposed themselves as legitimate, the characteristics of their authors, the seminars in which they meet to produce them, etc.

Ideally, the same tasks would be undertaken for social capital!

8 See Bourdieu (1986b, p. 243) where economic capital is what is "immediately and directly convertible into money" (quoted in Calhoun 1993, p. 70).

9 See also Bourdieu (1994, pp. 111 and 127; and 1996b, p. 265) and Bourdieu and Wacquant (1992, p. 97).

10 Beasley-Murray (1999) points to Bourdieu's fluid notion of capital in observing the latter's reference to the state as "the central bank of symbolic credit" (Bourdieu 1996b, p. 376).

11 See Lamont and Lareau (1988, p. 159).

12 As in the symbolic capital of the bachelor on a dance floor and his capacity to dress, dance and present himself (Bourdieu and Wacquant 1992, p. 165).

13 Compare with Becker's (1990, p. 41) reference to the problem of the source of hegemonic language:

> The speaker last night at the rational choice seminar spoke on why one specific language gets chosen as the official language in a multilingual situation. He said that he wasn't a rational choice person until he concluded that he could best explain the behaviour he was investigating with the rationality assumption. And that is OK to me.

See also Lazear (2000).

14 See also Bourdieu (1998b, p. 7): "agents are distributed ... according to the overall volume of the different kinds of capital they possess, and ... according to the relative weight of the different kinds of capital, economic and cultural."

15 See also Robbins (1991, p. 154):

> Bourdieu argues that the notion of "cultural capital" which he had used at that time (1964) has been necessary to differentiate his position from those of both the educational psychologists and the "human capital" economists. Although he does not explicitly say so (in 1979), however, it is clear that "cultural capital" was not wholly satisfactory because it was individualistic.

It is far from clear that such individualistic content has been both recognised and rectified in subsequent work.

16 See also Bourdieu (1981, p. 308) where the positions of the Sun King's courtiers are interpreted as "their power over the objectified degrees of the specific capital – which the king controls and manipulates within the room for manoeuvre the game allows him". The theme recurs in Bourdieu (1998b, p. 47) where it is applied to the twelfth and thirteenth centuries, but Louis XIV remains the favoured application. His possession of symbolic capital "makes one bow ... (and) allows him to demean, demote, or consecrate, etc." (p. 85).

17 See also Wacquant (1996). From a Marxist perspective, this is a remarkable inversion in that the categories of capitalism are explained by those attached to a lower form of development. A striking illustration of the use of such theory in advance of the object of theory is the case study provided by Kolankiewicz (1996). He deploys the notion of social capital (education, connections, etc.) to anticipate who will become capitalists in the Polish transition to capitalism. It is "interpreted as various networks brought into play by the absence of conventional capital" (p. 429).

18 See also Calhoun (1993, p. 65) and Postone et al. (1993, p. 5): "Economic capital can be more easily and efficiently converted into symbolic (that is, social and cultural) capital than vice versa, although symbolic capital can ultimately be transformed into economic capital."

19 Ryan (1992, p. 50) puts the issue well: "The problem for capital is that *commoditisation* of cultural objects erodes those qualities and properties which constitute them as cultural objects, as use values in the first place." See also Slater's (1997, p. 71) reference to Gresham's law of cultural taste – a parallel with money suggested by F.R. Leavis – in which the good is driven out of circulation by the bad. This paradox can,

however, be exaggerated as is revealed by Haug's notion of the aesthetic illusion being turned to commercial gain. See Fine and Leopold (1993, Chapter 2) for a discussion.

20 Consequently, Bourdieu (1998b, pp. 106–07) sees these two logics as confronting one another, with the logic of the economy undermining sentiment, collectivity, and solidarity. As a result:

> The family is subject to two contradictory systems of forces: on the one hand the forces of the economy ... and, on the other hand, the forces of cohesion which are in part linked to the fact that the reproduction of capital in its different forms depends, to a large degree, on the reproduction of the family unit.

Or, as Cantwell (1999, p. 219) opens his assessment of Bourdieu, "*Money can't buy me love* – the Beatles".

21 This has not prevented the emergence of a theory of religion within neoclassical economics. For a survey, see Iannacone (1998).

22 See Wu (1998) for the notion that corporate spending on the arts is a way of accumulating cultural capital.

23 In many ways, much of the content of Bourdieu's approach is captured in the following (Bourdieu 1996b, p. 318):

> Symbolic capital consisting of recognition, confidence, and, in a word, legitimacy has its own laws of accumulation that are distinct from those of economic capital ... [Such] durable capital tends to be ... misrecognised, recognised legitimate capital ... through conversion into better concealed forms of capital, such as works of art or education.

24 Thus, as Lamont and Lareau (1988, p. 156) lament, "In Bourdieu's global theoretical framework, cultural capital is alternatively an informal academic standard, a class attribute, a basis for social selection, and a resource for power which is salient as an indicator/basis of class position." See also Calhoun (1993, p. 65).

25 Most notably in Bourdieu (1986b, pp. 244–45) for cultural capital. See also Bourdieu (1994, p. 127) and Bourdieu (1986a, p. 177) for the hidden capital that generates distinct tastes for food.

26 Febrero and Schwartz (1995) implicitly claim that Becker too has discovered the invisible. In his case, ironically so from the perspective of political economy, for he is the most vulgar of economists, and merely identifies all of life itself as economic, an insight that is understandably beyond most normal visions (p. xliii):

> Becker's economics differs from traditional economics in two fundamental respects: scope and approach. Economic theory is a much more powerful tool than noneconomists and even professional economists tend to think, being not only the science of explicit markets and prices but a way of thinking. A whole new world of nonmarket activities is waiting to be fruitfully analyzed by economic tools. The economic theories of marriage, fertility, and criminal and political behaviour are outstanding examples of this *imperialistic* view of economics in which Becker has become a leading figure. Armed with the postulates of stable preferences, maximizing behaviour, and market equilibrium, the economist can offer insights into areas not traditionally viewed as the province of economics. More often than not, these insights are at variance with casual observation, conventional wisdom, or established propositions from other sciences.

27 For overviews of the new economic sociology, see collections edited by Swedberg. For a critique, see Ingham (1996).

28 Note, however, that DiMaggio (1991, p. 153) provides evidence for the interpretation

offered here of a transition away from the extremes of postmodernism in which concepts of capital play a leading role. In the context of cultural production but of more general applicability:

> The received terminology of lay and academic cultural criticism – phrases such as mass society, highbrow–lowbrow, postmodernism – will not get us very far in addressing such issues. Terms that have entered the sociological vocabulary during the past two decades – cultural capital, cultural industry systems, and others developed by Pierre Bourdieu … will provide more leverage. What such recent progress promises is an analytic sociology of culture, distinct from criticism and textual interpretation, sensitive to the structural and pragmatic aspects of the symbolic economy, rigorously empirical in method and temperament, and thus capable of a comprehension of contemporary cultural change.

29 It is noted that this leads to a chicken and egg problem as far as the definition of the field of a particular type of capital is concerned as well as its distribution across agents and activities (Bourdieu and Wacquant 1992, p. 108). It should also be observed that Bourdieu's categories of capital have proved far from temporary in his and other hands and that it is essential that their genealogy be uncovered irrespective of how temporary they are for him.

30 Note the Althusserian overtones and also that Bourdieu frequently does degenerate into economic reductionism, in part because this is immanent in the notion of convertibility between the various types of capital, so that one is equivalent to another (whether in changing form, as in the profit of non-economic capital, or in the balance of conflict where one form is set against another).

31 This methodological commitment is made more secure by Bourdieu's pre-occupation with cultural studies. The symbolic is perceived as the most complex form of capital and "his whole work may be read as a hunt for its varied forms and effects" (Bourdieu and Wacquant 1992, p. 119).

32 Portes (1998) agrees that Bourdieu has been dropped: "This lack of visibility is lamentable because Bourdieu's analysis is arguably the most theoretically refined amongst those that introduced the term in sociological discourse." Unfortunately, despite being translated and despite his prominence in use of other forms of capital, such as the symbolic and the cultural, an explanation is proffered in terms of Bourdieu's writing in French. Further, whilst correctly pointing to Bourdieu's use of fungibility between capitals, and much that goes with it, there is no apparent awareness of the contextual content of Bourdieu, in the social construction of meaning.

33 We leave aside the new economic geography that is simply the application of the theory of market imperfections to the location and level of economic activity, all uncritically understood. See the special issue edited by Venables (1998) for example and, within it, Krugman (1998) who correctly specifies the new economic geography as a synthesis of new growth and trade theories, incorporating increasing returns to scale and cumulative causation and other market imperfections so that, relative to earlier location theory (p. 9):

> They fail to explain how the spatial structures they describe would be either created or maintained by the actions of self-interested individuals. Again, by contrast, the new economic geography is all about what spatial equilibria might exist … when individuals are choosing locations to maximize their welfare given what other individuals are doing.

In short, the imperialism of economics as applied to geography. For a parallel treatment of the spatial nature of social capital, see Sampson et al. (1999). For a critique of the new economic geography, see Martin (1999).

34 Kearns and Philo (1993, p. ix) point to "*cultural capital* where 'capital' refers both to money and to 'capital' or sizeable cities".

35 Despite the use of terminology from Marxist political economy, the latter is clear that urban capital is no such thing, is at best fictitious capital, and derives its "valorisation" from the present value of a stream of income, unlike any other capital if such it were.

36 Equally of interest, if to anticipate, is the response to Castle across the social sciences. Salamon (1998) comments from an anthropological perspective that notions of cohesion and integration are long-standing, and so there is no need to jump on the social capital bandwagon, not least in avoiding economic reductionism. An illustration is offered in terms of migrant workers in agriculture, who can exhibit strong intra-community solidarity but can also suffer exclusion by old timers. Consequently, social capital is unevenly distributed and contested. A warning is issued against oversimplification of community culture but a welcome given to the broadened understanding of capital by an economist. For Summers and Brown (1998) social capital has emerged over the last fifteen years but is ancient in concept, the "glue" that bonds individuals. "Because it is used by so many people to mean so many different things, it seems quite predictable that rancorous debate over the proper definition will soon follow" (p. 642).

Further, it is perceived as a general abstraction with many potentially measurable dimensions and considerable heuristic value, but still leaving causal issues unresolved. It has the advantage of potentially bringing together a range of disparate theories. Its current prominence (when focusing on the local and associational) is possibly a consequence of dissatisfaction with more traditional forms of collective action and delivery – whether "religious, political, labor, ethnic, racial, or gender organization, or the state" (p. 642). This all anticipates in broad brush much that is to follow in Chapter 7.

37 It has also, of course, become appropriately common to understand the cultural and the symbolic not only in terms of meaning but also through contestation and conflict, each proving uncomfortable for social capital once departing Bourdieu. Thus, for example, whilst continuing to emphasise its economic convertibility, Thornton (1995) understands the subcultural capital, attached to youth, as more complex than a dialectic of submission and resistance – as in clubbing.

5 Bringing rational choice back in

1 It would, of course, be possible to trace social capital back further beyond social exchange but a line has to be drawn somewhere – and it is, as will be seen in the social capital literature, around Coleman. But see Chadwick-Jones (1976) for an overview of origins and influence of social exchange, with particular emphasis on the work of Thibaut and Kelley (1959). Yet he confesses that "they do not discuss exchange theory as such" (p. 5), setting a standard for the later predilection of social capital theory to incorporate any contribution to social theory wherever it has any resonance irrespective of broader analytical compatibility (Chapter 7).

2 Note that the literature has also been seen in terms of the macro/micro divide – my first issue – and reductionism, but the latter straddles the two issues laid out here.

3 Note that Lindenberg (1990) suggests that macro-sociological models of behaviour had become exhausted by the 1960s, thereby paving the way for a renewal of interest in economic models, albeit in unclean forms.

4 This is in debate with Zelizer (2000) and concerns the appropriate understanding of money and commodities in addressing how the personal can enter into the apparently impersonal world of market relations.

5 Thus, Ekeh (1974) observes a lack of scholarship in ignorance or neglect of earlier relevant writers in exchange theory. For an exception that proves the rule, see Mitchell (1978) who seeks a return to Mauss in order to resolve the contradictions of social exchange theory.

6 The continuing presence of social exchange theory within social psychology is marked, for example, in the volume edited by Burgess and Huston (eds) (1979) to which Homans contributed a foreword. In this case, social exchange theory incorporates a dual projection – from behaviourism to personal development and from the latter to social development.

7 The difference for Homans between humans and other species is the presence and extent of symbolic behaviour, which is dynamic and learnt, together with a capacity for conscious choice. Note, leaving aside the symbolic, the affinity with social capital as understood by economists. This is especially so for the interpretation of Homans – as in Chadwick-Jones (1976), for example – as dependent upon psychological reinforcement, which has an exact correspondence with the trust and credibility that accrues through repeated interaction.

8 Remarkably, in opening his chapter on human exchange, following the previous chapter concerned with a pigeon pecking in response to a seed feed stimulus, Homans (1961, p. 30) asserts:

> In this book we are less interested in individual than in social behaviour, or true exchange, where the activity of each of at least two animals reinforces (or punishes) the activity of the other, and where accordingly each influences the other. Yet we hold that we need no new propositions to describe and explain the social. With social behaviour nothing unique emerges to be analyzed only in its own terms. Rather, from the laws of individual behaviour, such as those sketched in out in the last chapter, follow the laws of social behaviour when the complications of mutual reinforcement are taken into account.

9 Mitchell (1978, p. 12) sees Homans' development of social exchange theory as only deriving in part from the desire for an individualistic theory, and hence psychological behaviourism and utilitarian economics, on which see below, the other parts being his method of deduction from induction, his anti-functionalism and anti-collectivism, and his aversion to functional anthropology. These, however, all seem to have common roots in the first part.

10 For Ekeh (1974, p. 191), Lévi-Strauss and Homans are mirror images of one another with, respectively, the one taking social structure as elementary and individualised exchange as its complex outcome, and the other viewing social structure as the complex outcome of individualised exchange.

11 Homans (1961, p. 68) confesses that "it should be clear by now that what we have been saying owes much to elementary economics".

12 Thus, more generally, Ekeh (1974) argues that the supposed importance of social exchange theory to sociology lies in its ability to address economic and social exchange, the structure of reciprocity, restricted and generalised exchange, exploitation and power, and social solidarity.

13 See also Cook and Emerson (1978) who wish to address power and equity by going beyond the dyadic exchange, associated with economics, to norms in order to determine an outcome, reflecting the orthodox confines of their economics, somewhere along, or otherwise in relation to, the Edgeworth contract curve (or points of Pareto-efficiency).

14 This is hopelessly fragmented and chaotic. As Friedman (1987, p. 47) notes, in reporting a colleague's comments on Emerson's, admittedly unfinished, paper, "I *loved* the first two pages and then, frankly, he lost me … Pointing out a problem is easier than solving it." Note that Homans was also distressed to be unable to make his contribution to this volume in honour of Emerson for "circumstances beyond my control" (Cook (ed.) 1987, p. 10). No doubt such circumstances and untimely death, as of Emerson, do prevent completion of papers. However, failure to finish is also related to the difficulty of what needs to be done. As, in this case, it is a matter of

squaring the circle of constructing the social out of the individual, failure to finish is consistent with the hypothesis that at some point, circumstance or death would inevitably interrupt proceedings. This is reminiscent of Ricardo's commitment to the labour theory of value – taken unresolved to his death-bed despite his having proven it to be wrong within his own approach; and also of Fermat's Last Theorem except that it has finally been proven to be true albeit with considerable difficulty (Singh 1997).

15 See also Gergen et al. (eds) (1980).

16 Here there is a parallel with the new institutional economics whether in the slightly different versions associated with Douglass North and Oliver Williamson, for example, where institutions and economic rationality are ultimately dependent on social values. See Fine (2000d) for a critical discussion. Note that Hodgson's (1994b) critique of methodological individualism highlights that it is arbitrary both methodologically and historically to allocate priority to rational choice once it is acknowledged to be symbiotic with continuing social outcomes.

17 Note that Emerson (1976, p. 359) sees, "social exchange theory as developing the conceptual tools needed (longitudinal exchange relations and network structure) to deal with exactly those topics that economic theory has trouble with: market imperfections". Apart from the previously observed ignorance even of the mainstream economics of the time, which is heavily committed to examining market imperfections, the new micro-foundations, which is concerned exclusively with market imperfections, would inevitably render social exchange theory redundant. Note this article appears in the *Annual Review of Sociology*, with Coleman then serving as an associate editor.

18 She refers explicitly to the work of Coleman (1986), discussed in the next section.

19 Turner (1987) also disagrees with Blau but for a different reason: he is happy with Emerson for his treatment of the macro-structural in its leading to network theory but less happy with the micro because of the limited set of processes drawn upon.

20 Note that Bourdieu (1991) essentially views such oppositions as obstacles to analytical progress.

21 Coleman primarily acknowledges his debt for social capital to Loury (1977 and 1987). But he also refers to Bourdieu (1980) and to Flap and de Graaf (1986), the latter a mundane application of social capital to the relationship between personal connections (networks) and occupational attainment. Note that the two authors of social capital come together in the 1990s in Bourdieu and Coleman (eds) (1991). In his epilogue, Bourdieu (1991, p. 373) considers the enterprise to have been a success in potentially breaching a dialogue of the mutually deaf. Despite this claim, there is little evidence of Bourdieu having been heard by the followers of Coleman.

22 See also Coleman and Hoffer (1987).

23 See Ramsay and Clark (1990).

24 For Swedberg (1990, p. 5):

> What is happening today is very significant: *the border between two of the major social sciences is being redrawn, thereby providing new perspectives on a whole range of very important problems both in the economy and in society at large.*

Even later, Smelser and Swedberg (1994) remain uncertain whether this will lead to an imperialism of economics.

25 Coleman's (1990a) presentation and assessment of social exchange theory is limited.

26 Smelser and Swedberg (1994, p. 17) report that Coleman initiated the journal *Rationality and Society* from 1989, Coleman (1994, p. 172) himself describing it as "directed wholly to work in rational choice sociology". See also "In Memoriam" in *Rationality and Society*, vol 7, no 3, 1995, pp. 253–54.

27 Turner (1987, pp. 223–24), thus, sees Emerson as having freed social exchange theory from the shackles imposed by Homans' behaviourism and Coleman's utilitarianism.

28 See also p. 363:

> Satisfactory *social* theory must attempt to describe behaviour of social units, not merely that of individuals … it must nevertheless be grounded in the behaviour of individuals … the central theoretical challenge is to show how individual actions combine to produce a social outcome.

29 For another example of Coleman's profound ignorance of neoclassical economics, see the bizarre statement of his fundamental difference with it on the grounds that it should use a Cobb–Douglas utility function rather than one of general functional form (Coleman 1990b, p. 57). He also inappropriately berates it for being incapable of making interpersonal comparisons.

30 On a different tack, in a review of his book, Frank (1992, p. 148) rebukes Coleman mildly for lack of originality and/or scholarship in failing to refer to Schelling's (1978) work, with Coleman's volume, "if not a clone of Schelling's, then at least its fraternal twin".

31 Something of a problem for his disciple, Putnam, who perceives social capital being laid down in Italy at least a century earlier!

32 See Coleman (1990a, pp. 590–95) where it is argued that women's working has been highly destructive for family life and children's social capital. More generally, empirical study leads him to the conclusion that the following factors can impair social and intellectual development: absence of a parent, more siblings (and hence less attention), talking personally, mother working before school age, and parental interest in child attending college. He also deplores the extent to which welfare provision undermines the interdependence associated with social capital (p. 321).

33 Yet another irony in Coleman's work is his unwitting parody of a position in favour of market socialism, only using state-determined price incentives to achieve parenting goals. There is, then, the added twist of a much more extensive scope for the market covered by the shadow pricing of the central planning board, to include economic and social reproduction!

34 See Portes (1998) for the idea that Coleman is concerned with the "process of social engineering that will substitute obsolete forms of control based on primordial ties with rationally devised material and status incentives".

35 Note that Coleman (1987a), in a contribution to a volume dedicated to social exchange theory, already has most of what he needs in place for social capital. Displaying an elementary command of economics, he addresses the problem of how both free-riders and altruists (or zealots) can exist in otherwise similar forms of organisation. He offers (for the latter) an answer in terms of regard for welfare of others within own welfare.

36 The possible exception, as observed earlier, is psychology since it is concerned with "the action of a natural person" (Swedberg (ed) 1990, p. 53). Even so, Coleman seems to think that it is possible that "the same structure exists *internal* to the individual, and the values of particular resources or events for the system are his interests, since he is the system." Elsewhere, Coleman (1991) sees constructed social organisation by way of physical analogy, as in nuclear fission and genetic engineering.

37 Although, as observed in Chapter 3, Becker's theory invariably relies upon an exchange economy without money.

38 Becker (1990, p. 40) himself sees the similarities to be greater than the differences with Coleman, with the emphasis on stable preferences being "a huge asset, surely not a handicap". Further, Becker (1990, p. 50) suggests:

> I think the differences between the various schools [of economics and sociology] are much smaller than the similarities. Basically, what the rational choice people do is to start with some unit of behaviour or actor that they assume is behaving rationally.

39 In this respect, the division, from the perspective of rational choice, between economics and sociology in dealing with the rational and irrational, respectively, is broken down. See Swedberg (1990, p. 13).

40 In this respect, the social is simply the systemic sum of the individual parts. As Heilbroner and Milberg (1995, p. 87) suggest:

> "Micro" and "macro", in that microbehaviour cannot be understood without taking cognizance of its social origins, and social forces remain empty abstractions unless they enter into the motivational concreteness of one or more individuals.

41 See also Coleman (1994, pp. 168–69). The prisoners' dilemma is deployed to suggest that social equilibrium can differ from social optimum and, hence, rational choice differs from functionalism. He concludes on the potential of social capital for addressing economic problems (p. 177):

> By the recognition that capital inheres not only in physical plant and in individuals, but also in the social relations that exist among individuals, rational choice theory provides economic analysis with a valuable conceptual tool, social capital.

None of this is at all foreign or enriching to an economics that increasingly includes game theory in its technical repertoire. Note that Swedberg (1990, p. 7) also reports Granovetter as civilising economics through network theory, with his refusing to accept "the economists' turf", and with sociologists handling traditional economics problems better than economists.

42 One interesting illustration – occasionally repeated elsewhere by others, and cited by reference to Coleman (1988, p. S99) in Portes (1998) – is that of diamond traders, and their need for mutual trust over quality. Crucially, however, nowhere is there any reference whatsoever to the extrinsic conditions that make this both possible and necessary, namely the unique and long-standing world cartel organised for the production and marketing of diamonds by de Beers.

43 See Sandefur and Laumann (1998) for social capital in these Colemanesque terms. See also Pérez-Sáinz (1997, p. 151), referring to Portes and Sensenbrenner (1993) and defining social capital "as expectations for action in a collectivity that, though not oriented toward the economic sphere, affects behaviour in business dealings per se and the general economic ends of its members".

44 Despite seeking to cover the foundations of social theory, issues such as (re)distribution and (in)equality are notably absent from his work, although it is recognised that inequality of resources may lead to inequality in outcomes as well as inability of the impoverished to counter the rich and powerful, not only for lack of resources, but because of the greater costs than benefits to them of doing so (p. 262). This, however, borders on tautology, with inequality of outcomes dependent upon inequality of initial endowments, no matter how complex the mechanisms connecting the two. Of course, in anything other than a world of economic and social equilibrium, this period's outcomes are next period's initial endowments. Note that Coleman (1990a) is also heavily concerned with rights but these are associated with power, the "control over whatever is of value in the system, that is, whatever interests others ... the capability of applying sanctions to enforce one's interests" (pp. 815–16).

45 By analogy with the question of whether merchants become producers or vice versa. To pursue the analogy the truly revolutionary route is from the latter to the former, and from economics to sociology.

46 Also cited in Foley and Edwards (1999).

47 The extent of his capital fetishism is revealed by Coleman's (1988, p. S100) commentary on human capital:

Probably the most important and original development in the economics of education in the past 30 years has been the idea that the concept of physical capital ... can be extended to include human capital as well. Just as physical capital is created by changes in materials to form tools that facilitate production, human capital is created by changes in persons that bring about skills and capabilities that make them able to act in new ways.

See also Coleman (1990a, p. 304).

48 For an illustration of how social capital serves these purposes whilst appearing to do otherwise, see Lyons (2000, p. 676):

Social capital acts as an umbrella term that covers a wide range of processes by which social relations are formed and form other institutions or relationships. It suffers, however, from being poorly defined and imprecisely applied. The concept of social capital does allows [sic] for an open debate about issues such as social structure, norms and habits in economics that challenge the concept of "methodological individualism".

In contrast, social capital is the latter, once stripped of lack of precision!

6 Making the benchmark work for social theory

1 See also Benjamin and Kochin (1982).
2 This is especially so of the literature attached to the non-accelerating inflation rate of unemployment (NAIRU), which rests on a path-dependent natural rate of unemployment around which the benefit–wage ratio has the B&K effect. For a broader critical discussion of such issues, see Fine (1998a, Chapter 2). There are also parallels with the notion that a higher minimum wage causes higher unemployment. See Fine (1998a, Chapter 9) for a critical review. Note that the Phillips' curve (inflation–unemployment trade-off) from which NAIRU and much other macroeconomics derives is itself a "benchkin", a term to be defined below. Empirically discovered on the basis of what subsequently proved to be misleading data, theory was constructed to address the (false) facts. With the breakdown of the Phillips' curve in the 1970s, due to stagflation, the theory was modified by the addition of expectations to explain the new evidence that contradicted the (false) evidence it was designed to explain in the first place. Such is the nature in practice of the verificationism and falsificationism attached to the (ab)normal science of economics. Note that Lawson (1997) implicitly suggests that all economics contains benchkin elements.
3 Billiet and Cambré (1999, p. 259) refer to social capital in *Distinction* purely in functional terms, Jordana (1999, p. 67) cites Coleman's citation of an obviously unread reference to Bourdieu (in French), and Newton (1999a, p. 18) makes a passing reference to Bourdieu's use of cultural capital.
4 Rather than taking opportunity here as well as elsewhere to address critiques, Gamm and Putnam (1999) is primarily a descriptive and statistical account of associational activity in the United States.
5 Alamazán (1999) addresses social capital in fifteenth- and early sixteenth-century Aztec society but only uses the term in the title to his paper!
6 See volume 86, no 2, 1997. For a rare reference to Banfield, see Guiso et al. (2000) who, following him and Putnam, seek to establish that financial development is distributed across Italy according to levels of social capital.
7 Putnam's continuing research falls under the "Social Capital and Public Affairs Project" of the American Academy of Arts and Sciences, which he directs with support from the Carnegie, Ford, and Rockefeller Foundations.
8 See also the discussion and references provided in Harriss and de Renzio (1997). As

Bayart (1999, p. 32) diplomatically suggests, "the use made of this concept by Putnam to analyse the governance of the Italian peninsula has captured the imagination of World Bank experts, even if it has not convinced every specialist on Italian affairs", including his Harvard colleagues.

9 As Tarrow (1996, p. 390) observes, for Putnam: "The same seeds of institutional innovation grow differently in different socioeconomic cultural soils to produce different kinds of institutional plants." Reminiscent of the Peter Sellers' character in "Being There", the simple gardener who inadvertently became economic adviser to the US President, Tarrow continues in a footnote, "the botanic metaphor is no accident; it was even more explicit in another report on [their] work in Italian". See Chapter 9 for continuing use of social capital as metaphor. Further, it is a short step from metaphor to what Tarrow refers to as "chamber-of-commerce enthusiasm" with Putnam relying upon the virtues of choral societies, soccer teams, bird-watching and Rotary clubs, and relatively honest leaders prepared to compromise (p. 392). Tarrow also observes the shift from prosaic to elegiac in shifting from north to south, as politicians become corrupt, undemocratic, cynical, etc.

10 As detailed by Tarrow in his footnote 6.

11 Similar considerations and more detail are provided by Brucker (1999) and Muir (1999), summed up by Rotberg (1999, p. 344):

> They disagree openly with Putnam, however, over what northern Italy city-states were like before the Risorgimento. They squarely criticize Putnam's assumptions about how northern Italy came to accumulate much more social capital than did southern Italy.

12 It would be interesting to speculate over the role of corruption in understanding development in light of revelations around the South Korea financial crisis of the late 1990s, let alone, at time of writing, those in the former West Germany surrounding the now disgraced former Chancellor, Helmut Kohl.

13 For even more devastating and wide-ranging criticism, see Jackman and Miller (1998), who draw upon a range of literature to comment on Putnam's Italian conclusions concerning measures of civic community and institutional performance as follows:

> Putnam's own data do not warrant this claim. His primary dependent variable, composite measure of institutional performance is flawed … [if] broken down to reflect individual dimensions of institutional performance, the evidence for social-capital effects is weak to non-existent … more qualitative historical evidence to argue that regional differences in social capital can be traced back to the Middle Ages … ignores considerable evidence that shifting regional differences have been structurally induced.

14 See Chapter 7.

15 See also Tarrow (1996, pp. 393–94) for brief reference to the "historiographic aspects of Putnam's analysis of southern Italy since the Norman conquests … [and] the criticisms they have raised".

16 The thesis is refined and generalised by Hemingway (1999) in suggesting that different forms of leisure activity have different implications for democracy depending upon the weight of their contribution to social capital.

17 See Putnam (1996b) in debate with Skocpol (1996). He tends to accept all criticisms as valid and as qualifications to his otherwise unchanged underlying approach.

18 Although Putnam (1996b) claims to have been caricatured in the overemphasis placed on television.

19 Uslaner (1998) argues that optimism, rather than rejecting television, is important in generating trust. Shah (1998) reasonably suggests that content of programmes is

important. Rahn and Transue (1998) suggest decline of US trust is a consequence of the rise of vulgar materialism.

20 See also McBride (1998) finding that individualism is heavily represented in the content of TV shows. This, however, raises the issue of the extent to which this is the responsibility of the system of media mega-corporations in much the same way that decline of communities can be dependent upon closure or relocation of plants, on which see below.

21 See also Rich (1999).

22 East Timor's exiled government website in Ireland was deliberately sabotaged by a conspiracy of worldwide access overload.

23 Contrast with the lack of doubt reported by Stamps (1998) for Tom Sander, executive director of the Saguaro Seminar, set up at Harvard out of Putnam's work. He opines that every measure of social capital has been on the wane from between 15% and 25% over the past thirty years. See also Paxton (1999) who, amongst other issues, is careful to distinguish measures based on trust as opposed to associations, points to definitional ambiguities in theory and hence in measurement, and finding no general decline in social capital over time.

24 Verba et al. (1997) also relate voting (less in US) and political participation (tilted towards the wealthy and educated) to the increasing role of funding as the form of participation which excludes the poor. On the other hand, van Deth (2000) implicitly sees political activity as an inferior good, decreasing as income rises, although subjective interest might increase.

25 Although, as Green and Brock (1998) observe, social capital can be ersatz.

26 See also Stolle and Rochon (1998).

27 Stolle (1998) finds that age of entry and length of membership of an association is important for trust, with the latter ultimately declining in old members.

28 La Due Lake and Huckfeldt (1998) find that different types of social capital are "politically relevant".

29 See also Berman (1997), Minkoff (1997), and Portney and Berry (1997).

30 See also Whittington (1998).

31 Booth and Richard (1998a) add that social capital can also be uncivil, as in the Ku Klux Klan.

32 An export of (negative) social capital from Italy to the United States before it was understood as such.

33 See also Putzel (1999) for a critical acceptance of social capital, as long as it is sufficiently modified (to an extent that effectively undermines it).

34 See also Duncan (1999) who seeks to explain in a comparative study why poverty should persist in some US rural communities but not in others. Whilst attracted by the notion of social capital, in terms of the presence of horizontally organised community activity (p. 153), she is critical of Putnam for having neglected the structure and history of class relations as the foundation for such activity, and the dependence of such structures on external factors, not least how many jobs are provided, by whom and how. Elites can block the formation of local horizontal associations (pp. 198–200 and pp. 206–07). See also Warren's (1998) discussion of the Industrial Areas Foundation that opposes, for example, plant closures and runs on the slogan, "no permanent allies, no permanent enemies". Warner (1999, p. 387) suggests the local state can build social capital by shifting "from acting as controller, regulator, and provider to new roles as catalyst, convener, and facilitator". This is in response to globalisation and through integration at other state levels. Here, there is a paradox of much of the globalisation literature, an emphasis on the powerlessness of the national state but the efficacy of the local state.

35 Note, however, that Helliwell and Putnam (1995) use Barro-type regressions to estimate growth rates for Italian regions, with greater autonomy unshackling social capital in the 1980s and perceived to be responsible for reversal of convergence in the

1960s and 1970s. Note that, if social capital effects were allowed to affect growth rates over the long run, differentials in per capita income would become enormous. Some extraneous effect will always be necessary to explain why divergence in economic performance does not keep on widening.

36 For reference and an addition to the critical literature, see Fine (1998a, Chapter 4). See also Fine (1995a). Note clothing, for example, can be seen either as familial cooperation or exploitation, subcontracting as efficient liaison between supply and demand or as subordination to big customer, etc. Interpreting the flexibility debate in terms of social capital adds nothing new to it.

37 Humphrey and Schmitz (1997) repay the compliment by retelling the story as social capital but without much by way of explicit reference to flec-spec. On the other hand, Schmitz and Nadvi (1999) introduce a special issue on industrial clustering without needing to rely upon social capital, the one minor exception in their collection being Weijland (1999) who sees it as providing sector-specific reductions in transaction costs and externalities unless overcrowding results.

38 Note that Cohen and Fields (1999) see the resonance between Putnam's social capital, flec-spec, and Alfred Marshall's industrial districts. But they warn against generalisation, arguing that Silicon Valley, for example, differs from both Italy and even Boston hi-tech, in gaining its degree of cooperation, trust and confidence in delivery for the overwhelming support provided by military contracts.

39 This does, however, appear to be a general weakness of the more culturally-inclined explanations of economic performance (weakness), not least Wiener's (1981) hypothesis of the British antipathy to industry and Perry Anderson's (1964) contested notion of the peculiarity of the British ruling class in view of its failure to launch a proper bourgeois revolution.

40 Fukuyama is a representative of what is a substantial scholarly downside characteristic of social capital illustrating, at one extreme, its first law: analytical acumen is in inverse proportion to popularisation. I blush to reproduce the following text of errors and unjustified qualitative and quantitative assertions (Fukuyama 1996, p. 13):

> Over the past generation, economic thought has been dominated by neoclassical or free market economists, associated with names like Milton Friedman, Gary Becker, and George Stigler. The rise of the neoclassical perspective constitutes a vast improvement from earlier decades in this [the twentieth] century, when Marxists and Keynesians held sway. We can think of neoclassical economics as being, say, eighty percent correct: it has uncovered important truths about the nature of money and markets because its fundamental model of rational, self-interested human behaviour is correct about eighty percent of the time. But there is a missing twenty percent of human behaviour about which neoclassical economics can give only a poor account. As Adam Smith well understood, economic life is deeply embedded in social life, and it cannot be understood apart from the customs, morals, and habits of the society in which it occurs. In short, it cannot be divorced from culture.

41 Of course, there is also the paradox to be explained away of what is perceived to be the unprecedented recent success of the US economy, its being noticed just as Putnam launches his account of decline.

42 In a particularly apt illustration for both human and social capital, Fevre et al. (1999) observe that educational motives are highly contextual and, even from an individualistic motivational perspective, highly "sociological", as in the rhythm of educational ethos attached to the Welsh working class, shifting between source of socialist solidarity and individual betterment.

43 See also Knack and Kropf (1998, p. 595) for an explicit statement of what is involved – and how limited it is:

This research provides further support for the inclusion of "civic norms of co-operation" in rational choice theory. Although methodological individualism provides important deductive theory to a point, it fails to account for empirically observed behaviors, such as contributing to public broadcasting or voting in elections. It is clear that the individual will consider more than narrow self-interest in any cost-benefit calculus. He or she will also consider the expectations of others, and those expectations become an integral part of the individual's analysis of the costs and benefits of participation.

44 The shift from such grand models is perceived, however, to be a "sociological" not a "scientific" issue.

7 The expanding universe of social capital

1 See Part III for a comprehensive assessment of the World Bank and social capital.
2 Note that Wall et al. (1998) are extremely rare in acknowledging the use of the notion of social capital in the theory of the fiscal crisis of the state, initiated by O'Connor (1973) and taken up by Gough (1979) in the context of the political economy of the welfare state. Whatever the merits of these analyses – and they are now being super-seded by Esping–Andersen welfare-regime analysis, on which see Fine (2000c) – their complete neglect in the social capital literature is highly indicative of the absence of systemic analysis wedded to political economy.
3 And, in what must be one of the longest ever footnotes, provides a bibliography.
4 As well as, not surprisingly, appropriate networks (Burt 1999).
5 As in the study of Belliveau et al. (1996) on top salaries, Leana and van Buren (1999) on employment practices, Chung et al. (2000) on inter-firm alliances, and Pennings et al. (1998) on firm survival. See also Falk (1999) for a "new community leadership model", based on social capital and other feel-good factors, and Ashman et al. (1998) for "civil society resource organisations". Margaret Dugan in Wallis et al. (1998) poses social capital in context of feel-good management for community development, with Putnam confessing of social capital to community development practitioners, "be-cause I believe in touching and feeling, I understand that there are important things that you can't measure". Whilst much of the work in management can be conceptu-ally and empirically sloppy, it can also be insightful when drawing critically upon social theory, leaping ahead of more supposedly scholarly fields. See Tsai and Ghoshal (1998), for example, and their argument that study of intra-firm networks needs to include the structural, the relational, and the cognitive. In a theme to be taken up in the concluding section to this chapter, Nahapiet and Ghoshal (1998) also throw everything from their field into social capital, including a good dose of Bour-dieu, to explain how social capital supports intellectual capital within organisations. On the other hand, see Dacin et al. (1999) for all of this essentially without any need to refer to social capital.
6 See especially Harriss and de Renzio (1997, p. 921) and Woolcock (1998).
7 See also Mondak (1998, p. 433) for a more general assessment:

> Coleman's work has, of course, been followed by a staggering flood of discourse in academia, the press, government, and elsewhere. Less staggering, unfortu-nately, has been the quality and quantity of empirical social research influenced by Coleman's model.

8 On a different tack, see Chin (2000) for the idea that success, in the sense of applying for high school, involves undue emotional effort on the part of children's parents in a contest for which they have scant respect but into which they believe they must enter.
9 For a selection of work other than that cited in the text, with their titles giving a feel

for its scope, see Meyerson (1994), Valenzuela and Dornbusch (1994), Zhou and Bankston (1994), Furstenberg and Hughes (1995), Hagan et al. (1995 and 1996), Smith et al. (1995), Lee and Brinton (1996), Teachman et al. (1996), Bianchi and Robinson (1997), White and Kaufman (1997), Runyan et al. (1998), Gandara (1999), McNeal (1999), Recchi (1999), Valenzuela (1999), and Volker and Flap (1999). Like empirical studies of human capital, those of social capital tend increasingly to diminish its impact as other factors are brought into play unless these are themselves interpreted as social capital. For Joshi et al. (1999), social capital simply derives from (increasing) diversity in family arrangements for raising children. But see also Hendricks (1999) who argues that the elderly can use their human capital better the more social capital they have.

10 Rounding up Coleman, Bourdieu, and others, they also argue that (Catholic) schools must not neglect social ethos in pursuing individual attainment, nor take public money that undermines the latter.

11   Difficulty in establishing causality is acknowledged in light of the small sample of diverse East Asians. See also Sun (1999) where an attempt is made to incorporate neighbourhood effects in a study of the impact of social capital.

12 Loizos (1999, p. 260) accepts that forced migrants "may well prefer to marry others like themselves and thus create communities of trust, shared values, and mutual aid which would rejoice social capital theorists", but he has already observed immediately before on the basis of a number of studies that:

> Survivors of violent displacement can usually benefit from a variety of forms of assistance – the granting of citizenship rights, housing aid, provision of land, working capital and jobs. In dealing with emotional and cognitive disruption, they will help each other by sympathy, empathy, and reciprocal support.

13 And, in doing so, incorporates a whole range of other variables in seeking to integrate rational choice with embeddedness.

14 See also Sanders and Nee (1996) who refer to the work of Granovetter (1985), Coleman (1988 and 1990a), and Bourdieu (1993) in addressing social capital.

15 They seek to explain relative success in self-employment. To address capital proper, they would need to examine access to exploitative labour markets, presumably equally dependent on ethnic networks and family membership!

16 In this respect, Fountain (1998a and 1998b) is a significant study for it addresses social capital, with emphasis on networks and information flows, in the context of research and development and innovation. Thus, at least, some implicit attention is offered on how social capital might raise productivity, something usually taken for granted in other studies. See also Gabbay and Zuckerman (1998). Barr (1998) referring to flec-spec and industrial district literature draws the distinction between using social capital to promote productivity and to smooth income uncertainty, and the potential trade-offs between them. These studies, however, do not tend to deal in the conflict and exclusion involved in access to technology and innovation, one central aspect, for example, of the national systems of innovation literature. For a critical overview of this approach, see Fine (1993b) and special issue of *Technology Analysis and Strategic Management*, vol 11, no 4, 1999 for a more recent contribution.

17 More informally, Munn (2000) sees social capital as value neutral, seeking, for education, "to link the micro processes of school life with macro economic and social structures".

18 Having been forced to acknowledge that social capital can have a downside or whatever, Putnam continues to wish to define it absolutely independently of its (positive or negative) effects (which effectively means context free). Informally, in email discussion, he argues:

I certainly agree that not all consequences of social capital are universally good. However, I suggest … that we phrase it as negative and positive *consequences* of social capital, not negative and positive social capital. The same empirical "bit" of social capital (e.g., an ethnic association in India) can have *both* negative *and* positive consequences, and I think we should avoid a definitional dispute about whether it is "really" a bit of "negative social capital" or "positive social capital".

Is this social theory through the looking glass – with something good unless it is bad and not really bad as opposed to its consequences being bad rather than itself?

19 This leads them to offer a new definition for social capital as:

> Social capital is the product of social interactions with the potential to contribute to the social, civic or economic well-being of a community-of-common-purpose. The interactions draw knowledge and identity resources and simultaneously use and build stores of social capital. The nature of the social capital depends on various qualitative dimensions of the interactions in which it is produced, such as the quality of the internal–external interactions, the historicity, futuricity, reciprocity, trust and the shared values of and norms.

It is a moot point whether this is able to deal with the three problems of unemployment, infrastructural decline, and withdrawal of government support, as delineated by Algie (n.d.) as the problems posed for social capital by Australian rural decline.

20 Their goal, similar to treatment of empirical studies in this chapter, is described as follows: "Ours is a theoretically driven review, that is, we review empirical work in hopes of clarifying the notion of social capital theoretically."

21 See Sullivan and Transue (1999) for an overview of the contribution of psychology to social capital and democracy.

22 See Furlong (1996) for the observation that trust, like social capital, is wide-ranging in meaning within and across different disciplines and, as such, contingent upon context.

23 They continue by listing the following examples that supplement previous discussion of the scope of application of social capital: dyads and informal networks (Burt 1997a and Heying 1997); voluntary associations (Eastis 1998); religious institutions (Wood 1997); communities (Bebbington 1997, and Schulman and Anderson 1999); cities (Portney and Berry 1997); and national (Minkoff 1997) or transnational (Smith 1997 and Smith et al. (eds) 1997) social movements.

24 See also Khan (1999) who suggests that social norms – represented by lessening litigation in New South Wales between 1860 and 1900 – are a product of development but can be disturbed by innovation. Consequently, "We can gain only partial – and potentially inaccurate – insights into the role of norms and social capital if ahistorical methods are adopted" (p. 173).

25 For use of the weaker form of context, see Greif (1997), for example, who integrates game theory and sociological concepts to demonstrate how path dependence is effected by culture, from the late mediaeval period to the present Third World, with individuals forming expectations about how others will respond in various contingencies. Note that, most revealingly, for Williamson (2000, p. 104), "Path dependency is another way of saying that history matters." Of course, history is much more than this. For a critique in the context of business history, see Fine (2000d); and, in the context of the work of Paul David, see Fine (2000e). See also Slater and Spencer (2000).

26 Rotberg (1999, p. 343) observes of historians that "some prefer to employ social capital and political culture as metaphors, not as theoretical propositions". See also Clemens (1999, p. 613):

> *Social capital* has proven exceptionally fruitful as a metaphor. By invoking financial imagery, this phrase points to the generative power of social ties, their

capacity to produce social goods such as economic growth or effective governance. But metaphors are also dangerous, not least because they assert multiple
dimensions of similarity, some of which may be inappropriate or positively misleading.

27 There will be more on metaphors later in Chapter 10 but, for the moment, consider
the discussion of Indian poverty by Morris (1998, p. 8) with social capital understood
as a pyramid of formal and informal concepts, from networks to trust:

> A positivistic parallel can be drawn between social capital and chemistry ... Like
> heat in the chemistry experiment, social capital speeds up the rate of reaction,
> making the system run faster and more smoothly.

Kilpatrick et al. (1998), in the context of social capital as (interactive) learning, cite
Cox (1998) as seeing it as lubricating oil, like a magic pudding that grows as it is
consumed. Schoen et al. (1997, p. 350) provide a striking statement of the colonisation of social sciences by economics but, in seeing children as a source of social
capital to their parents rather than the social capital of their parents as a support to
their progress, conclude: "Children are not seen as consumer durables; they are seen
as the threads from which the tapestry of life is woven." Note that Lewis (1999) sees
metaphor as inevitable in social theory, but requires that it should be generative of
further insight.

28 See, however, Tijhuis et al. (1995) for the early positing of a link between health and
social capital, and also Baum (1997), Kawachi et al. (1996, 1997a, 1997b, 1999a, and
1999b), Achat et al. (1998), Kennedy et al. (1998) and Lomas (1998). Note that
Kawachi et al. (1997b) pose the puzzle of why, as chance would have it, a close-knit
Pennsylvanian community of migrants from a small rural village in Italy from the
1880s should currently enjoy low rates of heart attacks. From there, it is a short step
to follow Putnam and correlate cross-state mortality with bowling league membership.
No wonder Marlon Brando and Al Pacino lived to ripe old ages in their respective
Godfatherdoms!

29 Rose and Clear (1998, p. 454) review social disorganisation theory, which has also
been used by Kawachi and Wilkinson together in Kawachi et al. (1999a), to argue
that it "is implicitly based upon the notions of social and human capital, even if the
terms have not been explicitly adopted". They themselves define social capital as "the
social skills and resources needed to effect positive change in neighborhood life".
Across the work of Kawachi in particular, there is a seamless move between social
capital, networks, and disorganisation suggesting both evidence in search of theory
and, ultimately, social capital as the explanatory umbrella. Note that in February 2000
Kawachi became guest moderator to the World Bank's Social Capital Email Discussion Group (see Chapter 9), specifically to solicit contributions on health. See references in issue 25 where it is confessed:

> The precise mechanisms underlying the connection between social capital and
> health still remain to be uncovered, but a great deal of evidence from epide-
> miology suggests that social support is an important determinant of longevity
> and quality of life.

The downside of social capital is also acknowledged as in emulative smoking. In issue
26, dated 1 March 2000, it is confessed by Kawachi that "we continue to be chal-
lenged by the question of how the notion of social capital might be operationalized in
terms of the [World] Bank's operations".

30 This is one of the pathways from inequality to poor health suggested by Kawachi and
Kennedy (1999), alongside its association with loss of human and social capital
(neither of which provides a direct route to medical outcomes).

31 For a similar critique, see Leeder and Dominello (1999) who call for complex and detailed epidemiological studies. But see also Veenstra (2000) who finds little effect of social capital on self-health reports from individuals, and Labonte (1999, p. 430) who perceptively asserts that social capital is not new but old ideas repackaged. Nor does it exist, but is constructed "by those aspects of social relations particular theorists or researchers choose to study in its name". Further, recognising that it does not challenge conventional economic thinking, "social capital ... allows elites who benefit from economic practices that undermine social cohesion to voice that loss without necessarily linking it back to those practices that privilege them."

32 See also Wilkinson (1999a) where a discussion is provided of the pathways to ill-health by comparison with primitive societies and animals, together with some discussion of the medical evidence.

33 As a result, social capital not only provides an explanation for health, it also incorporates social factors and analyses that have preceded it, as in Cooper et al. (1999, p. 45):

> The review of the literature relating to social support, social capital, health and health behaviour involved an extensive and systematic search of library catalogues and of journals published during the past 20 years in the fields of medicine, nutrition, nursing, dentistry and the social and behavioural sciences.

In milder form, this parallels the World Bank appropriation of social theory as social capital, discussed below. Note, however, the conclusion that (p. 145):

> A consistent finding in all of our analyses is the strong association between health status and socioeconomic position. For men and women, those living in the most materially disadvantaged conditions, the unemployed and those in manual occupations are most likely to report a chronic illness or poor subjective health ... The influence of social capital and social support on health, stress and health behaviour is much weaker than the influence of socioeconomic factors.

So why not deal with these more important problems rather than shifting policy emphasis to communities taking responsibility for their own health through building a nebulous social capital?

34 In a different context, see Svendsen and Svendsen (2000).

35 See also Kawachi (1999). Social capital and crime is a favoured topic in studying eastern Europe. See Hagan and Radoeva (1997–98), for example.

36 Note, however, that conservatives would disagree on the first of these in view of incentives, and social cohesion, as Muntaner and Lynch observe, can be extremely socially unhealthy as in Nazism and all other instances of perverse social capital to be discussed in more detail shortly.

37 See also Portes (1998). Note that he is much happier about social capital as a factor in explaining individual rather than social outcomes, especially if the gap between the two is not fully mediated. For the need for conceptual disaggregation for empirical purposes, see Newton (1997).

38 Whilst on the topic, it is worth quoting Putnam's view, from Wallis et al. (1998):

> If I wanted to use the term social capital to refer to the African American experience ... I would say that the institutions of slavery were designed to destroy social capital. They were designed to break up connections among people ... to keep a group of people down ... by breaking up the connections among them.

Of course, it was also designed to make profit out of trade in people and for the latter to pick cotton.

39 In this light, Wilkinson's (1999b) response to Muntaner and Lynch is significant. Either he seems to fail to understand that it is the causal structure of explanation that is at issue – positively welcoming the inclusion of class as a variable that might help to explain the incidence of ill-health (although he suggests that income causes class rather than vice versa). In short, he seeks "to avoid an infinite regress into causes of causes" in seeking out (social) correlates of ill-health. Or he seems to argue that the effect of income on health and the causes of the distribution of income can be examined separately. For he accepts that his work implies that income inequality should be reduced but sets this aside "as a task requiring separate expertise" focusing upon "the socioeconomic causes of ill health within developed countries". For further debate on the issue, ultimately calling for more precision and more factors to be taken into account, see Baum (1999 and 2000), Lynch et al. (2000), Popay (2000), and Wilkinson (2000), Popay adding the need for contextual content, presumably to allow for the postmodern condition.

40 See also Edwards and Foley (1998), and Schuller (2000a), who suggests that social capital "encourages questions and reflection rather than providing answers … this heuristic quality … is the primary, and very powerful, advantage of the concept". Note, though, that this leads to a compromise with long-standing objections to the notion of human capital. It appears to be rendered acceptable as long as it is complemented by social capital! See also Schuller (2000b). For a critique of human and social capital, both separately and as complements, see Fine and Green (2000).

41 By chance, in another context, Frank Stilwell suggested to me that appeal to heuristic analysis is a sneaky way of importing unjustified and generally illegitimate concepts.

42 Campbell (2000) views social capital as a heuristic device in its infancy. Schuller et al. (2000) "conclude by giving pride of place to the heuristic potential of social capital, its capacity to open up issues rather than to provide definitive answers". This promise is seen in terms of four key features over and beyond its investigative content: the shift from individual agents to social units and institutions; the links between micro, meso and macro; the impulse to multi- and inter-disciplinary study; and reinserting values into social scientific discourse. An alternative perspective is to see these elements as being brought back in again, having been taken out by the rational choice foundations underlying social capital, as argued in Chapter 5 and the previous section.

43 The new economics of crime, for example, appears to be based upon Becker's dilemma on whether to pay for legal parking. For other such sources of his inspiration, see Tommasi and Ierulli (eds) (1995).

44 See also Ostrom (1994).

45 See especially Narayan (1999a and 1999b).

46 See Rosenthal (1998) for the idea that women are more collaborative in leadership than men but this advantage in social capital may be eroded by professionalisation.

47 The same applies to social capital more generally. See Youniss et al. (1997).

48 Brown (1999) points to the lack of a clear definition of social capital despite its rapid rise to prominence in the new economic sociology and policy circles. An appeal is made for its systemic incorporation through a middle-range theory of micro, meso and macro, thereby allowing for embeddedness and contextual construction of content in the mode of Zelizer and DiMaggio.

49 See discussion in Chapter 2.

50 Lack of account of values or morality, other than as (socially and historically derived) self-interest, is a common critique of social capital theory. See Uslaner (1999). Note that Becker specifically criticises Sen (1977) for the suggestion that individuals might hold to a set of meta-preferences based on moral judgements as opposed to preferences for personal welfare alone. Becker's judgement is that there is no case that (p. 18):

> Higher-order rankings are either necessary or useful in understanding behaviour since ethics and culture affect behaviour in the same general way as do other

determinants of utility and preferences. In particular, considerations of price and cost influence ethical and moral choices – such as whether to act honestly – just as they influence choices of personal goods.

Accordingly, the moral dilemma of a gap between the preferences we do have and those we might like to have from ethical considerations is denied by Becker. Rather, the divorce between actual and desired preferences is reinterpreted as dissatisfaction with inherited personal and social capital just as, for example, we do not necessarily have different preferences over consumption goods because we choose differently both quantitatively and qualitatively when we enjoy different levels of income or wealth. Note that Hausman and McPherson (1996) argue that rationality involves morality and, hence, preferences and explanations should include moral reasoning. Further, just because the origins and determinants of social norms can be made logically reducible to self-interest in an essentially neoclassical fashion, this does not imply that they are so (pp. 56–57).

51 Jackman and Miller (1998), citing Samuelsson (1961, p. 25), suggest that social capital attempts to bond (and bridge and link?) the inconsistent:

> [Many] writers disposed to compromise, evidently believe that false concepts can be made into perfectly sensible ones simply by taking little bits of each and gluing them together into "between-the-two" or "as-well-as" joinery of totally opposed notions.

52 See also Woolcock (1998, p. 168) for social capital in correspondingly more abstract terms:

> In order to explore these different levels, dimensions, and combinations of social capital ... at the micro level, I will henceforth refer to embeddedness ... as Integration, and autonomy ... as Linkage. Embeddedness ... at the macro level will be referred to as Synergy, while autonomy ... as Organizational Integrity.

53 See also Paraskevopoulos (1998a and 1998b).

54 This has the effect of setting aside two of the crucial issues for analysing coproduction: (de)commodification and the formation of institutions. Outcomes for these must be presumed in order to construct public–private divide isoquants in the first place! Note that Heath et al. (1998) see commodification as a major factor in undermining familial social capital, in unwitting resonance with Coleman. More generally, commodification potentially undermines the ethos of voluntary work (Nowland-Foreman 1998), and of the public service (Gregory 1999). On the latter, see Fine (1997c) drawing particularly upon Haque (1996) for discussion in context of privatisation.

55 But, for a more upbeat approach to social capital, see de Renzio and Kavanamur (1999).

56 See Slemrod (1998) for an ingenious discourse on why people pay taxes or not, with the economy being caught in vicious or virtual circles around affluence, high trust, high government expenditure, and high voluntary tax compliance, or their opposites. On taxation, see also the treatment by Konrad (1995), for example, of infrastructure as social capital. An older generation provides it for the younger, not out of altruism, but as an intertemporal optimising exercise in view of the later higher taxes it can take from the next generation's higher earnings for use as social security transfers to themselves.

57 Consequently, Wang (1999) sees Evans as having brought civil society back in with his vertical use of social capital, having taken it out by unduly horizontally emphasising the state when previously bringing that back in (Evans et al. (eds) 1985).

58 See Wilson (1997) for whom social capital is free, invisible but real, involving

stakeholder participation, professional protocol, social learning, collaboration, trust, solutions to tragedies of the commons, collective responsibilities, etc. On the other hand, for Walker et al. (1997, p. 111), "social capital is a means of enforcing norms of behaviour ... and thus acts as a constraint as well as a resource."

59 He is designated as Director of the Ford Foundation's Governance and Civil Society Unit, having been Senior Civil Society Specialist at the World Bank. I return to Edwards' contribution in the concluding chapter since he addresses the motives that have informed social capitalists and their opponents.

60 Note that Lehning (1998, pp. 241–42) argues that "social capital is not a substitute for effective public policy but ... a prerequisite ... and a consequence" but, in doing so, rejects the dichotomy between civil society and the state.

61 See studies collected in van Deth et al. (eds) (1999), and also Cusack (1999) and Papadakis (1999) for Putnamesque studies of Germany and Australia, respectively. Hall (1999) for the UK, explicitly seeking to emulate Putnam, finds no overall evidence of decline of social capital, imputing this to increasing education, shifting class composition and government support for voluntary organisations. He also suggests that government may enhance social capital rather than vice versa.

62 Repeated from Chapter 6, note 40. For a critique of Fukuyama along the lines that it is the rule of law rather than custom that is important, see Fellmeth (1996, p. 169) who concludes, on the discovery that political culture matters to economic behaviour: "Fukuyama has merely rediscovered the wheel, although he has used it as an impediment rather than a mode of transport."

63 For a systematic overview, see Fine (2000a).

64 For an account in the wider context of the associated theoretical deficiencies of neoclassical growth theory, see Harcourt (1972 and 1976) and Fine (1980, Chapter 5).

65 Thus, most recently, as initiated by Young (1994 and 1996), attempts have been made to deny the East Asian productivity miracle by suggesting that increases in output have primarily been due to increases in human and physical capital.

66 See Barro and Sala-i-Martin (1995) and Aghion and Howitt (1998) for the most comprehensive and recent mainstream presentation.

67 Interestingly, with Putnam's informal (in email discussion) acceptance in explicitly citing Temple, "my general impression is that the current evidence for the non-economic effects of social capital is an order of magnitude stronger and broader than the current evidence for macroeconomic effects".

68 See Woolcock (1998, p. 191):

> In contemporary research, the importance of endogenous factors such as human capital and technology is stressed by the so-called New Growth Economics ... which has interesting and important complementarities with the social capital approach.

69 It should be added that, even if the mathematical and statistical issues involved could be resolved on the basis of available data, it is a moot point whether a general theory of growth and social capital is appropriate as opposed to a country-by-country case-specific study of how the various factors interact with one another.

70 Knack (1999) provides an excellent summary of those factors interpretable as social capital that, according to his survey, have been investigated for their impact on economic growth.

71 They close by seeking social and historical specificity in the following way (Jackman and Miller 1996b, p. 713):

> The more fruitful strategy, however, involves institutional analyses that address two basic questions. First, how do procedures and rules structure the choices made by different political actors? Second, how does political conflict generate

these procedures and rules? The analyses in this symposium have given us no reason to depart from these fundamental political issues.

See also Jackman and Miller (1998), and Booth and Richard (1998a and 1998b), who see government performance in Latin America as more dependent upon political activity, norms, and associations, or what they term political as opposed to social capital.

72 Their critique is also applied to the work of Inglehart (1997), but this rarely refers to social capital explicitly.

73 See Grootaert (1997, p. 78): "The term 'social capital' has found its way into economic analysis only recently, although various elements of the concept have been present under different names for a long time." Thus, the new concept of social capital is imposed retrospectively on all social theory, and not just economics, on which see later.

74 A particularly unselfconscious and revealing understanding of social capital from the economist's perspective is provided by Spagnolo (1999) because of simply getting down to the business of mathematical modelling on the basis of parsimonious assumptions. Social relations are anything that is not production, with social capital the non-market incidence of credible threats and monitoring in repeated games. See also Giusta (1999) for social capital as collective reputation and Guttman (2000) for social capital as evolutionary reciprocity. More informally and specifically, Szreter (2000) concludes:

> Social capital offers the prospect of a superior understanding of market eco-nomics and competition and of how to promote a nation's economic efficiency in the world's markets through the promotion of its citizens' communicative competence.

Maskell (2000), following Glaeser et al. (1999), defines trust "as the commitment of resources to an activity where the outcome depends upon the cooperative behavior of others". So:

> Social capital has mainly been seen as contributing to economic performance by reducing inter-firm transaction cost, i.e. search and information costs, bargaining and decision costs, policing and enforcement costs.

75 This example is anticipated by Coleman (1990a, p. 316) in arguing that moving from a neighbourhood undermines its social capital.

76 Lest this be seen as an early aberration, see Schiff (1999a), where a benefit of free trade is perceived to be the reduction of compensating indirect trade through labour migration, with consequent loss of social capital. The Amazonian example is reiter-ated with the interpretation that "the expansion of agribusiness in the Brazilian state of Mato Grosso do Sul has led to the breakdown of tribal social structures and has pushed Indian teenagers to high levels of alcoholism, violence, suicide, and 'a loss of touch with their gods' ", citing the *Washington Post* from 20 April 1991. See also Schiff (1999b).

77 Robison et al. (1999) adopt the same approach and test whether farmland trade in neighbouring properties is more likely and beneficial between those who know one another. In a different context, the private ownership of UK coal royalties, I have shown how productive efficiency can be highly impeded by relations across neigh-bouring properties despite long-standing familiarity and contracting (Fine 1990a).

78 At the suggestion of Ismail Serageldin, a leading World Bank social capitalist. See also Dasgupta (1988).

79 In view of discussion in the next part, it is worth pointing out that Paul Collier is

Director of the Development Research Group of the World Bank, having fallen immediately beneath Joe Stiglitz, Chief Economist, in the hierarchy.

80 In a remarkable flash of insight, Collier invents the notion of *social labour* for where the social interaction effect does not persist. The implication, of course, is that the vast majority of labour is non-social. Yet an intrinsic component of the Marxist theory of capital(ism) is that all (commodity) producing labour is social in a particular way, Fridayless Robinson Crusoe apart.

81 He continues:

> What is the implication for a pro-poor public policy? The different distributional consequences of differing mechanisms of internalisation suggests that public policy should both promote most heavily those mechanisms which are most distributionally progressive, and should attempt to redress the regressive aspects of the other mechanisms.

Who could disagree with such profundity?

82 See Fine (1998a, Chapter 3).

83 See Friedman and Krackhardt (1997) for the idea that discrimination can be explained by differential access to social capital.

84 On the other hand, note that Arnold and Kay (1995) suggest that large law firms embody social capital since they are more liable to be self-monitoring in establishing legal and ethical standards.

85 See also Gold (1995) for the idea that female Israeli emigrants to the US are required to build lost social capital for their families and, hence, are less liable to join the labour market.

86 Stone (1995) draws similar conclusions for social capital concerning problems of definition and causation in commenting upon the account by Hinrich (1995) of inequality and redistribution in health provision in Germany. See also Brown and Ashman (1996), Fox (1997), Brown (1998), and Buckland (1998) for discussion of social capital, often in the context of power and conflict, and the role of nongovernmental organisations (NGOs). As always, the latter are presumed to mediate and provide for positive-sum outcomes, for cooperation over conflict and, in addition, the corresponding creation of social capital.

87 Smith (1997) offers an interesting upside-down account of social capital through empirical study of misanthropy, finding no long-term rise in its incidence (loss of social capital) in the United States. It is, however, higher especially amongst the less educated, but also for those with less income, financial reversals, racial and ethnic minorities, southerners, migrants, and blacks with limited contacts with whites, victims of crime, violence or poor health, those not attending church other than fundamentalists, and the young (with implications for cohort replacement). It is not more prevalent for urbanites, for experience of divorce as child or spouse, the never married, geographical mobility, gender, trauma of death, unemployment or hospitalisation. That is, not all negative life events make us less charitably disposed to others.

88 See also Kuperman (1996).

89 Waldinger (1995) refers to the construction industry as "the quintessential ethnic niche" and shows how social capital incorporates closure as a result of the material factors connected to the nature of the industry itself, not least its casualised labour and product markets.

90 See Zulfacar (1998), Kyle (1999), and Rogers (1999), for example. In each case, the concern is much more penetrating in understanding what social capital is and Bourdieu-like in content. Bayart (1999, p. 32) uses "the term 'social capital' to refer to the ensemble of configurations and the texture of relationships which are the outcome of sub-Saharan Africa's long historical trajectory, or rather of the cluster of historical trajectories, distinct but acting upon one another over long periods, of an

entire sub-continent". There is, however, no reference to Bourdieu despite the fact that "we would emphasize the abundance of distinct and sometimes contradictory cultural repertoires". For Shetler (1995), as limited an object as a Kiroba text of popular history forms social capital in Tanzania since it depicts a constellation of networks and social relations that can inform and sustain those who draw upon it. Putterman (1995), also addressing Tanzania, seeks to generalise social capital as culture beyond a set of individual ties "to encompass the repertoires of entire material cultures" (p. 15). Indeed, "a society's division of labour with respect to the holding of its overall cultural capital stock can be regarded as a kind of collective memory algorithm."

91 Campbell et al. (1999) in their case study of social capital and health also seek conceptual and empirical refinement – along seven dimensions! These are: the diversity of trust and civic engagement; the porosity of social capital across community boundaries; the uneven impact of networks; the importance of informal networks; attention to the processes attached to facilities as well as their provision; the complexity of community cohesion, trust and identity; and differential access to social capital. Where does this leave the original concept?

92 Although I am generally perceived to be obsessive in hunting down social capital literature, I do confess to not being able to bear to go back to the database to sift out new additions for scrutiny following my first, early foray.

93 See also Portes and Sensenbrenner (1993), Portes (1998), Woolcock (1998, p. 160), and Bruni and Sugden (2000) – and Woolcock's subsequent discussion, which is even more rapacious, taking in Simmel and Parsons as well:

> The Durkheimian, Weberian, and Marxist traditions within classical sociology were all heavily influenced by the economic debates and issues of that period, and much of what we now refer to as "social capital".

Putnam is also guilty of imposing social capital where it is not already known. For, he accepts, in addressing community practitioners, that social capital is an alien term from their perspective. But, for Putnam, it does not matter what the idea is called as long as they build networks of shared values and reciprocal obligations. "In fact, these practitioners employ concepts and standards in their work that suggest acceptance of the task, if not of the term itself." Indeed, "they do it anyway whatever it is called" (Wallis et al. 1998).

94 At time of writing, the web page devoted to the definition is now described as, "Currently Under Construction".

95 Admittedly:

> We do not claim that our definition of social capital has produced the one correct definition. We may yet change it again. Nor do we claim that our definition of social capital has satisfied all the definition requirements we imposed on ourselves. Nevertheless, we have arrived at a definition that reflects near consensus among our group though we represent different disciplines. In addition, we have obtained measures of the influence of social capital using the definition and gain appreciation and insights from each other that help us reexamine our own disciplines in a new light.

8 Making the post-Washington consensus

1 This chapter draws heavily on a unit drafted for the distance learning programme from the School of Oriental and African Studies on development economics and also Fine (1999b, 2001a, and 2001c).

2 See Mosley et al. (1995), for example.

232 Notes for Chapter 8, pp. 139–149

3 See Carrier and Miller (eds) (1998).

.4 According to Harcourt (1997, p. 3), Stiglitz makes reference to one hundred or so examples of his own (or co-authored) work in providing, on the basis of market imperfections, "one of the most profound internal critiques of mainstream economics I have ever read" (p. 3).

5 This is brought out especially clearly by Agénor and Montiel (1996).

6 However, for an account of how the monetarist counter-revolution of the 1970s influenced the making of policy in Australia, see Pusey (1991). He points to the dominance of Keynesian-trained, "generously minded" economists in Australia in the post-war period. These were, however, displaced in the late 1970s by "a new genera-tion attached to the neoclassical curriculum that swept through the economics departments of Australian universities ... a passage through an economics curricu-lum in their early 20s is the single factor that most strongly sets these young forty-plus-year-old captains of a nation-building state against their historical mission" (pp. 5–6).

7 See also de Vries (1996, p. 238) who reports that the World Bank distributes one million books and papers, has a catalogue list of five hundred titles, and a scale of publishing equivalent to a sales volume of between $10 and $30 million. Significantly, however, the public relations budget is two to three times that for research, provoking the speculation about which is dog and which is tail.

8 See also Mwanza (1992, pp. 4–5) who observes on the first half of the 1980s that, although the IMF's staff are heavily deployed, particularly at the stage of policy formulation:

> The IMF usually adopts a more rigid position than the World Bank. It rarely de-ploys its staff in countries implementing its programmes ... The IMF approach to programming is, therefore, vulnerable to the criticism that it lacks a detailed appreciation of the local environment ... one IMF-designed policy framework paper could have sufficed for Malawi, Tanzania, Zambia and Zimbabwe ... lo-cal expertise does not participate in programme design. The IMF will usually draw up a list of loyal IMF technocrats to be employed in key ministries or in-stitutions for the purpose of implementing or overseeing the implementation of the SAP. In most cases these technocrats, most of whom are foreign, are paid from World Bank loans. This practice is more often than not accompanied by retrenchment of local experts made under the banner of making the civil service more efficient.

9 For a stronger, if implicit, account of the World Bank's role in promoting openness in trade policy in terms of how we learnt to embrace the Washington consensus and abandon inappropriate theory and misleading stylised facts, see Krueger (1997). For a review of the tensions between the new trade policy and the new trade theory, see Deraniyagala and Fine (2000). Note that Kapur et al. (1997, p. 22) tell the story in a slightly different way. The departure of McNamara as Bank President is followed by that of Hollis Chenery as Chief Economist. He is succeeded by Anne Krueger who, "in turn, replaces large fractions of the Bank's central economics establishment until she had a highly compatible staff".

10 For a critical assessment, see Fine and Rose (2001).

11 Note, however, that Stern and Ferreira (1997) make no mention of the World Bank's contribution to the economics of education and only mention human capital in a reference to new growth theory.

12 See also p. 234 and elsewhere.

13 Fine (1990a and 1990b) terms this the new synthesis on privatisation. See also Fine (1997c).

14 For a review of recent World Bank thinking, see Bayliss (1999). See also Bayliss and Fine (1998) and other references cited in these two pieces.

15 Discussion of World Bank research on individual countries is left aside. Here, there is influence from World Bank research, imposition of conditionality and incorporation of recipient country personnel. A particularly sharp example is provided by the resources that were devoted to making an impact upon South Africa with which the current author is well acquainted. In the words of an internal World Bank report on how its policies came to be owned by the new government (Cofino 1995):

> When the Bank began to re-establish formal relations with South Africa around 1990, its image in the country was very negative. Politicians, academics and even some business groups perceived the Bank as an inflexible, authoritarian sponsor of failed economic policies. By contrast, when the government headed by Nelson Mandela was inaugurated in 1994, the Bank was perceived as a flexible institution capable of effectively addressing the country's specific economic and social problems.

For relations between NGOs, as an external factor, and the World Bank, see Fox and Brown (eds) (1998).

16 See Coats (ed) (1996). Particularly disturbing is the declining number of US students taking PhDs in economics whilst the number of those studying there from abroad continues to increase (Coats 1996). See also Hodgson and Rothman (1999, p. F165) who report that over 70% of the editors of the "top" thirty economic journals are located in the United States, almost 40% in twelve institutions alone. Two-thirds of articles are of US authorship, the top twelve institutions accounting for over 20%. As they conclude, "the degree of institutional and geographical concentration of editors and authors may be unhealthy for innovative research."

17 By way of comparison and despite claims to the contrary (Polak 1996), the IMF can be judged to have failed to be at the forefront of macroeconomic research despite its role in stabilisation. This is a result of the obsessive, if institutionally determined, pre-occupation with financial programming, both analytically and as target. See Fine and Hailu (1999).

18 I am grateful to Jonathan Pincus for suggesting this point to me.

19 In what follows, discussion is confined to a number of works of Cernea. But see also Kardam (1993), favourably cited by Cernea (1994), who argues that the shift to accept the social within the World Bank was a result of internal and external factors, with the former including an important role for successful advocacy for which the World Bank's Sociology Group is seen as key. The one dissenting note is quoted from interview (p. 1784):

> The Sociology Group is seen as a minor gadfly for special interests, a continuous plea for more resources. The Sociology Group took a slave mentality and viewed itself as the keeper of humanistic qualities in economic development and claimed a place at the table. Otherwise, humanistic qualities would presumably be ignored. But sociology and anthropology do not have a monopoly on human qualities. This is the wrong approach, begging for recognition. It is also wrong to bring in anthropology whenever there is a marginal group like displaced populations or tribal people. Sociology should make contributions to mainline development analysis.

See also Miller-Adams (1999) who recognises the complexity of the World Bank and its rapid pace of change in policy stance, taking private enterprise, governance, and participation as case studies.

For a critical overview of different World Bank approaches to the social, see Francis (1999).

20 See also p. 19 and Cernea (1993, p. 15):

My conviction, relying on experience inside a major development agency, is that social research findings will become effective guidance for future practice only if they result in the *formulation and adoption of new or improved policy guidelines*. Social science knowledge must be used not just to evaluate program results but to craft policies. Only new policies have compelling *authority* over *planning*.

21 See also Cernea (1991a, p. 22).
22 See also Cernea (1994, p. 3):

> During the last eight to ten years, the Bank's corps of non-economic social scientists – mainly anthropologists, sociologists, and political scientists – has probably become *the largest group of this kind in the world that works together in one location actually practising development sociology and anthropology*. In this process they often break open new trails, chart untraveled territory, and push the frontiers of these disciplines forward.

Note how the World Bank's economists are emulated in relative weight of external academic presence, if not internally.

23 See also Cernea (1991a, pp. 22–23).

9 World banking on social capital

1 A third theme is by geographical area – Africa, East Asia and the Pacific, Latin America and the Caribbean, Middle East and North Africa, Europe and Central Asia, South Asia, OECD Nations, Global – but these lead directly to the database of abstracts and do not have dedicated pages on the internet. Nonetheless, the implication is that social capital has full scope of applicability, geographically as well as historically and conceptually!

2 Note that Bates' (1999) contribution on ethnicity to the Social Capital Initiative Working Papers Series only mentions social capital once in opening and then proceeds to argue that ethnicity is context specific, an implicit, possibly intended, double-slap to social capitalists. This is all the more significant for his being a leading representative of rational choice political economy, as in Bates (1981) and, especially, Bates (1988).

3 As Woolcock (1998, p. 156) puts it for individual motivation:

> If social capital can be rational, pre-rational, or even non-rational, what is it *not?* At the very least, these different conceptualizations suggest that there may be various forms or dimensions of social capital.

4 This comes from the foreword to the Social Capital Initiative Working Papers.

5 With its twenty-ninth issue, focusing on community development, the World Bank's Email Discussion Group on social capital (on which see later) became moderated by Cornelia and Jan Flora. In the thirtieth issue, they continue to lay out "four forms of capital (human social, natural, and financial/manufactured)", suggesting "a balance of bridging and bonding social capital is needed at all levels".

6 As Woolcock (1998, p. 196) observes, just as "if all behaviour is, by definition, utility-maximizing, then the assumption is rendered non-falsifiable … so too an indiscriminate application of social capital over-explains collective action."

7 Woolcock (1998, p. 196) correctly perceives:

> Ordinarily, a theory's parsimony – i.e., its capacity to explain the most with the least – is a desirable property; however, a single term is being adopted indiscriminately, adapted uncritically, and applied imprecisely.

8 We can always rely upon the conservatism of *The Economist* (1995) to check the progress of radical and innovative thinking. It severely attacks the notion that national accounts should be reconstructed to incorporate changes in social as opposed to material conditions, including social capital.

9 See also Narayan (1997). A further key reading in this vein is Moser and Holland (1997). This is a study of violence and poverty. Irrespective of its merits as a study, social capital is clearly appended as an analytical afterthought. Much the same is true of Narayan and Pritchett (1996) other than in the specific chapter devoted to social capital and assessment of its empirical effects. Similarly, social capital is appended to Wann's (1995) study of self-help. Social capital appears in the title alone, strangely common, or in a sentence or two, across a number examples of the literature.

10 But see also Narayan (1997, p. viii). By way of comparison, Putnam claims more immodestly if informally:

> In a correlational sense in large US data sets, getting married is the happiness equivalent of quadrupling your annual income and attending one club meeting a month is the happiness equivalent of doubling your income.

11 Essentially we have a prisoners' dilemma (or, more exactly, isolation paradox). Each village has an incentive to expand its levels of social capital irrespective of what other villages do, leading to an excess of social capital. Similarly, suppose government seeks to raise a given level of overall taxation, all efforts at evasion and avoidance merely redistribute the burden (thanks to the social capital provided by accountancy!). As has been discussed in the literature (for example, Woolcock 1998, p. 157), is social capital zero-sum? The same point is made by Knack (1999) in distinguishing between Olsonesque (Olson 1965) and Putnamesque approaches to collective action. See also Ostrom (2000) and Dasgupta (2000) for game-theoretic approaches to social capital. These inevitably impose the deterministic content of the rules of the game and cannot otherwise be contextual. Note the game-theoretic approach can be taken to absurd limits as in Barr's (1999) getting settled and re-settled villagers in Zimbabwe to play games to see which have greater levels of trust. Quite apart from the nature of social capital, this raises the issue of the nature of games and their relevance for non-games. Interestingly, Wittgenstein employed the notion of game in order to investigate the nature of categories. For him, games do not share a single collection of properties but they have what he termed "family resemblances", similarities to one another in a variety of ways. As a result, conclusions from Barr's games cannot be projected to other circumstances. For a simple elaboration, see Lakoff (1987). See also discussion in Fine (1997b) in the context of consumption.

12 Note, in this context, that the problem is equivalently one of how we measure social capital or what functional form we use to model its effects. For a fuller discussion, see Chapter 10.

13 See Molinas (1998), for example, for the idea that creation of social capital might be U-shaped in terms of benefits from numbers involved. This is, however, a standard result in that there is a trade-off between the costs of organising a network and the benefits that accrue from doing so as the numbers increase. As Dasgupta (2000) observes, in a paper seen after the first draft of this chapter was completed: "investigations on the matter have run cross-country *linear* regression, a methodologically questionable move, given that indices of civil and political liberties have no cardinal significance." Dasgupta suggests that such problems do not carry over to the measurement of local-level indices characteristic of Narayan and Pritchett (1996). Nonetheless, the problems for estimation do carry over.

14 Although Moser (1998) argues that social capital, along with other assets, reduces vulnerability to shocks.

15 See DiPasquale and Glaeser (1999) who suggest that home owners are more settled

and hence provide social capital as an externality in the form of more local citizen-ship and more investment in local amenities. Of course, in the Tanzanian context, this raises the issue of migration and the extent to which this undermines social capital. Is it not plausible that migration is a consequence of low local income opportunities with mixed effects depending upon remittances?

16　See, for example, Grootaert (1998a and 1998b), Narayan (1998), Grootaert and Narayan (1999), Krishna and Shrader (1999), Rillera (1999), and Szabo (1999), covering a wide range of countries.

17　See Fine and Rustomjee (1997).

18　Note that, by some measures, inequality has increased in the post-apartheid period as a minority of well-placed blacks have benefited (cashing in on what might be termed an anti-apartheid dividend). This is consistent with the idea of social capital working in the later period as well as with the broader context suggested here. Further, there is the prospective destruction of social capital, as many have suggested, with the instability that arises with growing inequality. Note also that their focus on KwaZulu-Natal raises considerable issues of context concerning the relationship between Inkatha and the ANC.

19　Hence the frequent reference here to his review.

20　In the World Bank's social capital newsletter, *Nexus* (vol 1, no 1), Woolcock is reported to be a social scientist in the World Bank's Development Research Group. The next four issues of the Email Discussion Group were moderated by Deepa Narayan, Chris Grootaert, Thierry van Bastalaer, and Phil Keefer prior to Woolcock resuming charge. At the beginning of the millennium, it is reported to have a circulation of nine hundred.

21　Apart from the two discussed, there is the social capital newsletter, *Nexus*. See also the website http://www.inform.umd.edu/iris/soccap.html for the IRIS Center at the University of Maryland. It works with the World Bank on social capital. It was previously run by Mancur Olson who died in 1998 and to whom the Social Capital Initiative Working Papers are dedicated. Note that he was trained as and was a professor in economics (Olson 1990, p. 177), with the following aim: "I like to get down, whenever possible, to the primitive entity of economic and social life: *the individual.*"

The orientation of the Center can be judged by a collection of papers edited by Clague (1997), of a 1994 conference. His opening piece begins with the heading, "From Physical Capital to Human Capital to Social Capital", and proceeds along the route of colonisation of the social sciences by economics through the new institu-tional economics and its synergies with social capital. Note also Olson and Kähkönen (eds) (2000), a collection devoted to, and arising out of, teaching India how to avoid "Big Bills Left on the Sidewalk" (Olson 2000). In their introduction, Olson and Kähkönen (2000) reject the idea that economics is perpetrating an imperialism on the other social sciences, since there is no use of armed force or denial of free choice. They prefer the equally revealing metaphor of economics as the metropolis, extend-ing its influence to the social science suburbs.

22　For Grootaert and van Bastelaer (1998b):

> The Social Capital Initiative aims to contribute to both the conceptual under-standing of social capital and its measure. Although there is a significant and rapidly growing literature on social capital and its impact ... it has not yet pro-vided an integrated and generally accepted conceptual and analytical frame-work.

See also World Bank (1998c, p. 2): "What is not clear is how this concept can be expressed in operational terms and fostered in a development context."

23　A later discussion paper (Rose 1999) extends the influence of social capital to address differences in levels of health, income, and food. Once again, the absolute drop in standards for all but the tiniest minority is surely more important than, and logically prior to, consideration of relative standards due to social capital. See also Rose et al. (1997) for discussion of Russia (and other east European countries) as an hourglass society, with a missing middle in the political system, high trust in immediate social networks, and low capability in state institutions. In the literature on transition in eastern Europe as much emphasis is put upon obedience as upon trust with a corresponding attention to vertical as opposed to horizontal associations (which are generally perceived to be rich if vertically disconnected). This is a consequence of the desire to establish property relations and legality. For a taster of some contributions on social capital and the transition from socialism, see Nichols (1996), Pahl (1996), Raiser (1997), Hagan and Radoeva (1997–98), King and Barnowe (1998), Holland (1998), Mondak and Gearing (1998), Stubbs (1998), Wong (1998), Neace (1999), and Volker and Flap (1999).

24 See also a special issue of *World Development* (vol 26, no 11, 1998) on the demographic crisis in the former Soviet Union, as cited by Sender (1999) in drawing its unfavourable comparison with Sub-Saharan Africa.

25 The discussion ranges over how social capital is both social and capital with a rare reference to the role played by Homans and social exchange theory, on which see Chapter 5. Note that why social capital is both social and capital is all too often, possibly inevitably, addressed tediously and superficially, especially by economists whom others are wont to mimic. Thus, for Narayan and Pritchett (1996, p. 1), "fashion aside, the popularity of 'capital'isms is due in part to the robust usefulness of the underlying metaphor: stuff that augments incomes but is not totally consumed in use", with social being associational interaction.

26 As for Bebbington, as discussed in Chapter 7, and, to a lesser extent as discussed later, for Woolcock and Narayan. See also Krishna (2000). See also Turner (2000, p. 94) who recognises that social capital includes everything, having observed, with explicit critical reference to Coleman, "efforts to redefine sociological variables as 'social capital' alongside other forms of capital ... tend to pour 'old sociological wine' in the 'new and smaller bottles' of economics" (p. 94). Of course, there are also those who, in some instances, want to refine social capital indefinitely and, in others, to criticise and even to reject it.

27 See also Fafchamps (2000) for a comparative study of ethnicity, gender, social capital (networks), and access to credit in manufacturing firms in Kenya and Zimbabwe.

28 See also Rillera (1999) and Dasgupta (2000). Note how the summary discussion of social capital by Serageldin and Grootaert (2000, p. 55), and of its interaction with other economic and social variables, essentially treats its diversity and complexity in terms of the technical characteristics of a production function.

29 Krishna and Shrader (1999) provide thirty-nine items of structural social capital covering density and character of networks and support organisations, exclusion, collective action, and conflict resolution. They also suggest twenty-one items of "cognitive" social capital such as solidarity, trust, reciprocity, and cooperation. Reid and Salmen (1999) look at social capital in terms of social cohesion: investigating village cleanliness (weeding), condition of mosque, prayer attendance, distribution of infrastructure, capacity to organise public infrastructure maintenance, number of associations, leadership. See also Pena and Lindo-Fuentes (1998) for a survey that runs slightly against the World Bank grain. Panamanians have social capital because they are poor. What they need is state-provided resources.

30 The suspicion must be that "down the line" in the previous Woolcock quote refers to a movement up the hierarchy (of economists) within the World Bank who are the ones to be targeted with social capital as ammunition.

31 Note that most of the metaphors are drawn from western experience prior to being imposed on developing countries, another analytical setback attached to social capital in the field of development studies!

32 Given the record of stabilisation and structural adjustment, diagnosis of failed development based on the Washington consensus might be one of iatrogenic policies – we caused it!

33 I am not in a position to assess the overall weight of social capital in the thinking and practice of the World Bank. Observe, however, that it does figure once in the World Development Report for 1997 (*The State in a Changing World*), with reference to the studies of Putnam (1993a) and Narayan and Pritchett (1996). It concluded:

> The debate about the contribution of social capital to economic and social development is just beginning and the early evidence is by no means unambiguous. But some studies are already demonstrating its potential impact on local economic development, on the provision of local public goods, and on the performance of public agencies.

For the Report of 1998–99 (*Knowledge for Development*), social capital warrants mention in three places with two of them to the study of Narayan (1997). There is, however, no reference in the proposed work programme for 1999–2000 (*Development Policy*) but social capital does figure a number of times in the text. By 2000–01 (*Poverty and Development*), there is a single mention in the programme, section 8.4 entitled "Social Capital, Inequality and Community", out of thirteen sections altogether and eighty-three subsections. Section 8 as a whole is entitled "Inequality, Social Cohesion and Poverty". In the first draft of the Report, released for consultative discussion in early 2000, social capital takes up a major part of one of ten chapters of the Report. The other, following part within the chapter is concerned with discrimination by ethnicity and gender and seems to have forgotten that social capital has preceded it. See Chapter 11 for further discussion of the draft.

34 Thus, leading and more circumspect neoclassical economists, such as Arrow (2000) and Solow (2000), have both explicitly expressed severe doubts about social capital.

35 Note that Narayan (1999a and 1999b) locates the rise of social capital to the increasing attention to social aspects of development inspired by Stiglitz. See Chege (1998) for the notion that Kenya is to be understood through post-Washington consensus and social capital.

36 Note that throughout his time at the World Bank, Stiglitz continued to produce mainstream papers in economics but none of these covered social capital. Ultimately, Stiglitz (2000a) is his most serious and exclusive focus upon the issue. It stands out for its lack of formal content compared to his normal, considered work. It is also remarkably vacuous whilst simultaneously reflecting both the post-Washington consensus approach to the social and the Colemanesque notion of how the social can make perfection out of market imperfection. Conclusions in full are (pp. 67–68):

(a) Social capital is a very useful concept, but an extremely complex one, in which different perspectives have much to contribute. I believe that the organizational perspective in particular provides a useful frame.

(b) There are reasons to believe that the composition, quality, and quantity of social capital of a society are not necessarily optimal.

(c) Social capital is affected by, and affects, the development process.

(d) There is an important public role in the enhancement of social capital, but who should undertake that public role, and how it should be done, are questions that will need a great deal more thought.

Personally, I find it extremely sad, yet appropriate and revealing, how touching social capital can turn the most technically proficient and insightful into the vacuous. Consider substituting almost any variable X for social capital in the above.

37 See Mehta (1999).

38 Thereby, as Hildyard (1998) and others have suggested, opening up for the Washington institutions more powerful levers for intervention for otherwise unchanged policies. Note that there is even a hint of self-criticism in deference to the neglect of social capital in the past; Grootaert and van Bastelaer (1998a) seek "to ensure that Bank programs avoid weakening existing, positive social capital (as they have sometimes done in the past)". Consequently, the research projects under the World Bank's Social Capital Initiative were selected:

> On the basis of their perceived ability to test two central hypotheses:
>
> 1. The presence of social capital improves the effectiveness of development projects; and
> 2. Through select donor-supported interventions, it is possible to stimulate the accumulation of social capital.

If both hypotheses are correct, it is about improving the effectiveness of projects through intervention in civil society!

39 See Unger (1998) for an attempt to interpret the Thai developmental state in terms of social capital.

40 This quote is followed by a footnote with the only reference in the piece to the World Bank, and the judgement (shared by myself at the time) of a "firm indication that the World Bank is beginning to construe development in these terms" (p. 208). The reference is to Serageldin (1996) which does, indeed, stake out a much broader economic compass for social capital in the first instance than has, as yet, been adopted by the World Bank.

41 I have been informed that social capital is now a thematic group within the World Bank, chaired across departments/sectors by Narayan, Bebbington, and Woolcock.

42 Note also that for Grootaert and van Bastelaer (1998b):

> Other aspects of social capital will be left relatively unexplored by the Initiative, such as the potential role of social capital in improving performance in the public sector, and issues related to welfare-decreasing forms of social capital (of which organized crime is an extreme example).

43 Note, however, that Woolcock's (1999) discussion of micro-finance, and how to learn lessons from its failures as well as its successes, essentially omits any discussion of social capital, presumably having been penned long before it was published. See also Schrieder and Sharma (1999) on micro-finance.

44 As coined by Merton (1957). For a critical discussion in the context of labour market segmentation, see Fine (1998a).

45 See also Gugerty et al. (1999) in the context of the role of NGOs in having a permanent effect rather than temporarily providing social capital themselves. Note linking has also been added to bridging and bonding (and perverse, etc.) as a broad genus of social capital.

46 See especially and most recently Narayan et al. (1999), and note how social capital flits in and out of the text.

47 See Chapter 11 for further discussion on this point.

48 For an account of the evolving position of social theory within the World Bank, the attempts of social scientists to gain a foothold against the economists, and their role as social engineers, see Francis (1999).

49 This is consistent with the broader more people friendly and social emphasis of the Comprehensive Development Framework launched by Wolfensohn, World Bank President, that is markedly silent on economic issues. See Edstrom (1999) for an inadvertent acceptance of all of this:

We acknowledge that too often in the past, the World Bank focused too much on the economics of growth, without a sufficient understanding of the social, the political, the environmental, and the cultural aspects of development. Nonetheless, the Bank has recognized, albeit later than some of our sister agencies in the United Nations, that development must be people centered – that is people must be the focus of the development agenda.

50 Soon after his resignation, in a keynote address to the American Economic Association, Stiglitz (2000b) reveals that he has embraced even greater freedom to criticise, arguing against labour market flexibility, "the not-so-subtle subtext was to lower wages and lay off workers", and the exclusion of workers from decision making in formulating adjustment policies. See also Stiglitz's (1999) views on trade liberalisation and how it has disadvantaged developing countries, leading Jordan (1999) to comment:

> Unfortunately, within the World Bank structure, Stiglitz is not able to influence the shape of lending operations or even the establishment of policies. In fact, his opinions are often accompanied by disclaimers from the public relations office of the World Bank.

Ultimately, in April 2000, Stiglitz was disowned even as a special advisor to World Bank president, Wolfensohn. Worse was to follow in June, 2000, with the resignation of Ravi Kanbur, the lead author for the World Bank's once in a decade World Development Report on Poverty. This was purportedly in response to editorial interference by Larry Summers, US Treasury Secretary. The latter is notorious for suggesting, when he was himself Chief Economist at the World Bank, that it made sound economic sense to use developing countries as a dumping ground for industrial waste. He is said to have been involved in redrafting and toning down the treatment of globalisation in the Poverty Report.

51 For a very clear indication of the extent to which this is so for the IMF, see Crockett (1999), who effectively sees the market mechanism as the "architecture" whose imperfections should not be unduly interfered with by plumbers (presumably, an unwitting reference to Joe Stiglitz). Crockett is General Manager of the Bank for International Settlements, and was widely, but wrongly, tipped as likely successor to Michel Camdessus, then the IMF's managing director. More substantively; for an IMF-inspired text of macroeconomics that fully incorporates the insights of the post-Washington consensus, see Agénor and Montiel (1996). For a critique, see Fine and Hailu (1999). Note also that, at the turn of the millennium, the IMF has become more people-friendly with a putative claim to be giving greater priority to poverty relief in its policies.

52 For an account of Stiglitz as a "renegade" with integrity from before the time of his joining the World Bank, see Chait (1999).

10 Measuring social capital – how long is a missing link?

1 See Fedderke et al. (1998) for a discussion of these issues.

2 Note also how many of the contributions to Dasgupta and Serageldin (eds) (2000) are cast in terms of how to satisfy economists with the notion of social capital, not least in progression from physical to human capital and beyond, and the need to measure impact in terms of an as if input (or sacrifice). For them: "It is difficult to think of an academic notion that has entered the common vocabulary of social discourse more quickly than the idea of social capital" (p. x). Further: "Whatever else social capital may be, it is emphatically an economic good. And yet, while the term has gained wide currency, it has not found favour among economists."

3 Alternatively, we could have different interactions that are not equivalent even if individuals are. Note, there is no need for $k_{rs} = k_{sr}$. Presumably, $k_{rr} = 0$, it is impossible for social interaction to be reflexive.

4 By analogy, "a" always comes before "baaaaaa ..." in the alphabet, so a strong connection with elite a always dominates the social capital of someone without it howsoever strong that might otherwise be through other connections.

5 See Kawachi in World Bank Discussion Group on Social Capital (Issue 27); "presumably, one would aggregate individual responses to obtain a measure of community social capital."

6 The second issue has been covered, for example, by Sen (1970a, 1970b, and 1979) and Fine (1974 and 1975b), the first by Fine (1974), and the two together by Fine (1996) who shows that there is an equivalence between them (varying an individual's ordinal measure, or intensity, is equivalent to a higher or lower interpersonal weight). Exactly the same issues arise in the context of measuring inequality (Fine 1985).

7 See, for example, Deaton and Muellbauer (1980), Blundell (1988), and Deaton (1997). Note that failure to keep abreast with such technical developments led the UK Ministry of Agriculture, Food and Fisheries (MAFF) to abandon estimation of demand elasticities for food. See Fine et al. (1996) for an account and a critique of such exercises in this context.

8 This is at best a partially correct memory, but it does capture the essence other than that Robinson was correct and accepted as such by opponents, especially Paul Samuelson, a close substitute for Solow and also Nobel prize winner.

9 For a full account, see Harcourt (1972 and 1976) and, for a more elementary exposition, Fine (1980, Chapter 5).

10 The account that follows is extremely favourable to the mainstream approach insofar as evaluation is attached to discounting a consumption stream rather than as a consequence of distributional relations between capital and labour over wages and profits.

11 In the simplest terms, the measure of capital is kv, where k is the physical quantity of capital and v is its relative price. One way of interpreting the Cambridge critique is that the standard neoclassical one-sector model treats kv as if it were k alone. Consequently, any change in v, theoretical or empirical, has to be treated as if it were a change in k.

12 Nor do we need to assume that resources are required for social capital as long as economic outcomes are measurably distinct from social capital, creating a relative value problem between the two.

13 See Hodgson (1997).

14 See also Chapter 7.

15 This section was drafted before the remarkable report of the Social Capital Conference at Michigan State University appeared in the World Bank's Email Discussion Group on Social Capital (no 13). Robison and Siles offer the following account:

> Not everyone accepts the metaphor of capital being associated with the product of social relations. Reflecting on a social capital workshop sponsored by the World Bank, economist and Nobel laureate Kenneth Arrow urged abandonment of the metaphor of capital and the term "social capital". He emphasized that the term, "capital" implied a deliberate sacrifice in the present for future benefit that he claimed social networks organized for reasons other than economic value to the participants fail. Regardless of whether one agrees or disagrees with Arrow's objections to the metaphor of capital and the term social capital, his recommendation that the term social capital be abandoned comes too late. The calves are out of the barn and into green pastures and not likely to return soon. The term social capital is now firmly entrenched in the language of social

scientists. Thus, for now and for some considerable time in the future, the term "social capital", will be in common use amongst social scientists if not economists.

Note that Arrow's Nobel prize was in part awarded for his pioneering work on social choice theory. Also, it is the use of social capital by economists that should be considered a source of alarm. Finally, in this heavy world of metaphors, is it by sticks, carrots, or hugs that we can get the calves back in the barn before we suffer mad cow disease (see Chapter 7)? Arrow (2000) provides a written account of his objections. It is complemented by that of Solow (2000) who is more concerned with the measurement of stocks and flows and rates of return as attached to social capital. Note also Stamps (1998) who cites Loury, generally cited as an original source for social capital, as "in accord with skeptical economists who wonder whether so murky a concept as social capital can ever be measured ... 'At the end of the day, I don't think it is measurable. It's like the weather. There's no single measure of what makes a good day or a bad day'."

16 Arrow (1951) is the classic reference, but see also Sen (1970a, 1975, and 1995). The Impossibility Theorem argues that no voting rule for coming to a decision is capable of satisfying a number of apparently reasonable axioms.
17 This is to reject the axiom of unrestricted domain. In voting for political parties, for example, preferences will tend to be from one extreme to another or from the middle ground outwards (or "peaked"). The same may be true across the various hierarchically ordered components of social capital.
18 See Fine and Fine (1974a and 1974b) and Fine (1974).
19 See Fine (1983), Fine et al. (1992a–e and 1993), and Fine and Simister (1995).
20 With use of degrees of trust, this will imply some restriction on the domain of individual orderings. It is not possible to have a second degree of trust before having first degree (just as it is not possible to own a second durable before owning a first).
21 Thus, the standard measure for determining the order of acquisition of consumer durables was shown to violate the axiom of monotonicity – in social capital terms, that the aggregate measure should be positively related to individual measures (Fine 1983).
22 For durables, see references in previous footnote; on food, see Fine et al. (1996) and Fine (1998d).
23 For increasingly dated reviews, see Fine and Leopold (1993) and Miller (ed) (1995).
24 This is wonderfully, if unwittingly, illustrated by Hirschman (1998) who observes the presence of commonsensality in the sharing of a meal, and the social significance of food and conviviality more generally. Yet it is equally conducive to good or bad outcomes (p. 27):

> The common meal or banquet contributed to the 'invention' of democracy in the age of classical Athens, on the one hand; in the Imperial Germany of Heinrich Mann, on the other, commonsensality could lead to the degradation of human relations and political life.

In short, as a source of social capital, the cultural content of food is sufficiently varied to undermine any general propositions concerning its nature and effects.
25 See references cited on consumption.
26 See Dasgupta (2000) on trust:

> Trust is central to the idea of social capital and, more generally, to all transactions ... I will be using the word "trust" in the sense of having correct expectations about those actions of others that have a bearing on one's own choice of action, when that action must be chosen before one can monitor the actions of those others.

Note the reductionism to the tools of the new (post-Washington) information-theoretic economics as also previously in Dasgupta (1988 and 1993).

27 And it is contested for downgrading the role of the horizontal. See the debate between Glennie and Thrift (1992 and 1993) and Fine (1993a). See also Fine et al. (1996) and Fine (1998d).

28 Here a different parallel is appropriate: the structuring of labour markets which also incorporates both horizontal (vocationally specific across sectors, for example) and vertical (sectoral specific across vocations) factors. See Fine (1998a).

29 See Onyx and Bullen (2000) for example. By comparing five communities, they essentially conclude that social capital is both conceptually and empirically slippery.

30 Lest the alternative offered in this paragraph be considered too weak, consider the conclusion drawn from a sympathetic commentator on social capital (Temple 2000):

> What can a policy-maker in Mexico or Turkey actually do, confronted with the evidence from the World Values Survey that they govern a low-trust society? Standard recommendations, such as attempting to eliminate corruption and improve the legal system, are nothing new, and make good sense quite independently of any emphasis on social capital.

Nonetheless, Temple holds out the hope for social capital that it will emulate the success of human capital, deemed just a decade earlier to have been in a similar ethereal and embryonic state. His view to the contrary, it is far from clear that human capital now successfully provides an "immediate message for education policies". See Fine and Rose (2001) where it can be seen that shifts in education policies are rationalised and not determined by human capital theory.

11 Social capital versus political economy

1 Yet, although primarily perceived at national or lower levels, Maskell (2000) opens his contribution:

> The contemporary process of globalization has dramatically enhanced the economic importance of what a diverse group of scholars (Bourdieu, Coleman, Burt, Putnam, Fukuyama and Woolcock) has called *social capital.*

2 See Gamarnikow and Green (1999b, p. 111) for a similar insight, in the context of Third Wayism, an aspect to be taken up later:

> Concerns about social capital thus represent a return to classical sociological preoccupations with community as the foundation of social solidarity and social cohesion. The journey from sociology to social capital does, however, indicate a key shift in discursive trajectories. Sociological explanations tend to incorporate, to varying degrees, the articulation of economic considerations with social structures and relations. By contrast, contemporary social capital theories tend to view society as pre-existing the economy and being causally implicated in its production. This sidelining of economic, material and structural effects or determinations opens the space for policy interventions in the realm of the social, political and cultural, so crucial to Third Way politics.

3 See Slater (2000) for the importance of the cultural in the definition of markets and, hence, as an irreducible part of the economic. He opens his paper extremely eloquently in addressing themes that will be taken up later in this chapter:

> The division between economic and socio-cultural analysis constitutes a kind of

deep structure of modern western thought. While it has been a favourite pastime of critical thinking since early modernity to attack the formalism of economic theory, we have been less good at reflecting on how critical and cultural analysis has itself been structured by this opposition. Essentially, critical thought has generally accepted the same terms of engagement as does economics, in which culture and economy are seen as macro-structures operating on each other as externalities; each sees the other as a global force or potential impurity pressing on it from outside.

4 I do not attempt here to unravel the complex and varied causal relations between the economy and culture. But see Fine (1998d and 2000b).
5 Note, however, that leading mainstream economists such as Arrow and Solow are dismissive of social capital because it does not even satisfy their limited criteria of what constitutes capital!
6 One of the reasons for critics treating all economics as if it were based exclusively on the virtues of laissez faire is the rise of neo-liberalism over the past few decades. This has encouraged non-economists to treat economics as if it were attached to the unchanging principles associated with the general equilibrium theory that pre-dated neo-liberalism's triumphant rise.
7 As one World Bank tactician put it to me, see below, X-thousand social scientists can't be wrong.
8 Different, directly commercial, pressures operate in the context of science as opposed to social science and are, arguably, greater and worse. See Press and Washburn (2000) for a journalistic account of the dangers to open science as examined by David (1998), for example.
9 Bowles' reservations could not be more orthodox:

> A good *term* it certainly is not. Capital refers to a thing possessed by individuals – even a social isolate like Robinson Crusoe had an axe and a fishing net ... Once everyone realized that market failures are the rule rather than the exception and that governments are neither smart enough or good enough to make things entirely right, the social capital rage was bound to happen.

This provides an excellent illustration of the loss of US radicalism and its incorporation by a colonising mainstream. For stronger, and more recent, evidence, see Bowles and Gintis (2000). Recall that this pair brought the theory of human capital to its knees (Bowles and Gintis 1976). Now, he has leapfrogged human to social capital. See Fine and Rose (2000), and also Fine (1998a) and Spencer (1998) in the context of labour markets. Note also how perceptive is Durlauf (1999) in response to Bowles: "Social capital has proven a useful lightening [sic] rod for the resocializing of the analysis of individual behaviour in the social sciences, notably in economics."
10 They also suggest that (p. 59):

> A fundamental criticism ... is that it ignores structured social inequalities, particularly those traditionally conceptualised as social class inequalities.

Whilst essentially correct, social capital is still slippery enough to throw this in as well if required. See also Gamarnikow and Green (1999b, p. 111, and 1999c, p. 10).
11 Note that Newton (1999b) locates the late 1990s as the point of departure from neo-liberalism and its concern for (economic) freedom as opposed to "underlying values, norms, and attitudes, and social conditions which create the capacity to trust and cooperate" (p. 169). With the 1980s having brought the state back in, as in Evans et al. (eds) (1985), the 1990s provided for social capital to take a turn, not least with Evans (1996a and 1996b) himself. Newton also observes from World Values data that

there is no strong systematic relationship between social trust and associational activity; and little between social and political trust, concluding that they always need to be distinguished from and have a complex relationship to one another and to other factors.

12 See Milonakis (2000) for a discussion of how the (Lange) market socialism debate has been transformed by the new micro-foundations of economics so that socialism, from a rational choice perspective, becomes egalitarianism married to appropriate incentive compatibility.

13 See Szreter (1998) for an explicit tying of social capital with the Third Way. Brown and Lauder (2000) quote Tony Blair (1998, p. 3 and p. 20):

> We can only realize ourselves as individuals in a thriving civil society, comprising strong families and civic institutions buttressed by intelligent government … This Third Way … will build its prosperity on human and social capital.

King and Wickham-Jones (1999) interpret Crosland's Keynesian-welfarism in terms of social capital and a failed attempt to build consensus. Interestingly, Blair's New Labour is perceived as significant only in informing the aims and discourse, but not the practice, of the Party. This is due to the "emphasis placed by the administration upon formal interventions, contractual exchanges, and potentially coercive arrangements" (p. 209). See also Gamarnikow and Green (1999b) and especially Gamarnikow and Green (1999c) for the hardness of the Third Way.

14 Perceptively understood as Third-Wayism by Standing (1999).

15 Edwards deploys the slogan, "Social development is dead … long live social capital" as their warning cry.

16 He continues somewhat romantically that "there is no other framework we can use to pursue the visions we hold in our hearts."

17 For an early, highly successful and well-motivated campaign in favour of social capital for the reasons laid out here, see Cox (1995).

18 See Fine (2000b) for a critique of the retreat to the cultural in the context of the study of consumption. See also Slater (2000).

19 For patriarchy as an investigative category, see Fine (1992).

20 With amendment, Scott's (1998) critique of the state as the enemy of the people can be applied to social capital, not least in the way in which it allows society to be "legible" both through over-simplifications of social space and through high-modernist ideology in the ordering of that space. He concludes with some relevance for social capital (p. 5):

> In sum, the legibility of a society provides the capacity for large-scale engineering, high modernist ideology provides the desire, the authoritarian state provides the determination to act on that desire, and an incapacitated civil society provides the leveled social terrain on which to build.

This is surely post-Washington consensus critically reconstructed through a postmodernist prism, not least because Scott accepts the case for high modernism if wedded to local knowledge and action and rejects the "illegibility" attached to neo-liberalism and its corresponding opposition to interventionism.

References

Achat, H. et al. (1998) "Social Network, Stress, and Quality of Life", *Quality of Life Research*, vol 7, no 8, pp. 735–50.

Adler, N. et al. (eds) (1999) *Socioeconomic Status and Health in Industrial Nations: Social, Psychological and Biological Pathways, Annals of the New York Academy of Sciences*, vol 896.

Adler, P. and S. Kwon (1999) "Social Capital: The Good, The Bad and the Ugly", World Bank Social Capital Library, Papers in Progress.

Agénor, P. and P. Montiel (1996) *Development Macroeconomics*, Princeton: Princeton University Press.

Aghion, P. and P. Howitt (1998) *Endogenous Growth Theory*, Cambridge: MIT Press.

Akerlof, G. (1970) "The Market for 'Lemons': Quality Uncertainty and the Market Mechanism", *Quarterly Journal of Economics*, vol 84, no 3, pp. 488–500.

Akerlof, G. (1984) *An Economic Theorist's Book of Tales*, Cambridge: Cambridge University Press.

Akerlof, G. (1990) "George A. Akerlof", in Swedberg (ed) (1990).

Algie, A. (n.d.) "Social Capital: An Overview", Social Responsibilities Commission, Australia.

Almazn, M. (1999) "The Aztec States-Society: Roots of Civil Society and Social Capital", *Annals of the American Academy of Political and Social Science*, vol 565, pp. 162–75.

Anderlini, L. and H. Sabourian (1992) "The Economics of Barter, Money and Credit", in Humphrey and Hugh-Jones (eds) (1992).

Anderson, P. (1964) "The Origins of the Present Crisis", *New Left Review*, no 23, pp. 11–52.

Anheier, H. and J. Gerhards (1995) "Forms of Capital and Social Structure in Cultural Fields: Examining Bourdieu's Social Topography", *American Journal of Sociology*, vol 100, no 4, pp. 859–903.

Arestis, P. et al. (eds) (1997) *Capital Controversy, Post-Keynesian Economics and the History of Economics: Essays in Honour of Geoff Harcourt, Volume I*, London: Routledge.

Arnold, B. and F. Kay (1995) "Social Capital, Violations of Trust and the Vulnerability of Isolates: The Social Organization of Law Practice and Professional Self-Regulation", *International Journal of the Sociology of Law*, vol 23, no 4, pp. 321–46.

Arrow, K. (1951) *Social Choice and Individual Values*, London: Chapman & Hall.

Arrow, K. (2000) "Observations on Social Capital", in Dasgupta and Serageldin (eds) (2000).

Arthur, C. (1998) "The Fluidity of Capital and the Logic of the Concept", in Arthur and Reuten (eds) (1998).

Arthur, C. and G. Reuten (eds) (1998) *The Circulation of Capital: Essays on Volume Two of "Capital"*, London: Macmillan.

Ashman, D. et al. (1998) "The Strength of Strong and Weak Ties: Building Social Capital for the Formation and Governance of Civil Society Resource Organizations", *Nonprofit Management and Leadership*, vol 9, no 2, pp. 153–71.

Astone, N. et al. (1999) "Family Demography, Social Theory, and Investment in Social Capital", *Population and Development Review*, vol 25, no 1, pp. 1–31.

Bain, K. and N. Hicks (1998) "Building Social Capital and Reaching out to Excluded Groups: The Challenge of Partnerships", World Bank, mimeo.

Banfield, E. (1958) *The Moral Basis of a Backward Society*, New York: Free Press.

Banfield, E. (1970) *The Unheavenly City*, Boston: Little, Brown.

Baron, J. and M. Hannan (1994) "The Impact of Economics on Contemporary Sociology", *Journal of Economic Literature*, vol XXXII, no 3, September, pp. 1111–46, reproduced in Swedberg (ed) (1996).

Baron, S. et al. (eds) (2000) *Social Capital: Critical Perspectives*, Oxford: Oxford University Press.

Barr, A. (1998) "Enterprise Performance and the Functional Diversity of Social Capital", Centre for the Study of African Economies, Working Paper Series, no 98–1.

Barr, A. (1999) "Familiarity and Trust: An Experimental Investigation", Social Capital Library, Papers in Progress.

Barro, R. and X. Sala-i-Martin (1995) *Economic Growth*, New York: McGraw-Hill.

Bates, R. (1981) *Markets and States in Tropical Africa: The Political Basis of Agricultural Policies*, Berkeley: University of California Press.

Bates, R. (1988) *Towards a Political Economy of Development: A Rational Choice Perspective*, Berkeley: University of California Press.

Bates, R. (1999) "Ethnicity, Capital Formation, and Conflict", World Bank Social Capital Initiative, Working Paper, no 12.

Baum, F. (1997) "Public Health and Civil Society: Understanding and Valuing the Connection", *Australian and New Zealand Journal of Public Health*, vol 21, no 7, pp. 673–75.

Baum, F. (1999) "Social Capital: Is It Good for Your Health? Issues for a Public Health Agenda", *Journal of Epidemiology and Community Health*, vol 53, no 4, pp. 195–96.

Baum, F. (2000) "Social Capital, Economic Capital and Power: Further Issues for a Public Health Agenda", *Journal of Epidemiology and Community Health*, vol 54, no 6, pp. 409–10.

Bayart, J. (1999) "The 'Social Capital' of the Felonious State: Or the Ruses of Political Intelligence", in Bayart et al. (eds) (1999).

Bayart, J. et al. (eds) (1999) *The Criminalization of the State in Africa*, Oxford: James Currey Press.

Bayliss, K. (1999) "Privatization, the World Bank and Africa: Time for a Rethink", mimeo.

Bayliss, K. and B. Fine (1998) "Beyond *Bureaucrats in Business*: A Critical Review of the World Bank Approach to Privatisation and Public Sector Reform", *Journal of International Development*, vol 10, no 7, pp. 841–55.

Bazan, L. and H. Schmitz (1997) "Social Capital and Export Growth: An Industrial Community in Southern Brazil", IDS Discussion Paper, no 361.

Beall, J. (1997) "Social Capital in Waste – A Solid Investment", *Journal of International Development*, vol 9, no 7, pp. 951–61.

Beasley-Murray, J. (1999) "Value and Capital in Bourdieu and Marx", mimeo.

Bebbington, A. (1997) "Social Capital and Rural Intensification: Local Organizations and Islands of Sustainability in the Rural Areas", *Geographical Journal*, vol 163, no 2, pp. 189–97.

Bebbington, A. (1999) "Capitals and Capabilities: A Framework for Analyzing Peasant Viability, Rural Livelihoods and Poverty", *World Development*, vol 27, no 12, pp. 2021–44.

Bebbington, A. and T. Perreault (1999) "Social Capital, Development and Access to Resources in Highland Ecuador", *Economic Geography*, vol 75, no 4, pp. 395–418.

Becker, G. (1958) "Competition and Democracy", *Journal of Law and Democracy*, vol 1, pp. 105–9.

Becker, G. (1990) "Gary S. Becker", in Swedberg (ed) (1990).

Becker, G. (1993) *Human Capital: A Theoretical and Empirical Analysis, with Special Reference to Education*, London: University of Chicago Press, third edition.

Becker, G. (1996) *Accounting for Tastes*, Cambridge: Harvard University Press.

Becker, G. and G. Becker (1996) *The Economics of Life*, New York: McGraw-Hill.

Belliveau, M. et al. (1996) "Social Capital at the Top: Effects of Social Similarity and Status on CEO Compensation Firms", *Academy of Management Journal*, vol 36, no 6, pp. 1–19.

Benjamin, D. and L. Kochin (1979) "Searching for an Explanation of Unemployment in Interwar Britain", *Journal of Political Economy*, vol 87, no 3, pp. 441–78.

Benjamin, D. and L. Kochin (1982) "Unemployment and Unemployment Benefits in Twentieth-Century Britain: A Reply to Our Critics", *Journal of Political Economy*, vol 90, no 2, pp. 410–36.

Berger, R. (1995) "Agency, Structure, and Jewish Survival of the Holocaust: A Life History Study", *Sociological Quarterly*, vol 36, no 1, pp. 15–36.

Berman, M. (1982) *All That Is Solid Melts into Air: The Experience of Modernity*, New York: Simon & Schuster.

Berman, S. (1997) "Civil Society and Political Institutionalization", *American Behavioral Scientist*, vol 40, no 5, pp. 562–74.

Berne Declaration (1998) "Mainstreaming Sustainability: The World Bank and the Rehabilitation of the Indian Coal Sector", http://www2.access.ch/evb/BD/coal.htm

Bianchi, S. and J. Robinson (1997) "What Did You Do Today? Children's Use of Time, Family Composition, and the Acquisition of Social Capital", *Journal of Marriage and the Family*, vol 59, no 2, pp. 332–44.

Billiet, J. and B. Cambré (1999) "Social Capital, Active Membership in Voluntary Associations and Some Aspects of Political Participation: An Empirical Case Study", in van Deth et al. (eds) (1999).

Blair, T. (1998) *The Third Way: New Politics for the New Century*, London: Fabian Society.

Blau, P. (1964) *Exchange and Power in Social Life*, New York: Wiley.

Blau, P. (ed) (1975) *Approaches to the Study of Social Structure*, New York: Free Press.

Blau, P. (1987) "Microprocess and Macrostructure", in Cook (ed) (1987).

Blaug, M. (1987) *The Economics of Education and the Education of an Economist*, New York: New York University Press.

Blaug, M. (1998a) "Disturbing Currents in Modern Economics", *Challenge*, vol 41, no 3, pp. 11–34.

Blaug, M. (1998b) "The Problems with Formalism: Interview with Mark Blaug", *Challenge*, vol 41, no 3, pp. 35–45.

Blundell, R. (1988) "Consumer Behaviour: Theory and Empirical Evidence – A Survey", *Economic Journal*, vol 98, no 1, pp. 16–65.

Boix, C. and D. Posner (1998) "Social Capital: Explaining Its Origins and Effects on Government Performance", *British Journal of Political Science*, vol 28, no 4, pp. 686–93.

Booth, J. and P. Richard (1998a) "Civil Society, Political Capital, and Democratization in Central America", *Journal of Politics*, vol 60, no 3, pp. 780–800.

Booth, J. and P. Richard (1998b) "Civil Society and Political Context in Central America", *American Behavioral Scientist*, vol 42, no 1, pp. 33–46.

Boskin, M. (ed) (1979) *Economics and Human Welfare: Essays in Honor of Tibor Scitovsky*, New York: Academic Press.

Bourdieu, P. (1980) "Le Capital Social: Notes Provisoires", *Actes de la Recherche en Sciences Sociales*, no 31, pp. 2–3.

Bourdieu, P. (1981) "Men and Machines", in Knorr-Cetina and Cicourel (eds) (1981).

Bourdieu, P. (1986a) *Distinction: A Social Critique of the Judgement of Taste*, London: Routledge & Kegan Paul, first published in French in 1979.

Bourdieu, P. (1986b) "The Forms of Capital", in Richardson (ed) (1986), first published in German in 1983.

Bourdieu, P. (1987) "What Makes a Social Class? On the Theoretical and Practical Existence of Groups", *Berkeley Journal of Sociology*, vol XXXII, pp. 1–17.

Bourdieu, P. (1991) "Epilogue: On the Possibility of a Field of World Sociology", in Bourdieu and Coleman (eds) (1991).

Bourdieu, P. (1993) "Concluding Remarks: For a Sociogenetic Understanding of Intellectual Works", in Calhoun et al. (eds) (1993).

Bourdieu, P. (1994) *Towards a Reflexive Sociology*, Cambridge: Polity Press, first published in French from 1987 onwards.

Bourdieu, P. (1996a) *The Rules of Art: Genesis and Structure of the Literary Field*, Cambridge: Polity Press, first published in French in 1992.

Bourdieu, P. (1996b) *The State Nobility: Elite Schools in the Field of Power*, Cambridge: Polity Press, first published in French in 1989.

Bourdieu, P. (1998a) *Practical Reasons: On the Theory of Action*, Cambridge: Polity Press.

Bourdieu, P. (1998b) *Acts of Resistance: Against the New Myths of Our Time*, Cambridge: Polity Press.

Bourdieu, P. and J. Coleman (eds) (1991) *Social Change for a Changing Society*, Boulder: Westview Press.

Bourdieu, P. and H. Haacke (1995) *Free Exchange*, Cambridge: Polity Press, first published in French in 1994.

Bourdieu, P. and L. Wacquant (1992) *An Invitation to Reflexive Sociology*, Cambridge: Polity Press.

Bowden, S. and A. Offer (1994) "Household Appliances and the Use of Time: The United States and Britain since the 1920s", *Economic History Review*, vol XLVII, no 4, pp. 725–48.

Bowden, S. and A. Offer (1999) "Household Appliances and 'Systems of Provision': A Reply", *Economic History Review*, vol LII, no 3, pp. 563–67.

Bowles, S. (1999) " 'Social Capital' and Community Governance", *Focus*, vol 20, no 3, pp. 6–10.

Bowles, S. and H. Gintis (1976) *Schooling in Capitalist America: Educational Reform and the Contradictions of Economic Life*, London: Routledge & Kegan Paul.

Bowles, S. and H. Gintis (2000) "Walrasian Economics in Retrospect", *Quarterly Journal of Economics*.

Branscomb, L. and J. Keller (eds) (1998) *Investing in Innovation: Creating a Research and Innovation Policy That Works*, Cambridge: MIT Press.

Brenner, R. (1998) "The Economics of Global Turbulence", *New Left Review*, no 229, pp. 1–264.

Brenner, R. and M. Glick (1991) "The Regulation School and the West's Economic Impasse", *New Left Review*, no 188, July–August, pp. 45–119.

Brewer, J. and R. Porter (eds) (1993) *Consumption and the World of Goods*, London: Routledge.

Brown, L. (1998) "Creating Social Capital: Nongovernmental Development Organizations and Intersectoral Problem Solving", in Powell and Clemens (eds) (1998).

Brown, L. and D. Ashman (1996) "Participation, Social Capital, and Intersectoral Problem Solving: African and Asian Cases", *World Development*, vol 24, no 9, pp. 1467–80.

Brown, P. (1995) "Cultural Capital and Social Exclusion – Some Observations on Recent Trends in Education, Employment and the Labour Market", *Work, Employment and Society*, vol 9, no 1, pp. 29–51.

Brown, P. and H. Lauder (2000) "Human Capital, Social Capital and Collective Intelligence", in Baron et al. (eds) (2000).

Brown, T. (1999) "Theoretical Perspectives on Social Capital", http://jhunix.hcf.jhu.edu/~tombrown/Econsoc/soccap.html

Brucker, G. (1999) "Civic Traditions in Pre-Modern Italy", *Journal of Interdisciplinary History*, vol XXIX, no 3, pp. 357–78.

Bruni, L. and R. Sugden (2000) "Moral Canals: Trust and Social Capital in the Work of Hume, Smith and Genovesi", *Economics and Philosophy*, vol 16, no 1, pp. 21–45.

Buckland, J. (1998) "Social Capital and Sustainability of NGO-Intermediated Development Projects in Bangladesh", *Community Development Journal*, vol 33, no 3, pp. 236–48.

Budlender, D. and N. Dube (1998) "Starting with What We Have – Basing Development Activities on Local Realities: A Critical Review of Recent Experience", Community Agency for Social Enquiry, South Africa, mimeo.

Burgess, R. and T. Huston (eds) (1979) *Social Exchange in Developing Relationships*, New York: Academic Press.

Burt, R. (1992) *Structural Holes*, Cambridge: Harvard University Press.

Burt, R. (1997a) "A Note on Social Capital and Network Content", *Social Networks*, vol 19, no 4, pp. 355–74.

Burt, R. (1997b) "The Gender of Social Capital", *Rationality and Society*, vol 10, no 1, pp. 5–46.

Burt, R. (1999) "The Social Capital of Opinion Leaders", *Annals of the American Academy of Political and Social Science*, vol 566, pp. 37–54.

Bynner, J. and R. Silbersen (eds) (1999) *Adversity and Challenge in Life in the New Germany and in England*, London: Macmillan.

Calhoun, C. (1993) "Habitus, Field and Capital: The Question of Historical Specificity", in Calhoun et al. (eds) (1993).

Calhoun, C. et al. (eds) (1993) *Bourdieu: Critical Perspectives*, Cambridge: Polity Press.

Campbell, C. (1993) "Understanding Traditional and Modern Patterns of Consumption in Eighteenth-Century England: A Character–Action Approach", in Brewer and Porter (eds) (1993).

Campbell, M. (1998) "Money in the Circulation of Capital", in Arthur and Reuten (eds) (1998).

Campbell, C. (2000) "Social Capital and Health: Contextualizing Health Promotion within Local Community Networks", in Baron et al. (eds) (2000).

Campbell, C. et al. (1999) *Social Capital and Health*, London: Health Education Authority.

Cantwell, R. (1999) "Habitus, Ethnomimesis: A Note on the Logic of Practice", *Journal of Folklore Research*, vol 36, no 2/3, pp. 219–34.

Carbonaro, W. (1999) "Opening the Debate on Closure and Schooling Outcomes: Comment on Morgan and Sørenson", *American Sociological Review*, vol 64, no 5, pp. 682–86.

Carrier, J. and D. Miller (eds) (1998) *Virtualism: The New Political Economy*, London: Berg.

Castle, E. (1998) "A Conceptual Framework for the Study of Rural Places", *American Journal of Agricultural Economics*, vol 80, no 3, pp. 621–31.

Cernea, M. (1991a) "Knowledge from Social Science for Development Policies and Projects", in Cernea (ed) (1991).

Cernea, M. (1991b) "Involuntary Resettlement: Social Research, Policy, and Planning", in Cernea (ed) (1991).

Cernea, M. (ed) (1991) *Putting People First: Sociological Variables in Rural Development*, Oxford: Oxford University Press, second edition.

Cernea, M. (1993) "Anthropological and Sociological Research for Policy Development on Population Resettlement", in Cernea and Guggenheim (eds) (1993).

Cernea, M. (1994) "Sociology, Anthropology and Development: An Annotated Bibliography of World Bank Publications, 1975–1993", Environmentally Sustainable Development Studies and Monographs Series, no 3, World Bank.

Cernea, M. (1996) "Social Organization and Development Anthropology: The 1995 Malinowski Award Lecture", Environmentally Sustainable Development Studies and Monographs Series, no 6, World Bank.

Cernea, M. and S. Guggenheim (eds) (1993) *Anthropological Approaches to Resettlement: Policy, Practice, and Theory*, Boulder: Westview Press.

Chadwick-Jones, J. (1976) *Social Exchange Theory: Its Structure and Influence in Social Psychology*, London: Academic Press.

Chait, J. (1999) "Shoeless Joe Stiglitz: Renegade at the Top", *The American Prospect*, no 45, pp. 52–56.

Champlin, D. (1997) "Culture, Natural Law, and the Restoration of Community", *Journal of Economic Issues*, vol 31, no 2, pp. 575–84.

Chege, M. (1998) "Introducing Race as a Variable into the Political Economy of Kenya Debate: An Incendiary Idea", *African Affairs*, vol 97, no 387, pp. 209–30.

Chin, T. (2000) " 'Sixth Grade Madness': Parental Emotion Work in the Private High School Application Process", *Journal of Contemporary Ethnography*, vol 29, no 2, pp. 124–63.

Chung, S. et al. (2000) "Complementarity, Status Similarity and Social Capital as Drivers of Alliance Formation", *Strategic Management Journal*, vol 21, no 1, pp. 1–22.

Clague, C. (1997) "Introduction", in Clague (ed) (1997).

Clague, C. (ed) (1997) *Institutions and Economic Development: Growth and Governance in Less-Developed and Post-Socialist Countries*, Baltimore: Johns Hopkins University Press.

Clarke, S. (1999) "Consumers and the Study of the Firm: The Experience of General Motors during the Great Depression", paper presented to Business History Conference, University of Glasgow, 3 July.

Clemens, E. (1999) "Securing Political Returns to Social Capital: Women's Associations in the United States, 1880s–1920s", *Journal of Interdisciplinary History*, vol XXIX, no 4, pp. 613–38.

Coats, A. (1996) "Comments", *History of Political Economy*, vol 28, Supplement, pp. 369–91.

Coats, A. (ed) (1996) "The Post-1945 Internationalization of Economics", *History of Political Economy*, vol 28, Supplement.

Cofino, R. (1995) "A Successful Approach to Participation: The World Bank's Relationship with South Africa", World Bank, mimeo.

Cohen, S. and G. Fields (1999) "Social Capital and Capital Gains in Silicon Valley", *California Management Review*, vol 41, no 2, pp. 108–30.

Coleman, J. (1972) "Systems of Social Exchange", *Journal of Mathematical Sociology*, vol 2, pp. 145–63.

Coleman, J. (1973) *The Mathematics of Collective Action*, Chicago: Alder.

Coleman, J. (1975) "Social Structure and a Theory of Action", in Blau (ed) (1975).

Coleman, J. (1986) "Micro Foundations and Macrosocial Theory", in Lindenberg et al. (eds) (1986).

Coleman, J. (1987a) "Free Riders and Zealots", in Cook (ed) (1987).

Coleman, J. (1987b) "Norms as Social Capital", in Radnitzky and Bernholz (eds) (1987).

Coleman, J. (1988) "Social Capital in the Creation of Human Capital", *American Journal of Sociology*, vol 94, Supplement, S95–S120, reproduced in Swedberg (ed) (1996).

Coleman, J. (1990a) *Foundations of Social Theory*, Cambridge: Harvard University Press.

Coleman, J. (1990b) "James S. Coleman", in Swedberg (ed) (1990).

Coleman, J. (1991) "Prologue: Constructed Social Organization", in Bourdieu and Coleman (eds) (1991).

Coleman, J. (1993) "The Rational Reconstruction of Society", *American Sociological Review*, vol 58, no 6, pp. 898–912.

Coleman, J. (1994) "A Rational Choice Perspective on Economic Sociology", in Smelser and Swedberg (eds) (1994).

Coleman, J. and T. Hoffer (1987) *Public and Private High Schools: The Benefit of Communities*, New York: Basic Books.

Coleman, J. et al. (1966) *Report on Equality of Educational Opportunity*, Washington: US Government Printing Office.

Coleman, J. et al. (1986) "Micro Foundations and Macrosocial Theory: General Discussion", in Lindenberg et al. (eds) (1986).

Collier, P. (1998) "Social Capital and Poverty", World Bank, Social Capital Initiative, Working Paper, no 4.

Connell, R. (1987) *Gender and Power: Society, the Person and Sexual Politics*, London: Polity.

Cook, K. (1987) "Emerson's Contribution to Social Exchange Theory", in Cook (ed) (1987).

Cook, K. (ed) (1987) *Social Exchange Theory*, London: Sage.

Cook, K. (1991) "The Microfoundations of Social Structure: An Exchange Perspective", in Huber (ed) (1991).

Cook, K. and R. Emerson (1978) "Power, Equity and Commitment in Exchange Networks", *American Sociological Review*, vol 43, no 5, pp. 721–39.

Cooke, B. and U. Kothari (eds) (1999) *Participation, the New Tyranny*, London: Zed Books.

Cooke, P. and D. Wills (1999) "Small Firms, Social Capital and the Enhancement of Business Performance through Innovation Programmes", *Small Business Economics*, vol 13, no 3, pp. 219–34.

Cooper, H. et al. (1999) *The Influence of Social Support and Social Capital on Health: A Review and Analysis of British Data*, London: Health Education Authority.

Corbo, V. et al. (eds) (1992) *Adjustment Lending Revisited: Policies to Restore Growth*, Washington: World Bank.

Cornia, G. and G. Helleiner (eds) (1994) *From Adjustment to Development in Africa: Conflict, Controversy, Convergence, Consensus?*, London: Macmillan.

Cox, E. (1995) *A Truly Civil Society*, Sydney: Australian Broadcasting Corporation.

Cox, E. (1998) "Measuring Social Capital as Part of Progress and Well-Being", mimeo.

Crilley, D. (1993) "Architecture as Advertising: Constructing the Image of Redevelopment", in Kearns and Philo (eds) (1993).

Crockett, A. (1999) "International Financial Arrangements: Architecture and Plumbing", David Finch Annual Lecture, University of Melbourne, 15 November.

Culpeper, R. et al. (eds) (1997) *Global Development Fifty Years after Bretton Woods*, London: Macmillan.

Cusack, T. (1999) "Social Capital, Institutional Structures, and Democratic Performance: A Comparative Study of German Local Governments", *European Journal of Political Research*, vol 35, no 1, pp. 1–34.

Dacin, M. et al. (1999) "The Embeddedness of Organizations: Dialogue and Directions", *Journal of Management*, vol 25, no 3, pp. 317–56.

Dasgupta, P. (1988) "Trust as a Commodity", in Gambetta (ed) (1988).

Dasgupta, P. (1993) *An Inquiry into Well-Being and Destitution*, Oxford: Clarendon Press.

Dasgupta, P. (2000) "Social Capital and Economic Performance", in Dasgupta and Serageldin (eds) (2000).

Dasgupta, P. and I. Serageldin (eds) (2000) *Social Capital: A Multifaceted Perspective*, Washington: World Bank.

Davern, M. (1997) "Social Networks and Economic Sociology: A Proposed Research Agenda for a More Complete Social Science", *Journal of Economics and Sociology*, vol 56, no 3, pp. 287–302.

David, P. (1998) "Common Agency Contracting and the Emergence of 'Open Science' Institutions", *American Economic Review*, vol 88, no 2, pp. 15–21.

de Hart, J. and P. Dekker (1999) "Civic Engagement and Volunteering in the Netherlands: A 'Putnamian' Analysis", in van Deth et al. (eds) (1999).

de Renzio, P. and D. Kavanamur (1999) "Tradition, Society and Development: Social Capital in Papua New Guinea", *Pacific Economic Bulletin*, vol 14, no 2, pp. 37–47.

de Vries, B. (1996) "The World Bank as an International Player in Economic Analysis", *History of Political Economy*, vol 28, Supplement, pp. 225–44.

Deaton, A. (1997) *The Analysis of Household Surveys: A Microeconometric Approach to Development Policy*, Baltimore: Johns Hopkins University Press.

Deaton, A. and J. Muellbauer (1980) *Economics and Consumer Behaviour*, Cambridge: Cambridge University Press.

Deraniyagala, S. and B. Fine (2000) "New Trade Theory versus Old Trade Policy: A Continuing Dilemma", *Cambridge Journal of Economics*.

Dezalay, Y. and B. Garth (1997) "Law, Lawyers and Social Capital: 'Rule of Law' versus Relational Capitalism", *Social and Legal Studies*, vol 6, no 1, pp. 109–41.

DiMaggio, P. (1990) "Cultural Aspects of Economic Action and Organization", in Friedland and Robertson (eds) (1990).

DiMaggio, P. (1991) "Social Structure, Institutions, and Cultural Goods: The Case of the United States", in Bourdieu and Coleman (eds) (1991).

DiMaggio, P. (1994) "Culture and Economy", in Smelser and Swedberg (eds) (1994).

DiPasquale, D. and E. Glaeser (1999) "Incentives and Social Capital: Are Homeowners Better Citizens?", *Journal of Urban Economics*, vol 45, no 2, pp. 354–84.

Dixon, H. (ed) (1997) "Controversy: Economics and Happiness", *Economic Journal*, vol 107, no 3, pp. 1812–14.

Dixon, J. and K. Hamilton (1997) "Introduction", in World Bank (1997), Chapter 1.

Dixon, R. (1986) "Uncertainty, Unobstructedness, and Power", *Journal of Post-Keynesian Economics*, vol 8, no 4, pp. 585–90.

Duncan, C. (1999) *Worlds Apart: Why Poverty Persists in Rural America*, New Haven: Yale University Press.

Durlauf, S. (1999) "The Case 'Against' Social Capital", *Focus*, vol 20, no 3, pp. 1–5.

Eastis, C. (1998) "Organizational Diversity and the Production of Social Capital: One of These Groups Is Not Like the Other", *American Behavioral Scientist*, vol 42, no 1, pp. 66–77.

Economist (1995) "No Accounting for Tastes", 23 September, p. 64.

Economist (1998) "New Economists: Journey Beyond the Stars", 19 December, pp. 143–46.

Edgell, S. et al. (eds) (1996) *Consumption Matters*, Oxford: Blackwell.

Edstrom, J. (1999) "Addressing Social Development by the World Bank", Statement delivered by Sector Manager, Social Development, World Social Summit, 16 February.

Edwards, B. and M. Foley (1997) "Social Capital and the Political Economy of Our Discontent", *American Behavioral Scientist*, vol 40, no 5, pp. 669–78.

Edwards, B and M. Foley (1998) "Civil Society and Social Capital Beyond Putnam", *American Behavioral Scientist*, vol 42, no 1, pp. 124–39.

Edwards, B. and M. Foley (eds) (1998) "Beyond Tocqueville: Civil Society and Social Capital in Comparative Perspective", *American Behavioral Scientist*, vol 42, no 1, pp. 1–139.

Edwards, M. (1999) "Enthusiasts, Tacticians and Sceptics: The World Bank, Civil Society and Social Capital", Social Capital Library, Papers in Progress.

Edwards, S. (1997) "Trade Liberalization Reforms and the World Bank", *American Economic Review*, vol 87, no 2, pp. 43–48.

Ekeh, P. (1974) *Social Exchange Theory: The Two Traditions*, Cambridge: Harvard University Press.

Ellerman, D. (2000) "Lessons from 'Voucher Privatization' ", World Bank, mimeo.

Elster, J. (1990) "Jon Elster", in Swedberg (ed) (1990).

Emerson, R. (1976) "Social Exchange Theory", *Annual Review of Sociology*, vol 2, pp. 335–62.

Emerson, R. (1987) "Toward a Theory of Value in Social Exchange", in Cook (ed) (1987).

Emirbayer, M. and J. Goodwin (1994) "Network Analysis, Culture, and the Problem of Agency", *American Journal of Sociology*, vol 99, no 6, pp. 1411–54.

Emmerij, L. (ed) (1997) *Economic and Social Development into the XXI Century*, Washington: Inter-American Development Bank.

Evans, P. (1996a) "Introduction: Development Strategies across the Public–Private Divide", *World Development*, vol 24, no 6, pp. 1033–37.

Evans, P. (1996b) "Government Action, Social Capital and Development Reviewing the Evidence on Synergy", *World Development*, vol 24, no 6, pp. 1119–32.

Evans, P. et al. (eds) (1985) *Bringing the State Back In*, Cambridge: Cambridge University Press.

Fafchamps, M. (2000) "Ethnicity and Credit in African Manufacturing", *Journal of Development Economics*, vol 61, no 1, pp. 205–35.

Fafchamps, M. and B. Minten (1999) "Social Capital and the Firm: Evidence from Agricultural Trade", World Bank Social Capital Initiative, Working Paper, no 21.

Falk, I. (1999) "Situated Leadership: A New Community Leadership Model", Social Capital Library, Papers in Progress, published in *Sociologia Ruralis*, vol 40, no 1, pp. 87–109.

Falk, I. and S. Kilpatrick (1999) "What Is Social Capital? A Study of Interaction in a Rural Community", Social Capital Library, Papers in Progress.

Febrero, R. and P. Schwartz (1995) "The Essence of Becker: An Introduction", in Febrero and Schwartz (eds) (1995).

Febrero, R. and P. Schwartz (eds) (1995) *The Essence of Becker*, Stanford: Hoover Institution Press.

Fedderke, J. et al. (1998) "Growth and Social Capital: A Critical Reflection", mimeo.

Feldman, T. and S. Assaf (1998) "Social Capital: Conceptual Frameworks and Empirical Evidence", World Bank, Social Capital Initiative, Working Paper, no 5.

Fellmeth, A. (1996) "Social Capital in the United States and Taiwan: Trust or Rule of Law?", *Development Policy Review*, vol 14, no 2, pp. 151–72.

Fevre, R. et al. (1999) "Some Sociological Alternatives to Human Capital Theory and Their Implications for Research on Post-Compulsory Education and Training", *Journal of Education and Work*, vol 12, no 2, pp. 117–40.

Field, M. (1995) "The Health Crisis in the Former Soviet Union: A Report from the 'Post-War' Zone", *Social Science and Medicine*, vol 41, no 11, pp. 1469–78.

Fine, B. (1974) "Individual Decisions and Social Choice", unpublished PhD thesis, University of London.

Fine, B. (1975a) "The Circulation of Capital, Ideology and Crisis", *Bulletin of the Conference of Socialist Economists*, no 12, pp. 82–96.

Fine, B. (1975b) "A Note on Interpersonal Aggregation and Partial Comparability", *Econometrica*, vol 43, no 1, pp. 169–72.

Fine, B. (1980) *Economic Theory and Ideology*, London: Edward Arnold.

Fine, B. (1983) "The Order of Acquisition of Consumer Durables: A Social Choice Theoretic Approach", *Journal of Economic Behaviour and Organization*, vol 4, no 2, pp. 239–48.

Fine, B. (1985) "A Note on the Measurement of Inequality and Interpersonal Comparison", *Social Choice and Welfare*, vol 1, no 4, pp 273–75.

Fine, B. (1989) *Marx's 'Capital'*, London: Macmillan, third edition.

Fine, B. (1990a) *The Coal Question: Political Economy and Industrial Change from the Nineteenth Century to the Present Day*, London: Routledge.

Fine, B. (1990b) "Scaling the Commanding Heights of Public Enterprise Economics", *Cambridge Journal of Economics*, vol 14, no 2, pp. 127–42.

Fine, B. (1992) *Women's Employment and the Capitalist Family*, London: Routledge.

Fine, B. (1993a) "Modernity, Urbanism, and Modern Consumption – A Comment", *Environment and Planning D, Society and Space*, vol 11, no 5, pp. 599–601.

Fine, B. (1993b) "Economic Development and Technological Change: From Linkage to Agency", in Liodakis (ed) (1993).

Fine, B. (1995a) "Flexible Production and Flexible Theory: The Case of South Africa", *Geoforum*, vol 26, no 2, pp. 107–19.

Fine, B. (1995b) "Reconsidering 'Household Labor, Wage Labor, and the Transformation of the Family' ", *Review of Radical Economics*, vol 27, no 2, pp. 107–25.

Fine, B. (1996) "Reconciling Interpersonal Comparability and the Intensity of Preference for the Utility Sum Rule", *Social Choice and Welfare*, vol 13, no 3, pp. 319–25.

Fine, B. (1997a) "The New Revolution in Economics", *Capital and Class*, no 61, Spring, pp. 143–48.

Fine, B. (1997b) "Playing the Consumption Game", *Consumption, Markets, Culture*, vol 1, no 1, pp. 7–29.

Fine, B. (1997c) "Privatisation: Theory and Lessons from the UK and South Africa", *Seoul Journal of Economics*, vol 10, no 4, pp. 373–414.

Fine, B. (1998a) *Labour Market Theory: A Constructive Reassessment*, London: Routledge.

Fine, B. (1998b) "The Triumph of Economics: Or 'Rationality' Can Be Dangerous To Your Reasoning", in Carrier and Miller (eds) (1998).

Fine, B. (1998c) "Value Theory: A Personal Account", *Utopia*, no 28, pp. 9–27, translated into Greek.

Fine, B. (1998d) *The Political Economy of Diet, Health and Food Policy*, London: Routledge.

Fine, B. (1999a) "From Becker to Bourdieu: Economics Confronts the Social Sciences", *International Papers in Political Economy*, vol 5, no 3, pp. 1–43.

Fine, B. (1999b) "The Developmental State is Dead – Long Live Social Capital?", *Development and Change*, vol 30, no 1, pp. 1–19.

Fine, B. (1999c) "A Question of Economics: Is It Colonising the Social Sciences?", *Economy and Society*, vol 28, no 3, pp. 403–25.

Fine, B. (1999d) " 'Household Appliances and the Use of Time: The United States and Britain since the 1920s': A Comment", *Economic History Review*, vol LII, no 3, pp. 552–62.

Fine, B. (1999e) "The Political Economist's Tale: Or, If Globalisation, (Welfare) State versus Market and Social Capital Are the Answers, Do We Have the Right Questions?", paper presented to conference, "Civilising the State: Civil Society, Policy and State Transformation", Deakin University, Melbourne, December.

Fine, B. (1999f) "Transition and the Political Economy of South Africa", paper presented to the African Studies Association of Australasia and the Pacific (AFSAAP), Perth, November.

Fine, B. (2000a) "Endogenous Growth Theory: A Critical Assessment", *Cambridge Journal of Economics*, vol 24, no 2, pp. 245 –65, a shortened and amended version of identically titled, School of Oriental and African Studies (SOAS) Working Paper, No 80, February 1998.

Fine, B. (2000b) "Consumption for Historians: An Economist's Gaze", SOAS Working Paper in Economics, no 91.

Fine, B. (2000c) "Whither the Welfare State: Public versus Private Consumption? ", SOAS Working Paper in Economics, no 92.

Fine, B. (2000d) "New and Improved: Economics' Contribution to Business History", SOAS Working Paper in Economics, no 93.

Fine, B. (2000e) "Critical Realism: It Ain't Critical and It Ain't Real", mimeo.

Fine, B. (2000f) "Bringing the Social Back into Economics: Progress or Reductionism?", University of Melbourne, Department of Economics Working Paper, no 731.

Fine, B. (2001a) "Neither Washington Nor Post-Washington Consensus: An Introduction", in Fine et al. (eds) (2001).

Fine, B. (2001b) "The Social Capital of the World Bank", in Fine et al. (eds) (2001).

Fine, B. (2001c) "The World Bank's Speculation on Social Capital: Bursting the Bubble", in Pincus and Winters (eds) (2001).

Fine, B. and K. Fine (1974a and 1974b) "Social Choice and Individual Ranking", Parts I and II, *Review of Economic Studies*, vol 41, no 3, pp. 303–22 and no 4, pp. 459–75.

Fine, B. and E. Leopold (1993) *The World of Consumption*, London: Routledge.

Fine, B. and J. Simister (1995) "Consumption Durables: Exploring the Order of Acquisition", *Applied Economics*, vol 27, no 11, pp. 1049–57.

Fine, B. and C. Stoneman (1996) "Introduction: State and Development", *Journal of Southern African Studies*, vol 22, no 1, March, pp. 5–26.

Fine, B. and Z. Rustomjee (1997) *South Africa's Political Economy: From Minerals-Energy Complex to Industrialisation*, Johannesburg: Wits University Press.

Fine, B. and D. Hailu (1999) "Convergence and Consensus: The Political Economy of Stabilisation and Growth", Occasional Paper Series, no 1, EMPAC, Ministry of Economic Development and Cooperation (MEDaC), Ethiopia.

Fine, B. and F. Green (2000) "Economics, Social Capital and the Colonisation of the Social Sciences", in Baron et al. (eds) (2000).

Fine, B. and C. Lapavitsas (2000) "Markets and Money in Social Theory: What Role for Economics?", *Economics and Society*, vol 29, no 3, pp. 357–82.

Fine, B. and P. Rose (2001) "Education and the Post-Washington Consensus – Plus Ça Change?", in Fine et al. (eds) (2001).

Fine, B. et al. (1992a) "Consumption Norms, Diffusion and the Video/Microwave Syndrome", SOAS Working Papers in Economics, no 19, May.

Fine, B. et al. (1992b) "Access to Phones and Democracy in Personal Communication: Myth or Reality?", SOAS Working Papers in Economics, no 20, May.

Fine, B. et al. (1992c) "Who Owns and Who Wants to Own a Car? An Empirical Analysis", SOAS Working Papers in Economics, no 21, May.

Fine, B. et al. (1992d) "Consumption Norms: A Definition and an Empirical Investigation of How They Have Changed, 1975–1990", SOAS Working Papers in Economics, no 22, May.

Fine, B. et al. (1992e) "Consumption Norms for Durables: Evidence from the General Household Survey", SOAS Working Papers in Economics, no 23, May.

Fine, B. et al. (1993) "Consumption Norms, Trickle-Down and the Video/Microwave Syndrome", *International Review of Applied Economics*, vol 7, no 2, June, pp. 123–43.

Fine, B. et al. (1996) *Consumption in the Age of Affluence: The World of Food*, London: Routledge.

Fine, B. et al. (1999) "Addressing the World Economy: Two Steps Back", *Capital and Class*, no 67, Spring, pp. 47–90.

Fine, B. et al. (eds) (2001) *Neither Washington nor Post-Washington Consensus: Challenging Development Policy in the Twenty-first Century*, London: Routledge.

Flap, H. and N. de Graaf (1986) "Social Capital and Attained Occupational Status", *Netherlands Journal of Sociology*, vol 22, no 1, pp. 145–61.

Fleetwood, S. (ed) (1999) *Critical Realism in Economics*, London: Routledge.

Flora, J. (1998) "Social Capital and Communities of Place", *Rural Sociology*, vol 64, no 4, pp. 481–506.

Flora, J. et al. (1997) "Entrepreneurial Social Infrastructure and Locally Initiated Economic Development in the Non-Metropolitan United States", *Sociological Quarterly*, vol 38, no 4, pp. 623–45.

Foley, M. and B. Edwards (1996) "The Paradox of Civil Society", *Journal of Democracy*, vol 7, no 3, pp. 39–52.

Foley, M. and B. Edwards (1997) "Escape from Politics? Social Theory and the Social Capital Debate", *American Behavioral Scientist*, vol 40, no 5, pp. 550–61.

Foley, M. and B. Edwards (1999) "Is It Time to Disinvest in Social Capital?", *Journal of Public Policy*, vol 19, no 2, pp. 141–73.

Fountain, J. (1998a) "Social Capital: A Key Enabler of Innovation", in Branscomb and Keller (eds) (1998).

Fountain, J. (1998b) "Social Capital: Its Relationship to Innovation in Science and Technology", *Science and Public Policy*, vol 25, no 2, pp. 103–16.

Fox, J. (1996) "How Does Civil Society Thicken? The Political Construction of Social Capital in Rural Mexico", *World Development*, vol 24, no 6, pp. 1089–1103.

Fox, J. (1997) "The World Bank and Social Capital: Contesting the Concept in Practice", *Journal of International Development*, vol 9, no 7, pp. 963–71.

Fox, J. and L. Brown (eds) (1998) *The Struggle for Accountability: The World Bank, NGOs, and Grassroots Movements*, Cambridge: MIT Press.

Francis, P. (1999) "A 'Social Development' Paradigm", in Cooke and Kothari (eds) (1999).

Frank, R. (1992) "Melding Sociology and Economics: James Coleman's 'Foundations of Social Theory' ", *Journal of Economic Literature*, vol XXX, no 1, March, pp. 147–70, reproduced in Swedberg (ed) (1996).

Friedland, R. and A. Robertson (eds) (1990) *Beyond the Marketplace: Rethinking Economy and Society*, New York: Walter de Gruyter.

Friedman, D. (1987) "Notes on 'Toward a Theory of Value in Social Exchange' ", in Cook (ed) (1987).

Friedman, R. and D. Krackhardt (1997) "Social Capital and Career Mobility: A Structural Theory of Lower Returns to Education for Asian Employers", *Journal of Applied Behavioural Science*, vol 33, no 3, pp. 316–34.

Fukuyama, F. (1995) "Social Capital and the Global Economy", *Foreign Affairs*, vol 74, no 5, pp. 89–103.

Fukuyama, F. (1996) *Trust: The Social Virtues and the Creation of Prosperity*, London: Penguin.

Furlong, D. (1996) "The Conceptualisation of 'Trust' in Economic Thought", IDS, University of Sussex, mimeo.

Furstenberg, F. and M. Hughes (1995) "Social Capital and Successful Development Among At-Risk Youth", *Journal of Marriage and the Family*, vol 57, no 3, pp. 580–92.

Gabbay, S. and E. Zuckerman (1998) "Social Capital and Opportunity in Corporate R&D: The Contingent Effect of Contact Density on Mobility Expectations", *Social Science Research*, vol 27, no 2, pp. 189–217.

Gamarnikow, E. and A. Green (1999a) "Developing Social Capital: Dilemmas, Possibilities and Limitations in Education", in Hayton (ed) (1999).

Gamarnikow, E. and A. Green (1999b) "Social Capital and the Educated Citizen", *The School Field*, vol X, no 3/4, pp. 103–26.

Gamarnikow, E. and A. Green (1999c) "The Third Way and Social Capital: Education Action Zones and a New Agenda for Education, Parents and Community?", *International Studies in Sociology of Education*, vol 9, no 1, pp. 3–22.

Gambetta, D. (ed) (1988) *Trust: Making and Breaking Cooperative Relations*, Oxford: Basil Blackwell.

Gamm, G. and R. Putnam (1999) "The Growth of Voluntary Associations in America, 1840–1940", *Journal of Interdisciplinary History*, vol XXIX, no 4, pp. 511–58.

Gandara, P. (1999) "Telling Stories of Success: Cultural Capital and the Educational Mobility of Chicano Students", *Latino Studies Journal*, vol 10, no 1, pp. 38–54.

Gergen, K. et al. (eds) (1980) *Social Exchange: Advances in Theory and Research*, New York: Plenum Press.

Gibbons, R. (1997) "An Introduction to Applicable Game Theory", *Journal of Economic Perspectives*, vol 11, no 1, pp. 127–49.

Giusta, M. (1999) "A Model of Social Capital and Access to Productive Resources", *Journal of International Development*, vol 11, no 7, pp. 921–34.

Glaeser, E. et al. (1999) "What is Social Capital? The Determinants of Trust and Trustworthiness", National Bureau of Economic Research, Working Paper, no 7216.

Glennie, P. and N. Thrift (1992) "Modernity, Urbanism, and Modern Consumption", *Environment and Planning D: Society and Space*, vol 10, no 4, pp. 423–43.

Glennie, P. and N. Thrift (1993) "Modern Consumption: Theorising Commodities and Consumers", *Environment and Planning D: Society and Space*, vol 11, no 5, pp. 603–6.

Gold, S. (1995) "Gender and Social Capital and Israeli Immigrants in Los Angeles", *Diaspora*, vol 4, no 3, pp. 267–301.

Goldberg, E. (1996) "Thinking about How Democracy Works", *Politics and Society*, vol 24, no 1, pp. 7–18.

Goodwin, M. (1993) "The City as Commodity: The Contested Spaces of Urban Development", in Kearns and Philo (eds) (1993).

Gough, I. (1979) *The Political Economy of the Welfare State*, London: Macmillan.

Granato, J. et al. (1996a) "The Effect of Cultural Values on Economic Development: Theory, Hypotheses, and Some Empirical Tests", *American Journal of Political Science*, vol 40, no 3, pp. 607–31.

Granato, J. et al. (1996b) "Cultural Values, Stable Democracy, and Economic Development: A Reply", *American Journal of Political Science*, vol 40, no 3, pp. 680–96.

Granovetter, M. (1985) "Economic Action and Social Structure: The Problem of Embeddedness", *American Journal of Sociology*, vol 91, no 3, pp. 481–510, reproduced in Swedberg (ed) (1996).

Granovetter, M. (1990a) "The Old and the New Economic Sociology: A History and an Agenda", in Friedland and Robertson (eds) (1990).

Granovetter, M. (1990b) "Mark Granovetter", in Swedberg (ed) (1990).

Granovetter, M. (1992) "Economic Institutions as Social Constructions: A Framework for Analysis", *Acta Sociologica*, vol 35, no 1, pp. 3–11, reproduced in Swedberg (ed) (1996).

Greeley, A. (1997a) "Coleman Revisited: Religious Structures as a Source of Social Capital", *American Behavioral Scientist*, vol 40, no 5, pp. 587–94.

Greeley, A. (1997b) "The Other Civic America: Religion and Social Capital", *The American Prospect*, no 32, pp. 68–73.

Green, M. and T. Brock (1998) "Trust, Mood, and Outcomes of Friendship Determine Preferences for Real versus Ersatz Social Capital", *Political Psychology*, vol 19, no 3, pp. 527–44.

Gregory, R. (1999) "Social Capital Theory in Administrative Reform: Maintaining Ethical Probity in Public Service", *Public Administration Review*, vol 59, no 1, pp. 63–75.

Greif, A. (1997) "Microtheory and Recent Developments in the Study of Economic Institutions through Economic History", in Kreps and Wallis (eds) (1997).

Grew, R. (1999) "Finding Social Capital: The French Revolution in Italy", *Journal of Interdisciplinary History*, vol XXIX, no 3, pp. 407–34.

Grootaert, C. (1997) "Social Capital: The Missing Link?", Chapter 6 in World Bank (1997), reproduced as World Bank, Social Capital Initiative, Working Paper, no 3.

Grootaert, C. (1998a) "Local Institutions and Service Delivery in Indonesia", Local Level Institutions Study, Social Development Department, Environmentally and Socially Sustainable Development Network, World Bank, mimeo.

Grootaert, C. (1998b) "Social Capital, Household Welfare and Poverty in Indonesia", Local Level Institutions Study, Social Development Department, Environmentally and Socially Sustainable Development Network, World Bank, mimeo.

Grootaert, C. and D. Narayan (1999) "Social Capital in Burkina Faso", World Bank, Local Levels Institutions Study.

Grootaert, C. and T. van Bastelaer (1998a) "The Social Capital Initiative", http://www. umd.edu/IRIS/Global/soccap.html

Grootaert, C. and T. van Bastelaer (1998b) "Expected Contributions from the Social Capital Initiative", IRIS website.

Grote, J. (1997) "Interorganizational Networks and Social Capital in the 'South of the South' ", European Institute Working Papers, Robert Schumann Institute, no 97/38.

Gugerty, M. et al. (1999) "The Impacts of Development Funding on Social Capital: The Kenya Local Community Action Project", World Bank Social Capital Initiative, Working Paper, no 19.

Guggenheim, S. and M. Cernea (1993) "Anthropological Approaches to Resettlement: Policy, Practice, and Theory", in Cernea and Guggenheim (eds) (1993).

Guiso, L. et al. (2000) "The Role of Social Capital in Financial Development", National Bureau of Economic Research, Working Paper, no 7563.

Guttman, J. (2000) "On the Evolutionary Stability of Preferences for Reciprocity", *European Journal of Political Economy*, vol 16, no 1, pp. 31–50.

Hagan, J. and D. Radoeva (1997–98) "Both Too Much and Too Little: From Elite to Street Crime in the Transformation of the Czech Republic", *Crime, Law and Social Change*, vol 28, no 3–4, pp. 195–211.

Hagan, J. et al. (1995) "Delinquency and Disdain: Social Capital and the Control of Right-Wing Extremism among East and West Berlin Youth", *American Journal of Sociology*, vol 100, no 4, pp. 1028–52.

Hagan, J. et al. (1996) "New Kid in Town: Social Capital and the Life Course Effects of Family Migration on Children", *American Sociological Review*, vol 61, no 3, pp. 368–85.

Hahn, F. and R. Solow (1995) *A Critical Essay on Modern Macroeconomic Theory*, Cambridge: MIT Press.

Hall, P. (1999) "Social Capital in Britain", *British Journal of Political Science*, vol 29, no 3, pp. 417–61.

Hallinan, M. and W. Kubitschek (1999) "Conceptualizing and Measuring School Social Networks", *American Sociological Review*, vol 64, no 5, pp. 687–93.

Hanifan, L. (1916) "The Rural School Community Center", *Annals of the American Academy of Political and Social Science*, vol 67, pp. 130–38.

Haque, M. (1996) "The Public Service under Challenge in the Age of Privatization", *Governance*, vol 9, no 2, pp. 186–216.

Harberger, A. (1992) "Comment", in Corbo et al. (eds) (1992).

Harcourt, G. (1972) *Some Cambridge Controversies in the Theory of Capital*, Cambridge: Cambridge University Press.

Harcourt, G. (1976) "The Cambridge Controversies: Old Ways and New Horizons – Or Dead End", *Oxford Economic Papers*, vol 28, no 1, pp. 25–65.

Harcourt, G. (1997) "Economic Theory and Economic Policy: Two Views", Discussion Paper, no 369, Centre for Economic Policy Research, Australian National University.

Hargreaves-Heap, S. (1992) *The Theory of Choice: A Critical Guide*, Oxford: Blackwell.

Harriss, J. and P. de Renzio (1997) " 'Missing Link' or Analytically Missing?: The Concept of Social Capital, An Introductory Bibliographic Essay", *Journal of International Development*, vol 9, no 7, pp. 919–37.

Harriss, J. et al. (eds) (1996) *The New Institutional Economics and Third World Development*, London: Routledge.

Harvey, D. (1989) *The Condition of Postmodernity: An Enquiry into the Origins of Cultural Change*, Oxford: Blackwell.

Hausman, D. and M. McPherson (1996) *Economics and Moral Philosophy*, Cambridge: Cambridge University Press.

Hayton, A. (ed) (1999) *Tackling Disaffection and Social Exclusion*, London: Kogan Page.

Heath, J. et al. (1998) "The Work of Families: The Provision of Market and Household Labor and the Role of Public Policy", *Review of Social Economy*, vol LVI, no 4, pp. 501–21.

Heilbroner, R. and W. Milberg (1995) *The Crisis of Vision in Modern Economic Thought*, Cambridge: Cambridge University Press.

Helleiner, G. (1994) "From Adjustment to Development in Sub-Saharan Africa: Consensus and Continuing Conflict", in Cornia and Helleiner (eds) (1994).

Heller, P. (1996) "Social Capital as a Product of Class Mobilization and State Intervention: Industrial Workers in Kerala, India", *World Development*, vol 24, no 6, pp. 1055–72.

Helliwell, J. and R. Putnam (1995) "Economic Growth and Social Capital in Italy", *Eastern Economic Journal*, vol 21, no 3, pp. 295–307, reproduced in Dasgupta and Serageldin (eds) (2000).

Hemingway, J. (1999) "Leisure, Social Capital, and Democratic Citizenship", *Journal of Leisure Research*, vol 31, no 2, pp. 150–65.

Hendricks, J. (1999) "Creativity over the Life Course – A Call for a Relational Perspective", *International Journal of Aging and Human Development*, vol 48, no 2, pp. 85–111.

Heying, C. (1997) "Civic Elites and Corporate Delocalization: An Alternative Explanation for Declining Civic Engagement", *American Behavioral Scientist*, vol 40, no 5, pp. 657–68.

Hildyard, N. (1998) *The World Bank and the State: A Recipe for Change?*, London: Bretton Woods Project.

Hinrich, K. (1995) "The Impact of German Health Insurance Reforms on Redistribution and the Culture of Solidarity", *Journal of Health Politics, Policy and Law*, vol 20, no 3, pp. 653–87.

Hirabayashi, L. (1993) *Cultural Capital: Mountain Zapotec Migrant Associations in Mexico City*, Tucson: University of Arizona.

Hirschman, A. (1998) *Crossing Boundaries: Selected Writings*, New York: Zone Books.

Hobsbawm, E. (1997) *On History*, London: Weidenfeld & Nicolson.

Hodgson, G. (1994a) "Some Remarks on 'Economic Imperialism' and International Political Economy", *Review of International Political Economy*, vol 1, no 1, pp. 21–28.

Hodgson, G. (1994b) "The Return of Institutional Economics", in Smelser and Swedberg (eds) (1994).

Hodgson, G. (1997) "The Fate of the Cambridge Capital Controversy", in Arestis et al. (eds) (1997).

Hodgson, G. and H. Rothman (1999) "The Editors and Authors of Economics Journals: A Case of Institutional Oligopoly?", *Economic Journal*, vol 109, no 453, pp. F165–86.

Holland, J. (1998) "Does Social Capital Matter?: The Case of Albania", *IDS Bulletin*, vol 29, no 3, pp. 65–71.

Homans, G. (1961) *Social Behaviour: Its Elementary Forms*, London: Routledge & Kegan Paul.

Huber, J. (ed) (1991) *Macro-Micro Linkages in Sociology*, London: Sage.

Humphrey, C. and S. Hugh-Jones (eds) (1992) *Barter, Exchange and Value: An Anthropological Approach*, Cambridge: Cambridge University Press.

Humphrey, J. and H. Schmitz (1997) "Trust and Inter-Firm Relations in Developing and Transition Economies", *Journal of Development Studies*, vol 34, no 4, pp. 32–61.

Hyden, G. (1997) "Civil Society, Social Capital, and Development: Dissection of a Complex Discourse", *Studies in Comparative International Development*, vol 32, no 1, pp. 3–30.

Iannacone, L. (1998) "Introduction to the Economics of Religion", *Journal of Economic Literature*, vol XXXVI, no 3, pp. 1465–95.

Ingham, G. (1996) "Some Recent Changes in the Relationship between Economics and Sociology", *Cambridge Journal of Economics*, vol 20, no 2, pp. 243–75.

Ingham, G. (1999) "Money Is a Social Relation", in Fleetwood (ed) (1999).

Inglehart, R. (1997) *Modernization and Postmodernization: Cultural, Economic and Political Change in 43 Countries*, Princeton: Princeton University Press.

Isham, J. et al. (1999) "What Determines the Effectiveness of Community-Based Water Projects?: Evidence from Central Java, Indonesia on Demand Responsiveness, Service Rules, and Social Capital", World Bank Social Capital Initiative, Working Paper, no 18.

Jackman, R. and R. Miller (1996a) "A Renaissance of Political Culture", *American Journal of Political Science*, vol 40, no 3, pp. 632–59.

Jackman, R. and R. Miller (1996b) "The Poverty of Political Culture", *American Journal of Political Science*, vol 40, no 3, pp. 697–716.

Jackman, R. and R. Miller (1998) "Social Capital and Politics", *Annual Review of Political Science*, vol 1, pp. 47–73.

Jameson, F. (1998) *The Cultural Turn: Selected Writings on the Postmodern, 1983–1998*, London: Verso.

Jones, P. (1992) *World Bank Financing of Education: Lending, Learning and Development*, London: Routledge.

Jordan, L. (1999) "The Death of Development", Bank Information Center, mimeo.

Jordana, J. (1999) "Collective Action Theory and the Analysis of Social Capital", in van Deth et al. (eds) (1999).

Joshi, H. et al (1999) "Diverse Family Living Situations and Child Development: A Multi-Level Analysis Comparing Longitudinal Evidence from Britain and the United States", *International Journal of Law, Policy and the Family*, vol 13, no 3, pp. 292–314.

Kähkönen, S. (1999) "Does Social Capital Matter in Water and Sanitation Delivery?: A Review of the Literature", World Bank Social Capital Initiative, Working Paper, no 9.

Kapur, D. et al. (1997) *The World Bank: Its First Half Century, Volume I: History*, Washington: Brookings.

Kapur, D. et al. (eds) (1997) *The World Bank: Its First Half Century, Volume II: Perspectives*, Washington: Brookings.

Kardam, N. (1993) "Development Approaches and the Role of Policy Advocacy: The Case of the World Bank", *World Development*, vol 21, no 11, pp. 1773–86.

Kaufman, J. and S. Tepper (1999) "Groups of Gatherings? Sources of Political Engagement in 19th Century American Cities", *Voluntas*, vol 10, no 4, pp. 299–322.

Kawachi, I. (1999) "Crime: Social Disorganization and Relative Deprivation", *Social Science and Medicine*, vol 48, no 6, pp. 719–32.

Kawachi, I. and B. Kennedy (1999) "Income Inequality and Health: Pathways and Mechanisms", *Health Services Research*, vol 34, no 1, pp. 215–27.

Kawachi, I. et al. (1996) "A Prospective Study of Social Networks in Relation to Total Mortality and Cardiovascular Disease Incidence in Men", *Journal of Epidemiology and Community Health*, vol 50, no 3, pp. 245–51.

Kawachi, I. et al. (1997a) "Long Live Community: Social Capital as Public Health", *The American Prospect*, no 35, pp. 56–59.

Kawachi, I. et al. (1997b) "Social Capital, Income Inequality, and Mortality", *American Journal of Public Health*, vol 87, no 9, pp. 1491–98.

Kawachi, I. et al. (1999a) "Crime: Social Disorganization and Relative Deprivation", *Social Science and Medicine*, vol 48, no 6, pp. 719–31.

Kawachi, I. et al. (1999b) "Social Capital and Self-Rated Health: A Contextual Analysis", *American Journal of Public Health*, vol 89, no 8, pp. 1187–93.

Kearns, G. (1993) "The City as Spectacle: Paris and the Bicentenary of the French Revolution", in Kearns and Philo (eds) (1993).

Kearns, G. and C. Philo (1993) "Preface", in Kearns and Philo (eds) (1993).

Kearns, G. and C. Philo (eds) (1993) *Selling Places: The City as Cultural Capital*, Oxford: Pergamon Press.

Kelly, M. (1994) "Towards Triumph: Social and Cultural Capital in the Transition to Adulthood in the Urban Ghetto", *International Journal of Urban and Regional Research*, vol 18, no 1, pp. 88–111.

Keman, H. (1999) "Foreword", in van Deth et al. (eds) (1999).

Kennedy, B. et al. (1998) "The Role of Social Capital in the Russian Mortality Crisis", *World Development*, vol 26, no 11, pp. 2029–43.

Kenworthy, L. (1997) "Civic Engagement, Social Capital, and Economic Cooperation", *American Behavioral Scientist*, vol 40, no 5, pp. 645–56.

Kern, M. (1997) "Social Capital and Citizen Interpretation of Political Ads, News, and Web Site Information in the 1996 Presidential Election", *American Behavioral Scientist*, vol 40, no 8, pp. 1238–49.

Khan, B. (1999) "Order with Law: Social Capital, Civil Litigation, and Economic Development", *Australian Economic History Review*, vol 39, no 3, pp. 172–90.

Kilpatrick, S. et al. (1998) "Groups of Groups: The Role of Group Learning in Building Social Capital", Social Capital Library, Papers in Progress.

King, A. (ed) (1996) *Re-Presenting the City: Ethnicity, Capital and Culture in the 21st Century Metropolis*, London: Macmillan.

King, D. and M. Wickham-Jones (1999) "Social Capital, British Social Democracy and New Labour", *Democratization*, vol 6, no 4, pp. 181–213.

King, G. and J. Barnowe (1998) "Social Capital in the Latvian Transition: Trust and Other Managerial Values", *Nationalities Papers*, vol 26, no 4, pp. 687–703.

King, J. (2000) "Has There Been Progress in Post-Keynesian Economics?", paper to the conference of the European Society for the History of Economic Thought (ESHET), Graz, February, in King (2001).

King, J. (2001) *The History of Post-Keynesian Economics, 1936–2000*, Cheltenham: Edward Elgar.

Knack, S. (1999) "Social Capital, Growth and Poverty: A Survey of Cross-Country Evidence", World Bank Social Capital Initiative, Working Paper, no 7.

Knack, S. and P. Keefer (1997) "Does Social Capital Have an Economic Payoff? A Cross-Country Investigation", *Quarterly Journal of Economics*, vol 62, no 4, pp. 1251–88.

Knack, S. and M. Kropf (1998) "For Shame! The Effect of Community Cooperative Context on the Probability of Voting", *Political Psychology*, vol 19, no 3, pp. 585–99.

Knorr-Cetina, K. and A. Cicourel (eds) (1981) *Advances in Social Theory and Methodology: Toward an Integration of Micro- and Macro-Sociologies*, London: Routledge & Kegan Paul.

Kolankiewicz, G. (1996) "Social Capital and Social Change", *British Journal of Sociology*, vol 47, no 3, pp. 427–41.

Konrad, K. (1995) "Social Security and Strategic Inter-Vivos Transfers of Social Capital", *Journal of Population Economics*, vol 8, no 3, pp. 315–26.

Kotz, D. (1994) "Household Labor, Wage Labor, and the Transformation of the Family", *Review of Radical Political Economics*, vol 26, no 2, June, pp. 24–56.

Kotz, D. (1995) "Analyzing the Transformation of the Family", *Review of Radical Economics*, vol 27, no 2, pp. 116–23.

Kreps, D. and K. Wallis (eds) (1997) *Advances in Economics and Econometrics: Theory and Applications: Volume 2*, Cambridge: Cambridge University Press.

Krishna, A. (2000) "Creating and Harnessing Social Capital", in Dasgupta and Serageldin (eds) (2000).

Krishna, A. and E. Shrader (1999) "Social Capital Assessment Tool", Conference on Social Capital and Poverty Reduction, World Bank, Washington, DC, 22–24 June.

Krishna, A. and N. Uphoff (1999) "Mapping and Measuring Social Capital: A Conceptual and Empirical Study of Collective Action for Conserving and Developing Watersheds in Rajasthan, India", World Bank Social Capital Initiative, Working Paper, no 13.

Krueger, A. (1997) "Trade Policy and Economic Development: How We Learn", *American Economic Review*, vol 87, no 1, pp. 1–22.

Krugman, P. (1998) "Two Cheers for Formalism", *Economic Journal*, vol 108, no 451, pp. 1829–36.

Kuperman, A. (1996) "The Other Lesson of Rwanda: Mediators Sometimes Do More Damage Than Good", *SAIS Review*, Winter–Spring, pp. 222–40.

Kyle, D. (1999) "The Otvalo Trade Diaspora: Social Capital and Transnational Entrepreneurship", *Ethnic and Racial Studies*, vol 22, no 2, pp. 422–46.

La Due Lake, R. and R. Huckfeldt (1998) "Social Capital, Social Networks, and Political Participation", *Political Psychology*, vol 19, no 3, pp. 567–84.

Labonte, R. (1999) "Social Capital and Community Development: Practitioner Emptor", *Australian and New Zealand Journal of Public Health*, vol 23, no 4, pp. 430–33.

Ladd, E. (1996) "The Data Just Don't Show Erosion of America's 'Social Capital' ", *Public Perspective*, vol 7, no 1, pp. 5–6.

Lakoff, G. (1987) *Women, Fire and Dangerous Things: What Categories Reveal about the Mind*, Chicago: Chicago University Press.

Lamont, M. and A. Lareau (1988) "Cultural Capital: Allusions, Gaps and Glissandos in Recent Theoretical Developments", *Sociological Theory*, vol 6, no 2, pp. 153–68.

Lang, R. and S. Hornburg (1998) "What Is Social Capital and Why Is It Important To Public Policy?", *Housing Policy Debate*, vol 9, no 1, pp. 1–16.

Lawson, T. (1997) *Economics and Reality*, London: Routledge.

Lazear, E. (2000) "Economic Imperialism", *Quarterly Journal of Economics*, vol 115, no 1, pp. 99–146.

Leach, W. (1993) *Land of Desire: Merchants, Power, and the Rise of a New American Culture*, New York: Pantheon Books.

Leana, C. and H. van Buren (1999) "Organizational Social Capital and Employment Practices", *Academy of Management Review*, vol 24, no 3, pp. 538–55.

Lee, F. and S. Harley (1998) "Peer Review, the Research Assessment Exercise and the Demise of Non-Mainstream Economics", *Capital and Class*, no 66, pp. 23–51.

Lee, S. and M. Brinton (1996) "Elite Education and Social Capital: The Case of South Korea", *Sociology of Education*, vol 69, no 3, pp. 177–92.

Leeder, S. and A. Dominello (1999) "Social Capital and Its Relevance to Health and Family Policy", *Australian and New Zealand Journal of Public Health*, vol 23, no 4, pp. 424–29.

Lehning, P. (1998) "Towards a Multicultural Civil Society: The Role of Social Capital and Democratic Citizenship", *Government and Opposition*, vol 33, no 2, pp. 221–42.

Lemann, N. (1996) "Kicking in Groups", *Atlantic Monthly*, no 277, pp. 22–26.

Levi, M. (1996) "Social and Unsocial Capital: A Review Essay of Robert Putnam's 'Making Democracy Work' ", *Politics and Society*, vol 24, no 1, pp. 45–55.

Lewis, P. (1999) "Metaphor and Critical Realism", in Fleetwood (ed) (1999).

Lindenberg, S. (1990) "Homo Socio-Oeconomicus: The Emergence of a General Model of Man in the Social Sciences", *Journal of Institutional and Theoretical Economics*, vol 146, no 4, pp. 727–48.

Lindenberg, S. et al. (eds) (1986) *Approaches to Social Theory*, New York: Russell Sage.

Liodakis, G. (ed) (1993) *Society, Technology and Restructuring of Production*, Athens: V. Papazissis.

Loizos, P. (1999) "Ottoman Half-Lives: Long-Term Perspectives on Particular Forced Migrations", *Journal of Refugee Studies*, vol 12, no 3, pp. 237–63.

Lomas, J. (1998) "Social Capital and Health: Implications for Public Health and Epidemiology", *Social Science and Medicine*, vol 47, no 9, pp. 1181–88.

Longhurst, B. and M. Savage (1996) "Social Class, Consumption and the Influence of Bourdieu: Some Critical Issues", in Edgell et al. (eds) (1996).

Loury, G. (1977) "A Dynamic Theory of Racial Income Differences", in Wallace and Le Mund (eds) (1977).

Loury, G. (1987) "Why Should We Care about Group Inequality?", *Social Philosophy and Policy*, vol 5, no 1, pp. 249–71.

Lynch, J. et al. (2000) "Social Capital – Is It Good Investment Strategy For Public Health?", *Journal of Epidemiology and Community Health*, vol 54, no 6, pp. 404–08.

Lyons, F. (2000) "Trust, Networks and Norms: The Creation of Social Capital in Agricultural Economies in Ghana", *World Development*, vol 28, no 4, pp. 663–81.

MacMillan, R. (1995) "Changes in the Structure of Life Courses and the Decline of Social Capital in Canadian Society: A Time Series Analysis of Property Crime Rates", *Canadian Journal of Sociology*, vol 20, no 1, pp. 51–79.

Macroeconomic Research Group (MERG) (1993) *Making Democracy Work: A Framework for Macroeconomic Policy in South Africa*, Cape Town: CDS.

Maloney, W. (1999) "Contracting Out the Participation Function: Social Capital and Chequebook Participation", in van Deth et al. (eds) (1999).

Maluccio, J. et al. (1999) "Social Capital and Income Generation in South Africa", Social Capital Library, Papers in Progress.

Marchand, R. (1998a) *Creating the Corporate Soul: The Rise of Public Relations and Corporate Imagery in American Big Business*, Berkeley: University of California Press.

Marchand, R. (1998b) "Customer Research as Public Relations: General Motors in the 1930s", in Strasser et al. (eds) (1998).

Martin, R. (1999) "The New 'Geographical Turn' in Economics: Some Critical Reflections", *Cambridge Journal of Economics*, vol 23, no 1, pp. 65–91.

Marx, K. (1965) *Capital: A Critique of Political Economy, Volume I, The Process of Capitalist Production*, London: Lawrence & Wishart. First German edition 1867.

Maskell, P. (2000) "Social Capital, Innovation and Competitiveness", in Baron et al. (eds) (2000).

Massey, D. and K. Espinosa (1997) "What's Driving Mexico–US Migration? A Theoretical, Empirical, and Policy Analysis", *American Journal of Sociology*, vol 102, no 4, pp. 939–99.

Matsusaka, J. (1995) "The Economic Approach to Democracy", in Tommasi and Ierulli (eds) (1995).

Mavroudeas, S. (1990) "Regulation Approach: A Critical Assessment", unpublished PhD thesis, University of London.

McBride, A. (1998) "Television, Individualism, and Social Capital", *Political Science and Politics*, vol 31, no 3, pp. 542–52.

McLennan, G. (1998) " 'Fin de Sociologie?' The Dilemmas of Multidimensional Social Theory", *New Left Review*, no 230, July–August, pp. 58–90.

McNeal, R. (1999) "Parental Involvement as Social Capital: Differential Effectiveness on Science Achievement, Truancy, and Dropping Out", *Social Forces*, vol 78, no 1, pp. 117–44.

Mehta, L. (1999) "The World Bank and Knowledge: Critical Reflections on the World Development Report (1998–99)", mimeo.

Merton, R. (1957) *Social Theory and Social Structure*, New York: Free Press.

Meyerson, E. (1994) "Human Capital, Social Capital and Compensation: The Relative Contribution of Social Contacts to Managers' Incomes", *Acta Sociologica*, vol 37, no 4, pp. 383–99.

Miller, D. (ed) (1995) *Acknowledging Consumption*, London: Routledge.

Miller-Adams, M. (1999) *The World Bank: New Agendas in a Changing World*, London: Routledge.

Milonakis, D. (2000) "Market Socialism: A Case for Rejuvenation or Inspired Alchemy?", paper to the conference of the European Society for the History of Economic Thought (ESHET), Graz, February.

Minkoff, D. (1997) "Producing Social Capital: National Social Movements and Civil Society", *American Behavioral Scientist*, vol 40, no 5, pp. 606–19.

Mitchell, J. (1978) *Social Exchange, Dramaturgy and Ethnomethodology*, New York: Elsevier.

Moesen, W. (1998) "The Macroeconomic Performance of Nations and Cultural Values", *Tijdschrift voor Economie en Management*, vol XLIII, no 3, pp. 379–94.

Molinas, J. (1998) "The Impact of Inequality, Gender, External Assistance and Social Capital on Local-Level Cooperation", *World Development*, vol 26, no 3, pp. 413–31.

Mondak, J. (1998) "Editor's Introduction", *Political Psychology*, vol 19, no 3, pp. 433–39.

Mondak, J. (ed) (1998) "Special Issue: Psychological Approaches to Social Capital", *Political Psychology*, vol 19, no 3.

Mondak, J. and A. Gearing (1998) "Civic Engagement in a Post-Communist State", *Political Psychology*, vol 19, no 3, pp. 615–37.

Morales, I. et al. (1999) "Preface: Civil Society and Democratization", *Annals of the American Academy of Political and Social Science*, vol 565, pp. 7–14.

Morgan, S. and A. Sørensen (1999a) "Parental Networks, Social Closure, and Mathematics Learning: A Test of Coleman's Social Capital Explanation of School Effects", *American Sociological Review*, vol 64, no 5, pp. 661–81.

Morgan, S. and A. Sørensen (1999b) "Theory, Measurement, and Specification Issues in Models of Network Effects on Learning: Reply to Carbonaro and to Hallinan and Kubitschek", *American Sociological Review*, vol 64, no 5, pp. 694–700.

Morris, M. (1998) "Social Capital In India", IDS Working Paper, no 61, University of Sussex.

Morrow, V. (1999) "Conceptualising Social Capital in Relation to the Well-Being of Children and Young People", *Sociological Review*, vol 47, no 4, pp. 744–65.

Moser, C. (1998) "The Asset Vulnerability Framework: Reassessing Urban Poverty Reduction Strategies", *World Development*, vol 26, no 1, pp. 1–19.

Moser, C. and J. Holland (1997) *Urban Poverty and Violence in Jamaica*, Washington: World Bank.

Mosley, P. et al. (1995) "Assessing 'Adjustment in Africa' ", World Development, vol 23, no 10, pp. 1583–1606.

Moy, P. et al. (1999) "Television Use and Social Capital: Testing Putnam's Time Displacement Hypothesis", *Mass Communication and Society*, vol 2, no 1–2, pp. 27–43.

Muir, E. (1999) "The Sources of Civil Society in Italy", *Journal of Interdisciplinary History*, vol XXIX, no 3, pp. 379–406.

Munn, P. (2000) "Social Capital, Schools and Exclusion", in Baron et al. (eds) (2000).

Muntaner, C. and J. Lynch (1999) "Income Inequality, Social Cohesion, and Class Relations: A Critique of Wilkinson's Neo-Durkheimian Research Program", *International Journal of Health Services*, vol 29, no 1, pp. 59–81.

Mwanza, A. (1992) "Theory and Practice of Structural Adjustment Programmes", in Mwanza (ed) (1992).

Mwanza, A. (ed) (1992) *Structural Adjustment Programmes in SADC: Experiences and Lessons from Malawi, Tanzania, Zambia and Zimbabwe*, Harare: SAPES Books.

Nahapiet, J. and S. Ghoshal (1998) "Social Capital, Intellectual Capital, and the Organizational Advantage", *Academy of Management Review*, vol 23, no 2, pp. 242–66.

Narayan, D. (1997) *Voices of the Poor: Poverty and Social Capital in Tanzania*, Washington: World Bank.

Narayan, D. (1998) "Social Capital Survey in Ghana – Preliminary Results", World Bank, mimeo.

Narayan, D. (1999a) "Complementarity and Substitution: Social Capital, Poverty Reduction and the State", World Bank, Poverty Group.

Narayan, D. (1999b) "Bonds and Bridges: Social Capital and Poverty", Social Capital Library, Papers in Progress.

Narayan, D. and L. Pritchett (1996) "Cents and Sociability: Household Income and Social Capital in Rural Tanzania", Environment Department and Policy Research Department, Washington, DC: World Bank.

Narayan, D. et al. (1999) *Can Anyone Hear Us?: Voices from 47 Countries*, Washington: World Bank.

Nauck, B. (1999) "Social Capital and Intergenerational Transmission of Cultural Capital within a Regional Context", in Bynner and Silbersen (eds) (1999).

Neace, M. (1999) "Entrepreneurs in Emerging Economies: Creating Trust, Social Capital and Civil Society", *Annals of the American Academy of Political and Social Science*, vol 565, pp. 148–61.

Neal, D. (1997) "The Effects of Catholic Secondary Schooling on Educational Achievement", *Journal of Labor Economics*, vol 15, no 1, pt 1, pp. 98–123.

Newton, K. (1997) "Social Capital and Democracy", *American Behavioral Scientist*, vol 40, no 5, pp. 575–86.

Newton, K. (1999a) "Social Capital and Democracy in Modern Europe", in van Deth et al. (eds) (1999).

Newton, K. (1999b) "Social and Political Trust in Established Democracies", in Norris (ed) (1999).

Nichols, T. (1996) "Russian Democracy and Social Capital", *Social Science Information*, vol 35, no 4, pp. 629–42.

Norris, P. (1996) "Does Television Erode Social Capital? A Reply to Putnam", *Political Science and Politics*, vol 29, no 3, pp. 474–80.

Norris, P. (ed) (1999) *Critical Citizens: Global Support for Democratic Government*, Oxford: Oxford University Press.

North, D. (1981) *Structure and Change in Economic History*, New York: Norton.

Nowland-Foreman, G. (1998) "Purchase-of-Service Contracting, Voluntary Organizations, and Civil Society", *American Behavioral Scientist*, vol 42, no 1, pp. 108–23.

O'Connor, J. (1973) *The Fiscal Crisis of the State*, New York: St Martin's.

Olson, M. (1965) *The Logic of Collective Action*, Cambridge: Harvard University Press.

Olson, M. (1990) "Mancur Olson", in Swedberg (ed) (1990).

Olson, M. (2000) "Big Bills Left on the Sidewalk: Why Some Nations Are Rich, and Others Poor", in Olson and Kähkönen (eds) (2000).

Olson, M. and S. Kähkönen (2000) "Introduction: The Broader View", in Olson and Kähkönen (eds) (2000).

Olson, M. and S. Kähkönen (eds) (2000) *A Not-So-Dismal Science: A Broader View of Economies and Societies*, Oxford: Oxford University Press.

Onyx, J. and P. Bullen (2000) "Measuring Social Capital in Five Communities", *Journal of Applied Behavioral Science*, vol 36, no 1, pp. 23–42.

Ostrom, E. (1994) "Constituting Social Capital and Collective Action", *Journal of Theoretical Politics*, vol 6, no 4, pp. 527–62.

Ostrom, E. (1996) "Crossing the Great Divide: Co-Production, Synergy, and Development", *World Development*, vol 24, no 6, pp. 1073–87.

Ostrom, E. (2000) "Social Capital: A Fad or a Fundamental Concept?", in Dasgupta and Serageldin (eds) (2000).

Pahl, R. (1996) "Comment on Kolankiewicz", *British Journal of Sociology*, vol 47, no 3, pp. 443–46.

Paldman, M. and G. Svendsen (1999) "Is Social Capital an Effective Smoke Condenser?: An Essay on a Concept Linking the Social Sciences", World Bank Social Capital Initiative, Working Paper, no 11.

Pantelic, J. and E. Pantoja (1999) "Exploring the Concept of Social Capital and Its Relevance for Community-Based Development: The Case of Coal Mining Areas in Orissa, India", World Bank Social Capital Initiative, Working Paper, no 15.

Papadakis, E. (1999) "Constituents of Confidence and Mistrust in Australian Institutions", *Australian Journal of Political Science*, vol 34, no 1, pp. 75–94.

Paraskevopoulos, C. (1998a) "Social Capital and the Public–Private Divide in Greek Regions", *West European Politics*, vol 21, no 2, pp. 154–77.

Paraskevopoulos, C. (1998b) "Social Capital, Institutional Networks and the Implementation of European Regional Policy: Evidence from Greece", *Regional and Federal Studies*, vol 8, no 3, pp. 31–64.

Parcel, T. and E. Menaghan (1993) "Family Social Capital and Children's Behavior Problems", *Social Psychology Quarterly*, vol 56, no 2, pp. 120–35.

Parcel, T. and E. Menaghan (1994) "Early Parental Work, Family Social Capital, and Early Childhood Outcomes", *American Journal of Sociology*, vol 99, no 4, pp. 972–1009.

Paxton, P. (1999) "Is Social Capital Declining in the United States? A Multiple Indicator Assessment", *American Journal of Sociology*, vol 105, no 1, pp. 88–127.

Pena, M. and H. Lindo-Fuentes (1998) "Community Organization, Values and Social Capital in Panama", World Bank, Central America Country Management Unit, Latin America and Caribbean Region, Economic Notes, no 9.

Pena, S. (1999) "Informal Markets: Street Vendors in Mexico City", *Habitat International*, vol 23, no 3, pp. 363–72.

Pennings, J. et al. (1998) "Human Capital, Social Capital, and Firm Dissolution", *Academy of Management Journal*, vol 41, no 4, pp. 425–40.

Pérez-Sáinz, J. (1997) "Guatemala: The Two Faces of the Metropolitan Area", in Portes et al. (eds) (1997).

Philo, C. and G. Kearns (1993) "Culture, History, Capital: A Critical Introduction to the Selling of Places", in Kearns and Philo (eds) (1993).

Pincus, J. and J. Winters (eds) (2001) *Reinventing the World Bank*, forthcoming.

Piore, M. and C. Sabel (1984) *The Second Industrial Divide: Possibilities for Prosperity*, New York: Basic Books.

Podolny, J. and K. Page (1998) "Network Forms of Organization", *Annual Review of Sociology*, vol 24, pp. 57–76.

Polak, J. (1996) "The Contribution of the International Monetary Fund", *History of Political Economy*, vol 28, Supplement, pp. 211–24.

Popay, J. (2000) "Social Capital: The Role of Narrative and Historical Research", *Journal of Epidemiology and Community Health*, vol 54, no 6, pp. 401–3.

Porter, R. (1993) "Baudrillard: History, Hysteria and Consumption", in Rojek and Turner (eds) (1993).

Portes, A. (1998) "Social Capital: Its Origins and Applications in Modern Society", *Annual Review of Sociology*, vol 24, pp. 1–24.

Portes, A. (ed) (1996) *The New Second Generation*, New York: Russell Sage Foundation.

Portes, A. and J. Itzigsohn (1997) "Coping with Change: The Politics and Economics of Urban Poverty", in Portes et al. (eds) (1997).

Portes, A. and J. Sensenbrenner (1993) "Embeddedness and Immigration: Notes on the Social Determinants of Economic Action", *American Journal of Sociology*, vol 98, no 6, pp. 1320–50.

Portes, A. and P. Landolt (1996) "The Downside of Social Capital", *The American Prospect*, no 26, pp. 18–21.

Portes, A. et al. (eds) (1997) *The Urban Caribbean: Transition to the New Global Economy*, Baltimore: Johns Hopkins University Press.

Portney, K. and J. Berry (1997) "Mobilizing Minority Communities: Social Capital and Participation in Urban Neighborhoods", *American Behavioral Scientist*, vol 40, no 5, pp. 632–44.

Postone, M. et al. (1993) "Introduction: Bourdieu and Social Theory", in Calhoun et al. (eds) (1993).

Powell, W. and S. Clemens (eds) (1998) *Private Action and the Public Good*, New Haven: Yale University Press.

Press, E. and J. Washburn (2000) "The Kept University", *The Atlantic Monthly*, vol 285, no 3, pp. 39–54.

Pribesh, S. and D. Downey (1999) "Why Are Residential and School Moves Associated with Poor School Performance?", *Demography*, vol 36, no 4, pp. 521–34.

Psacharopoulos, G. (1981) "The World Bank in the World of Education: Some Policy Changes and Some Remnants", *Comparative Education*, vol 17, no 2, pp. 141–45.

Pusey, M. (1991) *Economic Rationalism in Canberra: A Nation-Building State Changes Its Mind*, Cambridge: Cambridge University Press.

Putnam, R. (1993a) *Making Democracy Work: Civic Traditions in Modern Italy*, Princeton: Princeton University Press.

Putnam, R. (1993b) "The Prosperous Community: Social Capital and Public Life", *The American Prospect*, no 13, pp. 35–42.

Putnam, R. (1995) "Bowling Alone: America's Declining Social Capital", *Journal of Democracy*, vol 6, no 1, pp. 65–78.

Putnam, R. (1996a) "The Strange Disappearance of Civic America", *The American Prospect*, no 24, pp. 34–48.

Putnam, R. (1996b) "Robert Putnam Responds", *The American Prospect*, no 25, pp. 26–28.

Putnam, R. (1998) "Foreword to Social Capital: Its Importance to Housing and Community Development", *Housing Policy Debate*, vol 9, no 1, pp. v–viii.

Putterman, L. (1995) "Social Capital and Development Capacity: The Example of Rural Tanzania", *Development Policy Review*, vol 13, no 1, pp. 5–22.

Putzel, J. (1997) "Accounting for the 'Dark Side' of Social Capital: Reading Robert Putnam on Democracy", *Journal of International Development*, vol 9, no 7, pp. 939–49.

Putzel, J. (1999) "Survival of an Imperfect Democracy in the Philippines", *Democratization*, vol 6, no 1, pp. 198–223.

Rabin, M. (1998) "Psychology and Economics", *Journal of Economic Literature*, vol 36, no 1, pp. 11–46.

Radin, M. (1996) *Contested Commodities*, Cambridge: Harvard University Press.

Radnitzky, G. and P. Bernholz (eds) (1987) *Economic Imperialism: The Economic Method Applied Outside the Field of Economics*, New York: Paragon House Publishers.

Rahn, W. and J. Transue (1998) "Trust, Mood, and Outcomes of Friendship Determine Preferences for Real Versus Ersatz Social Capital", *Political Psychology*, vol 19, no 3, pp. 545–65.

Raiser, M. (1997) "Informal Institutions, Social Capital and Economic Transition: Reflections on a Neglected Dimension", European Bank for Reconstruction and Development, Working Paper, no 25.

Ramsay, W. and E. Clark (1990) *New Ideas for Effective School Improvement: Vision, Social Capital, Evaluation*, Basingstoke: Falmer Press.

Ranis, G. (1997) "The World Bank Near the Turn of the Century", in Culpeper et al. (eds) (1997).

Recchi, E. (1999) "Politics as Occupational Choice: Youth Self-Selection for Party Careers in Italy", *European Sociological Review*, vol 15, no 1, pp. 107–24.

Reid, C. and L. Salmen (1999) "Notes for 'Understanding Social Capital': Trust and Social Cohesion for Agricultural Extension in Mali", World Bank Social Capital Initiative, Working Paper, no 20.

Renshon, S. (2000) "Political Leadership as Social Capital: Governing in a Divided Culture", *Political Psychology*, vol 21, no 1, pp. 199–226.

Rich, P. (1999) "American Voluntarism, Social Capital, and Political Culture", *Annals of the American Academy of Political and Social Science*, vol 565, pp. 15–34.

Richardson, J. (ed) (1986) *Handbook of Theory and Research for the Sociology of Education*, New York: Greenwood Press.

Rillera, N. (1999) "The Magkasaka Programme: Farmers Trust Development in Conjunction with Joint Economic Enterprises for Productivity", Social Capital Library, Papers in Progress.

Robbins, D. (1991) *The Work of Pierre Bourdieu*, Buckingham: Open University Press.

Robison, L. and M. Siles (1997) "Social Capital and Household Income Distributions in the United States: 1980–1990", Michigan State University, Department of Agricultural Economics, Report no 595.

Robison, L. and M. Siles (1998) "Social Capital and Organizations", Department of Agricultural Economics, Michigan State University, Staff Paper, no 98–27.

Robison, L. et al. (1999) "Social Capital and the Terms and Likelihood of Farmland Trades", Social Capital Library, Papers in Progress.

Rogers, A. (1994) "Evolution of Time Preference by Natural Selection", *American Economic Review*, vol 84, no 3, pp. 460–81.

Rogers, N. (1999) "Money, Marriage, Mobility: The Big Bourgeoisie of Hanoverian London", *Journal of Family History*, vol 24, no 1, pp. 19–34.

Rojek, C. and B. Turner (1993) "Regret Baudrillard", in Rojek and Turner (eds) (1993).

Rojek, C. and B. Turner (eds) (1993) *Forget Baudrillard*, London: Routledge.

Rose, D. and T. Clear (1998) "Incarceration, Social Capital, and Crime: Implications for Social Disorganization Theory", *Criminology*, vol 63, no 3, pp. 441–79.

Rose, N. (1999) "Inventiveness in Politics", *Economy and Society*, vol 28, no 3, pp. 467–93.

Rose, R. (1998) "Getting Things Done in an Anti-Modern Society: Social Capital Networks in Russia", World Bank, Social Capital Initiative, Working Paper, no 6, reproduced in Dasgupta and Serageldin (eds) (2000).

Rose, R. (1999) "What Does Social Capital Add to Individual Welfare? An Empirical Analysis of Russia", World Bank Social Capital Initiative, Working Paper, no 23.

Rose, R. et al. (1997) "Social Capital in Civic and Stressful Societies", *Studies in Comparative International Development*, vol 32, no 3, pp. 85–111.

Rosenthal, C. (1998) "Determinants of Collaborative Leadership: Civic Engagement, Gender or Organizational Norms?", *Political Research Quarterly*, vol 51, no 4, pp. 847–68.

Rotberg, R. (1999) "Social Capital and Political Culture in Africa, America, Australasia, and Europe", *Journal of Interdisciplinary History*, vol XXIX, no 3, pp. 339–56.

Roy, W. (1984) "Class Conflict and Social Change in Historical Perspective", *Annual Review of Sociology*, vol 10, pp. 483–506.

Rubio, M. (1997) "Perverse Social Capital – Some Evidence from Colombia", *Journal of Economic Issues*, vol 31, no 3, pp. 805–16.

Rudebeck, L. and O. Törnquist (eds) (1998) *Democratization in the Third World: Concrete Case Studies in Comparative and Theoretical Perspective*, London: Macmillan.

Runyan, D. et al. (1998) "Children Who Prosper in Unfavourable Environments: The Relationship to Social Capital", *Pediatrics*, vol 101, no 1, pp. 2–8.

Ryan, B. (1992) *Making Capital from Culture: The Corporate Form of Capitalist Cultural Production*, New York: Walter de Gruyter.

Salamon, S. (1998) "The View from Anthropology: Discussion of Castle's Conceptual Framework", *American Journal of Agricultural Economics*, vol 80, no 3, pp. 637–39.

Sampson, R. et al. (1999) "Beyond Social Capital: Spatial Dynamics of Collective Efficacy for Children", *American Sociological Review*, vol 64, no 5, pp. 633–60.

Samuelsson, K. (1961) *Religion and Economic Action*, London: Heinemann.

Sandefur, R. and E. Laumann (1998) "A Paradigm for Social Capital", *Rationality and Society*, vol 10, no 4, pp. 481–501.

Sanders, J. and V. Nee (1996) "Immigrant Self-Employment: The Family as Social Capital and the Value of Human Capital", *American Sociological Review*, vol 61, no 2, pp. 231–49.

Schelling, T. (1978) *Micromotives and Macrobehavior*, New York: W.W. Norton.

Schelling, T. (1990) "Thomas C. Schelling", in Swedberg (ed) (1990).

Schiff, M. (1992) "Social Capital, Labor Mobility, and Welfare: The Impact of Uniting States", *Rationality and Society*, vol 4, no 2, pp. 157–75.

Schiff, M. (1999a) "Labor Market Integration and Welfare", Development Research Group, World Bank, mimeo.

Schiff, M. (1999b) "Labor Market Integration in the Presence of Social Capital", Social Capital Library, Papers in Progress.

Schmitz, H. and K. Nadvi (1999) "Clustering and Industrialisation", *World Development*, vol 27, no 9, pp. 1503–14.

Schneider, M. et al. (1997) "Institutional Arrangements and the Creation of Social Capital: The Effects of Public School Choice", *American Political Science Review*, vol 91, no 1, pp. 82–93.

Schoen, R. et al. (1997) "Why Do Americans Want Children?", *Population and Development Review*, vol 23, no 2, pp. 333–58.

Schrieder, G. and M. Sharma (1999) "Impact of Finance on Poverty Reduction and Social Capital Formation: A Review and Synthesis of Empirical Evidence", *Savings and Development*, vol XXIII, no 1, pp. 67–94.

Schudson, M. (1996) "What If Civic Life Didn't Die?", *The American Prospect*, no 25, pp. 17–20.

Schuh, G. (1993) "Involuntary Resettlement, Human Capital, and Economic Development", in Cernea and Guggenheim (eds) (1993).

Schuller, T. (2000a) "The Complementary Roles of Human and Social Capital", paper prepared for the OECD for Symposium on The Contribution of Human and Social Capital to Sustained Economic Growth and Well-Being, Human Development Canada, Quebec, March.

Schuller, T. (2000b) "Exploiting Social Capital: Learning about Learning", Text of an Inaugural Lecture, Birkbeck College, February.

Schuller, T. and J. Field (1998) "Social Capital, Human Capital and the Learning Society", *International Journal of Lifelong Education*, vol 17, no 4, pp. 226–35.

Schuller, T. et al. (2000) "Social Capital: A Review and Critique", in Baron et al. (eds) (2000).

Schulman, M. and C. Anderson (1999) "The Dark Side of the Force: A Case Study of Restructuring and Social Capital", *Rural Sociology*, vol 64, no 3, pp. 351–72.

Scott, J. (1998) *Seeing Like a State: How Certain Schemes to Improve the Human Condition Have Failed*, New Haven: Yale University Press.

Selle, P. (1999) "The Transformation of the Voluntary Sector in Norway: A Decline in Social Capital?", in van Deth et al. (eds) (1999).

Sen, A. (1970a) *Collective Choice and Social Welfare*, San Francisco: Holden-Day.

Sen, A. (1970b) "Interpersonal Aggregation and Partial Comparability", *Econometrica*, vol 38, no 3, May, pp. 393–409, reproduced in Sen (1982).

Sen, A. (1975) "Social Choice Theory: A Re-Examination", *Econometrica*, vol 45, pp. 53–89, reproduced in Sen (1982).

Sen, A. (1977) "Rational Fools: A Critique of the Behavioral Foundations of Economic Theory", *Philosophy and Public Affairs*, vol 6, no 3, pp. 317–44.

Sen, A. (1979) "Interpersonal Comparisons of Welfare", in Boskin (ed) (1979), reproduced in Sen (1982).

Sen, A. (1982) *Choice, Welfare and Measurement*, Oxford: Blackwell.

Sen, A. (1990) "Amartya K. Sen", in Swedberg (ed) (1990).

Sen, A. (1995) "Rationality and Social Choice", *American Economic Review*, vol 85, no 1, pp. 1–24.

Sender, J. (1999) "Africa's Economic Performance: Limitations of the Current Consensus", *Journal of Economic Perspectives*, vol 13, no 3, pp. 89–114.

Serageldin, I. (1996) "Sustainability as Opportunity and the Problem of Social Capital", *Brown Journal of World Affairs*, vol III, no 2, pp. 187–203.

Serageldin, I. (1997) "Preface", to Narayan (1997).

Serageldin, I. and C. Grootaert (2000) "Defining Social Capital: An Integrating View", in Dasgupta and Serageldin (eds) (2000).

Seron, C. and K. Ferris (1995) "Negotiating Professionalism: The Gendered Social Capital of Flexible Time", *Work and Occupations*, vol 22, no 1, pp. 22–47.

Shah, D. (1998) "Civic Engagement, Interpersonal Trust, and Television Use: An Individual-Level Assessment of Social Capital", *Political Psychology*, vol 19, no 3, pp. 469–96.

Shetler, J. (1995) "A Gift for Generations to Come: A Kiroba Popular History from Tanzania and Identity as Social Capital in the 1980s", *International Journal of African Historical Studies*, vol 28, no 1, pp. 69–112.

Shucksmith, M. (2000) "Endogenous Development, Social Capital and Social Inclusion: Perspectives from LEADER in the UK", *Sociologia Ruralis*, vol 40, no 2, pp. 208–18.

Siisiäinen, M. (1999) "Voluntary Associations and Social Capital in Finland", in van Deth et al. (eds) (1999).

Singh, S. (1997) *Fermat's Last Theorem*, London: Fourth Estate.

Sklar, K. (1998) "The Consumers' White Label Campaign of the National Consumers' League, 1898–1918", in Strasser et al. (eds) (1998).

Skocpol, T. (1996) "Unravelling from Above", *The American Prospect*, no 25, pp. 20–25.

Slater, D. (1997) *Consumer Culture and Modernity*, Cambridge: Polity Press.

Slater, D. (2000) "Capturing Markets from the Economists", paper for Cultural Economics Conference, Open University, UK, January.

Slater, G. and D. Spencer (2000) "The Uncertain Foundations of Transaction Cost Economics", *Journal of Economic Issues*, vol XXXIV, no 1, pp. 61–87.

Slemrod, J. (1998) "On Voluntary Compliance, Voluntary Taxes, and Social Capital", *National Tax Journal*, vol LI, no 3, pp. 485–91.

Smelser, N. and R. Swedberg (1994) "Introduction", in Smelser and Swedberg (eds) (1994).

Smelser, N. and R. Swedberg (eds) (1994) *The Handbook of Economic Sociology*, Princeton: Princeton University Press.

Smidt, C. (1999) "Religion and Civic Engagement: A Comparative Analysis", *Annals of the American Academy of Political and Social Science*, vol 565, pp. 176–92.

Smith, J. (1997) "Characteristics of the Modern Transnational Social Movement Sector", in Smith et al. (eds) (1997)

Smith, J. (1998) "Global Civil Society? Transnational Social Movement Organizations and Social Capital", *American Behavioral Scientist*, vol 42, no 1, pp. 93–97.

Smith, J. et al. (eds) (1997) *Transnational Social Movements and World Politics: Solidarity Beyond the State*, Syracuse: Syracuse University Press.

Smith, M. et al. (1995) "Social Capital, Place of Residence, and College Attendance", *Rural Sociology*, vol 60, no 3, pp. 363–80.

Smith, T. (1997) "Factors Relating to Misanthropy in Contemporary American Society", *Social Science Research*, vol 26, no 2, pp. 170–96.

Smith, T. (1998) "The Capital/Consumer Relation in Lean Production: The Continued Relevance of Volume Two of 'Capital' ", in Arthur and Reuten (eds) (1998).

Snell, S. (1999) "Social Capital and Strategic HRM: It's Who You Know", *HR. Human Resource Planning*, vol 22, no 1, pp. 62–65.

Social Capital Interest Group (1999) "Social Capital: A Position Paper", Social Capital Interest Group (SCIG), Michigan State University, http://www.ssc.msu.edu/~internat/soccap/position.htm

Solow, R. (1990) "Robert M. Solow", in Swedberg (ed) (1990).

Solow, R. (2000) "Notes on Social Capital and Economic Performance", in Dasgupta and Serageldin (eds) (2000).

Spagnolo, G. (1999) "Social Relations and Cooperation in Organizations", *Journal of Economic Behavior and Organization*, vol 38, no 1, pp. 1–25.

Spencer, D. (1998) "Economic Analysis and the Theory of Production: A Critical Appraisal", unpublished PhD thesis, University of Leeds.

Stamps, D. (1998) "Social Capital", *Training*, vol 35, no 11, pp. 44–50.

Standing, G. (1999) "New Development Paradigm or Third Wayism?: A Critique of a World Bank Rethink", mimeo.

Stanley, C. (1996) *Urban Excess and the Law: Capital, Culture and Desire*, London: Cavendish Publishing Company.

Stern, N. and F. Ferreira (1997) "The World Bank as 'Intellectual Actor' ", in Kapur et al. (eds) (1997).

Stiglitz, J. (1989) "Markets, Market Failures and Development", *American Economic Review*, vol 79, no 2, pp. 197–202.

Stiglitz, J. (1994) *Whither Socialism?*, Cambridge: MIT Press.

Stiglitz, J. (1998a) "More Instruments and Broader Goals: Moving Toward the Post Washington Consensus", the 1998 WIDER Annual Lecture, 7 January, Helsinki.

Stiglitz, J. (1998b) "Towards a New Paradigm for Development: Strategies, Policies and Processes", Prebisch Lecture, UNCTAD, Geneva.

Stiglitz, J. (1999) "Two Principles for the Next Round, Or, How to Bring Developing Countries in from the Cold", Geneva, 21 September.

Stiglitz, J. (2000a) "Formal and Informal Institutions", in Dasgupta and Serageldin (eds) (2000).

Stiglitz, J. (2000b) "Democratic Development as the Fruits of Labour", Keynote Address, Industrial Relations Research Association, AEA Meetings, January, Boston.

Stiglitz, J. and K. Hoff (1999) "Modern Economic Theory and Development", Symposium on Future of Development Economics in Perspective, Dubrovnik, 13–14 May.

Stolle, D. (1998) "Bowling Together, Bowling Alone: The Development of Generalized Trust in Voluntary Associations", *Political Psychology*, vol 19, no 3, pp. 497–525.

Stolle, D. and T. Rochon (1998) "Are All Associations Alike? Member Diversity, Associational Type and the Creation of Social Capital", *American Behavioral Scientist*, vol 42, no 1, pp. 47–65.

Stolle, D. and T. Rochon (1999) "The Myth of American Exceptionalism: A Three-Nation Comparison of Associational Membership and Social Capital", in van Deth et al. (eds) (1999).

Stone, D. (1995) "Commentary: The Durability of Social Capital", *Journal of Health Politics, Policy and Law*, vol 20, no 3, pp. 689–94.

Strasser, S. et al. (eds) (1998) *Getting and Spending: European and American Consumer Societies in the Twentieth Century*, Cambridge: Cambridge University Press.

Strathern, M. (1992) "Qualified Value: The Perspective of Gift Exchange", in Humphrey and Hugh-Jones (eds) (1992).

Stubbs, P. (1998) "Conflict and Cooperation in the Virtual Community: Email and the War of the Yugoslav Succession", *Sociological Research Online*, vol 3, no 3, http://www.socresonline.org.uk/socresonline/3/3/7.html

Sudarsky, J. (1999) "Colombia's Social Capital: The National Measurement with the Barcas", World Bank, mimeo.

Sullivan, J. and J. Transue (1999) "The Psychological Underpinnings of Democracy: A Selective Review of Research on Political Tolerance, Interpersonal Trust, and Social Capital", *Annual Review of Psychology*, vol 50, pp. 625–50.

Summers, G. and D. Brown (1998) "A Sociological Perspective on Rural Studies", *American Journal of Agricultural Economics*, vol 80, no 3, pp. 640–43.

Sun, Y. (1998) "The Academic Success of East-Asian-American Students – An Investment Model", *Social Science Research*, vol 27, no 4, pp. 432–56.

Sun, Y. (1999) "The Contextual Effects of Community Social Capital on Academic Performance", *Social Science Research*, vol 28, no 4, pp. 403–26.

Svendsen, G. and G. Svendsen (2000) "Measuring Social Capital: The Danish Co-operative Dairy Movement", *Sociologia Ruralis*, vol 40, no 1, pp. 72–86.

Swank, D. (1996) "Cultural, Institutions, and Economic Growth: Theory, Recent Evidence, and the Role of Communitarian Polities", *American Journal of Political Science*, vol 40, no 3, pp. 660–79.

Swartz, D. (1996) "Bridging the Study of Culture and Religion: Pierre Bourdieu and the Political Economy of Symbolic Power", *Sociology of Religion*, vol 57, no 1, pp. 71–85.

Swedberg, R. (1990) "Introduction", in Swedberg (ed) (1990).

Swedberg, R. (ed) (1990) *Economics and Sociology, Redefining Their Boundaries: Conversations with Economists and Sociologists*, Princeton: Princeton University Press.

Swedberg, R. (ed) (1996) *Economic Sociology*, Cheltenham: Edward Elgar.

Szabo, S. (1999) "Social Intermediation Study: Field Research Guide Exploring the Relationship between Social Capital and Microfinance", Aga Khan Foundation and CIDA, Canada.

Szreter, S. (1998) "Social Capital, the Economy and the Third Way", http://www.netnexus.org/debates/3wayecon/library/socialcap.htm

Szreter, S. (2000) "Social Capital, the Economy and Education in Historical Perspective", in Baron et al. (eds) (2000).

Tarrow, S. (1996) "Making Social Science Work across Time and Space: A Critical Reflection on Robert Putnam's 'Making Democracy Work' ", *American Political Science Review*, vol 90, no 2, pp. 389–97.

Teachman, J. et al. (1996) "Social Capital and Dropping Out of School Early", *Journal of Marriage and the Family*, vol 58, no 3, pp. 773–83.

Temple, J. (1998) "Initial Conditions, Social Capital, and Growth in Africa", *Journal of African Economics*, vol 7, no 3, pp. 309–67.

Temple, J. (2000) "Growth Effects of Education and Social Capital in the OECD", paper prepared for the OECD for Symposium on The Contribution of Human and Social Capital to Sustained Economic Growth and Well-Being, Human Development Canada, Quebec, March.

Temple, J. and P. Johnson (1998) "Social Capability and Economic Growth", *Quarterly Journal of Economics*, vol CXIII, no 3, pp. 965–90.

Tendler, J. (1997) *Good Government in the Tropics*, Baltimore: Johns Hopkins University Press.

Thibaut, J. and H. Kelley (1959) *The Social Psychology of Groups*, New York: Wiley & Sons.

Thornton, S. (1995) *Club Cultures: Music, Media and Subcultural Capital*, Cambridge: Polity Press.

Tijhuis, M. et al. (1995) "Social Support and Stressful Events in Two Dimensions: Life Events and Illness as an Event", *Social Science and Medicine*, vol 40, no 11, pp. 1513–26.

Tilly, C. (1998) *Durable Inequality*, Berkeley: University of California Press.

Tommasi, M. and K. Ierulli (eds) (1995) *The New Economics of Human Behaviour*, Cambridge: Cambridge University Press.

Torcal, M. and J. Montero (1999) "Facets of Social Capital in New Democracies: The Formation and Consequences of Social Capital in Spain", in van Deth et al. (eds) (1999).

Törnquist, O. (1998) "Making Democratization Work: From Civil Society and Social Capital to Political Inclusion and Politicization: Theoretical Reflections on Concrete Case Studies in Indonesia, Kerala, and the Philippines", in Rudebeck and Törnquist (eds) (1998).

Toye, J. (1994) "Structural Adjustment: Context, Assumptions, Origins and Diversity", in van der Hoeven and van der Kraaij (eds) (1994).

Toye, J. (1996) "The New Institutional Economics and Its Implications for Development", in Harriss et al. (eds) (1996).

Tsai, W. and S. Ghoshal (1998) "Social Capital and Value Creation: The Role of Intra-Firm Networks", *Academy of Management Journal*, vol 41, no 4, pp. 464–76.

Turner, J. (1987) "Social Exchange Theory", in Cook (ed) (1987).

Turner, J. (2000) "The Formation of Social Capital", in Dasgupta and Serageldin (eds) (2000).

Unger, D. (1998) *Building Social Capital in Thailand: Fibers, Finance, and Infrastructure*, Cambridge: Cambridge University Press.

Uslaner, E. (1998) "Social Capital, Television, and the 'Mean World': Trust, Optimism, and Civic Participation", *Political Psychology*, vol 19, no 3, pp. 441–67.

Uslaner, E. (1999) "Trust but Verify: Social Capital and Moral Behavior", *Social Science Information*, vol 38, no 1, pp. 29–55.

Valelly, R. (1996) "Couch Potato Democracy?", *The American Prospect*, no 25, pp. 25–26.

Valenzuela, A. (1999) " 'Checkin' Up on My Guy': Chicanas, Social Capital, and the Culture of Romance", *Frontiers*, vol 20, no 1, pp. 60–79.

Valenzuela, A. and S. Dornbusch (1994) "Familism and Social Capital in the Academic Achievement of Mexican Origin and Anglo Adolescents", *Social Science Quarterly*, vol 75, no 1, pp. 18–36.

van Bastelaer, T. (1999) "Does Social Capital Facilitate the Poor's Access to Credit? A Review of the Microeconomic Literature", World Bank Social Capital Initiative, Working Paper, no 8.

van der Hoeven, R. and F. van der Kraaij (eds) (1994) *Structural Adjustment and Beyond in Sub-Saharan Africa*, London: James Currey.

van Deth, J. et al. (eds) (1999) *Social Capital and European Democracy*, London: Routledge.

van Deth, J. (2000) "Interesting but Irrelevant: Social Capital and the Saliency of Politics in Western Europe", *European Journal of Political Research*, vol 37, no 1, pp. 115–47.

Veenstra, G. (2000) "Social Capital, SES and Health: An Individual-Level Analysis", *Social Science and Medicine*, vol 50, no 5, pp. 619–29.

Velthuis, O. (1999) "The Changing Relationship between Economic Sociology and Institutional Economics: From Talcott Parsons to Mark Granovetter", *American Journal of Economics and Sociology*, vol 58, no 4, pp. 629–49.

Venables, A. (1998) "The Assessment: Trade and Location", *Oxford Review of Economic Policy*, vol 14, no 2, pp. 1–6.

Verba, S. et al. (1997) "The Big Tilt: Participatory Inequality in America", *The American Prospect*, no 32, pp. 74–80.

Volker, B. and H. Flap (1999) "Getting Ahead in the GDR: Social Capital and Status Attainment under Communism", *Acta Sociologica*, vol 42, no 1, pp. 17–34.

Wacquant, L. (1996) "Foreword" to Bourdieu (1996b).

Waldinger, R. (1995) "The 'Other Side' of Embeddedness: A Case Study of the Interplay of Economy and Ethnicity", *Ethnic and Racial Studies*, vol 18, no 3, pp. 555–80.

Walker, G. et al. (1997) "Social Capital, Structural Holes and the Formation of an Industry Network", *Organization Science*, vol 8, no 2, pp. 109–25.

Wall, E. et al. (1998) "Getting the Goods on Social Capital", *Rural Sociology*, vol 63, no 2, pp. 300–22.

Wallace, P. and A. Le Mund (eds) (1977) *Women, Minorities, and Employment Discrimination*, Lexington: Lexington Books.

Wallis, A. et al. (1998) "Social Capital and Community Building: Building Healthier Communities, Ten Years of Learning, Part 2", *National Civic Review*, vol 87, no 4.

Wang, X. (1999) "Review of 'State–Society Synergy: Government and Social Capital in Development' ", *Comparative Politics*, vol 31, no 2, pp. 231–49.

Wann, M. (1995) *Building Social Capital: Self-Help in a Twenty-First Century Welfare State*, London: IPPR.

Warner, M. (1999) "Social Capital Construction and the Role of the Local State", *Rural Sociology*, vol 64, no 3, pp. 373–93.

Warren, M. (1998) "Community Building and Political Power", *American Behavioral Scientist*, vol 42, no 1, pp. 78–92.

Weijland, H. (1999) "Microenterprise Clusters in Rural Indonesia: Industrial Seedbed and Policy Target", *World Development*, vol 27, no 9, pp. 1515–52.

Weintraub, R. (1998) "Controversy: Axiomatisches Mißverständnis", *Economic Journal*, vol 108, no 451, pp. 1837–47.

White, M. and G. Kaufman (1997) "Language Usage, Social Capital, and School Completion among Immigrants and Native-Born Ethnic Groups", *Social Science Quarterly*, vol 32, no 1, pp. 3–30.

Whiteley, P. (1999) "The Origins of Social Capital", in van Deth et al. (eds) (1999).

Whittington, K. (1998) "Revisiting Tocqueville's America", *American Behavioral Scientist*, vol 42, no 1, pp. 21–32.

Wiener, M. (1981) *English Culture and the Decline of the Industrial Spirit, 1850–1980*, Cambridge: Cambridge University Press.

Wilkinson, R. (1996) *Unhealthy Societies: The Afflictions of Inequality*, London: Routledge.

Wilkinson, R. (1999a) "Health, Hierarchy and Social Anxiety", in Adler et al. (eds) (1999).

Wilkinson, R. (1999b) "Income Inequality, Social Cohesion and Health: Clarifying the Theory, A Reply to Muntaner and Lynch", *International Journal of Health Services*, vol 29, no 3, pp. 525–43.

Wilkinson, R. (2000) "Inequality and the Social Environment: A Reply to Lynch et al.", *Journal of Epidemiology and Community Health*, vol 54, no 6, pp. 411–13.

Williamson, J. (1990) "What Washington Means by Policy Reform", in Williamson (ed) (1990)

Williamson, J. (ed) (1990) *Latin American Adjustment: How Much Has Happened?*, Washington: Institute for International Economics.

Williamson, J. (1997) "The Washington Consensus Revisited", in Emmerij (ed) (1997).

Williamson, O. (1998) "Transaction Cost Economics: How It Works; Where It Is Headed", *De Economist*, vol 146, no 1, pp. 23–58.

Williamson, O. (2000) "Economic Institutions and Development: A View from the Bottom", in Olson and Kähkönen (eds) (2000).

Wilson, P. (1997) "Building Social Capital: A Learning Agenda for the Twenty-First Century", *Urban Studies*, vol 34, no 5–6, pp. 745–60.

Wilson, T. (1998) "Weak Ties, Strong Ties: Network Principles in Mexican Migration", *Human Organization*, vol 57, no 4, pp. 394–403.

Wong, R. (1998) "Multidimensional Influences of Family Environment in Education: The Case of Socialist Czechoslovakia", *Sociology of Education*, vol 71, no 1, pp. 1–22.

Wood, R. (1997) "Social Capital and Political Culture: God Meets Politics in the Inner City", *American Behavioral Scientist*, vol 40, no 5, pp. 595–605.

Woolcock, M. (1998) "Social Capital and Economic Development: Toward a Theoretical Synthesis and Policy Framework", *Theory and Society*, vol 27, no 2, pp. 151–208.

Woolcock, M. (1999) "Learning from Failures in Microfinance: What Unsuccessful Cases Tell Us about How Group-Based Programs Work", *American Journal of Economics and Sociology*, vol 58, no 1, pp. 17–42.

Woolcock, M. and D. Narayan (2000) "Social Capital: Implications for Development Theory, Research, and Policy", *World Bank Research Observer*, vol 15, no 2.

World Bank (1997) *Expanding the Measure of Wealth: Indicators of Environmentally Sustainable Development*, Washington: World Bank.

World Bank (1998a) "The Local Level Institutions Study: Overview and Program Description", Local Level Institutions, Working Paper, no 1.

World Bank (1998b) "The Initiative on Defining, Monitoring and Measuring Social Capital: Text of Proposals Approved for Funding", World Bank, Social Capital Initiative, Working Paper, no 2.

World Bank (1998c) "The Local Level Institutions Study: Overview and Program Description", Social Development Department and Environmentally and Socially Sustainable Development Network, World Bank, Local Level Institutions, Working Paper, no 1.

Wu, C. (1998) "Embracing the Enterprise Culture: Art Institutions since the 1980s", *New Left Review*, no 230, July–August, pp. 28–57.

Young, A. (1994) "Lessons from the East Asian NICs: A Contrarian View", *European Economic Review*, vol 38, pp. 964–73.

Young, A. (1996) "The Tyranny of Numbers: Confronting the Statistical Realities of the East Asian Growth Experience", *Quarterly Journal of Economics*, vol 110, no 3, pp. 641–80.

Youniss, J. et al. (1997) "What We Know about Engendering Civic Identity", *American Behavioral Scientist*, vol 40, no 5, pp. 620–31.

Yusuf, S. and J. Stiglitz (1999) "Development Issues: Settled and Open", Symposium on Future of Development Economics in Perspective, Dubrovnik, 13–14 May.

Zelizer, V. (1988) "Beyond the Polemics on the Market: Establishing a Theoretical and Empirical Agenda", *Sociological Forum*, vol 3, no 4, pp. 614–34, reproduced in Swedberg (ed) (1996).

Zelizer, V. (2000) "Fine-Tuning the Zelizer View", *Economy and Society*, vol 29, no 3, pp. 383–89.

Zhou, M. and C. Bankston (1994) "Social Capital and the Adaptation of the Second Generation: The Case of Vietnamese Youth in New Orleans", *International Migration Review*, vol 28, no 4, pp. 821–45, reproduced in Portes (ed) (1996).

Zukin, S. (1996) "Space and Symbols in an Age of Decline", in King (ed) (1996).

Zulfacar, A. (1998) *Afghan Immigrants in the USA and Germany: A Comparative Analysis of the Use of Ethnic Social Capital*, Münster: Lit Verlag.

Name index

Subject index